THE CROWD
IN THE FRENCH
REVOLUTION

rej ideology

Oxford University Press, Amen House, London E.C.4

GLASGOW NEW YORK TORONTO MELBOURNE WELLINGTON
BOMBAY CALCUTTA MADRAS KARACHI KUALA LUMPUR
CAPE TOWN IBADAN NAIROBI ACCRA

THE CROWD
IN THE FRENCH
REVOLUTION

BY

GEORGE RUDÉ

OXFORD
AT THE CLARENDON PRESS

FIRST PUBLISHED 1959
REPRINTED (WITH CORRECTIONS) 1960
REPRINTED LITHOGRAPHICALLY IN GREAT BRITAIN
AT THE UNIVERSITY PRESS, OXFORD
FROM SHEETS OF THE SECOND IMPRESSION
1961

ONULP

TO
GEORGES LEFEBVRE

PREFACE

THIS book is the outcome of frequent visits to Paris and to Parisian archives and libraries during the past nine years. I should like, therefore, to express my warmest appreciation to the archivists and staff of the Archives Nationales, Archives de la Préfecture de Police, the departmental archives of the Seine, Seine-et-Oise, and Seine-et-Marne, and of the Bibliothèque Nationale and Bibliothèque Historique de la Ville de Paris for their never-failing co-operation, sympathetic interest, good humour, and goodwill.

More particularly my thanks are due to my friends and collaborators, Richard Cobb and Albert Soboul, who have always been lavish with ideas, advice, and information and generous in putting at my disposal the fruits of their own researches. Our collaboration has, indeed, been so close in recent years that it is difficult to determine precisely, in the present instance, where their particular contribution ends and my own begins. In a real sense, therefore, this book is an expression of collective, rather than of purely individual, enterprise. And by no means least has been the contribution made to it by Professor Georges Lefebvre, whose example, wise counsel, and friendly encouragement have placed me, as countless other students of the French Revolution, deeply in his debt.

I also wish to thank Professor Alfred Cobban for his help and guidance over a number of years, and Mr. Alun Davies for much helpful advice and for sharing with me the ungrateful task of proof-reading. And finally, my special gratitude is due to my wife, whose patience, understanding, and concern for my well-being have made the writing of this book a pleasure rather than a burden.

G. R.

15 *June* 1958

CONTENTS

PART I

Introduction

I. INTRODUCTION   1

II. PARIS ON THE EVE OF THE REVOLUTION   10

PART II

The Revolutionary Crowd in Action

III. PRELUDE TO REVOLUTION   27

IV. JULY 1789   45

V. THE MARCH TO VERSAILLES   61

VI. THE 'MASSACRE' OF THE CHAMP DE MARS   80

VII. THE FALL OF THE MONARCHY   95

VIII. THE TRIUMPH OF THE MOUNTAIN   113

IX. THERMIDOR   128

X. GERMINAL-PRAIRIAL   142

XI. VENDÉMIAIRE   160

PART III

The Anatomy of the Revolutionary Crowd

XII. THE COMPOSITION OF REVOLUTIONARY CROWDS, 1787-95   178

XIII. THE MOTIVES OF REVOLUTIONARY CROWDS   191

XIV. THE GENERATION OF REVOLUTIONARY ACTIVITY   210

XV. THE 'REVOLUTIONARY CROWD' IN HISTORY   232

APPENDIXES

  I. Paris Sections of 1790–5   241
  II. The Population of the Paris Sections in 1791–5   242
  III. Paris Sections and Insurgents of 1787–95   244
  IV. Paris Trades and Insurgents of 1787–95   246
  V. Parisian Insurgents and Rioters of 1775–95   249
  VI. The Revolutionary Calendar   250
  VII. Prices and Wages in Paris 1789–93   251

GLOSSARY   253

BIBLIOGRAPHY   258

INDEX   261

MAP OF REVOLUTIONARY PARIS   *at end*

PART I

Introduction

I

INTRODUCTION

ONE aspect of the French Revolution that has been largely neglected by historians is the nature of the revolutionary crowd. It has, of course, long been recognized that the Revolution was not only a political, but a profound social upheaval, to the course and outcome of which masses of ordinary Frenchmen, both in the towns and countryside, contributed. Not least in Paris; and, in the history of revolutionary Paris, a particular importance has been justly ascribed to the great *journées*, or popular insurrections and demonstrations, which, breaking out intermittently between 1789 and 1795, profoundly affected the relations of political parties and groups and drew many thousands of Parisians into activity.

So much is common knowledge and has long been commonly accepted. But how were the crowds composed that stormed the Bastille in July 1789, marched to Versailles to fetch the king and queen to the capital in October, that overthrew the monarchy in August 1792, or silently witnessed the downfall of Robespierre on 9 Thermidor? Who led them or influenced them? What were the motives that prompted them? What was the particular significance and outcome of their intervention? It is not suggested that the great historians of the Revolution have had no answers to these questions: far from it; but, for lack of more precise inquiry, they have tended to answer them according to their own social ideals, political sympathies, or ideological preoccupations. In this respect we may distinguish between those writers who, like Burke and Taine, adopted a distinctly hostile attitude to the Revolution and everything that it stood for; Republican historians like Michelet and Aulard, for whom the Revolution marked a great regenerative upsurge of the French people; and, again, a Romantic like Carlyle who, while broadly sympathetic to the 'Nether Sansculottic World', was torn between admiration for its 'heroism' and fascinated horror at the 'World-Bedlam' or 'anarchy' that it appeared to unleash.

✳ To Burke the revolutionary crowd was purely destructive and presumed to be composed of the most undesirable social elements: the crowds that invaded the *château* of Versailles in October 1789 are 'a band of cruel ruffians and assassins, reeking with . . . blood'; and the royal family, on their return journey to Paris, are escorted by 'all the unutterable abominations of the furies of hell, in the abased shape of the vilest of women'. The National Assembly, having transferred to the capital, is compelled to deliberate 'amidst the tumultuous cries of a mixed mob of ferocious men, and of women lost to shame'.[1] Yet Burke's invective is far outmatched by Taine, the former Liberal of 1848, soured by his experiences of 1871, whose vocabulary of expletives has served the conservative historians of the Revolution ever since. The provincial insurgents of the early summer of 1789 are presented as 'contre-bandiers, faux-sauniers, braconniers, vagabonds, mendiants, repris de justice'. The Paris revolutionaries and the captors of the Bastille are the lowest social scum:

La lie de la société monte à la surface . . . la capitale semble livrée à la dernière plèbe et aux bandits . . . Vagabonds, déguenillés, plusieurs 'presque nus', la plupart armés comme des sauvages, d'une physionomie effrayante, ils sont 'de ceux qu'on ne se souvient pas d'avoir rencontrés au grand jour'.

The market women and others who marched to Versailles in October are thus described:

Les filles du Palais Royal . . . ajoutez des blanchisseuses, des mendiants, des femmes sans souliers, des poissardes raccolées depuis plusieurs jours à prix d'argent . . . la troupe s'incorpore les femmes qu'elle rencontre, portières, couturières, femmes de ménage, et même des bourgeoises. Joignez à cela des gens sans aveu, des rôdeurs de rue, des bandits, des voleurs, toute cette lie qui s'est entassée à Paris et qui surnage à chaque secousse . . . Voilà la fange qui, en arrière, en avant, roule avec le fleuve populaire.

[1] E. Burke, *Reflections on the Revolution in France* (London, 1951), pp. 66–69.

The insurgents of 10 August 1792, who drove Louis XVI from the Tuileries, become:

Presque tous de la dernière plèbe, ou entretenus par des métiers infâmes, spadassins et suppôts de mauvais lieux, accoutumés au sang . . . des aventuriers intrépides et féroces de toute provenance, Marseillais et étrangers, Savoyards, Italiens, Espagnols, chassés de leur pays.[1]

Following Taine, such terms as 'la canaille', 'la dernière plèbe', 'bandits', and 'brigands' have been commonly applied to the participants in these and similar events up to the present day.[2]

On the other hand, Michelet and the upholders of the Republican tradition have presented the revolutionary crowd in entirely different terms. Whenever it advanced, or appeared to advance, the aims of the revolutionary *bourgeoisie*, it has been presented as the embodiment of all the popular and Republican virtues. To Michelet the Bastille ceased to be a fortress that had to be reduced by force of arms: it became the personification of evil, over which virtue (in the shape of the People) inevitably triumphs: 'La Bastille ne fut pas prise . . . elle se livra. Sa mauvaise conscience la troubla, la rendit folle et lui fit perdre l'esprit.' And who captured it? 'Le peuple, le peuple tout entier.' Similarly, on 5 October, while the revolutionary leaders are groping for a solution to the crisis: 'Le peuple seul trouve un remède: il va chercher le Roi.' The role of the women takes on a more than merely casual significance: 'Ce qu'il y a dans le peuple de plus peuple, je veux dire de plus instinctif, de plus inspiré, ce sont, à coup sûr, les femmes.'[3] Louis Blanc, though lacking Michelet's exaltation, follows him closely;[4] and Aulard, the Radical professor of the Sorbonne, for all his sobriety of language and wealth of documentary learning, is in the same tradition: 'Paris se leva, tout entier, s'arma, s'empara de la Bastille.'[5]

---

[1] H. Taine, *Les Origines de la France contemporaine. La Révolution* (3 vols., Paris, 1876), i. 18, 53-54, 130, 272.

[2] See, for example, L. Madelin, who freely uses the terms 'bandits' and 'brigands' in relation to the Paris insurgents of July 1789 (*La Révolution* (Paris, 1914), pp. 60, 66, 68); and P. Gaxotte, *La Révolution française* (Paris, 1948), *passim*.

[3] J. Michelet, *La Révolution française* (9 vols., Paris, 1868-1900), i. 248, 377-9. The original edition dates from 1847 to 1853.

[4] L. Blanc, *Histoire de la Révolution française* (12 vols., Paris, 1868-70), ii. 352-3; iii. 184. The first edition is dated 1847-62.

[5] A. Aulard, *Histoire politique de la Révolution française [1789-1804]* (Paris, 1905), p. 37.

Great as has been the influence of these two rival schools on the historiography and teaching of the Revolution in France, in this country perhaps an even greater influence has been exerted on generations of students, teachers, and textbook writers by the striking imagery of Carlyle. The social forces unleashed by the Revolution and composing the active elements in each one of its decisive phases are variously described as an 'enraged National Tiger'; 'the World Chimera, bearing fire'; 'Victorious Anarchy'; and 'the funeral flame, enveloping all things . . . the Death-Bird of a World'. With all this, it is perhaps not surprising that he should gravely warn his readers against attempting a more precise analysis: 'But to gauge and measure this immeasurable Thing, and what is called account for it, and reduce it to a dead logic-formula, attempt not.'[1]

Yet, widely different as these interpretations are and the influences they have exerted, there is one common thread running through them all: whether the revolutionary crowd is represented as 'la canaille' or 'vile multitude' by Taine and Burke; as 'Victorious Anarchy' by Carlyle; or as 'le peuple' or 'tout Paris' by Michelet and Aulard—it has been treated by one and all as a disembodied abstraction and the personification of good or evil, according to the particular fancy or prejudice of the writer. This should perhaps not surprise us as, in the nineteenth century, to which most of these writers belonged, the debate on the French Revolution was conducted almost exclusively in political or ideological terms. This applied equally to constitutional monarchists like Mignet and Thiers in the 1820's; to those, like Michelet and Louis Blanc, who drew their inspiration from the events of February 1848; to a disgruntled Liberal like Taine in the 1870's; and even, though less obviously, to a Radical of the Third Republic like Aulard. Though differing profoundly in their attitude to the revolutionary tradition and in their hostility or reverence for the leaders or victims of the great Revolution, they have all been inclined to view these events and their participants 'from above'[2]

[1] T. Carlyle, *The French Revolution* (3 vols., London, 1869), i. 226, 258, 264–6 303. It is of some interest to note that Carlyle's first edition of 1837 bore the subtitle 'A History of Sansculottism'.

[2] The phrase has been frequently used in this connexion by Georges Lefebvre, most recently in his preface to W. Markov and A. Soboul, *Die Sansculotten von Paris* (Berlin, 1957), p. viii.

—that is, from the elevation of the committee room of the Committee of Public Safety, of the rostrum of the National Assembly or Jacobin Club, or of the columns of the revolutionary press. This being the case, the revolutionary crowd, whose voice was seldom reflected in the speeches of the politicians or the writings of the pamphleteers and journalists, tended to be lost sight of as a thing of flesh and blood and to assume whatever complexion accorded with the interests, opinions, or ideals of the revolutionary leaders, their critics, or adherents.

During the past half-century, however, the work of a number of eminent historians has made it possible to approach the subject in a more detached, or scientific, spirit. It is not so much that they have unearthed new archival materials that were unknown or inaccessible to their predecessors. This has sometimes been so, though, in the case of Paris, at least, rather the opposite is true: important materials that were available to Michelet and Mortimer-Ternaux, the historian of the Terror, have subsequently been destroyed. It is rather that the new social patterns and problems of the twentieth century have prompted historians to seek answers to new questions and, as the result of these considerations, to view the history of the Revolution from a new angle. An important consequence of their inquiries has been that the popular elements composing the sans-culottes—the peasants, craftsmen, journeymen, and labourers —have begun to appear as social groups with their own distinctive identity, interests, and aspirations, whose actions and attitudes can no longer be treated as mere echoes or reflections of the ideas, speeches, and decrees of the journalists, lawyers, orators, and politicians established in the capital. This new conception of the Revolution—seen as it were from below— was first given expression by Jaurès in his *Histoire socialiste de la Révolution française* which, in spite of its tendentious title, won the unstinting praise of Aulard, then holding the chair of French Revolution studies at the Sorbonne.[1] During the next fifty years this field of inquiry has been enormously widened by Albert Mathiez's work on the Parisian social movements of 1792–94,[2] Professor Labrousse's researches on prices and wages

[1] J. Jaurès, *L'Histoire socialiste de la Révolution française* (4 vols., Paris, 1901–4. Revised edition, 8 vols., 1922–4).
[2] A. Mathiez, *La Vie chère et le mouvement social sous la Terreur* (Paris, 1927).

during the eighteenth century,[1] and, above all, by Professor
Georges Lefebvre's studies on the peasantry, the psychology
of revolutionary crowds, and on the revolutionary panics of
1789.[2]

Without the new direction and stimulus that such work has
given to French Revolution studies, the present volume might
never have been attempted. Another determining factor has
been, of course, the availability of suitable documentation. It is
evident that the mass of participants in the great popular
movements of the Revolution have, unlike the journalists and
politicians, left few permanent records of their activities and
aspirations in the form of letters, pamphlets, speeches, or
committee minutes. In the case of Paris, too, a valuable source
has been removed by the destruction by fire in 1871 of the
great bulk of municipal and fiscal records, whose survival might
have yielded valuable information on the incomes, tax-assess-
ments, and working capital of the craftsmen and shopkeepers,
from whom the most militant elements among the Parisian
sans-culottes were to be drawn. Yet an important source, perhaps
even more valuable for the present purpose, remains to us—
the police records of the Archives Nationales and the Paris
Préfecture de Police; these have served as the main documentary basis for this volume. The French police system of the
eighteenth century was far more developed than that of this
country and has consequently left far more substantial archives.
In addition the method of cross-examination conducted by
the police, with its recording in the traditional procès-verbal,
provides the historian with detailed information regarding a
prisoner's occupation, address, province of origin, age, and his
degree of literacy and previous criminal record. Already fifty
years ago Alexandre Tuetey and Marcel Rouff, in a number
of studies, illustrated the great value of such records as a
source for social history.[3] Yet, unaccountably, they were neg-

---

[1] C.-E. Labrousse, *Esquisse du mouvement des prix et des revenus en France au XVIIIe
siècle* (2 vols., Paris, 1933); *La Crise de l'économie française à la fin de l'ancien régime et
au début de la Révolution* (Paris, 1944).

[2] G. Lefebvre, *Les Paysans du Nord pendant la Révolution française* (Paris-Lille,
1924); 'Foules révolutionnaires', *Annales historiques de la Révolution française*, xi
(1934), 1–26; *La Grande peur de 1789* (Paris, 1932).

[3] See, for example, A. Tuetey's Introduction to volume I of his *Répertoire général
des sources manuscrites de l'histoire de Paris pendant la Révolution française* (11 vols., Paris,

lected by Mathiez and his pupils,[1] and it is only in recent years that historians have begun to turn to them again. In the present instance, I have drawn largely on the *procès-verbaux* drawn up by the *commissaires de police* of the Paris Châtelet for 1787–90[2] and of the Paris Sections for 1790–5,[3] and—to a lesser extent—on the equivalent reports of the Committee of General Security of 1793–5.[4] These documents help to throw a new light on several of the popular movements arising on the eve of, and during, the Revolution in Paris, often inadequately treated by previous historians; and, above all, they make it possible to present a fuller and more accurate picture of the varying social elements that took part in them. While, of course, they relate only to a small minority of the participants—those arrested, killed, or wounded, or against whom information is laid with the police—the samples thus provided are often sufficiently large to allow one to draw general conclusions from them. For the participants in the major revolutionary movements of the period, however—those of July 1789, August 1792, May–June 1793, and the revolts of Prairial of the Year III and Vendémiaire of the Year IV (1795)—it has been found necessary to turn to other, additional, sources: to the lists of the *vainqueurs de la Bastille*,[5] to those of the claimants for pensions in August 1792[6] and for compensation for time lost under arms in June 1793,[7] and to the records of the military tribunals set up to judge the insurgents of Prairial and Vendémiaire.[8]

While the composition of revolutionary crowds may emerge, more or less clearly, from such records, it is, perhaps not surprisingly, more difficult to determine the motives that drew

1890–1914); also M. Rouff, 'Le Personnel des premières émeutes de '89 à Paris', *La Révolution Française*, lvii (1909), 213–31.

[1] Thus, even a great work of social history like *La Vie chère et le mouvement social sous la Terreur* is based almost entirely on reports of speeches in the National Convention, the Paris Commune, and the Jacobin Club.

[2] Archives Nationales, series Y: archives du Châtelet de Paris; series Z: juridictions spéciales et ordinaires.

[3] Archives de la Préfecture de Police, series Aa: sections de Paris. Procès-verbaux des commissaires de police.

[4] Archives Nationales, series F7 (police générale).

[5] The most useful of these is the list of 662 *vainqueurs de la Bastille* among the Osselin papers of the Archives Nationales, series T 514(1).

[6] Arch. Nat., F15 3267–74; F7 4426.

[7] Arch. Nat., BB1 80.

[8] Arch. Nat., W 546–8, 556–8.

them together and led thousands of Parisians to participate in these movements. For this purpose, too, the police records have been a far more fruitful source than the usually tendentious accounts of memorialists, journalists, deputies, and government reporters. In addition to the police archives just cited, a valuable source is provided by the collections of *rapports*, or public-opinion surveys, of police agents of the Paris Commune, the Central Bureau of Police and the Ministry of the Interior, variously compiled by Schmidt, Caron, and Aulard for the period 1792 to 1795.[1] These reports are a mine of information on the reactions of small property-owners and wage-earners, in particular, to the events of these years. For the earlier years, there is no exact equivalent, though Hardy's manuscript *Journal* is more than an adequate substitute for the eve and outbreak of the Revolution.[2]

The police surveys are, besides, a useful source for the movements of prices and wages, which play a considerable part in the present volume. The main source for these, however, are the various statistical lists and occasional data found in series F^{12} and F^{13} of the Archives Nationales.[3]

It may perhaps seem surprising that fuller use has not been made of the *cahiers de doléances* of 1789 and of the papers of the Paris Sections of 1790–5, which have been listed and (for the 'Year II') used to such good advantage by Albert Soboul.[4] But it must be remembered that the *sans-culottes*, from whom the great bulk of rioters and insurgents were drawn, had little to say in the drafting of the *cahiers*—least of all in Paris. Again, they played little or no part in the general assemblies or committees of the Sections until after August 1792 and a predominant part only during the brief period June 1793 to July 1794; and this, being a period of strong government, was, with the single exception of September 1793, a phase of the

[1] A. Schmidt, *Tableaux de la Révolution française* (4 vols., Leipzig, 1867–71); P. Caron, *Paris pendant la Terreur. Rapports des agents secrets du Ministre de l'Intérieur* (4 vols., Paris, 1910–49); A. Aulard, *Paris pendant la réaction thermidorienne et sous le Directoire* (5 vols., Paris, 1898–1902).

[2] S. Hardy, *Mes loisirs, ou journal d'événements tels qu'ils parviennent à ma connoissance* (MS. in 8 vols., Paris, 1764–89. Bibliothèque Nationale, fonds français, nos. 6680–7).

[3] For a fuller record of sources see Bibliography.

[4] A. Soboul, *Les Papiers des sections de Paris (1790–an IV)* (Paris, 1950); *Les Sans-Culottes parisiens en l'an II. Histoire politique et sociale des sections de Paris 2 juin 1793–9 thermidor an II* (to be published in autumn 1958); (with W. Markov), *Die Sansculotten von Paris: Dokumente zur Geschichte der Volksbewegung 1793–1794* (Berlin, 1957).

Revolution in Paris singularly unmarked by mass political disturbance.[1]

In the present volume, while dealing in the main with the revolutionary movements of 1789–95, I have attempted to bring into the picture the popular movements of the years 1787 and 1788 which, though preceding the outbreak of 1789, were a significant expression of the social and political ferment out of which the Revolution arose. Earlier historians, while appreciating the role of the *révolte nobiliaire* of those years as a curtain-raiser (if not an integral part) of the Revolution itself, have tended to neglect these movements—as they have tended, at the other end of the story, to neglect that of Vendémiaire of the Year IV (October 1795) which, though essentially a rising of middle-class property-owners, yet provoked a significant response from the Parisian *sans-culottes*. The present study may therefore perhaps claim to be original in so far as it attempts to present the Parisian revolutionary crowd (in its broadest sense) throughout the period 1787–95—showing how it behaved, how it was composed, how it was drawn into activity, what it set out to achieve, and how far its aims were realized. To do this it is proposed, in the first place, to relate those episodes of the Revolution in Paris, and of the years immediately preceding, in which a decisive factor was the mass intervention in streets and markets, of mainly ordinary men and women: these outbursts were, with the exception of the year 1790 (a period of remarkable social calm), an almost continuous feature of the life of the capital during the first six years of the Revolution and for nearly two years before its outbreak. Following this, some general conclusions will be drawn from the composition, behaviour, springs of action, and aims of the crowds engaged in these various movements.

But first the reader must be introduced, if only briefly, to the social and historical background against which the events of the Revolution in Paris took place.

[1] Some revision of Part II, chapter 9 (dealing with the period September 1793–July 1794) may, however, be called for with the publication of M. Soboul's work on *Les Sans-Culottes parisiens*.

PARIS ON THE EVE OF THE REVOLUTION

OUTWARDLY, on the eve of the Revolution, Paris was being radically transformed. It was not the first time in her history. The medieval city, once enclosed by the stout walls erected by Philippe-Auguste in the thirteenth century, had been' pushed farther outwards by Charles V who, in the fourteenth, had built the Bastille to guard its eastern approaches. Under Louis XIII, a new *enceinte*, or barrier of customs posts, to mark the official point of entry into the city, had been constructed along the line of the present Inner Boulevards.[1] In the eighteenth century the rapid pace of building and enhanced tempo of commercial and social life had necessitated further changes: the houses on the old bridges were pulled down or allowed to crumble; work was begun on the new Pont Louis XVI—the present Pont de la Concorde; medieval cemeteries were cleared from the city centre; street lamps began to replace the grim old *lanternes* on the street-corners; and pavements were slowly beginning to appear in imitation of London.[2] Above all, the boundaries of the city were further extended; and, in 1785, work was completed on the new *enceinte*, a ring of fifty-four customs posts, linked by a wall ten feet high, which encircled the capital over a span of eighteen miles. Not only did it push the city limits outwards to enclose the Faubourg Saint-Antoine to the east and the Faubourgs Saint-Martin and Saint-Denis to the north; but, for the first time, it added to the capital the villages of Passy and Chaillot to the west and the old *faubourgs* of Saint-Victor, Saint-Marcel, Saint-Jacques, and Saint-Germain to the south.[3] But the new barrier was intended to do more than merely mark the new contours of the city: its prime object was to tighten up the system of internal customs and, by checking smuggling, to increase substantially the royal revenues.

[1] A. Demangeon, *Paris. La Ville et sa banlieue* (Paris, 1933), p. 16.
[2] A. Babeau, *Paris en 1789* (Paris, 1889), p. 23; H. Monin, *L'État de Paris en 1789* (Paris, 1889), pp. 10–13.   [3] Demangeon, loc. cit.

Its importance in this respect may be judged by the fact that in 1789 the Paris customs yielded no less than 28–30 million *livres* of a national total of 70 millions.[1] This, of course, did little to add to the popularity of Calonne, the minister promoting the scheme, or of the Farmers General to whom its construction and its administration had been entrusted. 'Le mur murant Paris rend Paris murmurant', wrote the wits.[2] This hostility was soon to be voiced in the *cahiers de doléances* of the clergy of Paris 'beyond the walls' and by the Third Estate of several electoral districts.[3] It was also to find expression in the more violent action of the Parisian *menu peuple*, and the *barrières* were to fall. a victim to popular fury before even the hated Bastille.[4]

The new limits of Paris enclosed a population, whose size, for all the statistical experiments that marked the period, has defied calculation: the most reliable estimates range between 524,000 and 660,000.[5] One of the great difficulties, as Necker saw, was to determine not only the relatively settled population[6] (variously computed according to births and deaths, households, bread cards, or police reports), but the far more elusive floating population of the hotels and *chambres garnies*, which

[1] M. Marion, *Dictionnaire des institutions de la France aux XVIIe et XVIIIe siècles* (Paris, 1923), pp. 402–4.

[2] Babeau, op. cit., p. 28.

[3] C.-L. Chassin, *Les Élections et les cahiers de Paris en 1789* (4 vols., Paris, 1888–9); ii. 410, 421, 425, 432, 442–3, 444, 448, 455, 465, 519; iv. 406, 451.

[4] See pp. 48–49 below.

[5] The census of 1788–9, based on the counting of households, yielded 524,186 inhabitants (*Statistique de la France*, vol. 3: *Territoire. Population* (Paris, 1837), p. 277). Necker's private calculation of 1784 had been 640,000–660,000 (J. Necker. *De l'administration des finances de la France* (3 vols., Paris, 1784), i. 277). A census of 1792 gave a population of 635,504 (N. Kareiev, *La Densité de la population des différentes sections de Paris pendant la Révolution* (Paris, 1912), pp. 14–15). Two censuses of 1795, the one partly based on registrations for bread-cards, the other on the number of consumers, yielded 626,582 and 636,772 respectively (P. Meuriot, *Un Recensement de l'An II* (Paris, 1918), pp. 33–34; Archives Nationales, F⁷ 3688⁴). For a discussion of the possible reliability of these various estimates see G. Rudé, *The Parisian Wage-Earning Population and the Insurrectionary Movements of 1789–91* [hereafter cited as *Parisian Wage-Earners*] (unpublished Ph.D. thesis in 2 vols., London Univ., 1950), i. 34–43. For estimates of the population of the forty-eight Parisian Sections in 1790–1800 see Appendix II below.

[6] The term 'settled' is, of course, used only in a relative sense. There was a continuous movement of population to and from Paris (though mostly to Paris from the provinces) throughout the century. Records of police and other public authorities reveal the high proportion of provincial-born among the resident Parisian population of the revolutionary period.

varied from one season to another and for which official returns only rarely provided.[1] Bearing this in mind, Necker's
private estimate of a population of between 640,000 and 660,000[2]
may be nearer to the truth than the lower figure of 524,000
yielded by the census of 1788–9 and accepted by several writers
as a reasonable computation.[3]

In either case, the privileged, or wealthier classes, formed but
a small proportion of the population as a whole. Léon Cahen,
who made some attempt to calculate the size of the various
social groups or orders inhabiting Paris in the mid-eighteenth
century, concluded that the clergy numbered about 10,000,
the nobility 5,000, and the financial, commercial, manufactur-
ing, and professional *bourgeoisie* about 40,000;[4] the rest—the
great majority—were the small shopkeepers, petty traders,
craftsmen, journeymen, labourers, vagrants, and city poor,
who formed what later became known as the *sans-culottes*.[5]

To a large extent it was to promote the economic interests
and to flatter the social ambitions of the nobility and wealthy
bourgeoisie that the outward face of Paris was being transformed
and its fashionable centre was moving westwards; the clergy
had too large a stake in the 140 religious houses that still lay
scattered over the old city and *faubourgs*[6] to indulge in large-
scale plans of extension: it was even said that Louis XV's intention to demolish and rebuild the Cité had been blocked by
clerical obstruction.[7] Aristocrats, bankers, and wealthy mer-

---

[1] The number of *non-domiciliés*—those living in *hôtels garnis* and lodgings of various
types—are recorded in the first of the two censuses of 1795, but only in the case of
25 of the 48 Sections (Meuriot, op. cit., p. 32).   [2] Necker, op. cit. i. 277.

[3] See, for example, F. Braesch, *La Commune du 10 août 1792* (Paris, 1911), p. 14;
A. Landry, 'La Démographie de l'ancien Paris', *Journal de la société de statistique de
Paris*, lxxvi (1935), 34–45. Meuriot, however, favours the higher figure (op. cit.,
pp. 34–35).

[4] L. Cahen, 'La Population parisienne au milieu du 18 siècle', *La Revue de Paris*,
1919, pp. 146–70.

[5] After June 1792, this term was to take on a political sense, as well, and to be
applied to extreme Republicans in general—even to those of personal wealth. I
have tried, however, in the course of this study, to use it in a social sense only.

[6] According to Edmé Verniquet's map of Paris in 1789 (published by the Paris
Municipal Council in 1889) there were, at this time, 68 'couvents et communautés'
for men and 73 for women.

[7] Babeau, op. cit., p. 19. There were, however, exceptions: thus, the abbess and
community of the Abbaye Royale de Saint-Antoine-des-Champs built a new
street, a market, and fountain on their estates lying east of the Bastille (Monin,
op. cit., p. 16).

chants had no such qualms and had long vied with one another in building new town houses in the more fashionable western quarters of the Palais Royal, the Cours-la-Reine, and the Faubourg Saint-Honoré, which had begun to spring up with the court's removal to Versailles under Louis XIV.[1] The Marais, the old aristocratic quarter of the Right Bank which, in the time of Henri IV and Louis XIII, had been the centre of fashion, was becoming deserted; in the 1780's Sébastien Mercier described it as 'un triste quartier',[2] where the tower of the Hôtel de Bourgogne and the Hôtels de Sens and de Cluny, both converted to commercial uses, bore witness to past, rather than present, glories.[3]

Meanwhile, wrote Mercier, in the last twenty-five years, 10,000 houses had been constructed and one-third of Paris had been rebuilt.[4] Regiments of building workers had been enrolled from the central provinces and the speed of construction was often phenomenal: the Opéra was built in seventy-five days and the Château de Bagatelle in six weeks.[5] Whole new streets were being opened up, specially in the northern and western districts. Monin, the historian of Paris in 1789, gives us some idea of the scale and speed of this development during the last fifteen years of the old régime. Off the Champs Elysées, which then marked the extreme western fringe of the new fashionable residential areas, the Comte d'Artois, the king's younger. brother, opened up the rues de Berry and d'Angoulême, which .followed soon after by the rues du Colisée and Milet (the present rue Matignon). In the adjoining Faubourg Saint-Honoré, the rue d'Astorg was planned—though uncompleted by 1789; farther north and east beyond the boulevards, the banker Laborde obtained letters patent for building the rues de Provence, d'Artois (today's rue Laffitte), Taitbout, and Houssaye; and, farther eastwards still, followed the rues Martel, Richer, Saint-Nicolas, Montholon, de Buffault, and de Lancry. Near the Palais Royal, the Marquis de Chabanais and the Marquis de Louvois gave their names to streets constructed on the site of their town houses. The sale of a part of the Duc de Choiseul's

[1] Demangeon, op. cit., p. 16.
[2] L. S. Mercier, *Tableau de Paris* (12 vols., Amsterdam, 1783), i. 258-61.
[3] Babeau, op. cit., p. 18.
[4] Mercier, op. cit., viii. 190.
[5] Babeau, op. cit., p. 27.

estates on the boulevards paved the way for the erection of the
Comédie Italienne and the opening of the rues Neuve Saint-
Marc, Tournante, d'Amboise, and de la Terrasse. Two years
before the Revolution, the rues de Breteuil, Boynes, and Crosne
were built in the former grounds of the Hôtel de Boynes.[1] Even
more spectacular was the construction by the Duke of Orleans,
wealthiest and most popular of the princes of the blood, of the
magnificent arcades and gardens of the Palais Royal, shortly to
become a centre of lavish entertainment and a meeting place
of journalists, pamphleteers, and political gossips; while, on the
Left Bank, the Théâtre Français (the later Odéon) was built
in 1789 on the site of the Hôtel Condé, recently purchased for
3 million *livres*.[2] Yet from all this feverish construction, Jaurès
noted, it was the wealthy *bourgeoisie* that emerged as the largest
holders of real estate in the capital: 'Sauf quelques centaines de
grandes familles,' he wrote, 'la noblesse elle-même était locataire
de la bourgeoisie'; and he concluded: 'La bourgeoisie parisienne
était, à la veille de 1789, la force souveraine de propriété, de
production et de consommation.'[3]

Yet, for all these changes, the old medieval Paris remained
substantially intact, and was to remain so for seventy-five years
to come. The splendours of Notre Dame and the Sainte-Chapelle
still dominated the approaches to the Cité; the numerous
religious houses and the Temple and Châtelet prisons vied with
the Bastille, with its eight towers and eighty-foot walls, as
survivals from a feudal past. Above all there still remained
the old tenements, the courtyards and alleys, workshops, and
lodging houses in which nine out of every ten Parisians lived
and worked—in the Cité and central market districts and in the
faubourgs lying east of the great pilgrims' way and thoroughfare,
formed by the rues Saint-Martin, Saint-Jacques, and their ex-
tensions and cutting the city in two from the barrière Saint-
Martin in the north to the barrière Saint-Jacques in the south.
There were as yet no distinctive working-class areas: these
only fully emerged under the Second Empire.[4] At most, there

---

[1] Monin, op. cit., pp. 15–16. See also Babeau, op. cit., pp. 1–38.

[2] Babeau, op. cit., p. 24.

[3] J. Jaurès, *L'Histoire socialiste de la Révolution française* (8 vols., Paris, 1922–4), i. 149–50.

[4] L. Chevalier, *La Formation de la population parisienne au XIXᵉ siècle* (Paris, 1950), pp. 122 et seq.

were streets of lodging houses and *chambres garnies*, like the rue de la Mortellerie, adjoining the Hôtel de Ville, or the rues Galande and des Jardins, a stone's throw from Notre Dame, where riverside workers, porters, stonemasons, and other seasonal workers lived closely huddled in lodgings at one to four *sous* a night.[1] But, generally, small masters, independent craftsmen, and journeymen lived cheek by jowl: during the Paris revolution, we shall find masters and journeymen setting out from the same house in the rue de Lappe or in the rue du Faubourg Saint-Antoine to join in the siege of the Bastille.[2] In this *faubourg* even wealthy manufacturers like Réveillon, who owned a 'manufactory' employing 350 workers in the rue de Montreuil, and the famous brewer, Antoine-Joseph Santerre, lived in close proximity to their workpeople. In such districts, it was not so much the wage-earners, but the whole *menu peuple* of shopkeepers, craftsmen, and labourers, who could, broadly speaking, be identified by their lodging, speech, and dress, their mode of living, and their weekly outings to the wine-shops and taverns of La Courtille, Les Porcherons, or La Nouvelle France.[3]

Yet certain districts had taken on a distinctive character from the trades and occupations of their inhabitants. There were, of course, the famous fish-wives or market-women, the *poissardes* or *dames de la halle*, of the Place Maubert and the central markets; there were the goldsmiths and jewellers of the quai de l'Horloge, the quai des Orfèvres, and the Place Dauphine in the Cité, or in the arcades of the Palais Royal. The newly developed Faubourg de Chaillot was famous for the Périer Brothers' Compagnie des Eaux de Paris, equipped with steampower and the first firm in France to manufacture steamengines based on James Watt's model.[4] The area north of the markets formed by the rue des Lombards, the rue Saint-Denis, and the rue des Gravilliers was the main commercial centre, where lived also a large proportion of the city's home-workers,

[1] These amounts appear in various police reports for the period 1789–92; see also Babeau, op. cit., p. 158.   [2] See pp. 58–59 below.
[3] A. Soboul, 'Les Sans-culottes parisiens en l'an II', *Miroir de l'histoire*. July 1956, pp. 91–99.
[4] By 1791, they had produced forty and had begun to export (A. Mathiez, *La France économique dans la seconde moitié du 18ᵉ siècle* (Cours proposé à la Faculté de Lettres de Paris, 1927-8, pour le Cert. d'Ét. Sup. d'Hist. Mod., Paris, 1928), p. 84.

like those '20,000' ribbon-weavers who, in November 1791, petitioned the Legislative Assembly in protest against the introduction of mechanical frames.[1] The greater number of the new textile manufactories, several of which employed 400 or 500—even 800—workpeople, lay in the northern *faubourgs* on either side of the rue Saint-Martin and the rue Saint-Denis.[2] Porters, dockers, and seasonal building workers gave a distinctive quality to the busy, teeming streets around the Hôtel de Ville and the Place de Grève. The Faubourg Saint-Antoine, the traditional focal point of popular agitation,[3] had several breweries and a glassworks employing 500, but was, above all, a typical centre of petty crafts—particularly of small workshops engaged in furnishing and upholstery.[4]

More variegated and (some thought) even more turbulent was the population composing the Faubourg Saint-Marcel and the adjoining *faubourgs* of Saint-Jacques and Saint-Victor. For long its most conspicuous industry had been the tanneries, expelled by Colbert from the quays of the Cité to the slopes of the Montagne Sainte-Geneviève a hundred years previously; yet they appear to have declined in the years before the Revolution, as a return of 1791 records the existence of a mere dozen masters employing less than 200 assistants.[5] Other trades included dyeing, cloth-making and laundries, besides the famous Gobelins tapestry works installed by Louis XIV in 1662.[6] Many of the dyers and cloth-makers were of Flemish or Dutch origin, and beer flowed freely in the ale-houses dotted along the *faubourg*'s main thoroughfare, the rue Mouffetard, which wound its way up from the barrière de Fontainebleau to the place Contrescarpe on the Montagne Sainte-Geneviève. 'Ce peuple boit pour huit jours,' wrote Mercier, who thought them dangerous—'plus méchant, plus inflammable, plus querelleur, & plus disposé à la mutinerie que dans les autres quartiers.'[7]

These *faubourgs* included some of the poorest districts in the city and were frequently the recipients of the largest amounts of

---

[1] Arch. Nat., F[12] 1430; cited by F. Braesch, *La Commune du 10 août 1792*, p. 24.

[2] F. Braesch, 'Un Essai de statistique de la population ouvrière de Paris vers 1791', *La Révolution française*, lxiii (1912), 289–321.

[3] C. Lefeuve, *Les Anciennes maisons de Paris. L'histoire de Paris, rue par rue, maison par maison* (5 vols., Paris, 1875), vol. i, pp. iii, 147.

[4] F. Braesch, *La Commune du 10 août 1792*, pp. 6–8.

[5] Braesch, op. cit., p. 10.   [6] Ibid.   [7] Mercier, op. cit., i. 257–8.

poor-relief that were distributed from time to time during both the old régime and the Revolution. When, for example, in February 1790 the Paris Commune voted 64,000 *livres* for distribution to the poor, 7,000 *livres* were allotted to the District of Saint-Étienne-du-Mont, lying between the Faubourgs Saint-Marcel and Saint-Jacques; 5,300 *livres* to the Val-de-Grâce and Saint-Jacques-du-Haut-Pas Districts in the Faubourg Saint-Jacques; and sums of 5,100 and 4,800 *livres* respectively to the Enfants-Trouvés and Sainte-Marguerite Districts of the Faubourg Saint-Antoine: these were by far the largest allocations.[1] And, in 1791, nearly one-quarter of all those receiving poor-relief resided in the four sections of the Faubourg Saint-Marcel.[2]

It may be considerations such as these that have led even recent historians to speak of these *faubourgs*, soon to play so prominent a part in the Revolution, as working-class suburbs.[3] The term is misleading for more than one reason. In the first place, as M. Braesch has shown, the largest concentrations of wage-earners were to be found in the central market area and the northern *faubourgs* of the capital—and not in the Faubourg Saint-Marcel, still less in the Faubourg Saint-Antoine, or any other district in which the petty crafts predominated. This emerges from the results of an inquiry which the Paris Municipality conducted in early 1791 to determine the number of workers employed by each industrial undertaking in the forty-eight Sections of the capital.[4] The returns—though not fully complete—suggest that the total wage-earning population (workers and their families) at this time fell little short of 300,000. By relating the figures for each Section to those yielded by the

[1] A. Tuetey, *L'Assistance publique à Paris pendant la Révolution* (4 vols., Paris, 1895–7), vol. i, pp. cxxxiii–v.
[2] 27,158 out of 118,784 (Chabrol de Volvic, *Recherches statistiques de la ville de Paris* (4 vols., Paris, 1821–9), vol. i, Table 43). In April 1794 it was reported that 15,000 of 68,000 recipients of poor-relief resided in the Faubourg Saint-Antoine alone (Soboul, op. cit., p. 96).
[3] See, e.g., J. M. Thompson, *The French Revolution* (Oxford, 1947), pp. 49, 66.
[4] F. Braesch, 'Un Essai de statistique de la population ouvrière de Paris vers 1791', *La Révolution française*, lxiii (1912), 289–321. M. Braesch's findings are based on the returns made by 41 of the 48 Sections in response to a request by the Paris Municipality late in 1790 for information as to the number of *assignats* (revolutionary paper-money) of low denomination required for distribution to employers. These returns are in Arch. Nat., F[30], nos. 109–24, 129, 131–4, 136–60. For a discussion of M. Braesch's calculations see *Parisian Wage-Earners* i. 46–51.

census of 1792[1] we find that the wage-earners and their families
accounted for some two-thirds of the resident population in
seven northern and north-central Sections[2] and for nearly half
the population in four Sections of the central market area,[3]
while accounting for only one-third to one-half the population
of the Faubourgs Saint-Antoine and Saint-Marcel.[4]

But, even when they formed a majority of the local population, the wage-earners lacked the attributes of a distinctive
social class. In eighteenth-century France, the term *ouvrier* might
be applied as readily to independent craftsmen, small workshop masters—or even, on occasion, to substantial manufacturers—as to ordinary wage-earners; in its most frequent
use it was synonymous with artisan.[5] Such usage corresponded to
the social realities of the time, when the wage-earner had as
yet no defined and distinctive status as a producer and there
were often numerous intermediate stages between workman
and employer. The typical unit of production was still the small
workshop, which generally employed but a small number of
journeymen and apprentices. Even in Paris, where the proportion of workers to employers was larger and the restrictions
imposed by the guild-system had become more relaxed than
elsewhere,[6] the journeyman still often ate at his master's table
and slept under his roof.[7] The distinction between a wage-
earning journeyman and an independent craftsman, or even a
workshop master, was ill defined: the 2,000 Parisian stocking-
weavers who struck against wage-cuts in 1724, while depending

---

[1] N. Kareiev, op. cit., pp. 14–15.

[2] These are: Beaubourg, Gravilliers, Ponceau, Mauconseil, Bonne Nouvelle,
Poissonnière, Faubourg Saint-Denis.

[3] These are: Louvre, Oratoire, Marchés des Innocents (later Halles), Lombards.

[4] See *Parisian Wage-Earners*, i. 52–53, 277–80 (Appendix A).

[5] The *Dictionnaire de l'Académie Française* (1772 ed.) defines an *ouvrier* as 'celui
qui travaille de la main et fait quelque ouvrage'; and Diderot's *Encyclopédie* explains
that the term 'se dit en général de tout artisan qui travaille de quelque métier que
ce soit'. The earliest edition of the *Dictionnaire de l'Académie* which defines the term
in its modern sense of a wage-earner is that of 1935. For a recent discussion of the
difficulties of definition in the study of social history see Alfred Cobban, 'The
Vocabulary of Social History', *Political Science Quarterly*, lxxi (1956), 14.

[6] A. Franklin, *La Vie privée d'autrefois: comment on devenait patron* (Paris, 1889),
pp. 281–4.

[7] Besides the evidence of the police records we find the assertion in a *Motion
des artistes, artisans et ouvriers du district des Capucins de la Chaussée d'Antin* of July
1789: 'Notre domicile est chez nos maîtres, nos pères ou en chambre garnie'
(Bibliothèque Nationale, nouvelles acquisitions françaises, no. 2642, fols. 13–15).

for their living on a wage, still rented their frames from their - ·
employers and worked in their own homes;[1] and, in August
1789, we shall find a substantial body of hairdressers' journeymen in Paris insisting on their right to set up in business on their
own irrespective of their masters' wishes.[2]

About one-third of all the wage-earners recorded in the 1791
return were in the building trades;[3] they were largely composed
of seasonal workers or recent immigrants from the Creuse and
Limoges—hence their nick-name of *limousins*—and lodged in
barely furnished rooms in the rue Mouffetard or the city centre.[4]
Among them, too, we find the journeyman-employer, or
maître-ouvrier who, while himself living on a wage paid by the
building contractor, hired his own *compagnons* or *garçons* at a
daily or seasonal rate.[5] The great mass of porters, carriers, and
riverside workers, often recent immigrants from Picardy, Savoy,
or Auvergne, and lodging around the markets or in the
neighbourhood of the docks, are harder to define; yet there
must have been numerous grades and distinctions separating
the common labourers from such highly organized *communautés*
as formed by the *forts de la halle* or the more aristocratic of the
various types of *gagne-deniers*.[6] Even more variegated were the
14,000 inmates of the *hôpitaux* and alms-houses,[7] soon to be
reinforced by the many thousands of workless peasants, small
tradesmen, and country-workers who flocked into the capital on ·
the eve of revolution and were herded into the *ateliers de charité*
on the hill of Montmartre and elsewhere.[8] It is, in fàct, only

[1] F. Funck-Brentano, 'La Question ouvrière sous l'Ancien Régime', *Revue
rétrospective*, xvii (1892), 1–24.   [2] Arch. Nat., T 514 (¹).
[3] For this and other categories of workers in Paris at this time see *Parisian Wage-
Earners*, ii. 277–80 (Appendix A).
[4] G. Mauco, *Les Migrations ouvrières en France au début du XIXe siècle* (Paris, 1932),
pp. 29–31.
[5] J.-J. Letrait, 'La Communauté des maîtres maçons de Paris au XVIIe et au
XVIIIe siècle', *Revue historique de droit français et étranger*, 1945, pp. 256–7; 1948,
pp. 113–17.
[6] For the latter, see M. Rouff, 'Une Grève de gagne-deniers en 1786 à Paris',
Revue historique, cv (1910), 332–48. None of these categories of workers appear in
the returns of 1791 analysed by Braesch.
[7] This is the figure for 1791 (C. Bloch and A. Tuetey, *Procès-verbaux et rapports du
comité de mendicité de la Constituante, 1790–1791* (Paris, 1911), p. 482).
[8] Lafayette estimated the number of 'étrangers ou gens sans aveu' in Paris in
the week following the capture of the Bastille at 'over 30,000'; yet this may have
been exaggerated for partisan ends (*Mémoires, correspondance et manuscrits du Général
Lafayette* (6 vols., Paris, 1837), i. 272–3).

among the workers in the new textile manufactories of the northern *faubourgs*, who may have amounted to a quarter or a fifth of the total working population,[1] that we begin to find the distinctive characteristics of a modern industrial working class; but, as we shall see, unlike the small craftsmen and journeymen, they were to play a relatively minor role in the events of the Revolution.

Yet, for all their lack of cohesion as a social class, the Parisian journeymen and labourers had long since learned to express their particular economic demands—often by violent means. With the break-down in the purposes and organization of the old medieval guild, the journeyman had found himself reduced to the status of a wage-earner with nothing but the slenderest chance of ever becoming a master.[2] This gradual divergence in the material interests of masters and journeymen is reflected in the increasingly bitter strikes and social movements of the century, becoming all the more bitter as prices tended progressively to outstrip wages.[3] To take a few examples. In 1724 there was a strike of stocking-frame weavers against a reduction of wages, which was broken by the arrest of their leaders.[4] In 1737 the journeymen weavers rebelled against the new regulations governing, and restricting, entry to the *maîtrise*.[5] In 1749 the journeymen hatters were forbidden by an *arrêt* of the Paris *Parlement* to interfere with their employers' freedom to hire labour;[6] and, in 1765, a similar *arrêt* forbade these workers to carry swords and hunting-knives.[7] In 1776 there was a general strike among bookbinders for a fourteen-hour day.[8] In 1785 workers in the building trades, striking against a wage-cut imposed by the contractors, won a notable victory: the *Parlement* declared in their favour after several hundred of them had

---

[1] *Parisian Wage-Earners*, i. 58, and note 83.

[2] A. Franklin, op. cit., pp. 90–95, 173–217.

[3] Professor Labrousse has shown that whereas the prices of food and other essentials of popular consumption increased by 62 per cent. between the periods 1726–41 and 1771–89, nominal wages increased by only 22 per cent. between the same periods (C.-E. Labrousse, *Esquisse du mouvement des prix et des revenus en France au XVIIIᵉ siècle*, ii. 597–608).

[4] Funck-Brentano, op. cit.   [5] Rouff, op. cit., p. 333.

[6] A. Franklin, *Dictionnaire des arts, métiers et professions exercés dans Paris depuis le XIIIᵉ siècle* (Paris, 1906), p. 372.   [7] Ibid., p. 573.

[8] S. Hardy, *Mes loisirs, ou journal d'événements tels qu'ils parviennent à ma connoissance* (MS. in 8 vols., Paris, 1764–89. Bib. Nat., fonds français, nos. 6680–7), iii. 281.

argued with Lenoir, the lieutenant of police, and others had marched in search of the, king at the château de Bounoy.[1] The following year, Sébastien Hardy, the bookseller-diarist, reported a far wider movement embracing carpenters, farriers, locksmiths, bakers, and stonemasons;[2] and, the same year, striking porters and carriers, protesting against a rival monopoly set up by court favourites, marched to Versailles to petition the king and aroused widespread popular sympathy.[3] In June 1789, on the very eve of the Paris revolution, there was a further strike of hatters—this time over rival journeymen's associations.[4]

Such movements may, as Marcel Rouff has suggested, have contributed to the revolutionary temper of 1789;[5] but they were not decisive. In the conditions of the time conflicts between capital and labour were generally of secondary importance and the wage-earner was usually more concerned with the price of food—particularly of bread—than with the amount of his earnings. This was partly due to the absence of large-scale capitalist industry and of a national trade union movement: more particularly, it was due to the large part played by bread in the budget of the wage-earners, as of all small property-owners. In Paris, in 1789, a labourer's daily wage might be 20 to 30 *sous*, a journeyman mason might earn 40 *sous*, and a carpenter or locksmith 50 *sous*.[6] According to Professor Labrousse an eighteenth-century French worker would normally spend something like 50 per cent. of his income on bread; 16 per cent. on vegetables, fats, and wine; 15 per cent. on clothing; 5 per cent. on fuel; and 1 per cent. on lighting.[7] Thus the wage-earners, and other small income-earners, were vitally interested in the price of bread which, in Paris, in 'normal' times, would be eight or nine *sous* for the 4-lb. loaf. Should its price, as all too frequently happened, rise sharply to

---

[1] Ibid. vi. 149–50.   [2] Ibid. vi. 315.
[3] Rouff, op. cit., p. 334.   [4] Arch. Nat., Y 13016 (12 June 1789).
[5] Rouff, op. cit., p. 347.
[6] G. Rudé, 'Prices, Wages and Popular Movements in Paris during the French Revolution', *Economic History Review*, vol. vi, no. 3, 1954, p. 248. The worker's average 'effective' earnings were, however, considerably less than this owing to the large number of feast days during the old régime: these amounted to about 111 per year (ibid.). See also Appendix VII.
[7] Labrousse, op. cit. ii. 597–608; G. Lefebvre, 'Le Mouvement des prix et les origines de la Révolution française', *Annales historiques de la Révolution française*, xiv (1937), 289–329.

12 or 15 (or even to 20) *sous*, it is evident that the bulk of the wage-earners faced sudden disaster. It is not surprising, therefore, that they tended to think in terms of cheaper and more plentiful bread—rather than in terms of higher wages and better workshop conditions; and, with rare exceptions, this continued to be the case during the Revolution as well.[1] In consequence it was the food riot rather than the strike that was still the traditional and typical form of popular protest; and in this not only journeymen, labourers, and city poor, but small shopkeepers, craftsmen, and workshop masters joined in common opposition to farmers, millers, bakers, hoarders, grain-merchants, and city authorities. This basic identity of interest was to prove one of the most solid of the links that bound together the social groups forming the *sans-culottes* of the Revolution.

Paris, like other big cities, had, throughout the century, been continually threatened with such outbreaks. To avert them an elaborate system had been devised to ensure the regular and adequate supply of wheat to suburban millers and flour to the Paris bakers—often at the expense of the supplying areas themselves, or at the reputed expense of the villages lying on the rivers and roads along which food-convoys bound for the capital travelled.[2] But the margin of safety was rarely sufficient to withstand the onslaught or vagaries of bad harvests, drought, hail, frost, poor communications, or the peculations of grain-monopolists and speculators. In such cases the system broke down and panic-buying led to steep rises in the price of bread and outbursts of anger and violence by the Parisian *menu peuple*. In the great famine year of 1709 the break-down had been so nearly complete and so protracted that hundreds had died of starvation.[3] In August 1725 the Marquis d'Argenson recorded

[1] This tendency is clearly reflected in the few provincial *cahiers de doléances* of wage-earners that have come down to us. In Paris there is no such evidence, in view of the special regulations drawn up to exclude wage-earners and small property-owners from the Parisian preliminary assemblies (Chassin, op. cit. i. 373-6).

[2] L. Cahen, 'La Question du pain à Paris à la fin du XVIIIᵉ siècle', *Cahiers de la Révolution française*, no. 1 (1934), pp. 51-76. For the Parisian supply-routes and the frequent attacks on Paris-bound convoys by road and river in the period 1752-89, see R. C. Cobb, 'Les Disettes de l'an II et de l'an III dans le district de Mantes et la vallée de la Basse-Seine', *Mémoires de la fédération des sociétés historiques et archéologiques de Paris et de l'Île-de-France*, iii (1954), pp. 227-33.

[3] A. de Boislisle, 'Le Grand Hiver et la disette de 1709', *Revue des questions historiques*, lxxiii (June 1903), 442-509; lxxiv (December 1903), 486-542.

that the price of bread had risen higher than in 1709 and that to appease popular anger ('il y avait eu à Paris des séditions sérieuses') M. d'Ombreval, the minister responsible, had been relieved of his post.[1] In September 1740 the price of the 4-lb. loaf rose to 20 *sous* (equivalent to the daily wage of an unskilled worker); the king was assailed with cries of 'Misère! du pain! du pain!'; Cardinal Fleury was mobbed by a crowd of angry women; and fifty prisoners at Bicêtre were shot dead after rioting in protest against a reduction in their bread-ration.[2] In December 1752 bread riots were coupled with angry demonstrations against the Archbishop of Paris who had refused the sacrament to a dying nun suspected of Jansenism;[3] six months later the price of bread was still abnormally high and seditious leaflets were circulated, bearing the inscription, 'Vive le Parlement! meurent le Roi et les évêques!'[4] It was the same king— Louis XV—who was popularly believed to have devised the sinister *pacte de famine*.[5]

More widespread and even more alarming to the authorities were the food riots that broke out in Paris and its adjoining provinces in the spring of 1775. Turgot had been appointed Comptroller-General in August 1774. He started with no particular record of unpopularity as far as the common people were concerned: in fact, his predecessor and most vocal opponent, the abbé Terray, was, soon after his appointment,. burned in effigy in the Faubourg Saint-Antoine.[6] Yet, to the delight of his enemies at court, he was soon to lose any semblance of popular favour by his over-haste in applying Physiocratic doctrine to the grain-trade: an *arrêt* of 13 September

---

[1] *Journal et mémoires du Marquis d'Argenson* (9 vols., Paris, 1859), i. 54. According to another memorialist, the lawyer Barbier, the price of the 4-lb. loaf had risen to the almost fantastic sum of 28–32 *sous* (E. J. F. Barbier, *Journal historique et anecdotique du règne de Louis XV* (4 vols., Paris, 1847), i. 224–5).

[2] D'Argenson, op. cit. iii. 169–73.

[3] Ibid. vii. 353, 357.   [4] Ibid. viii. 35.

[5] L. Biollay, *Le Pacte de famine et les opérations sur les grains* (Paris, 1885).

[6] Métra, *Correspondance secrète, politique et littéraire . . . depuis la mort de Louis XV* (18 vols., London, 1787–90), i. 87. Terray, unlike Turgot, was an arch-exponent of State-intervention in the grain-trade; and as its administration, during his period of office, had been largely in the hands of a group of wealthy 'monopolists', his name had become popularly associated with the notorious *pacte de famine*. In November 1768, while Terray was in office, the price of the 4-lb. loaf in Paris had risen to 16 *sous*, and minor disturbances had followed (S. Lacroix, *Actes de la Commune de Paris* (2nd series, 8 vols., Paris, 1900–14), vi. 398).

restored freedom of trade in grain and flour. This, combined
with a bad harvest, led to a shortage and a rapid increase in the
price of corn, flour, and bread in the following spring and
summer. The price of the 4-lb. loaf in Paris rose to 11½ *sous*
in early March and to 13½ *sous* at the end of April. Grain riots
had already broken out at Bordeaux, Dijon, Tours, Metz,
Rheims, and Montauban—and in their wake sprang up that
particular series of riots known to history as 'la guerre des
farines'. The movement spread from market to market and took
the form of a popular price-control of wheat, flour, and bread—
the price of bread being generally fixed at 2 *sous* a pound, that
of flour at 20 *sous* a bushel, and wheat at 12 francs a *setier* (two
quintals). Starting on 27 April at Beaumont-sur-Oise, twenty
miles north of the capital, it reached Pontoise on the 29th,
Saint-Germain on 1 May, Versailles on the 2nd, and Paris
itself on the 3rd. Here the central flour and bread-markets
were ransacked and bakers in the city centre and *faubourgs*
pillaged or compelled to sell at the popular price, before the
troops were called out and order was restored. The movement
then spread eastwards and southwards up the valleys of the
Seine and Marne, lingered for several days in the markets and
villages of Brie, reached Beaumont-en-Gâtinais (fifty miles
south of Paris) on the 9th, and petered out somewhere near
Melun on the 10th.[1]

These riots gave a remarkable foretaste of certain episodes
of the Revolution—notably of popular price-control, or *taxation populaire*, of essential commodities, which became a regular
feature of the years 1789 to 1793. Yet they were far from being
directed against the existing order: they were rather a massive
protest against the new-fangled principle of allowing food-prices
to find their natural or market level, instead of being regulated
by considerations of social justice. It is perhaps hardly surprising that the movement yielded no tangible results. It was
essentially a movement of wage-earners, artisans, and village
and city poor: neither the *bourgeoisie* nor the bulk of the peasantry
played any part. However, it gave a severe jolt to the government and 'respectable' classes: twelve years later, Hardy, who
had witnessed the invasion of markets and bakers' shops in

[1] G. Rudé, 'La Taxation populaire de mai 1775 à Paris et dans la région
parisienne', *Annales historiques de la Révolution française*, April–June 1956, pp. 239–79.

Paris, referred to the dangers of a repetition of the scenes enacted in May 1775.[1] In Paris, at least, this was the last of the great popular revolts of the old régime. The twelve years that followed were years of comparatively stable food-prices and social peace.[2] The most that Hardy records are protests against the newly erected *barrières*, some grumbling in the markets about the price of meat and firewood, and a few significant incidents expressive of anti-clerical feeling.[3] For all their latent turbulence the inhabitants of the central markets and the *faubourgs* were no more prone to violence and disorder than the contemporary population of Southwark, Westminster, and the metropolitan parishes of Middlesex, who had rioted against excise and the Gin Act under Walpole and, in the 60's and 70's, acclaimed 'Wilkes and Liberty'. Paris, at all events, had a far more efficient and centralized police system, with considerably larger forces at its beck and call, than the cities of London and Westminster and the county of Middlesex, where the limited powers of magistrates and constables and the scattered and unwieldy machinery of repression were an almost standing invitation to riot and disorder. In Paris, on the other hand, the lieutenant of police, whose jurisdiction extended over the whole area of the capital, and the forty-eight commissioners of the Châtelet, who exercised powers of police in the various quarters of the city, had at their disposal substantial forces to deal with both crime and civil commotion. These included the 150 *archers du Guet*; three companies of the Garde de Paris, amounting to nearly 1,000 men; and 300 to 400 *exempts*—in all, some 1,500 men at their immediate command; with a further military reserve of 5,000 to 6,000 Gardes Françaises, Suisses, and Musketeers—the great majority stationed in the capital—who could be called upon in an emergency.[4] While these combined forces were greatly inferior to those later available to the revolutionary authorities,

---

[1] Hardy, *Journal*, vii. 123.

[2] During this period, the price of the 4-lb. loaf remained remarkably steady, generally ranging between 8 and 9 *sous*; it rose to 10½ or 11 *sous* only for brief spells in 1784 (ibid., vols. 3–7, *passim*).

[3] Ibid. v. 322–3, 394–5, 410; vi. 18, 35, 330, 332, 435, 479.

[4] H. de Montbas, *La Police parisienne sous Louis XVI* (Paris, 1949), pp. 78–84, 93–101. See also Monin, op. cit., pp. 479, 543.

as long as they remained loyal to the government and its local agents they constituted a far more formidable force than that which lay within easy call of the London magistrates.

So, when the Gordon Riots broke out in June 1780 and large parts of London were, for several days on end, at the mercy of the 'No Popery' rioters, French observers could afford to be complacent. Being wise after the event, we may laugh at the *naïveté* of Sébastien Mercier who, commenting on the London disturbances, wrote nine years before the assault on the Bastille that such terrors and alarms as were spread by Lord George Gordon in London would be inconceivable in a city as well policed as Paris;[1] yet, at the time of writing, he appeared to have reasonable grounds for self-satisfaction.

However, behind the apparent calm there were forces maturing, not immediately discernible to even the most enlightened and far-seeing observers, that would soon shatter these illusions and involve Parisians in events far more cataclysmic than any experienced in the preceding century. Though, in their outcome, these events left the outward appearance of Paris singularly untouched,[2] they drastically disturbed the lives and properties of its citizens.

[1] Mercier, op. cit., vi. 22–25.
[2] Monin, op. cit. pp. 11–12. The one notable exception was, of course, the Bastille, which was systematically demolished in 1789–91.

PART II

The Revolutionary Crowd in Action

III

PRELUDE TO REVOLUTION

TRADITIONALLY the French Revolution has been treated
as one single protracted episode, which opened with the
meeting of the States General at Versailles in May 1789,
or with the fall of the Bastille in July. In recent years, however,
historians have tended to revise this view and both to present
the Revolution as a series of distinct, though interrelated,
episodes and to ante-date its outbreak by two years—to May
1787, when the dismissal of the Assembly of Notables unleashed
the 'révolte nobiliaire' or 'révolution aristocratique'.[1] The
arguments in favour of presenting the Revolution as a gradual
unfolding of minor revolutions, by a sort of chain-reaction of
revolutionary explosions, need not detain us here; but a word
should be said about the date of its outbreak. The 'révolte
nobiliaire', it has been urged, must be seen as an intrinsic part
of the Revolution, as it was the aristocracy and the *Parlements*—
the *noblesse de robe*—that forced the king to convene the States
General, without which there would have been no revolution
of 1789; and it was they also who, by their open challenge to
the monarchy, drew into activity the classes mainly engaged in
the Revolution—the *bourgeoisie* and the peasant and urban
masses.[2] 'Les patriciens', wrote Chateaubriand, 'commencèrent
la révolution, les plébéiens l'achevèrent.'[3] This thesis contains an
important general truth in so far as every great revolution is
attended by deep divisions and crises within the governing
classes: students of the seventeenth century will find interesting

---

[1] See A. Mathiez, *La Révolution française* (3 vols., Paris, 1922–7), vol. i, chaps. 1
and 2; G. Lefebvre, *Quatre-vingt-neuf* (Paris, 1939), pp. 11 ff.

[2] Mathiez, loc. cit.   [3] Cited by Lefebvre, op. cit., p. 7.

parallels in our own national history. Yet the argument is not fully convincing: the divisions between the monarchy and privileged orders who launched the 'révolte nobiliaire', though deep, were not fundamental; and these divisions were rapidly healed as soon as the Third Estate—comprising both the *bourgeoisie* and the masses of town and countryside—joined forces in support of their own, more far-reaching, claims, as they began to do in the spring of 1789. According to this view, the real point of revolutionary outbreak was only reached when the separate and scattered actions of peasants, urban craftsmen and *bourgeois* journalists, lawyers, and deputies merged in common struggle in July 1789.[1]

In this study, therefore, the 'révolte nobiliaire' is presented as a prelude or curtain-raiser, rather than as the opening act of the revolutionary drama. Yet its profound significance and its particular importance for the present subject are not denied: not only did it pave the way directly for the triumph of the Third Estate but, by drawing the urban masses into activity, it ended the period of social peace which, in the case of Paris, had lasted, more or less undisturbed, since the 'guerre des farines' twelve years before. This new period of intense social struggle was to include both six years of revolution and the two years preceding it. This is therefore the point at which our study of the Parisian revolutionary crowd, in its wider context, must begin.

Ever since the American War, in which France became engaged in 1778, the country's finances had been in a desperate condition. In February 1787 an almost empty exchequer and a mounting deficit compelled the government to resort to drastic remedies: the Assembly of Notables was convened with the express purpose of finding some immediate solution to the financial crisis. Calonne, as Comptroller-General, proposed a number of far-reaching measures, including an extension of the stamp-duty and a new general tax on landed estates: the privileged orders were, in fact being invited, as by Turgot and Necker on earlier occasions, to make a belated contribution to save the State from bankruptcy. The Notables, with grievances and pretensions of their own, refused to co-operate. Calonne was dismissed on 8 April and succeeded by Loménie de Brienne, Archbishop of

[1] For a fuller treatment see G. Rudé, 'The Outbreak of the French Revolution', *Past and Present*, November 1955, pp. 28–42.

Sens and Toulouse, and soon to be promoted Cardinal. Brienne's proposals being no more acceptable than Calonne's and being met with similar obstruction, the Notables in turn were dismissed on 25 May, and the 'révolte nobiliaire' followed. As so often in the past, it was the Paris *Parlement*, with its vaguely defined constitutional powers, that fired the opening shot. While accepting Brienne's plan to relax controls on the sale and export of grain and endorsing, under protest, the stamp-duty, the *Parlement* refused categorically to register the decree on the land-tax and demanded that the States General be convened to deal with the matter. When the decrees were, none the less, promulgated in a *lit de justice* in August, the provincial *Parlements* rallied to the support of Paris, and Brienne was forced to capitulate: the decrees on the land-tax and stamp-duty were withdrawn on 21 September and the Paris *Parlement*, whose members had been exiled, was reinstated a few days later.[1]

The return of the *Parlement* to the capital was the occasion of wild scenes of jubilation in the Place Dauphine, the rue du Harlay, and other approaches to the Law Courts. Anti-royalist tracts had begun to appear in August[2] and the authorities were prepared for trouble: the Palais de Justice was ringed with 500 Gardes de Paris, supported by a regiment of Gardes Françaises. Hardy, himself a supporter of the *Parlement*, tells us that 'une jeunesse effrénée', composed of the clerks of the Palais and the apprentices and journeymen of the luxury trades of the Place Dauphine, crowded the Pont Neuf and its approaches, fired squibs and fireworks, and pelted the troops with stones. On 28 September, the climax of the disturbances, some soldiers were stung to open fire; the order was given by a sergeant of the Gardes Françaises in the brutally eloquent phrase: 'f--moi du plomb dans les fesses de cette canaille'. There were no casualties, though a passing lawyer had his coat pierced by a stray bullet. Five young men were arrested and were escorted, to the accompaniment of jeers and further volleys of stones, to the office of Commissioner Ferrand in the rue des Lombards for cross-examination.[3] From his report we learn that the prisoners, four of whom

[1] For a general account of the 'révolte nobiliaire' see Mathiez, op. cit., vol. 1, chaps. 1–2; Lefebvre, op. cit., pp. 24–42; A. Goodwin, *The French Revolution* (London, 1953), pp. 27–42. [2] Hardy, vii. 178.
[3] Ibid. 250–1. According to Hardy the soldiers who had opened fire were put in cells.

were committed to the Force jail, included two apprentices in small crafts, two journeymen goldsmiths and a master tailor; two lived in the immediate vicinity of the Palais, two others in the university quarter across the river.[1]

The disorders continued for a week, during which bonfires were lit in the square before the Palais, anti-royalist tracts were distributed, and Calonne and the Comtesse de Polignac, the governess of the royal children, were burned in effigy.[2] Finally, on 3 October, the *Parlement* issued an *arrêt*, solemnly proscribing all gatherings and firework displays in the neighbourhood of the Palais,[3] and the movement subsided—although Hardy recorded a further minor outbreak and the mustering of 600 troops as late as 12 November.[4] Though thus protracted, this had been a localized affair without widespread repercussions: only a small part of the *bourgeoisie* was engaged; and the *faubourgs* and markets, perhaps because the price of bread remained stable, were not yet involved.

In the following months, however, the crisis deepened—not least because the return to Turgot's free-trade measures had led to a sharp rise in the price of grain. To reach a settlement of the financial crisis Brienne fell back on the expedient of raising a loan, which the Paris *Parlement* was willing to accept provided that the States General be summoned. But negotiations broke down again in November; the popular Duke of Orleans and two *conseillers* were exiled; on his return in April the duke was welcomed with another round of fireworks.[5] In May 1788 the *Parlement* won further popularity by issuing a declaration condemning the whole system of arbitrary government, including the *lettres de cachet*. The government riposted by once more ringing the Palais with troops, forced the *parlementaires* to surrender their ringleaders to royal justice, and promulgated six edicts, drafted by Lamoignon, the *garde des sceaux*, which restricted the jurisdiction of the *Parlements*, reduced the number of *conseillers*, and vested the royal courts and officials with greater legal powers; on this occasion only the presence of troops prevented an angry crowd from burning

---

[1] Arch. Nat., Y 13014. In addition, a domestic servant had been brought before Commissioner Léger on 2 September, charged with inciting the crowd against the Garde de Paris (Arch. Nat., Y 10634, fol. 81).

[2] Hardy, vii. 252–5   [3] Brit. Mus., 27 d 13 (43).

[4] Hardy, vii. 287.   [5] Ibid. 411.

down the Law Courts.[1] A new phase of violence followed—at first mainly in the provinces: there were mass riots in Grenoble and Rennes in June; in Dauphiné nobility and Third Estate joined forces against the Crown in July. Early that month, angry placards threatening the king with mass revolt appeared in the Cité: 'Tremblez, Tyrans, votre Règne va finir'; and Hardy feared that a serious popular outbreak was pending.[2] Anticipating further trouble, the government began, in early August, to draft new regiments into the villages adjoining the capital—this time not so much for fear of the clerks and apprentices of the Palais as of the *menu peuple* of the markets and *faubourgs*.[3]

These fears proved well founded. The government, compelled to bow before the storm, promised that the States General should be called in May 1789; on 24 August Brienne was replaced by Necker and the *Parlement* was recalled soon after. This double victory was greeted two days later with another outburst of celebrations in the Place Dauphine and its neighbourhood: under the noses of the guards fireworks were let off in profusion, bonfires were lit, and the occupants of coaches crossing the Pont Neuf were made to bow low to the equestrian statue of Henri IV and to shout 'A bas Lamoignon!' A new factor, however, was to extend these disturbances far beyond the scope and limits of the previous year. On 17 August, the price of the 4-lb. loaf, after long remaining at 9 *sous*, rose to 9½ *sous*, on the 20th to 10 *sous*, on 2 September to 10½ *sous*, and on 7 September to 11 *sous*.[4] After the first increase Hardy noted a slight commotion in the Faubourg Saint-Antoine;[5] and, on 28 August, the *ouvriers* and *menu peuple* of the markets and *faubourgs* joined the riots started two days earlier by the Palais clerks in the Place Dauphine, and changed their whole character.[6] The next day they became more violent and spread into other districts: guard-posts on the Pont Neuf and on both sides of the river were ransacked and burned to the ground. Meanwhile supreme command of all troops stationed in the

---

[1] Ibid. 470. There was another minor disturbance in the rue des Lombards ten days later (ibid. 481).   [2] Ibid. viii. 10–11.
[3] Ibid. 35, 72–73.   [4] Ibid. 49–68.   [5] Ibid. 49.
[6] Ibid. 61–62. In Hardy's words: 'La populace du fbg St. Antoine et celle du fbg St. Marcel, étant venue augmenter le nombre des polissons du quartier, le désordre ne fait qu'augmenter progressivement.'

capital had been given to the Maréchal de Biron, 'hero' of the pacification of May 1775, and the Guards were ordered to meet force by force. That night a party of 600 demonstrators, operating in the Place de Grève, was fired on by the Garde de Paris; seven or eight were killed[1] and the rest were put to flight. For a fortnight Paris was comparatively calm.

But the dismissal, on 14 September, of the unpopular Lamoignon touched off a new round of disturbances that continued intermittently until the end of the month. The crowds were allowed, more or less unmolested, to voice their satisfaction by acclaiming Henri IV on the Pont Neuf and burning Lamoignon in effigy in the Place de Grève; but an attempt to attack the town house of the Chevalier Dubois, commander of the Garde de Paris, off the rue Saint-Martin, led to an ugly slaughter, when troops fired on a crowd hemmed in the narrow rue de Meslai: according to Hardy, fifty were killed and twenty-five taken prisoner; yet this appears to be an exaggeration.[2] The return of the *Parlement* a week later provoked further disorders: this time, there was a bloody affray in the university quarter, when 200 young people, carrying lighted torches and laurel-branches and chanting 'Vive Henri Quatre! Vive le Parlement et au diable les tristes à patte!',[3] were set upon by the Gardes Françaises in the rue de la Harpe, resulting in several casualties.[4] On 30 September the Chevalier Dubois tendered his resignation, having been rewarded with a sum of 10,000 *livres* and the lieutenancy of Péronne, and the disturbances came to an end.[5]

The lists of persons wounded, arrested, and sentenced as the result of these riots, later drawn up by the *Parlement* and the Châtelet, give us some idea of the sort of people taking part in them and of the districts from which they came. Occupations appear in some 50 cases: of these, 24 were journeymen, apprentices, labourers, and other wage-earners; 10 were master

---

[1] Arch. Nat., X I^b 8989: extrait du Parlement du 24 septembre 1788; cited by Monin, op. cit., pp. 482–7.

[2] Hardy, viii. 80. According to the police, however, there were no deaths, 14 were wounded in the rue Saint-Martin and the Faubourg Saint-Germain (where another collision took place) and 18 (of which 8 were wounded) were taken prisoner (Monin, op. cit., p. 486).

[3] A common, unflattering, term for the cavalry.

[4] Arch. Nat., Y 11206; Hardy, viii. 100.   [5] Monin, op. cit., p. 489.

craftsmen; and 16 were small traders and shopkeepers. The great majority came from the main centres of disturbance— the Cité, the Faubourg Saint-Germain, and the central and northern districts of the capital; surprisingly, not one was from the Faubourg Saint-Antoine, in spite of Hardy's insistence that the *menu peuple* of the *faubourg* had joined the riots at the end of August.[1] In short these records suggest that the Parisian *sans-culottes* had entered the struggle against the Government as a decisive force, but not yet as the ally of the *bourgeoisie*; the real revolutionary crisis was still to come.

This developed in the winter of 1788–9 and was to bring about a radical realinement of classes. The harvest was generally bad and, in the Paris region, crops had been flattened by a freak hailstorm in July. There followed a winter of pheno-menal severity which threw thousands out of work and brought further thousands of villagers flocking to the capital; in December Hardy wrote of 80,000 unemployed. The price of the 4-lb. loaf in the Paris markets rose to 12 *sous* on 8 November, to 13 *sous* on the 28th, to 14 *sous* on 11 December and, finally, to 14½ *sous* on 1 February; it was to remain at this level until after the fall of the Bastille.[2]

Meanwhile, the *bourgeoisie* had made its entry on the revolu-tionary stage. The cause of conflict had its roots deep in the old régime: while colonial trade, land-values, and luxury spending had enormously increased in the course of the century, capital investment and expansion of manufacture were everywhere im-peded by the restrictions imposed by privileged corporations, feudal landowners, and government on the elementary capitalist freedoms: the freedom to hire labour, the freedom to produce, and the freedom to buy and sell. Yet, while the ensuing con-flict owed its eventual sharpness and finality to these deeper social antagonisms, the clash between the *bourgeoisie* and the privileged orders arose, in the first instance, over representation and voting in the States General. Already in September the Paris *Parlement* had begun to lose its reputation as the spokesman for popular liberties by demanding that the States General be constituted as in 1614—i.e. that each order should have equal

---

[1] Bib. Nat., Collection Joly de Fleury, doss. 1113; Arch. Nat., Y 9491, 9989, 11206, 11517, 15309A, 18751, 18795; X I^b 8989 (cited by Monin, op. cit., p. 489.
[2] Hardy, viii. 154–5, 168, 408, 426.

representation and vote separately. An even more forthright insistence on the maintenance of privilege was voiced in the Manifesto of the princes of the blood in December. Necker, however, persuaded the Council to allow the Third Estate double representation; but the question of voting 'par tête' (as demanded by the *bourgeoisie*) or 'par ordre' (as insisted by the nobility and clergy) remained open and led to bloody clashes between nobles and commoners at Rennes. By January the new alinement of forces was becoming clear and Mallet du Pan noted that it was no longer a question of constitutional conflict between the king and the *privilégiés* but a 'war between the Third Estate and the two other orders'.[1] In February the conflict was raised to a higher pitch by the publication of the abbé Sieyès's pamphlet *Qu'est-ce que le tiers état?*, in which the *bourgeoisie* for the first time laid claim to control the destinies of the nation irrespective of the wishes or privileges of the other orders.

It was against this background of developing crisis and political ferment that the Réveillon riots took place in the Faubourg Saint-Antoine at the end of April; they have been called the first great popular outbreak of the Revolution,[2] though they might perhaps with equal justice be termed the last outbreak of the old régime. Réveillon was a successful manufacturer of wall-paper, whose main factory in the rue de Montreuil, off the rue du Faubourg Saint-Antoine, employed some 350 workers. He had won a Royal Medal for his services to industry. He was wealthy: his library contained 50,000 volumes, and his furniture alone was said to be worth 50,000 *livres*; even after his cellars had been ransacked in the riots, we are told that 2,000 bottles remained unscathed. He had the reputation of being a good employer: he claimed to pay none of his workers less than 25 *sous* a day, when it was still common for a labourer to receive no more than 20; and, during the arctic winter of 1788-9, when industry was almost at a standstill for lack of fuel, he had paid 15 *sous* unemployment pay to 200 of his workpeople who had been laid off.[3] Why then did such a solid citizen, good employer, and respected member of his local Electoral Assembly

[1] Cited by Lefebvre, *La Révolution française* (Paris, 1954), p. 113.
[2] Lefebvre, *La Révolution de 1789*, p. 69.
[3] G. Rudé, *Parisian Wage-earners*, ii. 36.

become the target for the destructive violence of the journey-men and labourers of the St. Antoine district? Let us consider the facts briefly.

On 23 April Réveillon made a speech in the Electoral Assembly of the Sainte-Marguerite District in which he re-gretted the high costs of production and the burden imposed on industry by the high level of wages; whether or not he advo-cated a reduction of wages is not certain, but he appears to have lamented the days when workpeople could make do on 15 *sous* a day. Similar views were expressed on the same day by Henriot, a powder manufacturer of the rue de Cotte, in the Assembly of the Enfants-Trouvés District, also in the Faubourg Saint-Antoine. That these remarks, whatever their intention, aroused immediate and spontaneous dissatisfaction among the wage-earners of the *faubourg* is evident from a report sent by Thiroux de Crosne, Paris lieutenant of police, to Louis XVI on the following morning:

Il y a eu hier soir sur les dix heures [he wrote] un peu de rumeur. dans un canton du faubourg St. Antoine; il n'était que l'effet du mécontentement que quelques ouvriers marquaient contre deux entrepreneurs de manufacture qui, dans l'assemblée de Ste. Mar-guerite, avaient fait des observations inconsidérées sur le taux des salaires.[1]

After a lull the storm broke on the 27th: being a Monday it was a workers' rest-day. At 3 o'clock in the afternoon, reported Thiroux de Crosne, five or six hundred *ouvriers* gathered near the Bastille; and, having hanged Réveillon in effigy, paraded dummy figures of the two manufacturers round different parts of the capital.[2] The same afternoon Hardy, whose bookshop, *A la Colonne d'Or*, in the rue Saint-Jacques was admirably situated for witnessing such processions, noted in his *Journal* that the 'insurrection' had spread to the Notre Dame district; later, he met several hundred workers, armed with sticks and headed by a drummer, in the rue de la Montagne Sainte-Geneviève; having recruited reinforcements in the Faubourg Saint-Marcel, they returned to the Place de Grève, before the Hôtel de Ville, some 3,000 strong.[3] Three Electors of the Third Estate subsequently

[1] Arch. Nat., C 221, no. 160/146, fol. 58.
[2] Ibid., fol. 53.   [3] Hardy, viii. 297-8.

described their meeting with the demonstrators later that evening as they set out once more for the Faubourg Saint-Marcel; they persuaded them to disperse.[1] But the crowds re-formed soon after near Réveillon's factory in the rue de Montreuil. Finding his house guarded by fifty men of the Royal Cravate Regiment, they made for Henriot's house in the rue de Cotte nearby and destroyed his furniture and personal effects. They were then dispersed by the troops—without loss of life, noted Thiroux de Crosne. In addition to the Guards posted in Réveillon's house, two further detachments of 100 men were brought in to guard different parts of the *faubourg*, while a reserve force of 100 mounted troops summoned from Charenton stood by in case of emergency. With this display of force, the authorities thought that the worst was over.[2]

But, early next day, the movement started up again and extended over a wider area, considerably alarming the house-holders. While more troops were called in, bands of workers went round the districts recruiting fresh supporters by persuasion or intimidation. No work was done that day in the docks; factory workers and workshop journeymen came out in the early afternoon, and many joined the rioters. The police had given express instructions that the 500 workers of the Royal Glass Manufactory in the rue de Reuilly—a bare 200 yards from Réveillon's factory—should be forcibly kept at work; but itinerant bands broke in the doors and persuaded or compelled the workers to join them. In the Temple district an attempt was made to fetch workers out from their lodgings.[3] By 5 o'clock, noted Hardy, demonstrators were assembling on the Pont Neuf, the Pont au Change (adjoining the Châtelet), the Porte Saint-Antoine, and off the boulevards.[4]

The climax came between six and eight in the evening. Réveillon's house was stormed, the fifty Guards of the Royal Cravate Regiment were swept aside, and the destruction of the previous night was repeated on a vaster scale. The Duc du Châtelet, commanding the Gardes Françaises, gave the order

[1] *Acte patriotique de trois électeurs du Tiers État* (Paris, 1789), Bib. Nat., L^b 39 1620.   [2] Arch. Nat., C 221, no. 160/146, fols. 49, 54.
[3] See cross-examination of Téteigne (port-worker), Gilles (marble-worker), Hallier (farrier), Guérin (paper-worker), Chelours (journeyman coppersmith) (Arch, Nat., Y 15101, 13454, 13582, 12218, 11033); also Arch. Nat., C 221, no. 160/146, fol. 51.   [4] Hardy, viii. 299.

to fire. In spite of the massacre that followed in the narrow congested streets with thousands crowding the windows and roofs, the crowd stood firm and fought back with shouts of 'Liberté . . . nous ne céderons pas,'[1] Others shouted, 'Vive le tiers état!', and even 'Vive le Roi! Vive M. Necker!'[2] The battle lasted until 8 o'clock; at 10, Thiroux de Crosne reported to the king: 'Le calme continue à se rétablir; il paraît qu'il ne reste plus dans le faubourg St. Antoine que quelques groupes.'[3] Hardy feared a repetition on the morrow and wrote that, before dispersing, the rioters had announced 'que le lendemain ils feraient grand tapage pour obtenir la diminution du pain'.[4]

There remained the judicial reckoning. On 29 April Gilbert, a blanket-maker, and Pourat, a porter, were hanged in the Place de Grève. Three weeks later Mary, a scrivener, was hanged at the Porte Saint-Antoine; a woman, Marie-Jeanne Trumeau, sentenced to share his fate, was found to be pregnant, respited, and eventually reprieved. Five others, found drunk in Réveillon's cellars and guilty of resisting the troops with violence and abusive language, were exhibited in stocks at the Porte Saint-Antoine alongside Mary's gallows, branded with hot irons, and sent to the galleys for life. Twenty-six other prisoners were eventually released, most of them three months later, as the result of public pressure.[5]

The numbers of killed and wounded in the Réveillon riots have never been established. In order not to inflame opinion further the authorities were careful to play down the number of victims and, in so doing, gave rise to the wildest rumours and speculation. The Marquis de Sillery, deputy for the nobility of Rheims, in reporting the events to his constituents, estimated the number of killed at 'several hundred'.[6] Hardy went one better and put the figure above 900.[7] Another writer speaks of seventy or eighty corpses being placed in the garden of one single house in the rue de Montreuil.[8] In contrast, the various reports of the commissioners of the Châtelet account for a

---

[1] J. Collot, 'L'affaire Réveillon', *Revue des questions historiques*, cxxi (1934-5), 35-55, 239-54.   [2] Arch. Nat., KK 641, fol. 17.
[3] Arch. Nat., C 221, no. 160/146, fol. 52.   [4] Hardy, viii. 299.
[5] Arch. Nat., Y 10530, fols. 129-33; Y 18795, fols. 444-5, 447-50, 457, 462; BB16 702; Hardy, viii. 303, 329-31.
[6] Arch. Nat., KK 641, fol. 16.   [7] Hardy, viii. 313.
[8] *Lettre au Roi* (Paris, 1789). Bib. Nat., Lb 39 7156, p. 15.

death-roll of only twenty-five and for twenty-two wounded survivors.[1] These figures are almost certainly incomplete, though we have no means of correcting them.

Yet, despite these deficiencies, these reports help us to establish both the nature of the rioters and the districts most directly involved in the disturbances. Historians have not been able to agree on the latter point. Jaurès thought the majority of the rioters came from outside the Faubourg Saint-Antoine;[2] while a more recent writer, J. Collot, has claimed that the main stimulus to them came from the other traditionally turbulent *faubourg* of Saint-Marcel.[3] Collot's contention is supported by Guérin, one of the accused, who, under cross-examination, told the police: 'Ce sont des gens du faubourg Marcel qui ont occasionné ce tumulte-là, qu'il l'a entendu dire à son frère et autres.'[4] Yet it is refuted by other evidence—not only by the reports of Thiroux de Crosne, who consistently speaks of the rioters as being largely drawn from the Faubourg Saint-Antoine;[5] but, more conclusively perhaps, by the reports of the commissioners of the Châtelet on those killed, wounded, and arrested. In fact, of sixty-three persons whose addresses appear in these reports, only five lived in the Faubourg Saint-Marcel.[6] This would seem to clinch the matter—unless, of course, it could be demonstrated that the people of Saint-Marcel had more than their share of skill or good fortune in dodging bullets or escaping detection!

Jaurès's contention is nearer the truth: of the same sixty-three persons, only thirty-two are known to have lived in the Faubourg Saint-Antoine—clearly a bare majority; yet if we add those residing in the adjoining and closely associated districts of Saint-Paul and Saint-Gervais, we shall account for a substantial majority of those whose records have been preserved. By and large, then, these riots may be said to have been largely a Saint-Antoine affair, drawing their main stimulus and most solid body of support from the Saint-Antoine districts. Yet as the

---

[1] Arch. Nat., Y 11033, 13582, 15101; C.-L. Chassin, *Les Cahiers et les élections de Paris en 1789*, iii. 72 ff.   [2] Jaurès, *Histoire socialiste* i. 142.

[3] Collot, op. cit., pp. 42–49.   [4] Arch. Nat., Y 12218.

[5] In a letter to Commissioner Joron of 8 May 1789, he writes: 'Vous leur ferez entendre que la plupart des séditieux étant 'du faubourg St. Antoine . . . ', &c. (Arch. Nat., Y 13981).

[6] Arch. Nat., Y 10491; 10530, fols. 131–3; 13582; 15019; 18795, fols. 444–5 447–50, 457, 462; Chassin, loc. cit.

remarks attributed to Réveillon had a significance in no way
peculiar to the *faubourg*, it proved an easy matter to recruit
support from neighbouring parishes—yet it remained a local
affair and its repercussions were not as widespread as those of
the previous August and September.

The Réveillon riots are unique in the history of the Revolution in that they represent an insurrectionary movement of
wage-earners. In them alone, of all the insurrections during the
period under review, the wage-earners clearly predominate and
an appeal is made, however confusedly, to the wage-earners as
a social group. The Revolution in Paris was to witness more
than one concerted wages movement of different trades—as in
1791 and 1794—but they were never to assume an insurrectionary form. We should certainly hesitate, after the warnings
voiced in the last chapter, to assume that the use of the term
ouvriers by Hardy and Thiroux de Crosne necessarily meant that
the persons so described were wage-earners in our modern
sense of the word;[1] but, in this instance, the terms prove substantially to coincide. We have already seen that a direct and
particular appeal was addressed by the demonstrators to
workers in docks, factories, and lodging-houses; and an examination of the police reports shows that of seventy-one persons
(arrested, wounded, or killed) whose occupations are given, no
less than fifty-eight were wage-earners—journeymen of the
small crafts of the *faubourg*, riverside and general workers of
Saint-Paul and Saint-Gervais, a sprinkling of workers in manufacture. The remainder included a sculptor, a wine-merchant,
a master upholsterer, and—somewhat incongruously—a Knight
of the Holy Roman Empire.[2] There was one woman among
them—one of the alleged ringleaders—Marie-Anne Trumeau
by name: she was supposed to have incited the rioters to burn
and loot with cries of 'Allons, vive le Tiers État!' and 'A la
Réveillon!'; as we saw, it nearly cost her her life.[3]

---

[1] See p. 18 above.
[2] See footnote 6, p. 38. In addition, Hardy records the arrest on 2 May in the rue
des Prêtres St. Séverin, in the university quarter, of two porters in connexion with this
affair (Hardy, viii. 307). If we add these to the other 35 men and women arrested
and recorded in the police reports, we find that as many as 32 out of 37 arrested
persons were wage-earners—an even more significant figure than that given above,
as these people were presumably more directly involved than the chance victims of
the soldiers' bullets.   [3] Arch. Nat., Y 13981, 13454.

What drove these journeymen, labourers, and petty craftsmen to such violent outbursts of anger and to behave with such
reckless courage? The immediate cause of the disturbance is, of
course, not in doubt: it flowed directly from the 'inconsiderate'
remarks attributed to Réveillon and Henriot concerning the
high level of wages. Whether they actually advocated a reduction, as was widely believed; or whether they merely regretted
the passing of happier days, as some of their apologists maintained;[1] or whether, as they themselves insisted, they never
made the reported remarks at all[2] does not really make much
difference. What is important is what they were believed to
have said by the wage-earners of the *faubourg* and the effect it
had on them. Some of the more coherent of the accused admitted under cross-examination that it was the veiled threat to
their wages that had made them join in the riots. For example,
the harness-maker, Le Blanc, who confessed to having entered
Réveillon's house and thrown furniture out of the window,
explained his reasons for joining the demonstrators as follows:

Qu'il y a été par curiosité et parce qu'il y a été entraîné par la
multitude, qu'il avait ainsi que les autres ouvriers du faubourg de
l'humeur contre le sr. Réveillon parce qu'il avait dit dans l'assemblée du tiers état à Ste. Marguerite que les ouvriers pouvaient vivre
avec quinze sols par jour, qu'il avait chez lui des ouvriers qui
gagnaient vingt sols par jour et avaient la montre dans le gousset et
qu'ils seraient bientôt plus riches que lui.

And he added, perhaps significantly, that it was his own employer, Olivier, a well-known porcelain manufacturer of the
rue de la Roquette, who had told him so.[3]

Taking place when they did, at a time of intense political
ferment, these riots were bound to appear to the authorities as
something more than a mere spontaneous outbreak over wages.
As none of the arrested workers appeared to be a leader, who
then had incited them by bribery, or other means? Hardy
refers to the rioters as '(des) ouvriers . . . soulevés par des

[1] Arch. Nat., KK 641, fol. 16.
[2] *Exposé justificatif pour le sieur Réveillon* and *Exposé justificatif pour le sieur Henriot*
(Paris, 1789). Bib. Nat., L⁵ 39 1618-19.
[3] Arch. Nat., Y 13319. Similar statements were made by Deldevèse, a sculptor,
and Verpy, a joiner (Arch. Nat., Y 12218). Olivier later achieved fame for his
porcelain models of the Bastille (see 'La Bastille et les faïenciers' in *La Révolution
rançaise*, i (1881), 116-18).

brigánds';[1] and the author of the pamphlet, *Courtes réflexions sur l' événement du 28 avril*, points to an aristocratic or clerical plot in which

un grand nombre d'ouvriers de différentes professions ont été contraints, les uns par argent, les autres par violence, à suivre cette troupe de forcenés.[2]

The reports of all the investigating commissioners show the same preoccupation with outside agents; and, having failed to obtain satisfaction on this score from any of the existing prisoners, the police proceeded to arrest on 3 May the abbé Roy, a man who had already been publicly denounced as a government agent and a personal enemy of Réveillon. But he proved a disappointing witness and was released a few days later.[3] The belief in clerical conspirators seems to have been strong at the Châtelet, for when one of the defendants, the paper-worker Sirier, claimed to have been given money in the rue Saint-Honoré some days after the riots, he was asked 'si ce n'était point un abbé ou d'autres particuliers qui le lui avait donné.'[4] Yet, as in the riots of 1775, the belief in a clerical plot appears to have had no solid foundation.

Nor did there prove to be any more substance in another aspect of the conspiracy theory—that the rioters had been bribed. Montjoie, the editor of the ultra-royalist *L'Ami du Roi*, reported that each of the wounded brought to the Hôtel-Dieu were found to have 12 *francs* in his possession, in most cases wrapped in paper as though newly counted.[5] It appears to have been a fabrication, as the police, who had every reason for wishing to confirm their own belief in a clerical, Orleanist, or other plot, found nothing suspicious on any one of the prisoners, all of whom were subjected to a personal search. On the eighteen corpses taken to Montrouge cemetery and examined by Commissioner Odent, not a brass farthing was found—only a few cheap tobacco-pouches, keys, trade instruments and, in one instance, a small silver object that may have been stolen.[6] The only person who admitted any monetary payment and who was

[1] Hardy, viii. 299.   [2] Bib. Nat., L[b] 39 7158.
[3] Hardy, viii. 308-9; Chassin, op. cit., iii. 104; Tuetey, *Répertoire général*, vol. i, pp. xliv-v. I have been unable to find Roy's dossier in the archives of the Châtelet.
[4] Arch. Nat., Y 14119.   [5] Tuetey, op. cit., p. xlv.
[6] Arch. Nat., Y 15019.

found to have considerable sums in his pockets was the paper-worker Sirier, and his connexion with the case only began a week after the riots ended.[1]

Nor, again, does Taine's charge that the rioters were 'brigands' stand up to investigation, unless the term is used in the widest sense. Among the prisoners, only three had incurred previous convictions of any kind and, in two cases, these had merely involved short terms of imprisonment at the Hôtel de la Force; only one man had a criminal record of any account— the port-worker Téteigne, who was found to be branded with a 'V'.[2] The majority of these prisoners appear, in fact, to have been ordinary working men of a variety of trades, most of them employed,[3] and to have come out of the affair without monetary gain or loot.

Yet there was a hidden hand behind these disturbances in so far as there lay at the back of them deeper economic causes than were immediately apparent. A few random remarks on wages by two local manufacturers could hardly in themselves have provoked a conflagration of such proportions. It is also a striking fact that not one of Réveillon's 350 workers were among the killed, wounded, or arrested and that no suggestion is made in any of the reports of attempts to bring them out with the other workers on 28 April. It would, therefore, be nonsense to try to explain the Réveillon riots in terms of a strike or simple wages protest against an unpopular employer. It was much more a violent, though partly unconscious, protest against the prevailing scarcity and high cost of bread: the 4-lb. loaf, as we saw, had since February remained at the phenomenally high price of 14½ sous. This protest was directed against Réveillon and Henriot, but not because they had shown themselves to be bad employers or because the workers had been agitated by clerical or aristocratic agents. Personal enemies of the two manufacturers may, as they themselves suspected, have played some part in stimulating popular anger; but they could only hope for success because Réveillon's offending remarks about wages had associated him and his colleague in the public mind with the

[1] Arch. Nat., Y 14119.
[2] Arch. Nat., Y 15101, 13454.
[3] Only 5 of 35 prisoners and 1 of 23 wounded are described as unemployed. Some historians may have been misled on this point by the fact that the riots began in earnest on a Monday, a workers' rest day.

hated *accapareurs*, or food-hoarders, the most ready target for popular fury. The author of the pamphlet *Lettre au Roi* seems to have appreciated this motive when he wrote: 'Sire, c'est à la cherté du pain que l'on doit attribuer nos derniers malheurs.'[1] We also note Hardy's entry in his *Journal* that, after wrecking Réveillon's house, the rioters had announced their intention of demanding a reduction in the price of bread;[2] and it is a remarkable feature of the riots that the only premises broken into, apart from Réveillon's and Henriot's own properties, were food-shops.[3] All the evidence, in fact, points to hunger as the main motive force behind the disturbances.

This does not, of course, rule out altogether the possibility that other outside agents intervened to fan discontent. Was popular anger deliberately fomented and directed against Réveillon and Henriot by political opponents or business rivals? The former seems unlikely: the rioters, as we saw, chanted the new fashionable slogan, 'Vive le Tiers État!', as they set about their work of destruction. This may seem all the more incomprehensible, as Réveillon himself was a prominent figure in the local Third Estate. But to the Réveillon rioters, as to the men who destroyed the Paris customs posts in the following July, the words 'Tiers État' had a more limited social application: in their mouths it appears to have been a rallying cry of the poor against the rich rather than of the nation as a whole against a handful of privileged persons, as conceived by the abbé Sieyès. In this sense, of course, the slogan 'Vive le Tiers État' could be used against a wealthy manufacturer like Réveillon.

More mysterious is the attitude of the porcelain-manufacturer Olivier, said to have reported Réveillon's indiscretions in the Sainte-Marguerite District Assembly to his own workpeople in the most lurid and provocative terms.[4] Had some local employers a personal grudge against Réveillon and did they deliberately stir up their workers and the poor of the *faubourg* against a successful business rival?

It is an interesting possibility, though it would offer no fundamental explanation: neither business rivals nor clerical adventurers, neither Orleanists nor Knights of the Holy Roman Empire played more than, at most, a very minor part in the

[1] Bib. Nat., L^b 39 7156.　　　　　　[2] Hardy, viii. 299.
[3] Arch. Nat., Y 11033, 16005.　　　　[4] Arch. Nat., Y 13319.

Réveillon affair. The primary cause of the disturbance, as so often in the riots of the old régime—and of the Revolution—lay in the shortage and the high price of bread, which already accounted for something like three-quarters of the wage-earner's budget.[1] A further cause, which gave the riots their special character, were the indiscreet remarks of the manufacturers which, by relating the question of bread to that of wages, roused the particular fury of the wage-earners.

Another important factor was, of course, the current political atmosphere, in which the ideas and slogans of the revolutionary *bourgeoisie*, already challenging the privileged orders for the control of the States General, were beginning to take root among the *menu peuple* and to be turned by them to their own advantage. This atmosphere was to be raised to an even higher pitch by the events of the next months.

[1] G. Rudé, 'Prices, Wages and Popular Movements in Paris during the French Revolution', *Econ. Hist. Rev.*, vol. vi, no. 3, April 1954, pp. 247-9. See also Appendix VII.

IV

JULY 1789

A VISITOR to France in the winter of 1788–9 might have been excused for not anticipating the cataclysm that was brewing or even for not observing any particular change in the attitude of the common people to the problems of the day. The privileged orders had, of course, taken resolute and vigorous action to assert their claims against the Crown; but this was part of the traditional pattern and had been done, though less successfully, under Louis XV. Again, the economic crisis had gravely deepened and the small consumers showed obvious signs of disaffection over the rising price of wheat, flour, and bread; but might not this end in much the same way as in 1740, 1768, or 1775? Even the severe frost of January 1789, which added to the already alarming industrial unemployment generally attributed to Vergennes's 'free' Trade Treaty with England,[1] did not substantially alter the picture. The talk of 'revolution', commonly voiced in fashionable-philosophic circles, had been going on for years. The government, it is true, had lately promised that the States General should meet in May—and this was certainly an event without recent precedent; but might not the Third Estate agree to accept submissively the humble role prescribed for it by the nobility and bishops who had taken the initiative in its calling? It was, in fact, not so much the decision to convene the Estates as the consequences that flowed (unexpected by its promoters) from this decision, that entirely transformed the situation and the perspective of future developments in France.

An intelligent traveller like Arthur Young or a shrewd native observer like Mallet du Pan could note this difference once the Third Estate had decided to accept the challenge—by demanding not only double representation in the Estates, which was soon conceded, but the right to vote *par tête*, i.e. as part of a

---

[1] C. Schmidt, 'La Crise industrielle de 1788 en France', *Revue historique*, xcvii (1908), 78–94. For a different view see L. Cahen, 'Une Nouvelle interprétation du traité franco-anglais de 1786–7', *Rev. Hist.*, clxxxv (1939), 257–85.

single deliberative body, in which the *Tiers* would inevitably carry the day provided it could win over even a small minority of nobles and clergy. It was to further this demand and to win support for it beyond the ranks of the *bourgeoisie* that the abbé Sieyès wrote his pamphlet *Qu'est-ce que le Tiers État?*, and that there was all this talk about 'Tiers État', 'la nation', and the Rights of Man. Once these ideas began to permeate the common people, as they did in the spring of 1789, a new direction and purpose were given to popular unrest, already nurtured on economic hardship and traditional grievances. The very realization, indeed, that the States General were about to meet and that the people's complaints, as voiced in the *cahiers de doléances*, should be heard, aroused what historians have called 'la grande espérance'.

Un événement si étrange [writes Lefebvre] a éveillé l'espoir, éclatant et nébuleux tout à la fois, d'une régénération nationale, d'une ère nouvelle où les hommes seraient plus heureux.[1]

An oft-quoted example is, of course, that given by Arthur Young of his meeting with an old peasant woman in Champagne who told him that

It was said that something was to be done by some great folks for such poor ones, but she did not know who nor how, but God send us better, *car les tailles et les droits nous écrasent.*[2]

The other side of the picture was the conviction that the privileged orders would stop at nothing to see that these hopes were defeated—and so the notion of the 'complot aristocratique', with its deep traditional roots, came simultaneously into being. How closely it was related to the old notion of the 'pacte de famine' is illustrated by Hardy, who tells us that when the price of bread rose, in February, to 14½ *sous*, people began to say

que les princes avaient accaparé les grains tout exprès pour mieux réussir à culbuter le sieur Necker qu'ils avaient un si grand intérêt de renverser.[3]

The events taking place at Versailles that summer were to deepen these fears and to stimulate the insurrectionary temper

---

[1] G. Lefebvre, *Quatre-vingt-neuf*, p. 112.

[2] Arthur Young, *Travels in France and Italy* (Everyman Library, London, 1915), p. 159.   [3] Hardy, viii. 250.

already developing in the capital.[1] The States General were deadlocked over the rival claims of the Third Estate—which soon constituted itself a National Assembly—and of the majority of the nobility and bishops. To force the pace and overawe Paris foreign troops were being concentrated on the outskirts of the city: on 3 June already Hardy had noted the arrival of German and Hungarian regiments, brought in on the pretext of preventing a renewed outburst of rioting in the Faubourg Saint-Antoine.[2] The intentions of the Court Party, grouped around Marie-Antoinette and the king's younger brother, the Comte d'Artois, were becoming clear: on the night of 22 June the king was persuaded to dismiss Necker and to overawe the National Assembly by a display of military force. The plot miscarried: thousands invaded the courtyard of the palace to demand that Necker be retained in office; soldiers under the command of the Prince de Conti refused to obey the command to fire; and the deputies, rallied by Mirabeau in an historic speech, refused to disperse. The king was compelled to yield.

Up to now the revolutionary temper developing in Paris had been without effective leadership. With the latest news from Versailles, however, the professional-and-commercial classes, who had hitherto been prepared to wait on events and had viewed the simmerings in the *faubourgs* and markets without sympathy, began to give a direction to affairs without which the July revolution could hardly have taken place. From this date the pamphleteers and journalists in the entourage of the Duke of Orleans (who had gone over to the Third Estate at Versailles) began to establish a permanent headquarters at the Palais Royal; here thousands congregated nightly and acquired the slogans and directives—and, possibly, too, the funds—of what Hardy called 'the extreme revolutionary party'.[3] Also at this time the 407 Electors of the Paris Third Estate, whose original task it had been to appoint the Parisian deputies to the Third Estate at Versailles, began to meet regularly at the Hôtel

---

[1] For the events of June–July 1789, the following authorities have been consulted: P. Caron, 'Une Tentative de contre-révolution en juin-juillet 1789', *Revue d'histoire moderne*, viii (1906–7), 5–34; 649–78; J. Flammermont, *La Journée du 14 juillet 1789* (Paris, 1892); P. Chauvet, *1789. L'insurrection parisienne et la prise de la Bastille* (Paris, 1946); G. Lefebvre, op. cit., pp. 107–38; J. M. Thompson, *The French Revolution* (Oxford, 1943), pp. 45–59. Documentary sources are separately indicated.   [2] Hardy, viii. 342.   [3] Ibid. viii. 362.

de Ville in the heart of the capital. These two bodies were to play distinctive, yet complementary, parts in the events of July. In the early days, however, it was the Palais Royal alone that gave a positive direction to the popular movement. Whereas the Hôtel de Ville contented itself with drafting paper schemes for the institution of a *milice bourgeoise*, or citizens' militia, the Palais Royal took effective measures, by public agitation and liberal expenditure, to win over the Gardes Françaises from their loyalty to the court. On 30 June crowds directed from the Palais Royal forcibly released from the Abbaye prison eleven guardsmen who had been jailed for refusing to fire on the people at Versailles on the night of 22–23 June.[1] Tracts supporting the standpoint of the Third Estate were distributed among the Paris garrisons: on 8 July a newsvendor was arrested for trying to sell such materials to officers and men encamped at the Champ de Mars.[2] On 10 July eighty artillerymen, who had broken out of their barracks in the Hôtel des Invalides, were publicly fêted in the Palais Royal and the Champs Elysées.

Reacting to these developments, the Court Party attempted a show-down: on 11 July Necker was sent into exile and replaced by the Baron de Breteuil. This proved to be the spark that touched off the insurrection in Paris. The news reached the capital at noon on the 12th. During the afternoon Parisians flocked to the Palais Royal, where orators—the young Camille Desmoulins among them—gave the call to arms. Groups of marchers quickly formed; the busts of Necker and the Duke of Orleans, the heroes of the hour, were paraded on the boulevards; theatres were compelled to close as a sign of mourning; in the Place Louis XV demonstrators clashed with cavalry commanded by the Prince de Lambesc, who had been ordered to clear the Tuileries gardens. Besenval, commander of the Paris garrison, withdrew to the Champ de Mars; the capital was in the hands of the people.

As the tocsin pealed—soon to become a frequent and familiar sound to Parisians—bands of insurgents joined those who, two days earlier, had begun to burn down the hated *barrières*, whose exactions were bitterly resented by shopkeepers, wine-merchants, and small consumers and which had already been the

---

[1] *Relation de ce qui s'est passé à l'Abbaye St. Germain* (Paris, 1789). Bib. Nat. L[b] 39 1882; Hardy, viii. 373, 383.　　　　[2] Arch. Nat., Y 13818.

scene of frequent disturbance and attempted smuggling.[1] From the proceedings opened against the raiders nine months later, in the course of which more than eighty witnesses were heard, we learn that no less than forty of the fifty-four customs posts were destroyed by fire in the course of four days' rioting.[2] The destruction was systematic: documents, registers, and customs receipts were burned, iron railings were pulled down, offices and furniture were fired, and the customs officers—where they had not already taken flight—were forcibly expelled. Many, taken by surprise, had no time to remove their personal belongings and suffered considerable loss: one official of the barrière du Trône later claimed for the loss of property valued at 25,413 *livres*, including 8,100 *livres* in cash; another for losses amounting to 27,470 *livres*, 10 *sous*.[3] Yet looting was not part of the plan as conceived by its organizers: at the barrière Saint-Martin, a looter was thus reprimanded by a fellow rioter: 'Brûlons, s'il le faut, puisque cela nous est ordonné, mais ne volons (pas), puisque cela nous est défendu.' From such and even more specific evidence it is clear that the Palais Royal had a hand in the affair: it is no doubt significant that two posts said to belong to the Duke of Orleans were deliberately spared by the incendiaries. It does not appear that the main purpose of 'the extreme revolutionary party' was so much to give free entry of consumers' goods into the capital—though this inevitably followed—as to destroy the monopoly of the Farmers General and to control the entry and exit of arms and persons. But the people carrying out their orders—and often acting independently of them—had their own accounts to settle with an institution that added substantially to the cost of wine, firewood, eggs, and livestock: they were the petty traders, wine-merchants, barrel and building workers, dockers, water-carriers, labourers, and workers employed on public-works schemes, who, the documents tell us, played a large part in this operation and, no doubt, affected its outcome.

That same night, too, armed civilians, Gardes Françaises and local poor broke into the monastery of the Saint-Lazare

[1] On 1 May ten smugglers had been arrested at the barrière Saint-Denis and, on 6 May, two others for causing a disturbance and insulting the officials (Arch. Nat., Y 18795, pp. 446–7; 18763).
[2] Arch. Nat., Z^{1a} 886. (See especially the document entitled *Information concernant l'incendie des Barrières. 29 mars, 1790 et jours suivans.*)   [3] Arch. Nat., Y 11987, 15403.

brotherhood on the northern fringe of the city, searched it for arms, released prisoners, and removed fifty-two cartloads of grain and flour to the central grain market.[1] The search for grain was the main object of the visit. An unemployed carter, who was later traced to Charolles in Burgundy, where he had escaped with 700 *louis* picked up in the monastery, described how he had been brought there 'par des gens qui avaient l'air comme il faut . . . pour conduire les grains qui y étaient à la Halle'.[2] Another carter, when questioned by the police, spoke of making two such trips for which he was paid at the rate of 40 *sous* per journey.[3] While this part of the proceedings was directed by the Palais Royal, the monastery was also completely ransacked by the local unemployed and *menu peuple*—the records speak of porters and labourers, rarely of workshop journeymen—for money, food, silver, and hidden treasure. Every conceivable object of real or imaginary value was pilfered: a butcher's boy, later convicted for theft, admitted removing a dried ram's head; and one zealot even came away with a skeleton which he dragged up five flights to his room! Such activities provided the police and the newly formed militia with a ready excuse for rounding up large numbers of suspects, mainly unemployed workers and vagrants, many of whom were later charged with participation in this affair.[4]

But the main feature of the night of 12–13 July was the search for arms: religious houses were visited and gunsmiths, armourers, and harness-makers were raided in different parts of the capital. A number of statements drawn up in support of their claims for compensation have come down to us. Thus, Marcel Arlot, master gunsmith of the rue Grénéta in the parish of Saint-Leu, reported that his shop was broken into at 2 a.m. by a crowd headed by a journeyman armourer of the rue Jean Robert; muskets, pistols, sabres, and swords to the value of 24,000 *livres* were removed. A harness-maker of the Pont Saint-Michel reported the theft of belts and shoulder-straps to the value of 390 *livres*. Brun, master gunsmith and sword-cutler of the rue Bar-du-Bec, parish of Saint-Jean-en-Grève, in submitting a

[1] *Information à la requête du Procureur fiscal du Bailliage de St. Lazare, 20 juillet 1789.* Arch. Nat., Z² 4691.

[2] Arch. Saône-et-Loire, B. 705.   [3] Arch. Nat., Z² 4691.

[4] The names of about fifty such persons appear in Arch. Nat., Y 10634, fol. 149; 10649, fols. 17–21; 18795, fol. 462; 11518; 12708; 12218; 14240; 15101; 15683.

claim for 4,348 *livres*, stated that his shop had been broken into no less than thirty times, in the course of which 150 swords, 4 gross of sword-blades, 58 hunting-knives, 10 brace of pistols, and 8 muskets had been removed; while another sword-cutler of the parish of Saint-Séverin complained that his shop had been invaded several times on both the 12 and 13 July and that a very considerable number of sabres, swords, and unmounted blades had been taken by persons who refused to pay for them on the ground 'that they would serve for the defence of the capital'; his losses amounted to 6,684 *livres*. The total losses eventually submitted to the National Assembly by the Parisian gunsmiths amounted to 115,118 *livres*. As far as we can tell, they never received their money: they were among the minor victims of the Revolution.[1]

Of considerable interest, too, is the eye-witness account of the events of that first night of the July revolution given by Jean-Nicolas Pepin, a tallow-chandler's labourer, who, as a subpoenaed witness in the Saint-Lazare affair, later told the story of how he was caught up in the milling throngs of civilians and Gardes Françaises that, all night long, surged through the streets, shouting the newly learned patriotic slogans, ringing the tocsin, and searching for grain and arms. From his account, too, it is doubly clear that, at this time, the guiding centre of the revolutionary movement lay in the Palais Royal to which, rather than to the Hôtel de Ville the angry, bewildered, but elated, citizens looked for leadership and guidance.[2]

On the morning of the 13th, however, the Electors made a firm bid to gain control of the situation. They formed a Permanent Committee to act as a provisional government of the city and determined to put a stop to the indiscriminate arming of the whole population. They had been alarmed by the burning of the *barrières* and the sacking of the monastery of Saint-Lazare. To them the bands of unemployed and homeless, who had played some part in these operations, were as great a menace to the security and properties of the citizens as the privileged orders conspiring at Versailles.[3] Accordingly the

- [1] Arch. Nat., Y 12218, 12698; C 134, doss. 8, pièce 12; D VI 6, no. 39, pièce 19.
  [2] Arch. Nat., Z² 4691.
  [3] These were soon to be increased by the release of prisoners from the Force and Bicêtre; some of these, however, not appreciating their freedom, surrendered to the police the next day (Arch. Nat., Y 13454).

plan to establish a regular citizens' militia, or *milice bourgeoise*, was hastily adopted with the dual object of defending the capital from the military threat without and from the danger of 'anarchy' within: it needs hardly be said that it was on the latter score alone that the king was persuaded to give his consent the next day.[1] Householders were summoned to meetings in the sixty Electoral Districts: each District was to contribute 200 (later 800) men. The same day, wrote Barnave, 13,200 citizens were registered and equipped;[2] two days later, he was happy to claim:

> La plus grande partie de la milice de Paris est bonne bourgeoise, et c'est ce qui la rend aussi sûre pour l'ordre public que formidable pour la tyrannie.[3]

In fact, while each District drew up its own conditions of enrolment, in most cases property and residential qualifications— even employers' certificates of good character—were imposed that virtually debarred a large part of the wage-earning population; certainly all unemployed and vagrants were excluded.[4] All *vagabonds*, *gens sans aveu*, and other 'irregulars' were to be immediately disarmed. An English observer, Dr. Rigby, recorded that this operation had already been largely carried through by the evening of the same day, 'at which time [he wrote] the regularly armed citizens almost exclusively occupied the streets'.[5]

The point is of interest as it illustrates the degree of authority quickly asserted by the Electors; yet it is doubtful if the process of disarming went so far as suggested by Dr. Rigby as long as the insurrection lasted. Even after its completion, the new city authorities felt compelled to invite the Paris workers and craftsmen to surrender their arms in return for a payment of 9 *livres* per head;[6] and, between 22 July and 3 August, the

---

[1] *Mémoires de Bailly* (2 vols. Paris, 1821), i. 267.

[2] Arch. Nat., W 12, fols. 197-9 (letter of 15 July 1789). On 14 July Hardy recorded that 30,000 had been enrolled (*Journal*, viii. 386); on 15 July Barnave estimated the enrolment at 48,000 (loc. cit.) and on 18 July at 90,000 (Arch. Nat., W 13, fol. 105).

[3] Arch. Nat., W 12, fols. 197-8.   [4] Arch. Nat., C 134, doss. 1.

[5] *Dr. Rigby's Letters from France etc. in 1789*, ed. Lady Eastlake (London, 1906), p. 55.

[6] *Procès-verbal des séances et délibérations de l'assemblée générale des électeurs de Paris, réunis à l'Hôtel-de-Ville, le 14 juillet 1789* (3 vols., Paris, 1790), ii. 156-8. Brit. Mus., F. 602-4. A large part of these minutes are reproduced in L. G. Wickham Legg, *Select Documents . . . of the French Revolution* (Oxford, 1905), i. 49-95.

District of Saint-Roch alone purchased 250 muskets and 12 pistols in this way.[1] Besides, crowds continued to besiege the Hôtel de Ville, demanding arms and gunpowder. Jacques de Flesselles, *prévôt des marchands* and acting head of the provisional city government, being anxious to limit their distribution, made vague promises and sent parties off on fruitless expeditions to the arsenal and the Carthusian monastery; this 'treachery' was to cost him his life on the morrow. Meanwhile, the Electors had deputed one of their number, the abbé Lefevre, to guard the considerable stocks of powder and ammunition that they had assembled in the vaults of the Hôtel de Ville. The abbé discharged his duties conscientiously, but he was compelled by the half-armed crowds surging round the building to hand out the powder in his custody with greater haste and less discrimination than he had wished. He kept a careful account of the transactions: we learn that he distributed 8 barrels of gunpowder on 13 July; 46 barrels—three of them 'pour prendre la Bastille'—on the 14th; and a further 42 barrels on the 15th. At the end of the record appears the sorrowful addendum:

Cette livraison a été faite avec tant de précipitation qu'il n'a pas été possible de faire ajouter aux bons des reçus. Les dits 96 barils pèsent ensemble 96.000 livres.[2]

The quest for arms and ammunition continued: on the morning of the 14th, a spectacular raid was made on the Hôtel des Invalides across the river. According to Salmour, the Saxon ambassador, who witnessed the affair, 7,000 to 8,000 citizens took part;[3] many, wrote Hardy, were crushed in the *mêlée*.[4] The Governor, the Marquis de Sombreuil, was abandoned by his troops and forced to open his gates. He later reported the removal of more than 30,000 muskets, of which 12,000 at least had fallen 'into dangerous hands'.[5] Meanwhile, the cry had gone up, 'to the Bastille!'

Royalist historians have scoffed at the picture of thousands of Parisians hurling themselves at the Bastille in order to release seven prisoners, all of them either lunatics or of unsavoury

[1] Bib. Nat., nouv. acq. franç., no. 2670, fol. 55.
[2] Ibid., no. 2678, fol. 47.
[3] A. Mathiez, *Les Grandes journées de la Constituante* (*1789–91*) (Paris, 1913), pp. 22–23.   [4] Hardy, viii. 390.
[5] *Procès-verbal de l'assemblée des électeurs*, i. 371.

character.[1] Such criticism falls wide of its mark. The immediate aim was not to release prisoners but to find the powder that was known to have been lately sent there from the arsenal. Other motives no doubt played a part. It was believed that the fortress was heavily manned; its guns, which that morning were trained on the rue Saint-Antoine, could play havoc among the crowded tenements. In the night it had been rumoured that 30,000 royalist troops had marched into the Faubourg Saint-Antoine and had begun to slaughter its citizens. Besides, though it had ceased to harbour more than a trickle of State prisoners, the Bastille was widely hated as a symbol of ministerial despotism: the *cahiers de doléances* of the Paris Districts bear witness to this fact.[2] Yet there does not appear to have been any serious intention to take it by storm,[3] least of all on the part of the Permanent Committee of Electors, who directed operations, with fumbling uncertainty, from the Hôtel de Ville. They made their intentions clear from the start: to negotiate with the Governor, de Launay, for the surrender of the gunpowder in his keeping and for the withdrawal of the guns from his battlements. That this plan failed, and that the Bastille fell only after the threat of a frontal assault, was due to circumstances outside their control.

Numerous eye-witness accounts of the siege of the Bastille, or accounts purporting to be such, have come down to us. Fact and fiction are often richly blended in them. Among the most trustworthy, perhaps, are those left by the Electors themselves.[4] From these it appears that the first deputation sent to parley with de Launay arrived at the Bastille at 10 o'clock. Having received a friendly welcome and an invitation to dine, they did not emerge for some time. The dense crowds waiting outside, fearing a trap, now raised a shout for the surrender or capture of the fortress. To allay suspicions, a second delegation, sent by the neighbouring District of La Culture, urged the Governor to surrender. Its leader, Thuriot de la Rozière, brought back word to the Permanent Committee that the Governor, while refusing to surrender, had withdrawn his cannon and had pro-

---

[1] A. Bégis, *Le Registre d'écrou de la Bastille de 1789 à 1792* (Paris, 1880).

[2] Ch.-L. Chassin, op. cit. ii. *passim.*

[3] But see Hardy: 'Les ouvriers du fauxbourg avaient entrepris de faire en forme le siège de ce château' (viii. 388).

[4] The essential passages appear in Wickham Legg, op. cit. i. 49–95.

mised not to fire unless attacked. Up to this point the crowds surging in from the rue Saint-Antoine had penetrated only into the outer of the two courtyards leading to the main draw-bridge and gate of the Bastille. The outer courtyard was, as usual, unguarded; it was separated from the inner Cour du Gouvernement by a wall and a drawbridge which de Launay had, unaccountably, left raised but undefended. Half an hour after Thuriot's departure, two men climbed the wall from a neighbouring building and lowered the drawbridge. Believing a frontal attack to be imminent, de Launay gave the order to fire. In the affray that followed, the besiegers lost ninety-eight dead and seventy-three wounded;[1] only one of the defenders was struck. Two further deputations, sent to the Bastille in the course of this affray, were fired on and failed to gain admittance.

The worthy Electors were now at their wits' end. Their policy of peaceful negotiations had proved a complete failure. Had it not been for the angry insistence of the bands of armed citizens who swarmed in the rooms of the Hôtel de Ville, in the Place de Grève outside, and along all the approaches of the Bastille, calling for vengeance for blood spilt and suspected treachery, they would certainly have abandoned their efforts. Meanwhile, two detachments of Gardes Françaises, drawn up outside the Hôtel de Ville, responded to the summons of Pierre-Augustin Hulin, a former non-commissioned officer, who marched them off to the Bastille with five cannon removed from the Invalides that morning. Joined at the fortress by a few hundred armed civilians, they fought their way under fire to the inner courtyard and trained their cannon on the main gate. This proved to be decisive. The Governor offered to surrender provided that the garrison were spared; but the angry crowds would not hear of conditions and the siege continued. At this point de Launay seems to have lost his head and threatened to blow up the fortress. He was, however, dissuaded by the garrison and, in desperation, gave orders for the main drawbridge to be lowered. So the Bastille fell.

It is perhaps surprising that the angry and triumphant crowds,

[1] These are the provisional figures given by Dussaulx in his first official report to the Constituent Assembly a few months later (*De l'insurrection parisienne et de la prise de la Bastille* (Paris, 1790), pp. 161–2. Bib. Nat. L^b 39 1972). Hardy's lower figures of 20–60 killed and 17 wounded were based on early hearsay (viii. 388).

pouring through the open gates of the Bastille, did not exact a more complete and indiscriminate vengeance. They had lived through days of nervous tension, continuously subject to the fear of sudden attack and disaster; they had been betrayed, they believed, by some of their leaders; over 150 of their fellows had been killed or wounded. Of 110 members of the defending garrison, six or seven were slaughtered. De Launay, though promised a safe-conduct to the Hôtel de Ville, was struck down on the way and his head severed with a butcher's knife. His assassin, Dénot, a cook of the rue Campalon, though claiming that de Launay had first kicked him, later boasted of his prowess: 'Que s'il en a agi ainsi, il a cru faire un acte patriotique, et mériter une médaille.'[1] De Flesselles, who had aroused popular fury by his reluctance to distribute arms, met a similar fate as he followed his accusers from the Hôtel de Ville.[2]

Such acts of popular vengeance—followed, a week later, by the murder of Foullon and Berthier—have, of course, been picked upon to discredit the captors of the Bastille and to represent them as vagabonds, criminals, or a mercenary rabble hired in the wine-shops of the Saint-Antoine quarter. This is a legend that dies hard; yet not only is there no evidence to support it, but all the available evidence directly refutes it. Nor should we, of course, be satisfied in describing them with such general terms as 'les ouvriers du faubourg St. Antoine', 'le peuple', or 'tout Paris'. There is, in fact, small excuse for so doing: those directly involved in the capture of the fortress were but a few hundred and, in their case at least, sufficient evidence has survived to enable us to get a reasonably clear picture.

The *vainqueurs de la Bastille*, as they came to be called, numbered between 800 and 900 persons. Those were they who managed, after careful sifting of evidence, to establish their claim to have taken a direct part in the capture of the fortress. Their names were carefully compiled and recorded and have come down to us in three separate lists, each one of which was, at various times during 1790, approved by the Constituent

[1] Arch. Nat., Y 12823. Dénot had, according to his own story, joined his local *milice* on 13 July and taken part in the attack on the Invalides.

[2] For *procès-verbaux* relating to these various victims see Arch. Nat., Y 11285; 14604; and 10634, fols. 149–51.

Assembly.[1] One of these lists—that drawn up and held by Stanislas Maillard, secretary of the *vainqueurs*—consists of the names of 662 survivors, of whom nearly 600 are those of civilians.[2] Although incomplete,[3] it is the only one that will serve our purpose, as here alone we find recorded the addresses and occupations, and even the militia units, of the persons concerned. It is, of course, only on the basis of such evidence that it is possible to build up a picture of the social or occupational status of the captors of the Bastille without resort to speculation or vague generalization.

There were few men of wealth among them. As Jaurès wrote:

On ne relève pas dans la liste des combattants les rentiers, les capitalistes pour lesquels en partie la Révolution était faite.[4]

Three manufacturers are listed, four merchants, the brewer Santerre, 3 naval officers, 4 termed 'bourgeois', and perhaps a handful of wealthy shopkeepers. The rest, apart from 61 soldiers and 15 cavalrymen of the *maréchaussée de la garde nationale*—whose civil occupations are not given—are almost all small tradesmen, artisans, and wage-earners. Of these, about two-thirds are small workshop masters, craftsmen, and journeymen drawn from about thirty petty trades;[5] the remainder are engaged in manufacture, distribution, building, the professions, and general trades.[6] The wage-earners cannot always be clearly identified, but they appear to be (as we should expect in this case) in a decided minority: perhaps 60 in the small crafts and

---

[1] *Tableau des citoyens vainqueurs de la Bastille* (871 names), Musée des Arch. Nat., no. 1166; *Tableau des vainqueurs de la Bastille* (954 names, many appearing twice) in F. Bournon, *La Bastille* (Paris, 1893), pp. 219–23; *Noms des vainqueurs de la Bastille* (662 names), Arch. Nat., T 514[(1)].

[2] Arch. Nat., T 514[(1)].

[3] Among notable omissions are Dénot, who chopped off de Launay's head; the abbé Fauchet; Fournier l'Américain; the architect Palloy; and Maillard himself.

[4] Jaurès, *Histoire socialiste*, i. 303.

[5] These include 49 joiners, 48 cabinet-makers, 41 locksmiths, 28 cobblers, 20 sculptors and modellers, 11 metal-chasers, 10 turners, 10 hairdressers and wig-makers, 7 potters, 9 monumental masons, 9 nailsmiths, 9 dealers in fancy ware, 8 printers, 7 braziers, 9 tailors, 9 founders, 5 jewellers, 5 goldsmiths, 5 stove-makers, and 3 upholsterers. For a similar classification see G. Bord, 'La Conspiration maçonnique de 1789', *Le Correspondant*, May 1905, pp. 521–44. M. Bord must have used Maillard's list to arrive at his results, but he gives no reference.

[6] These include 11 wine-merchants, 3 café-proprietors, 2 innkeepers, 21 shop-keepers, 9 hatters, 3 manufacturers, 4 businessmen, 6 gardeners, 3 carpenters, and 7 stonemasons.

85 or 90 in other occupations.[1] There was one woman among them—Marie Charpentier, *femme* Hauserne, a laundress of the parish of Saint-Hippolyte in the Faubourg Saint-Marcel.

These were the survivors; we know less about the ninety-eight said to have been killed during the siege. Jaurès, quoting the journalist Loustalot, wrote: 'Plus de trente laissaient leur femme et leurs enfants dans un tel état de détresse que des secours immédiats furent nécessaires.'[2] There is further evidence to suggest that those killed included wage-earners and city poor. Hardy reports a burial service for Charles Dusson, aged 31, a journeyman edge-toolmaker of the rue de la Huchette, in the church of Saint-Séverin on 18 July.[3] Again, Jean-Marie Silvain Gomy, aged 17, one of Santerre's brewers, was last seen alive when he set out for the Bastille under arms on the afternoon of 14 July.[4] Five further corpses of civilians were brought to the Châtelet for identification: they included a journeyman shoe-maker of the Faubourg Saint-Antoine, and a street-lighter of the rue des Noyers, off the Place Maubert; the rest remained unclaimed and unidentified.[5]

Of the survivors, at least, the great majority were citizens of the Faubourg Saint-Antoine. Four hundred, it is true, of the 635 whose origins have been traced, were of provincial birth;[6] yet most of them had become settled inhabitants of the *faubourg*: no less than 425, out of 602 whose addresses are given, lived in one or other of its parishes.[7] Of the remainder, 60 came from Saint-Gervais, Saint-Paul, and other districts adjoining the Bastille from the west, 30 from the central markets,[8] perhaps a dozen from the Faubourg Saint-Marcel. Very few came from more than a mile or two from the Bastille: among them were a locksmith from the Faubourg Saint-Honoré and a tinsmith from

---

[1] The largest categories are: cabinet-makers (8–10), joiners (8), locksmiths (7–9), cobblers (5), print and paper workers (4), stocking-weavers (4), gauze-workers (22), porters (17), riverside workers and bargemen (8), shipyard workers (5), coachmen (4), stonemasons (5), stonecutters (4), ribbon weavers (3).

[2] Jaurès, op. cit. i. 303.   [3] Hardy, viii. 388.

[4] Arch. Nat., Y 14119.   [5] Arch. Nat., Y 10634, fol. 150; 12698; 10598.

[6] J. Durieux, *Les Vainqueurs de la Bastille* (Paris, 1911), pp. 261 ff.

[7] Most of these were from the streets adjoining the Bastille—the rue du Faubourg Saint-Antoine and adjacent streets (245), rue de Lappe (53), rue de Charenton (44), rue de Bercy (12), rue de Montreuil (7).

[8] Fournier l'Américain's claim, therefore, to have led 400 of his band of 800 followers from the Saint-Eustache District to the siege must not be taken too literally (*Mémoires secrets. . . de C. Fournier, Américain*, Arch. Nat., F⁷ 6504).

the Gros Caillou, near the Champ de Mars. And all of these, whether from the Faubourg Saint-Antoine or elsewhere, far from being vagrants or down-and-outs, were men of settled abode and occupation. More surprisingly perhaps, the overwhelming majority of its captors went to the Bastille under arms as enrolled members of their local units of the newly formed *milice bourgeoise*, or Parisian National Guard.[1] This, of course, not only serves further to disprove the legend that the captors were vagrants or social riff-raff—such elements were, of course, rigorously excluded from the ranks of the militia—but it also suggests that the operation may have been a far less spontaneous affair than has usually been claimed.

Yet, in a wider sense, we may agree with Michelet that the capture of the Bastille was not just the affair of those few hundred citizens of the Saint-Antoine quarter who were most immediately involved, but of the people of Paris as a whole. At the peak of the insurrection there may have been a quarter of a million Parisians—some thought more—under arms;[2] and, taking an even broader view, we should not ignore the part played by the great mass of Parisian petty craftsmen, tradesmen, and wage-earners, in the Faubourg Saint-Antoine and elsewhere, whose revolutionary temper had been moulded over many months by the rise in living costs and, as the crisis deepened, by the growing conviction that the great hopes raised by the States General were being thwarted by an aristocratic plot.

Though of little military importance the capture of the Bastille had far-reaching political consequences. The National Assembly was saved and received royal recognition. The Court Party began to disintegrate and the Comte d'Artois went into voluntary exile. In the capital, power passed into the hands of the Committee of Electors, who set up a City Council with Bailly as mayor and Lafayette as commander-in-chief of its National Guard. On 17 July the king himself made the journey to Paris,

---

[1] In the case of 6 out of every 7 civilians on Maillard's list the name of the company and/or battalion of the National Guard is indicated. I have assumed that the remaining 1 in 7 (they include a boy of 14, another of 16 and a woman) were not enrolled in the *milice*.

[2] Nicolas de Bonneville, the original promoter of the *milice bourgeoise*, later wrote that, on 14 July, Paris had 300,000 men under arms (S. Lacroix, op. cit., 2nd series, v. 31); Barnave, on 18 July, wrote of 180,000 (Arch. Nat., W 12, fol. 105).

was received at the Hôtel de Ville by the victors and, in token of acquiescence in the turn of events, donned the red, white, and blue cockade of the Revolution. Though to Hardy the 14th had seemed 'une triste journée',[1] it was a week of public rejoicing and fraternal embraces. Yet it proved short-lived. Though a decisive step had been taken, the Revolution was far from completed; and the festivities and rejoicing soon gave way to a new round of solemn and tragic events.

[1] Hardy, viii. 390.

V

THE MARCH TO VERSAILLES

THE march to Versailles on 5 October, by ending in the king's return to the capital, completed the Paris revolution of July. As long as court and king remained at Versailles and an active minority of deputies were able, in alliance with the court, to frustrate the constitutional programme of the Assembly, effective power still remained divided between the revolutionary *bourgeoisie* (supported by a minority of liberal aristocrats) and the adherents of the old régime. The king's refusal to give his assent to the Declaration of the Rights of Man and to the Assembly's famous resolution of 4 August, which eventually led to the abolition of the feudal system of land-tenure, the long struggle over the 'veto', and the constant intrigues to abduct the king to a safe distance from Paris, showed how precarious as yet were the gains of the July revolution.

The October insurrection was to consolidate these gains. By placing the king under the watchful eye of the majority in the National Assembly, the Paris city government, and Districts and by destroying the influence of the conservative 'English Party' within the Assembly, it established the ascendancy of the constitutional monarchists which, in Paris, found its reflection in the long rule of Bailly as mayor and of Lafayette as commander-in-chief of the National Guard. It must, of course, be added that by placing the Assembly itself under the equally watchful eye of the Parisian *menu peuple*, whose more active elements began to crowd the tribunes and, often, to influence its debates, it opened the way for further developments that were neither foreseen, nor in the event welcomed, by the victors of October; but this, of course, lay still in the future.

Yet the constitutional monarchists, who were clearly the immediate beneficiaries of the insurrection, were not eager to boast of their successes or to show the world how they were achieved. When the Châtelet inquiry into the events of 6 October was published in March 1790,[1] it was with the full

[1] *Procédure criminelle au Châtelet . . . de Paris sur la journée du 6 octobre* (Paris, 1790). Bib. Nat., L^c 29 980.

consent of the Assembly's majority; yet, far from throwing a
bright light into dark corners, it served effectively as a smoke-
screen to divert attention from the real authors of the October
'days'. It suited the court, the police, the Paris administration,
and the dominant party in the Assembly to present the violence
and haste with which the king had been hustled to Paris as the
outcome of a vaguely defined Orleanist plot or of the sinister
machinations of the discredited Mirabeau; it would have been
impolitic to reveal it as the execution of plans long nurtured by
the respectable *bourgeois* and liberal aristocrats who controlled
the Assembly and Paris city government. Mystery undoubtedly
attaches to the exact part played by Mirabeau, Orleans, or
even Lafayette—a mystery which the Châtelet inquiry succeeded
in deepening. It is not the purpose of the present chapter to
seek to throw a fresh light on the respective guilt, or responsibility, of the various parties concerned: this has already been
attempted, with remarkable success under the circumstances,
by Albert Mathiez.[1] Suffice it here to say that it would be
strange indeed if those who benefited most directly from these
events did not have at least as effective a control of the October
insurrection as they had of the Paris revolution of July. Within
certain limits they would no more hesitate in October than in
July to turn to their advantage the anger and revolutionary
energies of the *menu peuple* in order to achieve defined political
objectives. Had not Academician Dussaulx, a highly respected
member of the Centre party in the Assembly, told Farmer
General Augeart already on 26 August that the king must be
brought to Paris—by violence if need be?[2] And did not Barnave's
letters written after the event explain to his Dauphinois constituents the necessity for the insurrection—however distasteful
certain of its features undoubtedly were—and praise the city of
Paris for once more saving 'la liberté publique'?[3]

So much, in brief, for the main political results and respon-
sibilities for the October days; but the *menu peuple* of Paris were

---

[1] A. Mathiez, 'Étude critique sur les journées des 5 et 6 octobre 1789', *Rev. hist.*
lxvii (1898), 241–81; lxviii (1899), 258–94; lxix (1899), 41–66. I have made
considerable use of this study in preparing this chapter.

[2] Quoted by Mathiez, op. cit. lxvii. 249.

[3] Arch. Nat., W 13, fols. 317–18. He, nevertheless, spoke of it as 'ce mouvement
terrible', which, he considered, might have ended in disaster, had it not been for
the part played by Lafayette and the Assembly (Arch. Nat., W 12, fols. 200–1).

no more helpless accessories, willing to stage an insurrection for the sole benefit of the constitutional monarchists in October, than they had been for the Palais Royal or the Paris Electors in July. While they might share the general alarm of all 'patriots' at the new 'conspiracies' hatching at Versailles, they also had their own particular preoccupations. Barnave, who often showed a deeper understanding of social realities than most of his colleagues, drew attention to this division of interest when he wrote to his constituents that while, in October, *bourgeoisie* and *peuple* acted together in a common cause, the former were actuated solely by the desire to defeat the plots of the aristocracy, whereas the latter, while sharing this desire, were equally concerned with the scarcity of bread.[1] This duality of interest was by no means peculiar to the events of October; but to be aware of it is to begin, at least, to understand an episode which, in some respects, is more shrouded in mystery than any other similar event of the Revolution. It will perhaps emerge more clearly if we first try to trace the origins of these separate trends, follow their development and see how they merged in common action on 5 October.

Again, as in July, it was the *menu peuple* rather than the *bourgeoisie* that was first involved in active protest; nor was their movement to cease with the realization of the immediate political objectives. For them the calm following the July revolution was short-lived. In terms of the political movement, the events of July and October, though linked by common ties, are clearly defined and distinctive episodes; in terms of the popular-social movement however, it would perhaps be more correct to speak of an almost continuous agitation, springing up in April or May, rising to a climax in July and again in October, but not finally subsiding until the early days of November. In this movement the problem of bread was uppermost, dominated all other considerations, and drew together the largest numbers in common protest. Yet there were other elements which, though affecting smaller groups, added to the general unrest and, therefore, must have contributed to the volume of anger and to the numbers of demonstrators on 5 October.

[1] Arch. Nat., W 12, fols. 200–1. The passage runs: 'Pendant que nous délibérions, l'impatience des Parisiens s'était portée à l'excès; la bourgeoisie et le peuple, les uns animés uniquement contre la dernière conduite du gouvernement et de l'aristocratie, *et les autres y mêlant l'intérêt du pain qui commençait à être rare*, se sont assemblés dans tous les districts' (my italics).

In the first place, there were the unemployed engaged on public-works schemes or merely herded in the *ateliers de charité*. Their numbers were rising sharply and, in August, there were already 22,000 in the public workshops, of which 18,000 were at Montmartre alone.[1] They had played a certain part in the July revolution, at the *barrières* and even at the Bastille,[2] but to the *bourgeois* revolutionaries they were unwelcome allies. So touchy were the authorities on their score that when a number of new recruits to Montmartre gathered outside the Duke of Orleans's estate at Monceaux on 9 August, waiting for a clerk to bring them work or pay, fifteen were arrested for forming an illegal assembly.[3] Shortly after there appeared a pamphlet by the Chevalier de Beaurepaire, alleging that the Montmartre workers were building fortifications for training artillery on the city.[4] Although a visiting deputation from the District of Petit Saint-Antoine denied the allegations in a reassuring report,[5] a demand was raised for the closure of the workshop. The city authorities agreed to do so on 12 August, and Lafayette was deputed to address the Montmartre workers on the subject on the 15th. He was not well received, possibly because the Assembly had just decided to reduce their wages.[6] Disturbances followed: later in the month two Montmartre navvies were jailed for threatening to kill their workshop manager; and ten Bastille workers, including three women, were arrested by Santerre for creating a disorder.[7] The Montmartre unemployed were duly disbanded, and the majority sent back to their native provinces, with the aid of the *volontaires de la Bastille* (a military force not to be confused with the *vainqueurs*);[8] but other workshops remained open and became, as we shall see, permeated by the political agitation that preceded the march to Versailles.

Meanwhile, a number of trades had decided to test the good faith of the new municipal authorities by putting forward claims for better wages and working conditions. These included

[1] *Mémoires de Bailly*, ii. 257.

[2] Maillard's list of *vainqueurs de la Bastille* includes four participants from the public workshops—two navvies, a foreman, and a *chef d'atelier* (Arch. Nat., T 514(1)).

[3] Arch. Nat., Y 12079.

[4] Chevalier de Beaurepaire, *Rapport à MM. du district des Petits Mathurins*. Bib. Nat., Lᵇ 40 285.   [5] Bib. Nat., nouv. acq. franç., no. 2654, fol. 156.

[6] *Mémoires de Bailly*, ii. 265.

[7] Arch. Nat., Y 15102; 18766; 18795, fols. 463, 466-7.

[8] Jaurès, op. cit. i. 356.

bakers, wig-makers, tailors, shoe-makers, apothecaries, and domestic servants. In general they were to find the new city government no more sympathetic to their claims than their predecessors: their requests for permission to hold meetings were curtly refused, sometimes with the aid of the National Guard;[1] the tailors alone, according to Hardy, won their demand for an increase of wages—in this case, of 10 *sous* per day.[2]

The wig-makers and domestic servants, as might be supposed, were suffering severely from the decline in the luxury trades and the growing volume of emigration. 4,000 wig-makers met in the Champs Elysées to demand a reorganization of their labour exchanges; after a scuffle with the National Guard a deputation was received at the Hôtel de Ville, a joint meeting with the masters was arranged, and a new code was eventually drawn up.[3] The servants' demands were, in the main, political: they requested full citizen rights, the right to attend District Assemblies, to enrol in the National Guard (from which as servile dependents they were debarred), and the exclusion of Savoyards from their calling. They were persuaded to disperse quietly and did not carry out their original threat to demonstrate 40,000 strong in the Champs Elysées, or on the Place du Temple, the next day.[4] Nevertheless, feelings ran high: a few days later Eugène Gervais, an unemployed cook, was arrested at the Palais Royal for inciting domestic servants and workers in general against the *bourgeois* National Guard; he was eventually condemned to be branded and to spend nine years in the galleys, a sentence later commuted to one of two years' prison.[5]

A feature of the scenes that took place at Versailles on 5 October, when the women burst in on the meeting of the

---

[1] Hardy, viii. 434, 438–9, 455; S. Lacroix, op. cit., 1st series, i. 123–4, 381, 416, 547; G. M. Jaffé, *Le Mouvement ouvrier à Paris pendant la Révolution française* (Paris, 1927), pp. 65–73.   [2] Hardy, viii. 438–9.
[3] Ibid., p. 439.   [4] Ibid., p. 455; Arch. Nat., Y 18766.
[5] Arch. Nat., Y 18767. He was reported to have said: 'Que toute la garde bourgeoise et toutes les personnes qui portaient l'uniforme étaient tous des j. f. et que 10.000 domestiques étaient capables de f. le bal à tous les j. f. qui portaient des habits bleus à revers blanc; et que tous les bourgeois étaient tous j. f. sans en excepter un; et que l'on ne voyait qu'un tas de freluquets faire des faquins au Palais Royal, et qu'il y avait 60.000 domestiques à Paris qui pourraient se réunir aux ouvriers des différents états et que l'on verrait tous ces j. f. se cacher chez eux avec leurs f. habits.' Though denying having used the exact words, Gervais admitted saying something similar.

Assembly, was the contempt and hostility shown to the clerical deputies, who were greeted with shouts of 'à bas la calotte!' and 'à mort les calottins!'[1] While this hostility had been recently stimulated by the clergy's refusal to give up their tithes, it had, of course, far deeper roots. Hardy heard the slogan 'à bas la calotte!' in the Palais Royal on 12 July;[2] and, early the same month, the pamphlet *Premier dialogue entre une poissarde et un fort de la halle* showed the degree of disrespect for the Church that, it may be assumed, had by this time become general in the markets.[3] A month later Hardy noted that a procession held on the Feast of the Assumption was threatened in the neighbourhood of Notre Dame with cries of 'à bas la calotte!' and 'Il faudrait les mettre à la lanterne!'[4] That this anti-clerical feeling was on the increase among the *menu peuple* is suggested by the incidents that took place at the end of September at the churches of Saint-Jacques-de-la-Boucherie and Saint-Nicolas-des-Champs, both in the area of the central markets. When the *curé* of Saint-Jacques refused to bury a journeyman carpenter without the payment of the full fee of 23 *livres*, the church was taken by storm and the *curé* compelled to submit. A solemn *requiem* was sung for the deceased to approving shouts of 'bravo' from the assembled crowds. The mood soon changed to one of fury when the choir-leader of the neighbouring church of Saint-Nicolas-des-Champs announced that he had been dismissed for taking part in the service. The church was stormed by a large crowd who threatened to hang the *curé*; it was only dispersed by the National Guard after the arrest of one of the rioters and the promise that the choir-leader would be reinstated.[5] This sharp hostility to the ministers of the Church—arising, in the first place, over such economic issues as the payment of tithe or of funeral expenses—was, of course, highly significant for the future. Hardy had perhaps good cause when he expressed alarm at the discipline, pageantry, and magnitude of the almost daily processions of market women, laundresses, tradesmen, and workers of different Districts that, during August and September, wound up the rue Saint-Jacques to the newly built church of Sainte-Geneviève for thanksgiving services.

---

[1] Mathiez, loc. cit. *Rev. hist.* lxviii. 261.   [2] Hardy, viii. 385.
[3] Bib. Nat., L^b 39 1882.   [4] Hardy, viii. 435.
[5] Arch. Nat., Y 10650; 10649, fol. 42; Hardy, viii. 493–4, 497.

Despite their quasi-religious objects, there is already a foretaste of the march to Versailles in these great demonstrations of the *menu peuple* of the markets and *faubourgs*. Hardy seems to have sensed these potentialities when he writes of the Faubourg Saint-Antoine procession in mid-September, in which 1,200 people took part:

> Bien des gens trouvaient qu'il avait quelque chose d'effrayant par son arrangement, sa composition et son immensité. Les personnes sensées trouvaient bien ridicules ces actes publics dont il était impossible d'interrompre le cours et dont la Piété ne formait pas malheureusement tout le motif.[1]

The price of the 4-lb. loaf had been reduced, on 22 July, from 14½ to 13½ *sous*.[2] The period of calm that followed did not last long. With brief interludes the popular movement that flared up again over the high price or shortage of bread in early August was to continue until November. It was to take the form of acts of violence against bakers and alleged hoarders and of protest meetings or deputations to the municipal authorities. On 2 August Châtel, the major's lieutenant of Saint-Denis, to the north of Paris, was massacred by an angry crowd of small tradesmen, craftsmen, and wage-earners: he had, they said, caused an artificial scarcity of corn and refused, in insulting and contemptuous terms, to reduce the price of bread— 'qu'il ne fallait point donner à la canaille du pain à deux sols la livre'. Châtel, it appears, was chased to the steeple of the parish church, where he was stabbed to death; his head was severed by a soldier of the Provence Regiment. As a result of the murder 21 persons, including 4 women, were arrested: among them were 2 master craftsmen, 4 tradesmen, 9 wage-earners. Another 12 wage-earners were among 18 others who, having evaded arrest, were charged in their absence. In April 1790 two of these, a print worker and a journeyman tailor, were found guilty and hanged in effigy.[3]

On 8 August after great demonstrations outside the Hôtel de Ville, the 4-lb. loaf was further reduced to 12 *sous*.[4] This was a considerable gain. To take two examples: it meant that a

[1] Ibid., pp. 429, 431, 437–8, 441, 443, 445–6, 453, 455–6, 462, 469–70, 473, 475.   [2] Ibid., p. 401.
[3] Arch. Nat., Y 12079; 10479; 10649, fol. 27; 10530, fols. 181–3; 18795, fols. 463, 470–1; Hardy, viii. 417.   [4] Ibid., p. 426.

builder's labourer who, between February and July, had been compelled to spend 80 per cent. of his effective earnings on bread, could now purchase the same amount with 67 per cent. of his income; whereas a journeyman locksmith or carpenter (earning twice the wage of a Réveillon labourer) would now be spending 40 per cent. on bread where he previously spent 48 per cent.[1] Consequently, during the second and third weeks in August, Hardy was able to report a lull in the bread crisis: supplies were more plentiful, the quality of the flour had improved and armed guards were withdrawn from the bakers' shops.[2] On 21 August, however, the crisis had returned in full strength: the harvest had been good, but owing to a prolonged drought, millers were unable to grind their corn. The price of bread remained stable, but the resulting scarcity caused hungry stomachs and ever-lengthening queues in the markets and shops. On 24 August a master wig-maker of the rue de la Cossonnerie was charged with threatening a baker with the dreaded *lanterne*; on the 25th, a cooper of the rue Basse du Rempart was arrested for blaming the city government for deliberately causing the flour shortage; and, two days later, a domestic servant was arrested in a bread-queue and charged with causing a disturbance.[3] Another brief lull followed; but, on 1 September, the guards reappeared in the bakers' shops and were to remain there for sixteen days in the month. Meanwhile, Hardy bitterly complained that he was reduced to buying 'la moitié d'un pain de 4 livres ayant fort mauvais goût'.[4] On 3 September a journeyman roof-maker was arrested in the rue de la Ferronnerie for publicly accusing Lafayette of being a party to a plot to cause scarcity and force up the price of flour— 'qu'il était un traître; qu'il filait sa corde et qu'il fallait le pendre'.[5] The *pacte de famine* had returned with a vengeance!

Nerves were becoming frayed, as working men waited in queues and lost part of their day's pay in consequence.

Pour y avoir du pain [wrote Hardy] les hommes plus pressés cherchaient à écarter les femmes et allaient même jusqu'à les maltraiter pour s'en procurer les premiers.[6]

---

[1] G. Rudé, 'Prices, Wages and Popular Movements in Paris during the French Revolution', *Econ. Hist. Rev.*, vol. vi, no. 3, April 1954, p. 248.
[2] Hardy, viii. 429–40.   [3] Arch. Nat., Y 18795, fols. 465–7; 18766.
[4] Hardy, viii. 458.   [5] Arch. Nat., Y 18767.   [6] Hardy, viii. 460.

On 13 September a bread riot took place at Versailles, where an angry crowd tried to hang a baker for selling good-quality loaves to his wealthier customers at 18 *sous* and poor-quality bread to the rest at a cheaper price. The baker was cut down in the nick of time by the local militia. The king was brought along 'pour calmer les esprits'. Several people were injured and twenty-one arrested, of whom three were hanged ten days later.[1] By now, the women had begun to take a hand. The bread crisis was peculiarly their own and, from this time on, it was they rather than the men that played the leading role in the movement. On 16 September Hardy recorded that women had stopped five carts laden with grain at Chaillot and brought them to the Hôtel de Ville in Paris. On the 17th, at midday, the Hôtel de Ville was besieged by angry women complaining about the conduct of the bakers; they were received by Bailly and the Municipal Council. 'Ces femmes [wrote Hardy] disaient hautement que les hommes n'y entendaient rien et qu'elles voulaient se mêler des affaires.' The next day the Hôtel de Ville was again besieged, and promises were made. The same evening Hardy saw women hold up a cartload of grain in the Place des Trois Maries and escort it to the local District headquarters.[2] This movement was to continue up to and beyond the political demonstration of 5 October.[3]

Meanwhile, as in June, a political movement had begun to develop in Paris in response to the new deadlock that had arisen between Court and Assembly at Versailles. Once more it was the journalists and lawyers in the entourage of the Duke of Orleans, with their headquarters at the Palais Royal, that took the lead. According to Mathiez, the leading part among the Parisian 'patriots' was played by Duport, Desmoulins, Danton, and Loustalot, the editor of *Les Révolutions de Paris*; Marat, with his *Ami du peuple*, played, as usual, a lone hand. It was they who, through their press, clubs, and Districts, launched and popularized the slogan that the king should be removed from the intrigues of the Court at Versailles and brought to Paris.[4]

---

[1] Arch. Seine-et-Oise, series B. Prévôté de l'Hôtel du Roi. Procédures, 1789. Fifteen accused (all men) included 2 wheelwrights and a mattress-worker (hanged), 2 building workers, 4 porters, 2 waiters, a soldier, 2 labourers, and a saddle-maker.
[2] Hardy, viii. 478–80.
[3] See Hardy's entries for 3–7 and 12 October 1789 (viii. 499–505, 512). The *Journal* ends on 14 October.   [4] Mathiez, op. cit. lxvii. 266–8; lxviii. 269–73.

The idea that the king should return to his capital and reside among his subjects in 'la bonne ville de Paris' was not a new one: it had been voiced in the *cahier* of the Parisian Third Estate and in a pamphlet in July; it was perhaps in the minds of many that gave Louis XVI so vociferous a welcome when he visited the revolutionary capital on 17 July. Now it was revived, and with greater insistence, to respond to a new and particular political situation. The immediate issue was the 'veto'—the question as to whether the king should have the power, under the Constitution being debated at Versailles, to amend, suspend, or permanently reject, the legislative proposals of the National Assembly. Broadly speaking, the Right, or moderates, wished to invest the king with an absolute right of veto; while the 'patriots', among whom Barnave was emerging as leader, upheld the legislative supremacy of the Assembly; yet, unlike their allies in the Palais Royal, they were prepared to negotiate with the help of a Centre group, who favoured a compromise. It was while these negotiations were going on, at the end of August, that Academician Dussaulx is reported to have made his declaration that the king must be brought to Paris, if need be by violence, in order to break the deadlock. When, three days later, negotiations broke down Duport launched a public campaign against the veto in the Palais Royal, and Desmoulins, though without Barnave's approval, put out the slogan that the king should be made to return to the capital.

Thus the extreme 'patriots' of the Palais Royal, perhaps with some secret support in the Assembly, tried to force the pace; the result was the first, abortive, attempt to stage a march to Versailles on the last day of August. It is an obscure episode, but it appears from the police reports of the Châtelet that the leading parts in it were played by the Marquis de Saint-Huruge, the Baron Tinto, the abbé Bernard, a certain Saint-Génie and the patrons of the Café Foy, known to the police as 'le rendezvous de gens vifs et séditieux qui troublaient la tranquillité publique', and to others as 'le centre des négociants et des capitalistes'.[1] It appears, too, that a deputation tried to persuade the Commune to issue a declaration demanding the king's return to the Louvre;[2] and that speeches were made in the

[1] Arch. Nat., Y 18767.
[2] *L'Ancien Moniteur (réimpression)*, li. 417; Mathiez, op. cit. lxvii. 251.

Palais Royal and the Café de Foy, urging that the tocsin be sounded, the Districts alerted, and the citizens called to arms. There was certainly no mystery about the precise objects of these manœuvres: the abbé Bernard was specifically charged with saying in the Café de Foy:

Qu'il fallait aller chercher le Roy et le Dauphin à Versailles pour les amener à Paris, aux Thuileries, sous la sauve-garde parisienne et de la nation; ·

and, though he denied using these words, he admitted that he had intended to call the citizens to District meetings 'pour empêcher le Véto'.[1]

The project came to nothing because the 'patriots' in the Assembly had not yet given up hope of a settlement by negotiation; and, even more important, because the project still lacked the degree of support among the Parisian *menu peuple* that alone could give it reality. The situation changed radically during September. The anger roused by the bread crisis had, as we saw, been directed, in the first place, against bakers and city authorities; at times it found expression in violent outbursts of denunciation of the Hôtel de Ville or the National Guard, or of Lafayette in person as its commander-in-chief: in August and early September numerous arrests on such charges were made of craftsmen, clerks, servants, and other wage-earners.[2] While the journalists—both Marat and those associated with the Palais Royal—were not averse to allowing Lafayette, whom they distrusted, to become the target of popular abuse, the 'patriots' of both Assembly and Paris Districts had a common interest in focusing this discontent into channels that better suited their immediate political aims. The results were soon to be seen. In early September Malouet noted: 'On vit des porteurs de chaise à la porte de l'Assemblée dans une grande agitation sur le véto.'[3] On the 17th Joseph Pergaud, a military pensioner of the rue Troussevache, was arrested in the Place de Grève on a charge of having said:

Que le Roi avait un château à Versailles et un Louvre à Paris; qu'il fallait l'aller chercher et l'amener à Paris et qu'il irait volontiers le chercher.[4]

[1] Arch. Nat., Y 18767.
[2] Arch. Nat., Y 18795, fols. 463–4, 467–9; 10530, fols. 149–51; 18766; 18767.
[3] *Mémoires de Malouet* (Paris, 1823), ii. 367.   [4] Arch. Nat., Y 18767.

The unemployed, too, were being won by the agitation. In a letter to La Tour du Pin, one of the king's ministers at Versailles, Bailly wrote on 22 September:

> J'apprends à l'instant que les malheureux employés aux ateliers de charité à l'école militaire proposaient de partir pour Versailles, pour cela seul qu'ils étaient instruits de l'arrivée des troupes.[1]

This last point is significant: though Barnave and his colleagues were prepared to compromise on the basis of a 'suspensive' veto, the Court, supported by the 'moderates' in the Assembly, had decided to break the deadlock by a new display of force. The Flanders Regiment was summoned to cope with possible disorders. It had the effect of driving the 'patriots' to resort to extreme measures and to rouse to a higher pitch the revolutionary movement in the capital. What finally decided the 'patriots' to act was the display of royalist arrogance at the banquet of the Gardes du Corps held at Versailles on 2 October, when (it was alleged) the national cockade was trampled underfoot and the queen and her children were received with almost mystical fervour. The incident was widely reported in Paris the next day, and the 'patriot' press called for vengeance. Danton carried a resolution in the Cordeliers Club, urging Lafayette to go to Versailles with an ultimatum; and Desmoulins repeated his call to Parisians to fetch the king to the capital. On Sunday, 4 October, groups of women 'of the middling sort' were seen in the Palais Royal; one, in her middle thirties and 'dont la mise indiquait une femme d'une classe au-dessus du médiocre', addressed a meeting; there was talk of going to Versailles on the morrow.[2] So the October insurrection began.

The main source for the events of 5 and 6 October is the inquiry conducted by the Châtelet and published in March 1790 after 388 witnesses had been heard. Such a report would seem to provide admirable material for a study of not only the events themselves, but of the composition and aims of the participants. Taine, indeed, made ample use of it for his descriptions of the men and women who fetched the royal family back to Paris.[3] Yet, as we noted before, it is an extremely one-sided

---

[1] Arch. Nat., C 31, no. 262, fol. 3.
[2] *Procédure criminelle...*, witness no. 62; Mathiez, op. cit. lxviii. 292–4.
[3] Taine, *Les Origines de la France contemporaine. La Révolution*, i. 130–6.

report; in fact, on its publication, it met with the condemnation of the majority of the Paris Districts: in the words of the Cordeliers District, which initiated the protest, 'sur la liste des témoins, on ne voit guère que des noms aristocratiques'.[1] While this is an exaggeration, the Châtelet inquiry had a clearly tendentious purpose and, as such, must be treated with caution and supplemented, where possible, from other sources—from the handful of surviving police reports (only two persons were arrested during these proceedings) and the accounts of other witnesses.

On the morning of 5 October the revolt started simultaneously in the central markets and the Faubourg Saint-Antoine; in both cases women were the leading spirits; and, from numerous and varying accounts, it appears that in the activities that followed women of every social class took part—both fishwives and stall-holders of the markets, working women of the *faubourg*, smartly dressed *bourgeoises*, and 'des femmes à chapeau'.[2] In the markets, according to a Châtelet witness, the movement was started by a small girl, who set out from the District of Saint-Eustache beating a drum and declaiming against the scarcity of bread; this drew together a large crowd of women, whose numbers rapidly increased.[3] Fournier l'Américain, Captain of the local National Guard and the leading agitator of the District, heard the tocsin at 7 o'clock and rushed to the Town Hall.[4] Meanwhile, in the Faubourg Saint-Antoine, women compelled the bellringer of the Sainte-Marguerite church to ring the tocsin and call the citizens to arms; among them, he said, were two well dressed men and a woman, 'qui ne paraissait pas être du commun'.[5] Between 7 and 8 o'clock a lawyer of the *faubourg* saw a crowd of forty to fifty women, who were crying out for bread at the Porte Saint-Antoine.[6] Almost simultaneously Stanislas Maillard led a squad of *volontaires de la Bastille* to quell a disturbance among the Bastille demolition

[1] *Extrait des délibérations de l'assemblée du District des Cordeliers* (Paris, 1790). Brit. Mus. R. 655 (6).
[2] See *Procédure criminelle*, witnesses nos. 62, 35, 91, 92, 119, 126; Hardy, viii. 501-2, 506; the Marquis de Paroy's letter to his wife of 6 October 1789 (*Revue de la Révolution*, i (1883), 1-7).
[3] *Procédure criminelle* . . . , witness no. 43.
[4] *Mémoires secrets de Fournier, Américain.* Arch. Nat., F⁷ 6504.
[5] *Procédure criminelle* . . , witness no. 92.   [6] Ibid., witness no. 12.

workers nearby; the workers, doubtless remembering that the same force had forcibly dispersed their comrades at Montmartre a few weeks earlier, were inclined to be truculent; but Maillard (so he tells us) was able to persuade them to disperse without bloodshed.[1]

From these beginnings the women now converged on the Hôtel de Ville.[2] Their first object was bread, the second probably arms and ammunition for their men. A merchant draper, passing by the old market hall at half past eight, saw groups of women stopping strangers in the streets and compelling them to go with them to the Town Hall, 'où l'on devait aller pour se faire donner du pain'. The guards were disarmed and their arms handed to the men who followed behind the women and urged them on. Another eyewitness, a cashier in the Hôtel de Ville, described how, about half past nine, large numbers of women, with men amongst them, rushed up the stairs and broke into all the offices of the building. One witness said they bore sticks and pikes, while another insisted they were armed with axes, crowbars, bludgeons, and muskets. A cashier, who had the temerity to remonstrate with the invaders, was told 'qu'ils étaient les maîtres et maîtresses dud. Hôtel de Ville'. In their search for arms and powder the demonstrators tore up documents and ledgers, and a wad of a hundred 1,000-*livres* notes of the Caisse des Comptes disappeared from a cabinet. But their object was neither money nor loot: the City Treasurer later told the police that something over 3½ million *livres* in cash and notes were left untouched; and the missing banknotes were returned intact a few weeks later. Having sounded the tocsin from the steeple, the demonstrators retired to the Place de Grève outside at about 11 o'clock.[3]

It was at this stage that Maillard and his *volontaires* arrived on the scene. According to his account, the women were threatening the lives of Bailly and Lafayette. Whether it was to avert such a disaster or merely to promote the political aims of the 'patriots', Maillard let himself be persuaded to lead them on the twelve-miles march to Versailles to petition the king and

[1] Ibid., witness no. 81 (Stanislas Maillard).

[2] Hardy, however, describes it merely as 'une insurrection de femmes des Halles et de différents marchés accourues à l'Hôtel de Ville' (viii. 501).

[3] For the above account see the evidence of twelve witnesses in Arch. Nat., Y 13319; see also Tuetey, *Répertoire*, vol. i, no. 950.

the Assembly to provide bread for Paris.[1] As they set out, in the early afternoon, they removed the cannon from the Châtelet and (wrote Hardy) compelled every sort and condition of woman that they met—'même des femmes à chapeau'—to join them.[2]

Thus reinforced, the contingents crossed the river to the Cité, followed the quai des Orfèvres to the Pont Neuf, crossed over again to the Louvre, passed through the Tuileries Gardens and halted, 6,000 or 7,000 strong, in the Place Louis XV. At the Place des Armes in the Champs Élysées, Maillard tells us, the women agreed to go on unarmed. According to the traditional account, the marchers then continued along the Right Bank to Chaillot, and so to Sèvres, Viroflay, and Versailles.[3] However, it would seem from other evidence that, while the main body of marchers accompanied Maillard through Chaillot, another contingent may have broken off at the Place des Armes and followed the southern route via Vaugirard. This is suggested, at least, by the statement made to the Versailles police by Bernard Salabert, a mill-worker at the École Militaire and one of two wage-earners arrested for looting swords and other weapons at the Hôtel des Gardes du Corps at Versailles. From this it appears that Salabert was picked up at Vaugirard, where he was having his dinner, by a band of 3,000 or 4,000 women who compelled him to join them on the march.[4]

Arriving at Versailles in the early evening, the marchers made straight for the meeting of the Assembly, crowded into the benches alongside the startled deputies and, with swords and hunting-knives slung from their skirts,[5] waited for Maillard to present their petition. In his speech, Maillard quoted liberally from the new popular pamphlet *Quand aurons-nous du pain?*, in which the authorities rather than the bakers were held

---

[1] For this and much that follows see *Procédure criminelle* ..., witness no. 81 (Maillard). Hardy, viii. 502.
[3] This version, based on Maillard's evidence before the Châtelet, is that followed by M. L. Batiffol, *Les Journées des 5 et 6 octobre 1789 à Versailles* (Paris, 1891), pp. 15–17.
[4] *Interrogatoire du Né Salabert. 6 8bre 1789.* Arch. Seine-et-Oise, series B. Prévôté de l'Hôtel du Roi, Greffe 1789. *Les Révolutions de Paris*, while not mentioning Vaugirard, also maintained that the women divided into two separate contingents taking separate routes: 'les unes avaient passé par Saint-Cloud; les autres avaient pris la route de Seves' (no. xiii, 3–10 October 1789, p. 15).
[5] Hardy, viii. 506.

responsible for the shortage.[1] He ended with two demands—the provision of bread for the capital and the punishment of the *gardes du corps* who had insulted the national cockade. Various deputies gave reassuring replies. There were angry shouts of 'A bas la calotte!' at the clergy; but Robespierre was heard in respectful silence, and there were calls for 'notre petite mère, Mirabeau'.[2] A deputation of six women were elected to wait on the king—the Marquis de Paroy considered two of them 'assez bien'[3]—and the meeting broke up in more or less orderly fashion.

Meanwhile, in Paris, the National Guard, summoned by the tocsin, had crowded into the place de Grève. There were cries of 'To Versailles!' The intentions of Lafayette in this episode are obscure. It seems that he hesitated for many hours to put himself at the head of what was only too clearly an armed insurrection; he temporized and, according to Fournier, made long speeches; but in the end, in response to popular clamour, he gave the order to march.[4] The forces that entered Versailles that night, between ten and midnight, consisted of three companies of grenadiers, one company of fuseliers, with three cannon, 20,000 National Guards of the Paris Districts, and a motley band of 700 to 800 men armed with muskets, sticks, and pikes.

Early next morning there was a clash between the Parisians and the *gardes du corps* guarding the palace. Some demonstrators had managed to enter the *château* and penetrated as far as the antechamber to the queen's apartments. In the course of this incident, a *garde du corps*, from a window, shot dead Jérôme Lhéritier, a 17-year-old volunteer and journeyman cabinet-maker of the Faubourg Saint-Antoine, who was in the courtyard below.[5] Provoked to anger, the crowd slaughtered two of the *gardes du corps* and cut off their heads.[6] Order was restored by the Parisian National Guard, while great crowds

---

[1] Bib. Nat. L^b 39 2344; Mathiez, op. cit. lxix. 42–43.

[2] *Procédure criminelle* . . . , witness no. 81; Taine, op. cit. i. 131.

[3] *Revue de la Révolution*, i (1883), 1–7.

[4] *Mémoires secrets de Fournier, Américain.* See also Barnave (Arch. Nat., W 12, fol. 201).

[5] Arch. Seine-et-Oise, series B. Prévôté de l'Hôtel du Roi, Greffe, 1789.

[6] Lhéritier's burial, as well as that of the two *gardes du corps*, is recorded in the *Registre des actes de sépulture de la Paroisse Royale de Notre Dame de Versailles*, fol. 82 (Arch. S.-et-O., series E). Of the three, Lhéritier alone received full military honours.

surged outside the *château* awaiting a solution. To the National Guard—to the tradesmen, small masters, and journeymen at least, who had lost a day's work to accompany Lafayette to Versailles—there could only be one solution: the king must be made to come back to Paris, whether their commander-in-chief was willing or not.[1] So much appears, too, from the evidence of Elizabeth Girard, 'bourgeoise de Paris', who later told the Châtelet

qu'à Versailles tout le peuple indistinctement, et principalement des compagnons serruriers au grand nombre, disaient qu'ils avaient perdu leur journée; que si le roi ne venait pas à Paris, et les gardes du corps n'étaient pas tués, il fallait mettre la tête de Lafayette au bout d'une pique.[2]

The women may have needed more persuading. At any rate, Fournier thought it necessary to indoctrinate a group of fish-wives in the language that he thought they would most readily understand: 'Sac ... B ... esses, vous ne voyés pas que Lafayette et le Roi vous couillonnent. ... Il faut emmener à Paris toute la sacrée boutique.'[3] However that may be, when the king, queen, and Lafayette appeared on the palace balcony, there was a great shout of 'To Paris!' A few hours later the royal family, escorted by the Parisian National Guard and the marching women, made their triumphal return to the capital.

[1] Mathiez, op. cit. lxix. 45–46. In this respect, it would be of great interest to know the social or occupational composition of the Parisian National Guard at this time; but unfortunately only a handful of lists have survived to enlighten us. The battalions of the Faubourg Saint-Antoine and of the central market Districts, who were probably the main promoters of the armed insurrection of the National Guard on 5 October, appear to have included a fair sprinkling of journeymen, porters, and labourers as well as a majority of shopkeepers and masters or independent craftsmen. We know, for example, that the journeyman cabinet-maker Lhéritier was a volunteer of the Sainte-Marguerite District and that Edmé Farcy, a journeyman goldsmith, also arrested for pillaging the Hôtel des Gardes du Corps, was a volunteer of the neighbouring District of Saint-Gervais. Besides, the enrolments made in August 1789 to the Battalion of Sainte-Opportune, in the central markets, included, together with a host of small masters and tradesmen, 26 merchant's clerks, 4 *commis* and 4 *employés*, 2 market-porters, a journeyman jeweller, a journeyman gunsmith, and a journeyman gilder (Brit. Mus., F. 830 (6)). By way of contrast, of 105 grenadiers recruited to the Battalion of Les Filles Saint-Thomas, near the Bourse, in November 1789, 25 were 'bourgeois' (usually applied to a man of independent means), 29 civil servants, 6 lawyers, 7 merchants, 2 bankers, and 3 stock exchange jobbers, while only 16 were tradesmen—and not one of these wage-earners (Arch. Nat., W 357, no. 750, 1st part, pièce 100).

[2] *Procédure criminelle* ..., witness no. 90.

[3] *Mémoires secrets de Fournier, Américain.*

The traditional account of the women's march to Versailles has it that, as they marched, the women chanted, 'Allons chercher le boulanger, la boulangère et le petit mitron!' It was supposed that the king would, by his very presence among his subjects, ensure a plentiful supply of bread. These hopes were not immediately realized: the bread crisis continued for another month. The day after the royal family's return, crowds of women invaded the corn-market and dumped 150 barrels of rotten flour into the river after samples had been shown to the king.[1] On 21 October, during a bread riot in the Hôtel de Ville area, the baker François was hanged from the notorious lamp-post on the Place de Grève; for his murder, F. Blin, a market porter, was sentenced to death and J. Advenel, a metal-gilder, to nine years' prison.[2] The next day in the rue Thibault-au-dé, off the central markets, women caused a riot by insisting on searching a house for hidden grain and flour.[3] On 2 November Bailly had to order military protection for a baker in the Marché Saint-Germain;[4] the next day a woman was arrested for causing a disturbance outside a baker's shop in the rue des Cordeliers.[5] Finally, ten days later, Nicolas Billon, a mill-worker, was arrested on a charge of creating riots and threatening to hang the baker at the École Militaire on two occasions in October and November.[6]

But the majority in the Assembly, having driven out the 'moderates' and established itself in the capital, had no further use for the insurrectionary energies of the *menu peuple*: these had served their purpose. Accordingly, on 21 October new measures were introduced to curb social disorder and the agitation conducted by Marat's *Ami du peuple*: they included the death penalty for 'rebellion', a press censorship and martial law. The first victim of these restraints on liberty, Michel Adrien, a Bastille labourer, was hanged the same day for attempting to stir up a 'sedition' in the Faubourg Saint-Antoine.[7]

But, simultaneously, energetic measures were taken by both Commune and Assembly to solve the food crisis. Though the price of bread remained at 12 *sous* for many months to come,

[1] Hardy, viii. 505.
[2] Arch. Nat., Y 18795, fols. 476–7; 10530, fols. 157–9; 18768.
[3] Arch. Nat., Y 18768.   [4] Arch. Nat., AF¹¹ 48, no. 375, fol. 2.
[5] Arch. Nat., Y 13172.   [6] Arch. Nat. Y 18769.
[7] Arch. Nat., Y 10530, fol. 157; 18768.

the regular supply of flour to bakers was ensured. There followed a remarkable period of social calm, while the Assembly continued, relatively undisturbed, with its task of giving the nation a constitution. The first Festival of the Federation, celebrated in the Champs de Mars on 14 July 1790, was a great symbol of national unity and peaceful advance. To most it must have seemed that the Revolution was all but completed.

VI

THE 'MASSACRE' OF THE
CHAMP DE MARS

THE violent affray that took place on the Champ de Mars in July 1791 marked an important stage in the struggle for power between constitutional monarchists (Feuillants) and Jacobins, between liberal *bourgeoisie* and revolutionary democrats. In Paris it led directly to the eclipse of Bailly and Lafayette as the leaders of the city administration; yet, in the National Assembly, the defeat of the 'constitutionalists' was delayed by the outbreak of war and was not completed until the fall of the monarchy in August 1792. In terms of the social history of Paris the Champ de Mars affair both represented the first bloody clash within the Third Estate—the growing divisions within which have already been noted—and the culmination of several months of social upheaval and of revolutionary agitation, at the end of which the democrats organized in the Jacobin and Cordeliers Clubs appear as the undisputed leaders of the Parisian *sans-culottes*. In the course of this movement the tradesmen, artisans, and wage-earners of the capital emerge more clearly as elements which the main protagonists in the struggle for power cannot afford to ignore and whose interests the revolutionary democrats, at least, must affect to espouse.[1] In this sense, then, the Champ de Mars demonstration itself should be seen as the culmination of a process and, as in the case of the October insurrection, treated in the context of the varied social and political movement that preceded it.

The period of social calm lasted, with minor eruptions, until the spring of 1791. In June 1790 the price of bread had fallen to 11 *sous*; soon after, controls were removed and the price fell,

---

[1] In Jaurès' words: 'En obligeant la faction bourgeoise plus ardente à chercher dans le peuple un point d'appui contre la puissance formidable du modérantisme bourgeois, les divisions de la bourgeoisie grandissaient le rôle des prolétaires: ceux-ci, bien faiblement encore, commençaient à apparaître comme les arbitres possibles de la Révolution' (Jaurès, op. cit. i. 367). I assume that the term 'prolétaires' is here intended to mean *sans-culottes* or *menu peuple*, rather than 'wage-earners'.

for the first time since early 1788, to its normal level of 8 *sous*.[1] It was not to rise appreciably again until August 1791—a month after the Champ de Mars affray. In this case, at least, the price or supply of bread was to play no great part as a stimulant to revolutionary activity.

The first serious breach of the peace occurred on 28 February, when an attempt was made to demolish a part of the Château de Vincennes, which was being converted into a temporary overflow prison for the capital. With memories of its former use as a prison for those detained by *lettres de cachet*, 'patriots' began to protest and, on 28 January, there was talk in the Jacobin Club of a projected assault by 'one of the faubourgs'.[2] A month later the movement came to a head when over 1,000 *ouvriers* of the Faubourg Saint-Antoine, among whom Bastille demolition workers were in evidence,[3] placed Santerre as commander of the Enfants-Trouvés battalion of the National Guard in much the same position as Lafayette had found himself in in October 1789: they compelled him to lead them, escorted by his battalion, to Vincennes, where they proceeded to demolish the *donjon*. Before long, however, Lafayette arrived with 1,200 troops, publicly reprimanded Santerre, and marched back to Paris with sixty-four prisoners and to the accompaniment of the jeers of the people of Saint-Antoine.[4] The prisoners were lodged in the Conciergerie, whence they were released three weeks later after considerable agitation by the democrats, among whom a prominent part was played by Buirette-Verrières, Santerre's defence-counsel and a leading figure in the Cordeliers Club.[5]

This is but one example of the continuous efforts made by the

---

[1] *Extrait du registre des délibérations du corps municipal. Arrêté concernant le prix et la vente du pain* (17 August 1791). Brit. Mus., F. 59* (18).

[2] Bib. Nat., fonds français, no. 11697, p .130 (Bailly–Lafayette correspondence).

[3] Bib. Nat., nouv. acq. franç., no. 2656, fols. 159–62 (account of day's events by Desmottes, Lafayette's A.D.C.). According to one eyewitness there were also people from the Faubourgs Saint-Marcel and Saint-Martin among them (*Heures sauvées: journée révolutionnaire du 28 février 1791. MS. account by Alexis Houzeau, cultivateur*, now in the custody of M. Estabert of Fontenay-sous-Bois, to whom I am indebted for its use).

[4] For an 'official' account see *P/v. de l'événement arrivé à Vincennes, le lundi, 28 février 1791, publié par l'ordre de la municipalité de Vincennes, 4 mars 1791.* Arch. Nat., F⁷462, fol. 201; for an apologia by Santerre see *Rapport de M. Santerre . . . relativement à l'affaire de Vincennes* (ibid., fol. 202).

[5] Arch. Nat., F⁷ 4622, fols. 151–6 (Verrières papers).

democrats in the course of the spring and summer of 1791 to indoctrinate and to win the allegiance of the small tradesmen, craftsmen, and employed and unemployed workers of the capital. This agitation was to culminate in the great meeting on 17 July, when people gathered from all parts of the city for the purely political purpose of signing a petition drawn up by the Cordeliers Club.[1]

Among the many persons arrested in Paris during this whole period, one is struck by the large number of unemployed, several of them from the public workshops maintained by the Municipality, arrested and imprisoned for their declared hostility to the city administration and the National Guard. This illustrates both the development of a certain political consciousness among the wage-earners and the growth of unemployment in a number of trades: one finds, among such persons, former painters, sculptors, tailors, barbers, domestic servants, jewellers, joiners, and basket-makers.[2] Meanwhile the numbers of those admitted to the public workshops were continually increasing: in January Bailly put their number at 24,000; by June it had risen to 31,000.[3] Apart from the expense of their maintenance they were seen as a constant threat to the newly established order: they were widely believed to be the ready tools of counter-revolutionary intrigue (even extreme democrats like Marat shared this view);[4] they were frequently involved in skirmishes with customs officials at the *barrières*, which the authorities still hoped to keep in being;[5] and such episodes as the march of the Bastille workers to Vincennes did little to allay public disquiet. In brief the administration did not need much persuasion to decide on their dispersal: on 8 May Bailly announced the decision to close down the Bastille workshop, where 800

[1] For the best detailed account of this process see A. Mathiez, *Le Club des Cordeliers pendant la crise de Varennes et le massacre du Champ de Mars* (Paris, 1910).

[2] Of 238 persons arrested in the Paris Sections between 14 April and 15 November 1791, and whose occupations are given, 45 were unemployed (or newsvendors unemployed from other trades), 10 of them engaged on public works. Among them there were 8 domestic servants and coachmen, 2 painters, 2 joiners, 2 tailors, and several others formerly engaged in luxury trades. (See Archives de la Préfecture de Police, series Aa (various cartons) and Ab 324, pp. 7–60.)

[3] Bib. Nat., nouv. acq. franç., no. 2673, fol. 229 (printed text); Arch. Nat., C 71, no. 695.

[4] *L'Ami du peuple*, no. 422, 7 April 1791, p. 6.

[5] Bib. Nat., fonds français, no. 11697, pp. 235, 239, 246–8 (Bailly-Lafayette correspondence).

workers had been continuously engaged since July 1789; and, in mid-June, the Constituent Assembly decreed the general closure of the *ateliers de charité*, while making certain indefinite promises to open other workshops to absorb the unemployed.[1] The workers, faced with the prospect of losing their bare sub-sistence of 20 *sous* a day, reacted vigorously; the Bastille workers, though dispersed by troops, carried on a lively agitation for some weeks to come and sought support among the journey-men of the Faubourg Saint-Antoine.[2] The closure of the other workshops aroused a far greater commotion, in which the democrats in the Jacobin and Cordeliers Clubs played a certain part. Three separate petitions were presented to the Assembly urging them to reconsider their decision. The first, presented on 28 June and drafted with the aid of the Point Central des Arts et Métiers, a Cordeliers Club affiliate, was extremely moderate: it justified the eventual closure of the *ateliers* in the interest of public security, while begging for a postponement.[3] The second petition was presented by Camille Desmoulins in the name of the Bastille workers on 3 July and had, he claimed, been approved by Robespierre: it demanded subsistence as a citizen's right and suggested that the workshops be maintained from a portion of the profits accruing from the sale of Church lands.[4] A third petition, following closely after the second, was threatening, almost violent, in tone: the workers (it declared) must have bread by one means or another; 'c'est le besoin, c'est le plus pressant besoin, et rien autre qui leur fait tenir un pareil langage'.[5]

The Assembly took no notice; but, meanwhile, the unem-ployed had resorted to more direct forms of pressure. In a demonstration in the Place Vendôme, on 24 June, there had been calls for a Republic.[6] After two more demonstrations in the following week, there was talk of a projected turn-out of 22,000 unemployed in the rue Saint-Honoré on 3 July.[7] Two days later a hostile gossip-sheet, *Le Babillard*, reported a march of 400

[1] Bibliothèque Historique de la Ville de Paris, MS. 10441; Arch. Nat., C 71, no. 695.   [2] Bib. Nat., fonds français, no. 11697, pp. 254–9.
[3] Arch. Nat., C 71, no. 700.
[4] S. Lacroix, op. cit., 2nd series, v. 261; Arch. Nat., F⁷ 4622, plaq. 1, fol. 14.
[5] Arch. Nat., DXXIXᵇ 36, no. 376.
[6] *Le Babillard*, no. xxi, 25 June 1791, pp. 6–7.
[7] Arch. Nat., DXXIXᵇ 36, no. 376, fol. 28.

workless on the Hôtel de Ville, a riot in the Place Vendôme, and the arrest of two workers in the Place Louis XV for seditious talk.[1] The result was a growing atmosphere of tension, in which respectable citizens began to say openly that the unemployed should be taught a lesson by the use of military force.

Les ouvriers [wrote *Le Babillard* on 6 July] commencent à lasser la patience des citoyens de tous les états. La garde nationale, les marchands, les fabricants, les bourgeois, les artisans crient contre ces gens soudoyés par les séditieux. . . . On dit hautement qu'il faut les balayer à coups de canon.[2]

Such an attitude does, of course, a great deal to explain the ferocity with which the *bourgeois* and *marchands* of the National Guard dispersed the Champ de Mars demonstrators less than a fortnight later.

A parallel movement to that of the unemployed, in which the democrats and Cordeliers Club were also involved, was that of the journeymen of various trades in support of higher wages; these, as we saw, had not risen appreciably since the July revolution. The movement began in April with a concerted attempt by the carpenters to secure a minimum daily wage of fifty *sous*; to the annoyance of an active minority the main body of contractors appear to have accepted the journeymen's terms fairly readily. The Municipality, invited by the journeymen to arbitrate, condemned their association as illegal, and rejected the proposal for a minimum wage as being contrary to liberal principles; later, its journal went so far as to threaten the journeymen's leaders with prosecution as disturbers of the public peace; yet the threat remained a dead letter.[3]

The carpenters' example was quickly followed by that of other workers—hatters and typographers among them. In early June the master farriers, in a petition addressed to the Assembly, warned of the existence of 'une coalition générale' of 80,000 Paris workers, including locksmiths, joiners, and cobblers as well as their own workpeople.[4] These numbers may

[1] *Le Babillard*, no. xxiii, 5 July 1791, p. 7.
[2] Ibid., no. xxiv, 6 July 1791, p. 3.
[3] *Les Révolutions de Paris*, no. xcvi, 7–14 May 1791; Lacroix, op. cit., 2nd series, iii. 700 ff; G. M. Jaffé, op. cit., Part II.   [4] Jaffé, op. cit., p. 124.

have been exaggerated—the master farriers were naturally inclined to overstate their case—but the movement is of interest
for a number of reasons. In the first place, it was the most
extensive wages movement in the capital until that of 1794,
which played some part in unseating Robespierre; secondly, it
was the petitions of the master farriers and carpenters that led
the Assembly to adopt the famous Loi Le Chapelier, making
'coalitions ouvrières', or trade unions, illegal—an Act, it should
be noted, that not even the Revolutionary Government of the
'Year II', at the height of Jacobin democracy, thought fit to
repeal; in fact, it remained law for nearly a hundred years to
come.[1] Thirdly, and of greater moment to our present argument, the journeymen carpenters received considerable aid
and encouragement from the revolutionary democrats. Thus
we find the carpenters not merely meeting in the same hall
as that used by the Cordeliers Club; but it turns out that the
'Union Fraternelle des Ouvriers en l'Art de la Charpente',
which directed their campaign, was an affiliate of the Comité
Central set up by the club in May 1791. Moreover, the secretary
of the Comité Central was François Robert who, with his wife
Louise, edited the *Mercure national et étranger*, which, though
objecting in principle to the journeymen's attempt to enforce a
minimum wage, gave some support to their cause.[2] Marat, too,
had opened the columns of his paper to workers' correspondence
and, on 12 June 1791, while the wages movement was at its
height, a violently worded letter, purporting to represent the
views of 560 building workers engaged on the construction of
the church of Sainte-Geneviève, appeared in *L'Ami du peuple*:
in it, the contractors were roundly assailed as 'oppresseurs igno-
rants, rapaces et insatiables', as 'vampires', and as 'hommes vifs
qui dévorent dans l'oisiveté le fruit de la sueur des manœuvres et qui n'ont jamais rendu aucun service à la Nation'.[3]
    The Cordeliers Club, however, did considerably more than
merely intervene in economic disputes in which the wage-
earners were already engaged. Through its Fraternal Societies,
also linked to Robert's Comité Central, it began, quite deliberately, to educate the Parisian *menu peuple* in the political

[1] Until an Act of 1884.
[2] *Mercure national et étranger*, no. xxv; 11 May 1791.
[3] *L'Ami du peuple*, no. 487, 12 June 1791, pp. 1–5.

ideas of the revolutionary democrats—a process that was to be of enormous significance for the future:

C'est par les sociétés fraternelles [wrote Mathiez] que s'est faite l'éducation politique des masses. Ces sociétés furent le berceau et l'asile de la sans-culotterie.[1]

The new societies, while firmly under *bourgeois* direction, opened their doors to wage-earners and other passive citizens.[2] The Cordeliers Club itself charged a subscription of only 2 *sous* a month; and, among those arrested by the National Guard that summer, we find a fancy-ware worker, a cook, and a domestic servant that attended its meetings.[3] In this period, too, the Club des Indigents and other Fraternal Societies are described as being composed of 'pauvres porteurs d'eau', 'artisans' and 'simples ouvriers'.[4] Far greater, of course, were the numbers touched by the public agitation of the democrats and their press on every imaginable political question—including such burning topical issues as the denial of the vote to 'passive' citizens, the virtual exclusion of manual workers from the National Guard, or the restrictions imposed on the right of petitioning.[5]

A single example from the police records will serve to illustrate the influence that such agitation might exert on the minds and ideas of many ordinary Parisians. Constance Evrard, a 23-year-old cook of 64 rue de Grenelle, was arrested on 17 July for abusing the wife of a National Guardsman, who had taken part in the 'massacre' of the Champ de Mars the same afternoon. Her cross-examination by the police commissioner of the Fontaine de Grenelle Section may be paraphrased as follows:

Q. Had she been to the Champ de Mars?
A. Yes, she had been there with Madame Léon and her daughter.

---

[1] Mathiez, op. cit., p. 66.

[2] That is, citizens not paying the equivalent of three days' labour in taxes and, as such, excluded from the franchise under a law of December 1789. This provision became later incorporated in the Constitution of 1791. Its repeal was one of the last acts of the Legislative Assembly before its dissolution in September 1792.

[3] Arch. Préf. Pol., Aa 148, fol. 30; 206, fols. 217–9; 220, fol. 142. Another servant claimed to have suscribed 24 *sous* in 4 months to the funds of the Jacobin Club (ibid., Aa 206, fols. 365–6).

[4] *Le Babillard*, no. xxi, 25 June 1791; *Mercure national et étranger*, no. viii, 23 April 1791. See also I. Bourdin, *Les Sociétés populaires à Paris pendant la Révolution* (Paris, 1937), pp. 15–44.   [5] Mathiez, op. cit., pp. 31–32.

Q. Why had she been there?

A. To sign a petition 'comme tous les bons patriotes'.

Q. What was the petition about?

A. She understood its aim was 'à faire organiser autrement le pouvoir exécutif'.

Q. Did she often go to public meetings?

A. She had sometimes been to the Palais Royal and the Tuileries.

Q. Did she belong to any club?

A. She had sometimes been to the Cordeliers Club, though not actually a member.

Q. Had she been with any particular group in the Champ de Mars?

A. She had been on the 'autel de la patrie' and signed the petition.

Q. Had she thrown stones or seen any stones thrown?

A. No.

Q. Who had invited her to sign the petition?

A. No one, but she had heard various people say that there was a petition to sign in the Champ de Mars.

Q. Was it true that her name had appeared in the papers?

A. Yes, her name had appeared in *Les Révolutions de Paris*, because she had expressed grief at the death of Loustalot.

Q. What papers did she read?

A. She read Marat, Audouin, Camille Desmoulins and, very often, *L'Orateur du peuple*.[1]

The political movement that ended with the Champ de Mars 'massacre' had its immediate origins in the king's attempted flight to the Imperial border on 20 June. From this time on, the agitation of the democrats and radical journalists had a clearly defined objective—to rouse popular opinion on the future of the king and the executive power. For the first time those journalists and others who, before the flight to Varennes, had been almost alone in their advocacy of Republican ideas, were able to command a certain following: their influence can be seen in the Republican slogans shouted at meetings of the unemployed and other workers in late June and early July, and in a number of resolutions and petitions of the Fraternal Societies.[2] Yet it has probably been exaggerated; and even the Cordeliers Club, which included known Republicans among its members, was

---

[1] Arch. Préf. Pol., Aa, 148, fol. 30.

[2] *Le Babillard*, no. xxi, 25 June 1791, pp. 6–7; Lacroix, op. cit., 2nd series, v. 378; Mathiez, op. cit., p. 53.

guarded in expressing views which could, as yet, hope to find little support among the *menu peuple*: certainly there is little trace of such a body of opinion among the fifteen or twenty persons arrested in the Sections for expressing seditious views during the week following the king's flight and ignominious return from Varennes.[1]

But the Club was certainly not slow to react to the new developments: on 21 June it called on the Assembly to delay a decision on the king's future until the Departments had been consulted; this, the first of seventeen similar petitions by the club, was posted all over Paris.[2] Three days later there followed the so-called 'Petition of the 30,000' which, according to Madame Roland, was supported by the Faubourg Saint-Antoine in full strength.[3] During July the agitation continued; but, on the 15th, the Constituent Assembly, with its Feuillant majority, declared in favour of letting well alone and of renewed confidence in Louis XVI as the head of the executive power.

The decision led to a breach in the ranks of the democrats. A protest demonstration, called for in a petition drafted by the Cordeliers Club on 16 July, was approved by the Jacobin Club; but the same evening, on Robespierre's initiative, the Jacobins withdrew their support.[4] The Cordeliers, now faced with the alternative of cancelling the demonstration or of going ahead on their own, decided on the latter course. The result was the petition of 17 July, drafted by François Robert and couched in more radical terms: while not specifically demanding a Republic, it called on the Assembly 'de convoquer un nouveau corps constituant pour procéder au remplacement et à l'organisation d'un nouveau pouvoir exécutif'.[5] Signatures were immediately canvassed;[6] and the societies and clubs were invited to muster in full strength at the Porte Saint-Antoine at ten or eleven in the morning,[7] and to march from there to the Champ de Mars to hold a peaceful demonstration.

[1] Arch. Préf. Pol., Aa 74, 84, 134, 157, 167, 172, 182, 206, 215.
[2] F. Braesch, 'Les Pétitions du Champ de Mars', *Rev. hist.* cxliii (1923), 17–18.
[3] Mathiez, op. cit., p. 52.
[4] Ibid., pp. 118–20.
[5] *Les Révolutions de Paris*, no. cvi, 16–23 July 1791, pp. 60–61.
[6] A. E. Primery, a fancy-ware worker and member of the Société des Halles et de la Liberté, was arrested in the rue du Faubourg Saint-Antoine the same day for collecting signatures (Arch. Préf. Pol., Aa 220, fol. 142).
[7] Ibid., *Les Révolutions de Paris*, no. cvi, p. 157.

Unfortunately for the petitioners, before their arrival, a curious incident took place that morning in the Champ de Mars that, in the tense political atmosphere prevailing, provided the authorities with a pretext for intervention. Two individuals who had hidden under the 'autel de la patrie'— possibly with the intention of getting a better view of the ladies' ankles—were pulled out by suspicious bystanders and unceremoniously hanged from a nearby window. During the afternoon a peaceful demonstration of 50,000 citizens gathered according to plan;[1] of these, over 6,000 had signed the petition before the troops arrived.[2] Meanwhile Bailly had been alerted of what was going on by his municipal officers and put into operation a plan that appears to have been premeditated.[3] Martial law was declared, the red flag of executive violence was unfurled and 10,000 Guardsmen, under the command of Lafayette, advanced on the demonstrators.[4] Accounts of what followed vary; but it appears that stones were thrown at the Guards (including Lafayette himself), and that perhaps fifty persons were killed and a dozen wounded.[5] In the words of a tailor, arrested two days later in the Henri IV Section for protesting at the Guard's conduct: 'on tirait sur les ouvriers comme de la volaille'.[6] Many arrests were made: only a dozen in the Champ de Mars itself; but maybe another 200 in the Sections, including a handful of Cordeliers Club members and other supposed ringleaders, and a far greater number of ordinary petitioners who presumed to criticize the administration or the Guard for their behaviour.[7] Many of these were released within a month; the rest were discharged under a general amnesty of 13 September.[8] Such was the demonstration and 'massacre' of the Champ de Mars.

[1] Ibid., pp. 53 ff. (F. Robert's account of events).
[2] Buchez et Roux, *Histoire parlementaire de la Révolution française* (40 vols., Paris, 1833–8), xi. 113.   [3] Mathiez, op. cit., pp. 138–9.
[4] *Les Révolutions de Paris*, no. cvi, pp. 53 ff.
[5] Contemporary estimates of those killed range between an official figure of 13 and one, based on the wildest rumour, of 3,000 (Arch. Nat., W 294, no. 235; Arch. Préf. Pol., Aa 215, fol. 460). *Les Révolutions de Paris* (Robert's account) gives 50 (loc. cit.). According to the official account, 11 or 12 persons (including a National Guardsman) were taken to the nearby Gros Caillou Military Hospital for treatment for wounds (*P/v. des 17 et 18 juillet*, p. 12 (printed text). Arch. Nat., C 75, no. 737).   [6] Arch. Préf. Pol., Aa 215, fol. 463.
[7] Arch. Préf. Pol., Aa, Ab (for details see page 91, note 5, below); Mathiez, op. cit., p. 132.   [8] *Le Journal de la Révolution*, no. 402, 18 September 1791.

Perhaps we should hesitate to qualify these peaceful petitioners as a 'revolutionary crowd'. Yet, in a wider sense, the term is apposite; and it is certainly of interest to our present study to inquire how they were composed and from which parts of the capital they came. The direct evidence on this point, though more plentiful than in the case of the October insurrection, is rather slight. Among the 6,000 signatures collected before the arrival of the military, the organizers claimed that more than 2,000 were those of *gardes nationaux*, municipal officers, and electors.[1] On the other hand, Buchez and Roux, who saw the completed petition before its destruction by fire in 1871, maintained that 'la masse des signatures est de gens qui savaient à peine lire', and pointed, in support of their contention, to the many crosses appearing on the petition sheets.[2] Again, *Le Babillard* wrote of the demonstrators with customary venom: 'Parmi tous ces hommes . . . pas un, je crois, ne sçait lire.'[3]

Even if we allow for exaggeration in the highly partisan account presented by *Le Babillard* and the uncertainty of the literacy test as a guide to social analysis, we should perhaps accept Buchez's and Roux's inference that the demonstrators were composed in the main of the poorer sections of the Parisian population. Such a picture is confirmed by the few surviving documents in the Paris archives which directly relate to participants in the demonstration. For instance the report prepared by municipal officer Filleul on those killed in the Champ de Mars and examined by him in the Gros Caillou Military Hospital nearby reveals that, of nine identified corpses, three were of workshop journeymen, one of a woman with 'a skirt of many colours and of many pieces', while others were of a master saddler, a wine-merchant's son, and of two relatively well-dressed *bourgeois*.[4] The police reports of the Paris Sections mention only one corpse, that of a cobbler of the Invalides Section brought to the police commissariat of the Palais Royal on 17 July.[5] Unfortunately the prison register of the Hôtel de la Force gives the occupation of only one of the twelve persons arrested in the Champ de Mars itself: he was an *abbé*, Parochet

[1] *Les Révolutions de Paris*, loc. cit.   [2] Buchez et Roux, op. cit., xi. 113.
[3] *Le Babillard*, no. xxxvi, 19 July 1791, p. 4.
[4] Arch. Nat., W 294, no. 235.   [5] Arch. Préf. Pol., Aa 85, fol. 768.

by name.[1] Of those arrested in the Sections after the demonstration, the only five who admitted having been in the Champ
de Mars that afternoon were a cook, a tailor, a journeyman
cabinet-maker, a café-waiter, and an unemployed boot-black.[2]
Of these the boot-black described the resistance offered to the
military by 'tous les ouvriers perruquiers et autres'; and the
tailor, as we already saw, claimed 'qu'on tirait sur les ouvriers
comme de la volaille'. Further evidence of the attendance of
wage-earners at the Champ de Mars is suggested by *Le Babillard's* report that port-workers had visited journeymen in their
workshops and lodgings to bring them along to the demonstration;[3] and Buirette-Verrières, when accused of inciting *ouvriers*
to assemble in the champ de Mars, replied 'qu'il est faux . . .
parce que ceux auxquels il aurait prêché (?) étaient prêts à
y entrer'.[4]

We have, besides, the far more considerable, though largely
circumstantial, evidence of the police commissioners' reports,
and the prison register of the Hôtel de la Force, relating in all
to some 250 persons arrested for political offences in the Paris
Sections in the months preceding and following the Champ de
Mars demonstration.[5] Admittedly these cannot furnish any
clear proof of attendance or of willingness to sign the Cordeliers'
petition; but they provide a rich source for the study of the
popular movement of the period and of the classes of people and
parts of the capital that were drawn into the political movement
that had as its climax the petition and demonstration of 17 July.

Only a handful of these persons were arrested for remarks
that might, even remotely, be construed as counter-revolutionary; in nearly every case they were charged with abusing or
criticizing the administration, the National Guard, or Lafayette
in person in terms which reveal the influence exerted by the
democrats and popular societies on the small tradesmen, craftsmen, and wage-earners of Paris during this period. Thus, of 52

[1] Arch. Préf. Pol., Ab 324, p. 60.
[2] Arch. Préf. Pol., Ab 324, pp. 33, 38; Aa 148, fol. 30; 215, fol. 463; 182, fol.
312; Arch. Nat., T 214⁽³⁾.   [3] *Le Babillard*, no. xxxvi, 19 July 1791.
[4] Arch. Nat., F⁷ 4623, fol. 104.
[5] Arch. Préf. Pol. Aa 56, 72, 74, 76, 84, 85, 134, 137, 148, 153, 155, 157, 166,
167, 172, 173, 182, 198, 205, 215, 216, 219, 220, 224, 239; Ab 324, pp. 7–60.
A few additional cases appear in Arch. Nat., W 294, no. 235 (Bailly papers);
T 214 [3] (*procureur* Bernard's papers), and DXXIXᵇ, nos. 34 and 36 (Comité
des Recherches).

persons arrested between 14 April and 15 July 1791, and for whom details of occupation are available, 34 were wage-earners, both employed and unemployed; the rest were, in the main, shopkeepers, workshop masters, or independent craftsmen. Of another 186 persons arrested between 16 July and 15 November (the great majority for criticizing the National Guard or the administration for the violence used against the Champ de Mars petitioners), 102 were wage-earners; while the rest were petty employers, craftsmen, and other small property-owners. This evidence, indirect though it be, seems to support the view already suggested by a perusal of the documents directly relating to the Champs de Mars affair, that the petitioners and demonstrators of 17 July were typical of the *menu peuple*—tradesmen, craftsmen, and wage-earners—that made up the bulk of the population of the *faubourgs* and crowded central districts of the city.

Which parts of the capital were, in fact, involved in this movement? As far as the Champ de Mars rally is concerned it was certainly the intention of the organizers to make it an all-Paris affair. While the Cordeliers Club itself was in the rue Dauphine on the Left Bank, the rallying-point for the clubs and societies was the Porte Saint-Antoine, and the petition of 16 July, which issued the first call to a demonstration, was canvassed in places as widely apart as the rue Saint-Honoré, the Porte Saint-Martin, and the rue du Faubourg Saint-Antoine.[1] How far this object was realized it is hard to tell from the comparatively few documents directly relating to attendance at the Champ de Mars. Yet, even from these, one striking fact emerges: the poor response given to the demonstration by the Faubourg Saint-Antoine. Lafayette had filled the Place de la Bastille with troops, and this may well be why Fournier l'Américain found so few people assembled there early that morning; but Primery, the commissioner appointed by the Société des Halles, not only found a poor attendance at the rallying-point, but met with little response in the *faubourg* when he tried to arouse interest.[2] The distance from the Champ de Mars—three and a half miles, as the crow flies, from the Porte Saint-

[1] Arch. Préf. Pol., Aa 206, fols. 363–9; 220, fol. 142; Arch. Nat., DXXIXᵇ 36, no. 372, fols. 7–10.
[2] *Les Révolutions de Paris*, no. cvi; Arch. Préf. Pol., Aa 220, fol. 142.

Antoine—may have played some part; again, the withdrawal of Jacobin support may have influenced many—for example, Santerre, whose behaviour appeared to Fournier to be evasive.[1] Yet an examination of the indirect evidence of the police reports suggests that the *faubourg* was relatively little involved in the political movement of the whole period: of some 240 persons arrested between April and November, and whose addresses are given, only ten resided in the Faubourg Saint-Antoine, of whom but three in Santerre's Section, the Quinze Vingts.

Admittedly there are considerable gaps in the records, which may produce a false picture: the relevant police reports have survived for only twenty-five of the forty-eight Paris Sections. Yet we can redress the balance somewhat by adding the information contained in the police register of the Hôtel de la Force, to which nearly 130 of the prisoners were committed; besides, the Sections in which the arrests were made were, in many cases, not those in which the arrested persons lived. On the basis of this combined evidence we find that these 240 Parisians, either killed in the Champ de Mars or arrested over the whole period under review, were drawn from no less than forty-seven Sections—only the Île-Saint-Louis is not accounted for. This is in itself striking proof of the wide dissemination of the political ideas of the democrats among the *menu peuple* of the capital; and, this being the case, we may perhaps assume that supporters flocked to the Champ de Mars from every part of the city.

The evidence does not suggest, however, that this support was evenly distributed; we saw already that the Faubourg Saint-Antoine was lukewarm in its response. Not surprisingly the most concentrated body of support appears to have come from a number of Sections on the Left Bank and not far distant from the Cordeliers Club itself: in this quarter three Sections alone (Quatre Nations, Thermes de Julien, and Sainte-Geneviève) account for thirty-eight arrests. Another fifty arrested persons were from the five central and north-central Sections of the Arcis, Ponceau, Gravilliers, Louvre, and Oratoire. These appear to have been the two main areas of support. The crowded central districts between the Hôtel de Ville and the Louvre had, as usual, made a substantial contribution to a movement with

[1] *Crimes de La Fayette en France* (printed text, 1791). Arch. Nat., F⁷ 6504.

more than a purely local appeal; but what is of greater interest is the emergence on the political scene of the Faubourg Saint-Marcel. Only a few months before, the citizens of that *faubourg* had been singled out for particular praise by the city administration for their peaceful and orderly behaviour ever since the outbreak of the Revolution.[1] This reputation was never to be regained: from now on, the Faubourg Saint-Marcel was to remain in the forefront in every political commotion of the period.

We have seen that the supply and price of bread can have played little part in stimulating support for the Champ de Mars petition or for the other political activities of the democrats. It only reappeared as an issue after the political movement had been crushed and its leaders had been arrested or had gone abroad. In mid-August, however, owing to a bad harvest and the bakers' shortage of flour, the price of the 4-lb. loaf began once more to rise and appears, by September, to have reached 12 *sous*, or even more.[2] On 7 September *Le Journal de la Révolution* reported that Bailly had been given a hostile reception at the corn-market, threatened with 'la lanterne' and forced to withdraw.[3] The next day, Pinché, a button-maker, was arrested in the Mail Section, adjoining the central markets, and sent to the Force for saying: 'Il nous faut le pain français à deux sols ou se battre.'[4]

But by this time the political movement had spent its force, and the fears of the authorities that the poor would stage a spectacular vengeance for the Champ de Mars slaughter were not to be realized.[5] Had the bread crisis appeared in May or June, it might have been otherwise and the issue of the Champ de Mars affair been more decisive. As it was, the police agent Delaborde was able to report to the Assembly's Comité des Recherches on 9 August: 'Paris jouit toujours d'un grand calme.'[6]

---

[1] 'Le Corps municipal saisit . . . cette occasion d'applaudir à l'ordre et à la tranquillité qui n'ont cessé de régner depuis la Révolution dans l'étendue du faubourg St. Marcel' (*Extrait du registre des délibérations du corps municipal, le 4 mars 1791* (printed text): Arch. Nat., F⁷ 4622, fols. 149–50).
[2] Lacroix, op. cit., 2nd series, vi. 455–63.
[3] *Le Journal de la Révolution*, no. 391, 7 September 1791.
[4] Arch. Préf. Pol., Aa 167, fol. 73.
[5] Arch. Nat., DXXIXᵇ 33, no. 347, fols. 9–10.
[6] Ibid., no. 348, fol. 10.

VII

THE FALL OF THE MONARCHY

THE king's flight to Varennes, though its immediate effects were masked by the Assembly's attempts to forget and forgive and to unite the nation round the Constitution of 1791, had far-reaching consequences. In August, the Courts of Vienna and Berlin, incited by the French *émigrés*, issued the joint Declaration of Pillnitz with the purpose of rallying the European Great Powers against the Revolution. Though not involving any immediate armed intervention, the Declaration both served to unite the forces of counter-revolution at home and abroad by giving them a programme, and provided the new Left within the Assembly, centred around Brissot and the deputies of the Gironde, with the necessary pretext to prepare the nation for an offensive crusade against the crowned heads of Europe. Their agitation, added to the effects of internal economic difficulties, met with enthusiastic response among the militants in the Paris Sections; and, when war broke out in April 1792, it had the overwhelming support of the political democrats (Robespierre was at first a notable exception) and the Parisian *menu peuple*. This state of revolutionary elation was further stimulated by military defeat, the effects of inflation, and the growing conviction that the court, guided by the *parti autrichien*, was using the war to inveigle the enemy into destroying the Revolution by military force. It was this combination of factors which, in the spring and summer of 1792, kept the popular movement in almost continuous effervescence, culminating in its overthrow of the monarchy in August and the massacres carried out in the prisons of Paris in September.[1]

Once more, as in 1789, it was the economic crisis that first drew the *menu peuple* into activity; but, this time, it was not so much a shortage of wheat or flour as inflation that forced up prices and provoked popular disturbance. The war was to intensify this process; yet, long before its outbreak, the value of

---

[1] For the political background to this chapter and the main sequence of events see G. Lefebvre, *La Révolution française*, pp. 217–56.

the *assignat*[1] had begun to decline and the exchange-rate of the French *livre* had begun to fall heavily abroad. Selling at 70 per cent. of its nominal value in London in June 1791, the *livre* had fallen to 50 per cent. in March; in Paris, the *assignat*, from 82 per cent. of its nominal value in November 1791, had declined to 63 per cent. in January and to 57 per cent. in June 1792.[2] Yet the more immediate cause of the outbreak of renewed disturbance in the capital was a shortage of sugar, and certain other colonial products, arising from the civil war that had broken out between the planters and natives in the West Indies. In January the price of sugar rose in a few days from 22–25 *sous* to 3 *livres* or 3½ *livres* a pound;[3] and riots broke out in the Faubourgs Saint-Antoine, Saint-Marcel, and Saint-Denis, and in the central Sections of Gravilliers and Beaubourg. The rioters, believing—with some justice—that the real reason for the shortage was the withholding of supplies by the merchants and that colonial disturbance was the pretext rather than the cause, broke into the shops and warehouses of some of the large wholesalers and dealers and demanded that sugar be sold at its former price of 20, 22, 24, or 26 *sous* a pound; while, in some districts, extending their operations to bread, meat, wine, and other wares.[4] It was the first great movement of *taxation populaire* in the capital since the riots of 1775.

The police reports of the Paris Sections for January and February throw some light on these events. In the Section de Beaubourg we learn that, on 20 January, a dozen women— 'ayant l'air de femmes de marché, passablement vêtues'— entered the shop of a wholesaler, Commard Senior, in the Cloître de Saint-Merry, and displayed a list on which were entered the names of certain dealers and wholesalers whom the people held particularly responsible for the rise in the price of sugar and coffee: the only remedy, they claimed, was to

---

[1] Originally issued as interest-bearing bonds to finance the public auctioning of Church lands, the *assignats* gradually became the recognized paper-money of the Revolution and were used for all financial operations.

[2] Mathiez, *La Vie chère et le mouvement social sous la Terreur*, p. 55; R. G. Hawtrey, 'The Collapse of the French Assignats', *The Economic Journal*, no. 111, vol. xxviii (1918), pp. 300–14.   [3] Mathiez, op. cit., p. 31.

[4] For a general account of the disturbances see Mathiez, op. cit., pp. 36–49. For those in the Faubourg Saint-Marcel in mid-February see J. Godechot, 'Fragments des mémoires de Charles-Alexis Alexandre sur les journées révolutionnaires de 1791 et 1792', *Ann. hist. Rév. franç.*, no. 126, April–June 1952, pp. 148–61.

pillage and burn their shops. Madame Commard, however, had the resource to offer them money, which they willingly accepted as compensation for time lost 'pour le bien public', and departed peacefully.[1] Three days later crowds gathered at the shop of Bailly, a merchant grocer of the rue Sainte-Marguerite, off the rue du Faubourg Saint-Antoine, and compelled him to sell them sugar at 25 *sous* a pound; they explained to Dumont, the police-commissioner of the Montreuil Section,

que la subite augmentation du sucre les avait mis dans la nécessité de faire cette démarche pour en faire diminuer le prix et faire punir les accapareurs.

Meanwhile, half a dozen grocers in the same Section had similarly been compelled to sell sugar at a reduced price before the police arrived with the National Guard, who cleared their shops and took prisoners.[2]

Another wave of rioting broke out in February: in the Faubourg Saint-Antoine, on the morning of the 14th, the police and *gendarmerie* were at first overwhelmed—'l'insurrection étant générale dans le faubourg'—and over twenty grocers in the rue du Faubourg Saint-Antoine alone were threatened with invasion; several were forced to sell their sugar at 20 *sous* a pound before order could be restored. At night cartloads of merchandise bound for Lyons were held up by crowds as they passed through the *faubourg*, and the authorities had to appeal to the National Guard to overcome their reluctance to protect the merchants' property.[3]

Meanwhile an even more explosive situation had developed in the Faubourg Saint-Marcel. Since the previous November two dyers, Auger and Monnery, of the Gobelins Section, who had recognized the potentialities of the rising market in sugar, had been laying up large stocks—it was said, 80,000 lb.—in a warehouse in the rue Saint-Hippolyte. In January a protest demonstration had been easily dispersed; but matters came to a head when, on 14 February, the rumour spread that the stocks were going to be distributed all over Paris. Crowds formed early in the morning, seized the first loads of sugar as they left the warehouse under military escort, and sold them in

[1] Arch. Préf. Pol., Aa 72, fol. 54.
[2] Arch. Préf. Pol., Aa 173, fol. 39.
[3] Ibid.

H

the street at 25 or 30 *sous* a pound.[1] This was followed, the next day, by attempts to break into the warehouse itself, which was guarded, somewhat unwillingly, by a detachment of the local National Guard. Women, laundresses among them, sounded the tocsin in the church of Saint-Marcel. This, in turn, had the effect of stirring the Municipality into action, and Pétion, newly elected mayor of Paris, arrived on the scene with a considerable armed force, which cleared the streets and took prisoners. Details of these and of other persons arrested during the disturbances appear in the police records: in January fourteen persons committed to the Conciergerie prison were composed mainly of craftsmen, journeymen, and labourers of the central Sections; in February five persons—of whom three or four were women—were sent to the Conciergerie for taking part in the events of the Faubourg Saint-Marcel.[2] The prisoners commanded considerable local sympathy: a petition for their release, sent to the Legislative Assembly on 26 February, contained the names of 150 local citizens, two of them clerics.[3]

It was the citizens of the two *faubourgs* again who were to play the leading part in the next great popular demonstration, which took place at the Tuileries on 20 June the same year. Ostensibly it was a purely political affair—its purpose was to compel the king to accede to the wishes of the Paris Sections and Jacobin Club—yet it may well be that irritation with growing economic hardship added to the numbers of demonstrators that, on this occasion, filed menacingly past Louis XVI in his own palace. Yet this is supposition. There were other, even more tangible, grounds for discontent and disquiet: the succession of military defeats; the king's refusal to assent to the law providing for the banishment of non-juring priests; and now, on 13 June, the dismissal of the 'patriot'—Girondin—ministers whom he had been compelled, much against his will, to include in Dumouriez's war government. This last act provided the pretext for the demonstration of 20 June. On the 16th Pétion received a request, signed by a small number of citizens of the Gobelins Section, but purporting to represent the collective wishes of the Faubourgs Saint-Marcel and Saint-Antoine, for

[1] See Godechot, op. cit., pp. 148–61.
[2] Arch. Préf. Pol., Aa 9 (arrestations), fols. 103–37, 200–4.
[3] Arch. Nat., D III 256 (⁴).

enfants' that we noted earlier.[1] From other accounts, however, it would appear that the main impetus to the demonstration was given by the shopkeepers, workshop masters, and artisans of the *faubourgs*, with the full support of the journeymen and working women. In the Faubourg Saint-Antoine, for example, shops and workshops remained closed for nearly a week;[2] and, in the Faubourg Saint-Marcel, it is evident from Alexandre's detailed relation of events that the main driving force was provided by the active citizens organized in the National Guard, from which most wage-earners and smaller property-owners were at this time excluded. At the same time Alexandre relates an incident that both shows the active interest taken in the event by the working women of the *faubourg* and provides an interesting link with the grocery riots of the previous February: when an order was sent out for his own arrest in connexion with the demonstration, the bearer was nearly lynched and he was saved from arrest by some of the same women against whom, a few months previously, he had defended the properties of Auger and Monnery.[3]

It is simple enough, in retrospect, to present the events of 10 August, when the Tuileries was captured by armed force and the king suspended from office, as the logical and inevitable outcome of the humiliation inflicted on the monarchy in June. In one sense it is true enough: the anti-royalist agitation in the *faubourgs* persisted and, in the course of July, both gained local momentum and spread to the other Sections: by the end of the month, forty-seven of them had declared for abdication. Besides, the dignity of the king's office, despite his personal display of courage, had been severely undermined; the federal volunteers, too, who were to play a prominent part in the attack on the Tuileries, had already been invited to the capital; and, perhaps even more important, a small group of determined Republicans had long decided to follow up the preliminary skirmish of 20 June with a more decisive, and final, blow when a

---

[1] Other accounts refer to 'un fort de la halle, armé d'un sabre' (Arch. Nat., BB³⁰ 17) and to 'un homme couvert d'un habit déchiré' (Godechot, loc. cit.); but this is, of course, very little to go by. One of the more suggestive descriptions is that given by some of the Tuileries servants, who claimed to have recognized among the demonstrators 'les gens de Mr. d'Orléans et portant des moustaches' (Arch. Nat., F⁷ 4387, doss. 2).
[2] Arch. Nat., F⁷ 4774⁷⁰, fols. 472–600.   [3] Godechot, op. cit., p. 179.

favourable opportunity should arise. So much appears evident from the *Mémoires* of Fournier l'Américain who, having been sent to confer with the leaders of the Marseillais at Charenton on their arrival on 29 July, told them

> qu'un grand coup préparatoire avait été jeté le 20 juin, et qu'il n'était plus question que d'achever . . . que ce plan consistait à aller s'emparer de l'individu nommé roi, ainsi que de sa famille royale et de chasser du château tous les scélerats et brigands qui conspiraient la perte totale des français et leur esclavage.[1]

Yet, thus presented, the picture is an incomplete one. For one thing, while the agitation against the monarchy in the Sections was a constant factor, the aims and composition of the leaders were not. The initiative in threatening the king with removal from office had been taken by the Girondins; Robespierre and the other topmost leaders of the Mountain (as the non-Girondin Jacobins began to be called) had played no part in the affair of 20 June. Pétion was still the hero of the day at the Festival of the Federation on 14 July; and it was only after mid-July, when the Girondins, alarmed at the social consequences of their own actions, drew back in defence of the monarchy, that the Mountain took over the leadership of the movement; yet, even at the end of July, Robespierre stressed that the future of the monarchy, as of the Constitution as a whole, should be decided by a popularly elected Convention, rather than by armed insurrection.[2] Again, the monarchy still had important cards to play: a stream of resolutions from the Departments denounced the affront to the king's person committed on 20 June; in Paris 20,000 signatures of 'active' citizens were quickly collected for a petition of protest; the commander-in-chief of the National Guard and several of its divisional commanders (including that of the Faubourg Saint-Marcel) were avowed king's men; Lafayette was well received by the Legislative Assembly on 28 June, when he proposed that active measures be taken to destroy the democrats, and only narrowly missed his chance of mobilizing a large part of the Parisian National Guard for a *coup de force* against the Jacobins: the queen, for one, with characteristic folly, refused his help.[3] but, even after

---

[1] *Mémoires secrets de Fournier, Américain.*
[2] Lefebvre, op. cit., p. 246.
[3] Godechot, op. cit., pp. 177–87.

Lafayette's failure and return to the army, the initiative still often remained with the 'loyalists'. Pétion was suspended from office early in July (though, admittedly, he was reinstated a week later); young men of the western Sections showed some determination to uphold the monarchy by volunteering for defence duties at the Tuileries; 'loyalist' battalions of the National Guard even felt secure enough to beat up peaceful crowds in the Tuileries Gardens;[1] while the air was thick with rumours of impending punitive measures against 'patriots', and a flood of denunciations of royalist 'conspiracies' poured into the Paris Commune and Department of Police.[2]

That such matters were taken seriously by 'patriots', and even by more or less uncommitted neutrals, is clear from the *Mémoires* of Alexandre for this period. Alexandre himself, although a royalist who had been a lukewarm—if not, unwilling—participant in the events of 20 June, was drawn by the fear of a counter-revolutionary *coup*, which he considered imminent, into active support for the insurrection of 10 August.[3] Such fears were, of course, given only too real a substance by the Brunswick Manifesto of 1 August, which threatened the Parisian Sections and National Guard with summary vengeance, should the invaders find them arms in hand. In this sense, then, the August revolution, far from being the logical outcome of a consistently conceived and conducted plan of operations, was an act of self-defence against dangers, both real and imagined.[4]

By the last week in July, however, a more or less decided plan of action had taken shape; and the outbreak of 10 August was the climax to a series of false starts. In the night of 26–27 July there was a call to arms by federal volunteers parading in the Montreuil Section of the Faubourg Saint-Antoine; *ouvriers* sounded the tocsin at the church of Sainte-Marguerite; Santerre was pulled out of bed; and workshops remained closed next day.[5] On the 30th additional impetus was given to the

---

[1] Arch. Préf. Pol., Aa 226, fol. 30.   [2] Arch. Nat., F⁷ 4387, doss. 2.
[3] Godechot, op. cit., pp. 187–221. See the passage: 'La Cour . . . continuait ses manoeuvres sourdes, ses persécutions et ses calomnies, en attendant qu'elle pût leur faire une guerre plus sérieuse . . . tandis que le parti contraire se tenait sur la défensive, mais avec l'intention très prononcée de la soutenir vigoureusement' (op. cit., pp. 187–8).
[4] Lefebvre, op. cit., p. 247.   [5] Arch. Préf. Pol., Aa 220, fol. 63.

movement and to its chances of success by an Assembly decree, admitting 'passive' citizens into the National Guard. There were further false starts, or rumours of such, on 30 July,[1] and on 1 and 5 August.[2] On 6 August a huge meeting of Parisians and *fédérés* in the Champ de Mars demanded the abdication of Louis XVI.[3] The Faubourg Saint-Antoine, which, since mid-July had taken the lead in the sectional movement, now warned the Assembly that the king must be deposed or suspended by the 9th, or the Sections would take armed action.

The same night the tocsin sounded. While the 'correspondence' committee of the forty-eight Sections formed themselves into a new, revolutionary Commune and kept Pétion a prisoner in his room, the armed formations of the National Guard advanced on the Tuileries.

Though the final outcome was hardly in doubt, the defenders might have put up a sterner resistance. Guarding the *château* were 900 Swiss, 200 to 300 Knights of Saint-Louis, and —before their wholesale desertion to the attackers—2,000 National Guardsmen. The besiegers had mustered a far larger force: by 9 o'clock, soon before the attack started, they may have been 20,000 men, including 400 Marseillais and smaller contingents from Brest, Rouen, and other cities.[4] Before a shot was fired, Roederer, the *procureur-syndic* of the Paris Department, who was in attendance on the king, persuaded him to seek refuge with his family in the Assembly, meeting nearby: thus bloodshed might be avoided and a solution found by the deputies without the dictation of armed rebellion. Abandoned by the king, only the Swiss and a handful of grenadiers of the financial quarter prepared to resist. The Marseillais advanced to fraternize with the defenders, but were raked by fire from the Swiss. As at the Bastille the cry of treachery went up. The attack was started in earnest. Before the *château* was reduced, the king sent word ordering a cease-fire; but it did not save the Swiss from

[1] According to Fournier, the plan failed for lack of support by Santerre and Pétion (*Mémoires secrets* . . .).

[2] Arch. Nat, F⁷ 4774⁷⁰: *Lettres et pièces relatives au dix août.* There was a strike of building workers in the Faubourg Saint-Antoine on 3 August, but it does not appear to have been connected in any way with the August insurrection (Arch. Préf. Pol., Aa 219, fol. 30).

[3] Bib. Nat., Lᵇ 39 10728ᵃ (printed text).

[4] For these figures, and those of other historians and observers, see P. Sagnac, *La Chute de la royauté, 1792* (Paris, 1902), pp. 277 ff.

wholesale massacre: 600 were slaughtered, 60 of them by order, or with the tacit approval, of the revolutionary Commune at the Hôtel de Ville, to which they were sent under armed escort. Of the besiegers some 90 *fédérés* and nearly 300 Paris *sectionnaires* were killed and wounded;[1] among the latter were 3 women, of whom one was Louise-Reine Audu of the Bibliothèque Section, a veteran of 5 October.[2]

Hostile eyewitnesses and historians have been particularly liberal in their use of lurid epithets to describe the federal volunteers and the men of the Paris Sections that took part in the attack on the Tuileries. These range from Madame de Tourzel's 'cette armée de bandits' and Bigot de Sainte-Croix's 'brigands révoltés' to Taine's 'presque tous de la dernière plèbe, ou entretenus par des métiers infâmes' and Peltier's 'ramas d'hommes perdus, de Barbaresques, de Maltais, d'Italiens, de Génois, de Piémontais'.[3] In so far as these descriptions purport to throw a light on the occupations or social origins—or even on the nationality—of the persons described, we can check their validity by reference to the lists of dead and wounded sent in by the Paris Sections and of those later recognized by the National Convention as having qualified for pensions for themselves or their dependants.[4]

It is not proposed here to attempt a detailed social analysis of the federal volunteers, whose dead and wounded may have accounted for rather less than a quarter of the total casualties recorded.[5] Suffice it to say that those appearing on these lists have typical French-sounding names and that the label of Italian or other foreigner was, no doubt, devised to create prejudice. Among a little over 300 Parisians[6] occupations are given in some 120 cases;[7] this, then, is the sample on which we have to base any estimate of the professional or social status of the participants. Of this number as many as ninety-five are drawn from fifty of the petty trades and crafts of the capital

---

[1] For the killed and wounded among the besiegers see A. Tuetey, *Répertoire général*, vol. iv, pp. i–xxi; see also Sagnac, op. cit., pp. 300 ff.

[2] Tuetey, op. cit., vol. iv, pp. iv–v.

[3] Cited by Sagnac, op. cit., pp. 134–6, 181, 190, 300–2.

[4] Arch. Nat., F¹⁸ 3269–74; F⁷ 4426.

[5] Of 376 casualties among the attackers recorded by Tuetey, the *fédérés* account for 89 (op. cit., vol. iv, p. xxi).

[6] Tuetey's figure of 287 Parisians appears to be an under-estimate.

[7] Tuetey lists only 84 occupations (op. cit., vol. iv, pp. xxiv–xxv).

either as shopkeepers, small traders and manufacturers, master craftsmen, artisans, or journeymen.[1] There are only two *bourgeois* and three that may be termed professional men among them: an architect, a surgeon, and a drawing-master. The rest are clerks (2), musicians (2), domestic servants (9), port-workers, labourers, and carters (7), and glass-workers (2). Considering the exclusion of 'passive' citizens from the National guard until a few days previously, there are surprisingly many wage-earners among them: thirty-three journeymen and eighteen other workers. Yet, even so, they form considerably less than half the total.[2] In all, then, they are typical *sans-culottes*, with a sprinkling of more or less prosperous citizens; but by no means 'de la dernière plèbe', as the jaundiced imagination of Taine would have us believe.

They are typical, too, in the sense that they are drawn from nearly every Section in the capital: all but four of these appear on the lists—the exceptions are the Roule Section in the west; the Place Royale in the centre of the old aristocratic quarter of the Marais; and the two island Sections of Henri IV (now re-named Pont Neuf) and the Île-Saint-Louis (Fraternité). This time the Faubourg Saint-Antoine reappears in its traditional role: no less than 8 killed and 50 wounded are from the Quinze Vingts Section alone; next on the list come Montreuil (18 killed and wounded), Finistère (19), and Observatoire (18)—the last two in the Faubourg Saint-Marcel. The two *faubourgs* between them account for between one-third and one-half of all the casualties suffered.

Behind these bare statistics lies many a story of personal heroism and sacrifice and of days spent in anxious expectation, terror, and deprivation. The late J. M. Thompson has recorded the anxieties and fears of Lucile, the wife of Camille Desmoulins, as she waited in a lodging-house in the Cordeliers district for the outcome of the assault on the Tuileries on the night of 9–10 August.[3] But Desmoulins was a popular journalist with an assured public: he might suffer physical danger,[4] but his family

---

[1] Among them there are 12 shoe-makers, 8 cabinet-makers, 6 gauze-workers, 4 wig-makers, 4 hatters, 3 carpenters, 3 locksmiths, 3 painters.

[2] Tuetey, surprisingly, describes the majority as belonging to 'la classe ouvrière' (op. cit., vol. iv, p. iii).

[3] J. M. Thompson, *Leaders of the French Revolution* (Oxford, 1948), pp. 118–21.

[4] Mathiez doubted it: 'Si Camille Desmoulins était sorti avec un fusil,' he writes, 'ce n'était pas pour s'en servir' (*Le Dix Août* (Paris, 1931), p. 119).

were not likely to face economic hardship. Quite different was the case of the small tradesmen, craftsmen, journeymen, and labourers who, as we saw, formed the majority of the assailants. To them and their families even the successful outcome of the events of that night would entail hardship and suffering if they should return wounded or maimed; and if they were killed in action, there were long months of waiting before the authorities might decide on a pension for the widow and children. Thus, Pierre Dumont, aged 50, gauze-worker of 254 rue du Faubourg Saint-Antoine, listed by his Section, the Quinze Vingts, as maimed in October 1792, died of his wounds two years later; his wife failed to obtain a pension. Antoine Lobjois, aged 39, master glazier of the rue de Beaune, Fontaine de Grenelle Section, left a wife and five children, of whom only two qualified for a pension. Louis Le Roy, aged 21, a journeyman goldsmith of the rue du Petit Saint-Jean in the Section des Invalides, left a dependent mother and father, a widow, and two small children. Pierre Homette, aged 49, a journeyman cabinet-maker of 20 rue du Faubourg du Temple, accompanied his employer, Legros, to the Tuileries on 10 August: though a wage-earner, he had been a member of the National Guard for a year and eight months; he left a widow and two children.

There are cases which show that the authorities were as chary of spending public money and as inclined to drive a hard bargain with applicants for compensation as they are today: Louis Chauvet, water-carrier of 22 rue de la Coutellerie, in the Arcis Section, was refused a grant because he failed to produce a doctor's certificate that showed the nature of his treatment, as prescribed by law; and Philippe Bouvet of the Popincourt Section was also refused compensation, as the hernia from which he was suffering a year later did not appear to have been caused by the events of 10 August. Others were more fortunate, yet the compensation was usually small compared with the sacrifice made. Thus, Jean Daubanton of the Montreuil Section, though wounded at the Tuileries, enlisted for the army and was sent to the frontiers before his wound had healed; he received 143 days' treatment and was subsequently awarded 50 *livres* as frontier pay and a grant of 214 *livres*. Another hardened warrior appears to have been Henri Buté, aged 41, a jeweller of 87 rue des Gobelins, who had been wounded in his left hand at the

Bastille and been given six months' sick leave from work to recover; wounded again at the Tuileries, he was treated for two and a half months and awarded a compensation of 112 *livres*, 10 *sous*. Another *vainqueur de la Bastille* (there are four of them in these lists) was less fortunate: E. Benoit, aged 52, a port-worker of the rue Deligre in the Quinze Vingts Section, was killed at the Tuileries after a long career as a combatant—he held the rank of *maréchal des logis* in the professional army, in which he served between 1761 and 1779, retired to the Faubourg Saint-Antoine as a dyer and fought at the Bastille in July 1789.[1]

Enrolment for the frontiers followed hard on the heels of the capture of the Tuileries; and many a Tuileries fighter must have had little time to recover before he was once more in the firing line, this time against the Prussians. We saw such a case above; another is that of Louis Chauvin, a master locksmith of the rue Traversière in the Faubourg Saint-Antoine, also of the Quinze Vingts Section, who had first been reported dead at the Tuileries. His wife's brother had been seriously wounded and, shortly after his departure, one child had died and the other fallen sick. The anguished state of mind of his wife as, after these experiences, she writes a pathetic and illiterate letter to the Comité des Secours Publics, begging for assistance for herself and family, is evident: her husband, she writes

fut obligé de partir avec les Citoyent pour aidé avangé la patrie jours trop funeste a mon souvenir puisqu'il est vrai qu audameurant mon frère nommé Damois aussi du distric des enfant trouvé étant blessé et presque mort il me fut annoncé que mon mari étoit tué.[2]

Such events as these and the fear and anguish that they engendered may perhaps help to explain the state of feverish agitation in which many of the citizens continued even after the fear of a *coup* directed from the Tuileries had been removed. The king had been suspended from office, the Swiss (his most loyal defenders) had been massacred or imprisoned; many open supporters of the court had been rounded up and their homes searched for hidden arms or correspondence. Yet the foreign enemy was a few hundred miles from the gates; and the prisons were full (and believed fuller) of refractory priests, political

---

[1] Arch. Nat., F15 3269–70, 3272.
[2] Arch. Nat., F15 3274, no. 1592, fol. 111.

enemies of the Revolution, and a host of forgers whose faked *assignats* were held responsible for rising prices and inflation. These were thought to be so many allies for the Duke of Brunswick, who were but waiting for the volunteers to leave for the frontiers in order to break out of prison and massacre the aged, women, and children left behind. Thus grew among the militants of the Sections—of the same kind, no doubt, as those who had stormed the Tuileries—the mentality that led to the gruesome extermination of prisoners in the early days of September. It was by no means a sudden eruption, carried out in a momentary fit of passion or as the result of a short-lived panic. Already on 11 August, the day after the capture of the Tuileries, a letter from two police administrators, Perron and Vignet, warned Santerre, newly appointed commander-in-chief of the Parisian National Guard:

> On nous informe dans le moment, Monsieur, que l'on forme le projet de se transporter dans toutes les prisons de Paris pour y enlever tous les prisonniers, et en faire une prompte justice.[1]

Six days later, Pétion wrote to Santerre:

> On me prévient . . . que cette nuit le tocsin doit sonner dans les fbgs. St. Ant. et St. Marceau pour réunir les citoyens, les porter sur les prisons et immoler les personnes qui sont détenues.[2]

But the movement was not limited to the *faubourgs*: the same day, similar threats were reported from the Gravilliers and Ponceau Sections in the centre of the city;[3] and, on 2 September, the day that Verdun fell to the Prussians, the general assembly of Poissonnière decided to send to the other forty-seven Sections copies of a resolution that declared:

> Qu'il n'y avait d'autre moyen à prendre pour éviter le danger et augmenter le zèle des citoyens pour partir aux frontières que faire sur le champ une justice prompte de tous les malfaiteurs et conspirateurs détenus dans les prisons.[4]

The same afternoon, prisoners being brought under armed

[1] Arch. Nat., F⁷ 4622: *Pièces relatives au 10 août*, fol. 29.
[2] Arch. Nat., F⁷ 4774⁷⁰, fol. 603. Neither of these two documents is cited by Caron (see page 110, note 1, below).
[3] Tuetey, op. cit., vol. v, no. 3874.
[4] Arch. Préf. Pol., Aa 266, fol. 203. The massacres had, however, started before this resolution could have had any effect (P. Caron, *Les Massacres de septembre*, pp. 338-9).

escort to the Abbaye prison near the church of Saint-Germain-des-Prés, were seized on arrival by waiting crowds and summarily executed. The massacre spread to the Carmes, a religious house in the rue de Vaugirard; and, during the night, to the Conciergerie, the Châtelet, and the Hôtel de la Force; at the latter, it went on spasmodically until the 6th or 7th. On the 3rd, executions were carried out at the Seminary of Saint-Firmin, in the rue Saint-Victor, and at the Bernardins monastery, where common criminals were awaiting their transfer to the galleys at Toulon, Brest, and Rochefort. The same afternoon and the next day, prisoners were slaughtered at Bicêtre, a prison-hospital for the poor, vagrants, and lunatics; and, though few in number, at the Salpêtrière, a place of detention for female thieves and prostitutes. Two prisons alone were untouched—the debtors' prison of Sainte-Pélagie in the rue de la Clef, and Saint-Lazare, now a women's prison, in the rue du Faubourg Saint-Denis. The massacres stopped on the 6th or 7th; by that time, between 1,100 and 1,400 prisoners (only 37 of them women) had been slaughtered out of a total of 2,800 in the nine prisons concerned. A slightly larger number—perhaps 1,500 or 1,600—had been spared by hastily constituted courts of justice, of which the most famous is that presided over by Maillard at the Abbaye. Surprisingly, only one-quarter of the prisoners were priests, nobles, or 'politicals'; the great majority were common-or-garden thieves, prostitutes, forgers, and vagrants.[1]

While the massacres were going on, and for some days after, there were persons in authority who were prepared to applaud them as a necessary act of popular justice, and even to recommend them as an example for others to follow. The circular sent to the Departments on 3 September in the name of the Paris Commune (often associated with the pen of Marat) is well known: 'et sans doute la nation entière . . . s'empressera d'adopter ce moyen nécessaire de salut public'. Again, the general assembly of the Finistère Section, in the Faubourg Saint-Marcel, did no more than express the prevailing opinion in Paris[2] when it called upon all forty-eight Sections on 6 September

de déclarer hautement que le peuple est vengé, qu'il livre au glaive

[1] P. Caron, *Les Massacres de septembre* (Paris, 1935), pp. 3–7, 76–102.
[2] For contemporary opinion on the massacres up to the end of September see Caron, op. cit., pp. 121–65.

des lois ce qui pourrait avoir échappé de conspirateurs à la juste vengeance.[1]

But once the moment of crisis was past, there was no party or faction that would justify or claim credit for the massacres; and the charge of having provoked or organized them—or even of having merely failed to put a stop to them—became an accepted weapon in the struggle between parties, in which the Mountain sought to discredit the Gironde and the Gironde to blacken the Mountain; while royalists and 'moderates' hurled the accusation at both Gironde and Mountain indiscriminately. After Robespierre's fall in Thermidor, the struggle became more bitter, and the most common epithet to attach to a Jacobin, apart from being a terrorist or a *buveur de sang*, was to have been a *septembriseur*. It has become all the more difficult to identify the real *massacreurs*. Were they many? were they a small band of resolute fanatics? were they, in any sense, typical of Paris as a whole? No certain answer is possible. Pierre Caron, in the course of a detailed study of the affair, examined every possible piece of evidence that he could lay hands on to determine the authenticity of the numerous documents purporting to give full lists and details of the *septembriseurs*; he concluded that the great majority, even when put forward in good faith, were apocryphal. Apart from eyewitness accounts of the presence of federal volunteers, *gardes nationaux*, and other individuals— many of which may be authentic enough—the only solid evidence is provided by the records of the judicial proceedings taken against thirty-nine persons in the Year IV (1796) for believed participation in the massacres of 1792. Though all but three were acquitted for lack of evidence—thus reducing an already small sample to derisory proportions—the list is significant as showing the sort of persons and classes from which contemporary opinion was willing to believe that the *massacreurs* might have been recruited: they comprise, in the majority of cases, small masters and craftsmen, shopkeepers, and a sprinkling of ex-soldiers and *gendarmes*; nearly all, at the time of their trial, were over 30 years old. From all this Caron concludes that Fabre d'Églantine was nearer to the truth than most when he declared in the Jacobin Club on 5 November 1792: 'Ce sont

[1] Arch. Préf. Pol., Aa 266, fol. 42.

les hommes du 10 août qui ont enfoncé les prisons de l'Abbaye, et celles d'Orléans, et celles de Versailles.'[1]

Unsavoury as the episode must appear in itself, the massacres were an event of historical importance: they completed the destruction of the internal enemy some weeks before the volunteers at Valmy, on 20 September, routed Brunswick's army and drove it back across the frontier. Thus the Republic, proclaimed that autumn, became established on what seemed at first a solid enough foundation—by the victory of the Revolution over its enemies at home and abroad.

[1] Caron, op. cit., pp. 103–20.

VIII

THE TRIUMPH OF THE MOUNTAIN

T HE overthrow of Louis XVI had profound social consequences. Not only was the Republic proclaimed, but
all citizens were, for the first time in modern history,
granted equal political rights: the old distinction between
'active' and 'passive' citizens—so dear to the 'constitutionalists'
of 1789–91—was swept aside, and every adult male was henceforth eligible to vote in all local, departmental, and national
elections.[1] Thus the concept of Equality, proclaimed in the
Declaration of the Rights of Man of 1789, was given more solid
substance. Yet, for all this, the period now under review was
one of intense internal conflict rather than of harmony: quite
apart from the foreign war, which was supported with a greater
or a lesser degree of enthusiasm by all groups in the newly
elected Convention, new antagonisms had arisen to take the
place of the old. The Girondin deputies had emerged from the
elections as the majority party in the Assembly and enjoyed
considerable support in the country; but, in Paris, their equivo-
cal behaviour in the August revolution had lost them their
following among the militants. Against them stood the Mountain—whose leaders, Robespierre, Danton, and Marat, now
all sat in the Convention—which was strongly backed by the
Paris Sections and clubs, where their credit stood high for the
role they had played in August. Gradually unfolding in the
autumn, the conflict became more bitter with the new round
of treacheries and defeats in the winter and spring, and broke
into open violence in the early summer. It was only resolved by
the revolution of May–June 1793, when the leaders of the
Girondins were forcibly expelled from the Convention by the
Parisian *sans-culottes* enrolled in the National Guard. The Jacobin dictatorship, however, only became consolidated, and its

[1] Workers and others living in furnished rooms and lodging-houses seem, however, to have been debarred from voting until the revolution of May–June 1793
(Arch. Nat., F7* 2520, fol. 53). Women and domestic servants, of course, remained
without the vote.

instrument, the Revolutionary Government of the Year II, only emerged after a further popular insurrection in September.

Yet this alliance between the Mountain and the Parisian *sans-culottes*, which was to be so remarkable a feature of the next phase of the Revolution, was not realized without difficulty and without stress. Apart from the gain of political rights, the *sans-culottes* had won little from the August revolution. The new Commune, which had conducted the insurrection with their active participation, was neither of their making nor made in their image: although fewer lawyers and merchants sat in it than in the Communes of 1789 and 1791, only one-third of its members were small shopkeepers, masters, or journeymen; and the lawyers and journalists, although in a minority, held the leading posts.[1] This, however, would be changed in the near future. There were more immediately pressing problems, such as work and food prices. In November the president of the Popincourt Section in the Faubourg Saint-Antoine appealed to the Convention to provide bread and work for 'la classe nombreuse de citoyens ouvriers'.[2] The rise in food prices, which had caused the outbreak of February 1792, had slowed down in the summer and autumn,[3] but it took another sharp upward turn in the early months of 1793: this time it was far more drastic and covered a far wider range of consumers' goods than in the previous spring. By February refined sugar (1790 price: 24 *sous*) was selling at 47–60 *sous*; unrefined sugar (1790 price: 12 *sous*) was selling at 40 *sous*; tallow candles (15 *sous*) at 18½–20 *sous*; coffee (34 *sous*) at 40 *sous*; soap (12 *sous*) at 23–28 *sous*. The consequence was a popular outburst, far more extensive and insistent than the sugar riots of the previous year, in which all, or nearly all, the Parisian Sections were involved and which, perhaps more clearly than any other incident in the Revolution, marked the basic conflict of interests between the *menu peuple* and the possessing classes, including the extreme democrats that spoke or applauded at the Jacobin Club, or sat with the Mountain on the upper benches of the National Convention.[4]

[1] F. Braesch, *La Commune du 10 août 1792*, p. 267; J. M. Thompson, *The French Revolution*, pp. 297–8.   [2] Tuetey, op. cit., vol. viii, no. 395.

[3] S. E. Harris, *The Assignats* (Harvard Univ. Press, 1930), p. 102.

[4] For a detailed account, mainly based on the police reports of the Paris Sections in the archives of the Préfecture de Police, see G. Rudé, 'Les Émeutes des 25, 26 février 1793', *Ann. hist. Rév. franç.*, no. 130, 1953, pp. 33–57.

There had been two deputations of women to the Convention on Sunday, 23 February, one of which was composed of laundresses, who complained of the price of soap;[1] and there had been local disturbances, followed by arrests, on the morrow. But the real outbreak began on the morning of the 25th; it took the form of the mass invasion of grocers' and chandlers' shops and the forcible reduction of prices to a level dictated by the insurgents. Starting in the central, commercial, quarter—formed by the Lombards, Gravilliers, and Marchés Sections[2]—at 10 o'clock in the morning, the movement spread with remarkable speed to every part of the city.[3] From surviving police reports we can follow its progress from Section to Section. First eastwards: soon after 10, in Maison Commune (Hôtel de Ville); at midday, in Place des Fédérés (Place Royale); at 2 o'clock in Arsenal; at 3, in Droits de l'Homme; between 3 and 4, in Quinze Vingts; at 4 o'clock, in Montreuil and l'Homme Armé (Marais). Meanwhile, northwards, the movement reached Amis de la Patrie at 2.30; and Bondy and Mont Blanc at 5 o'clock. In the west it reached the Gardes Françaises at 2.30, the Muséum (Louvre) at 4 o'clock, the Butte des Moulins (Palais Royal) at 7, the Tuileries at 8, and République (Roule) at 10. From the Tuileries it may have crossed the Pont National (the former Pont Louis XVI) to the Left Bank; at any rate, there were disturbances in the Fontaine de Grenelle Section between 8 and 9 that night. The next day there followed minor incidents in a number of Sections, in which the market women of the centre and laundresses of the rue de Bièvre, in the Faubourg Saint-Marcel, played a conspicuous part. But Santerre, who had been away at Versailles on the 25th, mobilized the National Guard at an early hour and soon succeeded in dispersing the crowds and restoring law and order.

This time it was not only sugar that was aimed at, but a whole

[1] A. Mathiez, *La Vie chère et le mouvement social sous la Terreur*, pp. 145–6.

[2] Unfortunately these 3 Sections are among the 30 for whom no *procès-verbaux* exist for the period covering the riots. However, there are some indications given in the case of 14 of them in police and prison registers and in the general reports of the Bureau de Surveillance de la Police.

[3] Cf. an address presented to the National Convention by the Paris Commune on 27 February 1793: 'Le désordre a éclaté subitement avec violence; il s'est propagé avec la rapidité de la foudre; du centre où il avait pris naissance aux extrémités de la ville les propriétés ont été violées' (Arch. Nat., C 247, no. 360, fol. 36).

number of other groceries and colonial products, as well. This was general; general, too, was the remarkable concordance between the level at which prices were fixed in one part of the city and another—all of which suggests concerted action. The following were the goods most commonly demanded by the rioters and the range of prices imposed by them: sugar at 18–25 *sous*; unrefined sugar at 10–12 *sous*; tallow candles at 12 *sous*; soap at 10–12 *sous*; and coffee at 20 *sous*. Had these amounts been strictly adhered to, we should expect the shopkeepers to have received something like two-fifths or one-half of the market-value of their goods; but this, in fact, was rarely the case. There were undoubtedly persons mingling with the rioters who saw a glorious opportunity for pillage—particularly as only a small part of the National Guard had turned out (some Guardsmen even joined in the riot). Besides, in the mêlée that ensued, even with the best intentions in the world, it was often easier to help oneself to goods than to leave the money and obtain a receipt for payment. Yet we find a merchant grocer of the rue Saint-Martin presenting the police with the following account of his receipts and losses:

Savoir, 420 livres sucre à 54 s.	1,134 livres
Cassonnade, 70 livres à 40 s.	140
Chandelle, 229 livres à 20 s.	229
Savon, 248 livres Blanc Bleu à 28 s.	347 l. 8 s.
	1,850 l. 8 s.
Avoir comptant	754 l. 5 s.[1]—

showing a receipt of nearly two-fifths of the market value of the goods distributed. Another grocer, Pierre Merville of the Place Royale Section, was able to show that he had received 521 *livres*, 15 *sous* in return for goods priced at 1,547 *livres*.[2] But these shopkeepers were exceedingly lucky: others received a bare tenth (or less) of the market value of their wares—for example, Cain of the Arcis Section, whose receipts amounted to 2,829 out of 26,267 *livres*, and Commard of the Gardes Françaises, who only managed to collect 1,158 *livres*, 4 *sous* 'in *assignats* wrapped in a tea-towel' for goods currently priced at 27,043 *livres*.[3]

---

[1] Arch. Préf. Pol., Aa 48, fol. 563.   [2] Ibid., Aa 205, fol. 265.
[3] Ibid., Aa 59, fols. 92–94; 153, fols. 78–81.

These riots had other remarkable features. Their main victims were, as one would expect, the big merchants and wholesalers, who were generally considered responsible for hoarding and forcing up prices. This probably explains why the movement started in the Gravilliers and Lombards Sections, where there was a concentration of such dealers. But as the riots spread outwards, there appears to have been less discrimination shown, and the shops of small chandlers and grocers suffered with the rest. In the Quinze' Vingts Section, for example, the police-commissioner drew up a list of twenty-five grocers, of whom thirteen had incurred losses of some kind or another—in some cases amounting to only a few *livres*.[1] Another significant fact that emerged was that-not-only-the-very-poor-took-part-in-what was largely a spontaneous protest against high prices. There are plenty of examples, quoted by witnesses, it is true, of wage-earners and city poor taking part in the disturbances: we hear of butcher's boys, building-workers, water-carriers, porters, market-women, cooks, and domestic servants playing con-spicuous parts in various quarters of the city; and among the forty-nine persons arrested as the result of the riots, twenty-eight were wage-earners of one kind or another; the rest were small shopkeepers and artisans.[2] Yet there is ample evidence to show that other shopkeepers—and even occasional *bourgeois*—were quite willing to take advantage of the unhappy plight of the grocers in order to send their cooks or servants, *garçons* or journeymen, along to mingle with the invading crowds and buy sugar, soap, candles, or coffee at prices highly favourable to themselves.[3]

It is hard to determine how far the riots were the outcome of a concerted plan of action. The Municipal Council, the Jacobin Club, and the various parties in the Convention, who all denounced them in most downright terms, while admitting that hardship had arisen from rising prices, sought to explain them in terms of a 'hidden hand', counter-revolutionary intrigue, or

[1] Ibid., Aa 220, fols. 240–1.
[2] There is evidence to suggest that the number of arrests was far greater, but the relevant documents (like so much other material in the former keeping of the Hôtel de Ville) must have disappeared in the fire of 1871.
[3] We find the same sort of thing happening in the corn riots of 1775, when small farmers took advantage of the *taxation populaire* to buy wheat from the wealthier *laboureurs* at something like two-fifths of the market price.

the machinations of their political opponents. Barère, for example, who had not yet joined the Mountain, spoke darkly of 'the perfidious incitement of aristocrats in disguise'; and, to underline his point, insisted that such 'luxury' articles as sugar and coffee were not likely in themselves to excite popular passions; but he showed his main preoccupation when he added:

N'oublions pas les principes de toutes les sociétés; car là où je ne vois point le respect des propriétés, je ne reconnais plus d'ordre social.[1]

The Mountain and the Commune, perhaps to draw attention away from Marat, whose paper had recommended hanging a number of grocers over their own doorsteps, picked on Jacques Roux, the 'red priest' of the Gravilliers Section, which, as we saw, had been a starting-point of the disturbances, as the main instigator of the riots. Mathiez is inclined to share this view.[2] Roux had certainly demanded for some time that an upper limit be placed on the prices of all consumers' goods; but how far his influence spread beyond his own Section it is impossible to say; and anyway there is no real evidence that he played any direct part in this affair whatsoever.

The riots had no immediate results: a report of the Bureau de Surveillance de la Police of 27 February insisted that the price of sugar, coffee, oil, leather, soap, and suet remained at the same 'exorbitant' level as before;[3] but the Commune took the opportunity, on 4 March, to fix the price of the 4-lb. loaf at 12 *sous* and maintained it at this level, in spite of the increase in other consumers' goods and of wages, by subsidies to bakers.[4] Yet, as police reports for the coming weeks show, the authorities continued to fear and to expect, for some time to come, another outbreak of *taxation populaire*.[5]

But soon other issues crept in to stoke up the agitation. In mid-April there was a temporary shortage of bread: there was talk of a women's protest march to the Hôtel de Ville and the Convention; and a baker's shop in the rue Saint-Honoré was

---

[1] *Archives parlementaires* (1st series, 1789–1799, 80 vols., Paris, 1868–1914), lix. 272–4.   [2] Mathiez, op. cit., pp. 139–61.

[3] Arch. Nat., AF[IV] 1470.

[4] P. Caron, *Paris pendant la Terreur*, i. 9, n. 1. Henceforth, the price of bread ceased to be an issue until the winter of 1795 (see Chapter X below).

[5] Arch. Nat., AF[IV] 1470 (reports for 1, 4, 7, 18 March 1793).

invaded and most of its contents pillaged by angry women. In April and May there were reports that market-women and others were preparing for a new prison massacre; and, from this time on, Marat, the arch-advocate of speedy revolutionary justice, becomes the hero of the *menu peuple*. On 2 May a deputation of 10,000 unarmed citizens of the Faubourg Saint-Antoine paraded before the Convention and demanded that prices be controlled in the interests of the small consumers; and women from Versailles rioted in the Convention and refused to leave the building.[1] It was against this background that the Convention, with considerable reluctance, voted the first law of the Maximum which controlled the price of bread and flour throughout the country.[2]

And now, as so often in the past, the party contending for power began to turn this movement to its own advantage and to guide it into channels that accorded with its own political interests. The struggle between Gironde and Mountain had reached a point of open breach, and it is evident from the Girondin's attempt to incriminate Danton over the treachery of Dumouriez and their subsequent arrest of Marat and his summons before the Revolutionary Tribunal that, had the Mountain not struck when the occasion arose, they would themselves have fallen a victim to their opponents.

At first, however, it was not the Mountain or the Jacobin Club, but the extreme revolutionary group of Enragés, whose leaders were Jean Varlet and Jacques Roux, that did the running and tried to push the Paris Commune and Sections into a premature insurrection. Varlet's speeches on the Terrasse des Feuillants, within earshot of the Tuileries, drew great crowds of supporters; but the attempt made by Varlet's insurrectional Committee to stage a popular *journée* on 10 March with the object of settling accounts with the Girondin leaders, Roland and Brissot, and of introducing the death penalty for hoarders and speculators, proved still-born: the resolute opposition of the Jacobin Club, the Commune, and the Faubourg Saint-Antoine doomed it to failure.[3] Yet the Enragés continued to have a following and there was talk, for several weeks to come, of the

[1] Ibid. (reports for 15–16 April, 4 April, 14 May, 5–8 April, 2–3 May).
[2] *Archives parlementaires*, lxiv. 56–57.
[3] Lefebvre, op. cit., p. 340.

need for a popular insurrection to purge the Convention wholesale and to control the prices of all essentials.[1]

But the Mountain and Jacobin leaders were in no immediate
hurry. They had learned wisdom from past experience; while,
unlike their Girondin opponents, they were both willing and
able to use the popular movement to promote their political
ends, they had no intention of allowing its direction to pass into
other hands—either to the Enragés or to Hébert, the editor of
the *Père Duchesne*, whose influence was steadily increasing in the
Cordeliers Club and the Paris Commune. Besides, they feared
that a premature rising would entail too drastic a purge of the
Convention, whose Rump would be powerless to resist the
economic demands of the *sans-culottes*; that it would be accompanied by a new outbreak of prison massacres and leave
Paris isolated in the face of the combined hostility of the provinces.[2] So they proceeded with caution; but by early April they
were ready to formulate their programme, win the support of
the Sectional assemblies (in which they could count on a
majority), and wrest the leadership of the popular movement
from either group of 'extremists'. Accordingly, on 5 April, in the
Jacobin Club, Robespierre's younger brother, Augustin, publicly
invited the Sections to present themselves at the bar of the
Convention and 'nous forcer de mettre en arrestation les
députés infidèles'.[3] The response was immediate: three days
later, a deputation of the Bon Conseil Section called on the
Convention to bring to justice the best-known of the Girondin
leaders—Vergniaud, Guadet, Buzot, and others; and, on the
10th, the neighbouring Section of the Halle au Blé went one
better by naming twenty-two deputies,[4] whose removal from
the Assembly would both meet the popular demand for a
purge of a discredited Convention and assure the Mountain of
a working majority within it. This now became the slogan
around which the insurrection of May–June took shape. Already, by mid-April, thirty-five of the forty-eight Sections had
given their individual support; the Paris Commune endorsed
the demands and, on 19 May, invited the Sections to send commissioners to discuss their operation. It was from the assembly

---

[1] Arch. Nat., AF[IV] 1470 (reports of 11–16 March, 16 April).
[2] Lefebvre, op. cit., p. 333.
[3] Buchez et Roux, op. cit. xxv. 294.   [4] *Moniteur* (*réimpr.*), xvi. 100.

thus formed that eventually emerged the Central Revolutionary Committee which organized and directed the Parisian revolution of 31 May–2 June.[1] While it is easy enough to follow the course of these preparations in the Sectional assemblies, we have far less knowledge of of how the Parisian *menu peuple* reacted to these developments and what steps were taken by the organizers to draw them into active support. That this support was forthcoming seems likely enough. They were, as we have seen, alarmed at the level of food prices, and demands were already being voiced, sometimes with the Enragés as spokesmen, for the control of the price and supply of not only bread and flour, but of all essential consumers' goods. While the Mountain had shown no great enthusiasm for such a programme, the main opposition to it came, as all those who crowded the upper tribunes of the Assembly could see and hear for themselves, from the Gironde and its supporters in the Convention. Prices continued to rise, and police reports of April and May reflect the popular view that a purge of the Convention, as proposed by the Jacobins, might lead to more energetic measures to deal with hoarders and to ensure supplies.[2] At the same time there are indications that the Jacobins and their affiliates were using the clubs and popular societies to draw in support from the men and women of the *menu peuple.* Thus a police agent reports to the Minister of the Interior on 13 May that

Les femmes persévèrent dans le projet de demander la retraite des 22 députés . . . ; elles ont même l'espoir qu'elles seront secondées par les hommes;[3]

and, on 29 May, we hear that an ex-Jacobin bookbinder of the Panthéon district

trouve scandaleux que l'on veuille substituer aux bourgeois tous les ouvriers de l'église Sainte-Geneviève, qui se sont formés en clubs et se réunissent en dehors et après l'assemblée de la section.[4]

When it came to the point, the organizers of the Revolution found, as we shall see, a more practical expedient for ensuring

---

[1] For a scholarly, yet somewhat tendencious, account, see P. Sainte-Claire Deville, *La Commune de l'an II* (Paris, 1946), pp. 42–76.
[2] Arch. Nat., AF^{IV} 1470 (reports for April–May); F7 3688³, doss. 2.
[3] Ibid.
[4] A. Schmidt, *Tableaux de la Révolution française* (4 vols., Leipzig, 1867–71), i. 330.

that there should be no defection from the ranks of their armed supporters owing to anxiety over time lost from work; yet this was a last-minute measure and played no part at all in stimulating support before the event itself.

Meanwhile the insurrection developed more or less according to plan. The Central Revolutionary Committee had gone into permanent session on 29 May; the next night the Commune became officially represented on it, and Hanriot, a former customs clerk, was given the command of the National Guard. In addition it was decided to raise in the Sections a revolutionary militia of 20,000 *sans-culottes* to be paid at the rate of 40 *sous* per day spent under arms.[1] On the 31st the tocsin pealed at 3 a.m., and the *barrières* were closed—the certain prelude to great events. But it was a working day (Friday) and, as yet, few craftsmen and workers responded. Consequently, the Convention found itself under comparatively little external pressure and was able to win time and save its face by passing on the inevitable petition to its newly formed Committee of Public Safety for a report. The Central Revolutionary Committee, however, decided to force the pace: on Sunday, 2 June, they surrounded the Tuileries with loyal battalions of the National Guard, supported by additional detachments of *sans-culottes*. The deputies, after attempting an heroic sortie and finding every exit blocked, surrendered ignominiously to the insurgents' demands. Twenty-nine deputies and two ministers of the majority party were placed under house arrest.[2] There was nothing said, for the moment, about food prices, but the Mountain had achieved its immediate aims.

Like the capture of the Bastille and the siege of the Tuileries the expulsion of the Girondin deputies was a largely military operation, carried out by organized military formations. In such cases, of course, we cannot hope to obtain a picture of the insurgents from police records;[3] nor, in this case, are there lists

[1] Arch. Nat., BB³ 80, doss. 16.

[2] Lefebvre, op. cit., pp. 341–2; Sainte-Claire Deville, op. cit., pp. 77–97.

[3] The police were, however, on the look-out for women armed with knives or pistols who, it was suspected, were lying in wait to ambush unsuspecting deputies of the Right—encouraged, it was supposed, by the agitation that had been carried on by Claire Lacombe's Société des Femmes Révolutionnaires. So much appears from the cross-examination of two working women—one arrested on 31 May near the Jacobin Club, the other on 2 June outside the Tuileries (Arch. Préf. Pol., Aa 90, fols. 562–3; 138, fol. 476).

of either *vainqueurs* or of dead and wounded to guide us. We do, however, get a certain impression of both the numbers and composition of the forces specially enrolled and armed by the ·Sections for the occasion from the often heated correspondence of the Sections with the Committee of Public Safety of the Paris Department;[1] this relates to the claims made for compensation on behalf of those who had lost work by taking up arms. We learn, for example, that, of thirty-one Sections putting in for a total claim of 114,291 *livres*,[2] and of another two Sections separately listed,[3] the following were able to muster the largest contingents of *sans-culottes*:

Montreuil .	. 2,946	Montmartre	. 1,438
Quinze Vingts	. 2,039	Bon Conseil	. 1,400
Croix Rouge	. 1,458	Invalides .	. 1,358
Gravilliers .	. 1,457	Popincourt	. 970

In fact once again the Faubourg Saint-Antoine is in the lead with nearly 6,000 applicants out of a total of a little over 22,000; while the Faubourg Saint-Marcel—with 907 claimants from the Observatoire and 660 from Finistère—seems to have played a smaller part. Yet the point must not be pressed too far: there are considerable gaps in the figures;[4] and, while they are a rough guide to the number of *sans-culottes* enrolled by the Sections making claims, we have no means of knowing what proportion they formed of the total numbers under arms.

But, while we may be reasonably certain that the numbers here listed are of *sans-culottes*—though not necessarily as members

[1] This was the new name given to the former Central Revolutionary Committee, purged of Varlet and his associates, after the uprising.
[2] Arch. Nat., BB³ 80, doss. 7.
[3] The Bon Conseil Section claimed, in a separate note, to have had 1,400 men under arms on 2 June (Arch. Nat., BB³ 80, doss. 11); while Bonne Nouvelle, which had requisitioned on behalf of its 'frères d'armes' 490 4-lb. loaves from 11 bakers on 1 June and 213 loaves from 4 bakers on 2 June (Arch. Préf. Pol., Aa 77, fol. 45), insisted that it had returned a list which the Committee had, presumably, lost (Arch. Nat., BB 80, doss. 7). Montreuil had gone one better in the provision of food for its 'volontaires indigents': on 2 June, we find them raising 56 4-lb. loaves, 44½ lb. of sausage, 30 lb. of cheese, &c., to a total value of 542 *livres*, 8 *sous* (Arch. Préf. Pol., Aa 173, fols. 92–93).
[4] Thus, apart from the 15 Sections sending no returns at all, the Panthéon Section gives a return for only 20 out of 33 companies and Muséum admits to having sent in only a partial return (Arch. Nat., F⁷* 2520, fols. 52, 54; BB³ 80, doss. 7).

of separate *sans-culottes* formations—it is not possible to distinguish masters from journeymen or the wage-earners and city poor from the shopkeepers and independent craftsmen. In a few cases, it is true, the distinction appears: among thirteen applicants listed by the Pont Neuf Section, among craftsmen and shopkeepers we find a tobacco-worker and a shop assistant; and we read of a farmer of the 5th company of the Invalides Section (an unusual occupation for a Parisian!) arranging a rota of attendances under arms for himself and his two farm-hands.[1] Again, in the military force mustered by the Unité Section, at least, there must have been a fair number of journeymen, as it was decided at dawn on 31 May to close every workshop and to order 'tous les ouvriers' to report to their respective companies; but this, of course, included small employers as well as workpeople.[2]

Yet Henri Calvet has thought it possible to show from these figures the proportion of proletarians among the armed citizens of the various Sections.[3] His argument is based on the assumption that the applicants for compensation for work lost were necessarily needy and, therefore, proletarians. Undoubtedly the Central Revolutionary Committee, in putting the scheme before the Convention, had intended that the 40 *sous* a day should be paid only to those whose attendance would otherwise entail hardship;[4] and the Commune, in asking the newly formed Revolutionary Committees of the Sections to draw up lists, stressed that they should be only of such as were in need of assistance.[5] Yet, while some Sections acted strictly according to the letter of these instructions,[6] others—for a variety of reasons—decided to do otherwise; and we find them returning not only *volontaires indigents, citoyens peu aisés,* or *citoyens journaliers,* but shopkeepers and employers—including farmer Guerre of

---

[1] The farmer made one attendance himself and fixed up a total of four attendances for his two labourers (ibid.).

[2] Arch. Nat., F7* 2507, fol. 22.

[3] H. Calvet, 'La Participation des sections au mouvement du 31 mai–1er–2 juin 1793', *Ann. hist. Rév. franç.* v (1928), 366–9.

[4] 'Que tous les ouvriers qui n'ont pas le moyen de faire à la république le sacrifice de leurs jours recevront 40s. par jour', &c. (Arch. Nat., BB3 80, doss. 16).

[5] 'Faites une liste de tous ceux qui sont sous les armes et qui peuvent avoir besoin de secours' (Arch. Nat., F7* 2517, fol. 14).

[6] Cf. returns of Halle au Blé, Montreuil, Droits de l'Homme Sections (Arch. Nat., BB3 80, doss. 5, 7; F7* 2497, fol. 29).

the Invalides Section!—and even whole companies without discrimination.[1]
Meanwhile the problems of food and prices remained. The revolution of May–June had done nothing to solve them and the upward movement of prices and downward spiral of the *assignat* went on as before. The *assignat*, having fallen to 36 per cent. of its nominal value in June, slumped further to 22 per cent. in August.[2] While the wages of skilled journeymen may have doubled since the early days of the Revolution, the prices of food and other essentials tended to outstrip them—at a pace that became increasingly precipitous between June and September, as the following comparative figures will show:

Commodity	June 1790	June 1793	September 1793
Wine (litre) . .	10 s.	16 s.	20 s.
Meat (lb.) . .	12 s.	19 s.	20 s.
Butter (lb.) . .	14 s.	26½ s.	35 s.
Eggs (25) . . .	21 s.	27½ s.	50 s.
Sugar (lb.) . .	24 s.	100 s.	110 s.
Coffee (lb.) . .	34 s.	80 s.	90–100 s.
Tallow candles (lb.) .	15 s.	40 s.	44 s.
Soap (lb.) . .	12 s.	23–28 s.	70 s.[3]

What these figures do not reveal are the sudden fluctuations in price that roused sudden spontaneous outbursts of anger. A bare week after the June revolution there was further talk of a general assault on grocers and butchers. A few days later queues began to form again at bakers' shops; and even police agents spoke of the need to curb the greed of the wealthy shop-keepers and wholesalers: 'on sait que cette classe en masse est la seule qui ait profité de la Révolution'.[4] There were soap riots between 25 and 28 June: in one such incident, on the 25th, a crowd in the rue Saint-Lazare held up a lorry loaded with ten crates of soap and sold its contents in the street at 20 *sous*

---

[1] Cf. returns of Panthéon, Pont Neuf, and Muséum Sections (Arch. Nat., F7* 2520, fols. 52, 54; BB³ 80, doss. 7). According to the latter: 'que tous avaient besoin et qu'aucun ne voulait en recevoir si tous ne participaient à ces secours.'
[2] Harris, op. cit., pp. 166–76.
[3] G. Rudé, 'Prices, Wages and Popular Movements in Paris during the French Revolution', *Econ. Hist. Rev.*, vol. vi, no. 3, 1954, pp. 254–7. With bread, of course, the issue was one of shortage and not of price.
[4] Arch. Nat., AF[IV] 1470 (reports for 7–10, 14, 16–17, 25, 27–29 June).

a pound, while the police stood by, powerless to intervene.[1] The same day, Jacques Roux was howled down in the Convention for accompanying a petition which he was presenting on behalf of the Cordeliers Club with attacks on the Mountain for failing to feed the poor. The shortage of bread continued, after a lull in July, during August and September: among various persons arrested in the course of these months for disorderly behaviour we find several wage-earners and small shopkeepers taken into custody for abusing the National Guard or for creating disturbances in bakers' shops.[2]

There followed the 'insurrection' of 4 and 5 September, which the Paris Commune took under its wing to further its own political plans.[3] It began at 5 o'clock in the morning in the Temple and Saint-Avoie districts, north of the Hôtel de Ville, where workers were fetched out from workshops and building sites. Meanwhile another demonstration seems to have started on the boulevards, near the Ministry of War, where Vincent, one of Hébert's lieutenants, had his offices. Calling for bread, the demonstrators advanced on the Place de Grève.[4] The Commune's leaders, Hébert and Chaumette, tried at first to fob them off with a display of oratory; but it was agreed, on Hébert's suggestion, that they should reassemble the next morning at 11 o'clock in order to march to the Convention to demand severe measures against hoarders and political suspects; the Jacobins also promised to join in. The same evening the Commune ordered workshops to close on the morrow, so that masters and journeymen might attend the demonstration. But, in case we should therefore be tempted to consider, with Daniel Guérin, that the 'insurrection' of 4 September was a largely working-class affair,[5] we should note that, at the same session, the Commune gave instructions that a military force should be mustered to disperse building workers who were demonstrating for bread and higher wages![6]

---

[1] Arch. Préf. Pol., Aa 226, fols. 329–30. See also Mathiez, op. cit., pp. 226–7.
[2] Arch. Préf. Pol., Ab 327 (registre de la Force), pp. 367–75.
[3] Mathiez, op. cit., pp. 322 ff.; E. Soreau, 'Les Ouvriers aux journées des 4 et 5 septembre 1793', Ann. hist. Rév. franç. xiv (1937), 436–47.
[4] There were various arrests at bakers' shops during the day (Arch. Préf. Pol., Aa 39, fol. 134; 139, fol. 96; 208, fol. 143).
[5] D. Guérin, La Lutte de classes sous la 1ᵉ République (2 vols., Paris, 1946), i. 130.
[6] Moniteur (réimpr.), xvii. 577–8.

In the flood of rhetoric that accompanied the demonstration on the 5th the questions of prices and supplies, though they had been the prime movers in the early agitation on the 4th, were once more conveniently forgotten. Yet important decisions were taken: Sections were to meet only twice a week, but needy *sans-culottes* were to be compensated with 40 *sous* per attendance; suspects were to be rounded up; and the long-delayed *armée révolutionnaire* was set on foot, which, as an instrument of the Terror, was to ensure the adequate provision of supplies of grain and meat to Paris from the neighbouring countryside. Yet the immediate problem remained and the crisis and agitation continued unabated.[1] At last, having tried or debated every other expedient, the Convention yielded to popular pressure and, on 29 September, passed the famous law of the Maximum Général, which put a limit on the prices of a large range of essential goods and services, including labour.[2]

The new problems thus created were of the future. For the moment shopkeepers, masters, and journeymen welcomed the Maximum, their own creation, with enthusiasm. 'Le peuple', wrote an agent of the Ministry of the Interior, 'a reçu avec transport les décrets de la Conv. Nat° sur la taxe des denrées de première nécessité.'[3] It seemed to augur well for the alliance of Jacobins and *sans-culottes* which, in Paris at least, was the foundation on which emerged the Revolutionary Government of the Year II.

[1] See National Guard and police agents' reports for September: Arch. Nat., AF^{IV} 1470; F^7 3688^3, doss. 1; Caron, op. cit. i. 56–210.
[2] *Moniteur (réimpr.)*, xvii. 775–6.   [3] Caron, op. cit. i. 210.

IX

THERMIDOR

ROBESPIERRE had joined the Committee of Public Safety on 26 July 1793, just a year before his downfall. Saint-Just and Couthon, who were to become his closest associates, were already members of the Committee; and, after the 'insurrection' of 4–5 September, they were joined by two leading members of the Cordeliers Club, Billaud-Varenne and Collot d'Herbois.[1] These men were to form the central core of the Revolutionary Government of the Year II, which ruled the country during the most critical year of the Revolution, arrested the disastrous course of inflation, fed and supplied the armies, and saved France from invasion and defeat. So much has been conceded by even the most hostile of their critics.

Here we are not concerned with the general history of this government or even with the general causes of its dissolution in Thermidor (27–28 July) of the Year II—but rather with its loss of support among the Parisian *sans-culottes* and their defection from the side of its leading members on the eve of their downfall.[2] It is realized, of course, that to approach the question in this way is to reverse the process that has been followed up to this point, which has been to trace the development of the human and material factors making for a revolutionary situation, to present the revolutionary crowd in action and to analyse its composition. Here, on the other hand, it is proposed to examine the causes of the abstention, rather than of the participation, of the persons most concerned. Yet this may be justified in the present instance by the fact that Robespierre's overthrow was the result rather of the defection of his former allies than of the revolutionary action of his opponents, if we except a small handful who planned the operation from on top.

The essential question facing us is, then, how was the alliance between Jacobins and *sans-culottes* gradually undermined and

[1] The other members of the 'great' Committee of Public Safety were Barère, Carnot, Robert Lindet, Jeanbon Saint-André, Prieur de la Côte d'Or, and Prieur de la Marne.

[2] For the most detailed, recent and thoroughly documented study of the whole question, the reader is referred to Albert Soboul's work, *Les Sans-Culottes parisiens en l'an II* (see p. 8, notes 4–5, above).

how was this reflected in the dramatic events of 9th–10th
Thermidor?

In the first place, there can be little doubt of the government's vigour and of the confidence and support that its actions
at first aroused among the Parisian *menu peuple* and their militants in the clubs and Sectional committees. Mention has
already been made of the enthusiasm that the mere enactment
of the law of the Maximum evoked among them. The law of
29 September, supplemented by an amending law of 1 November, provided for the increase of prices at the point of production
by one-third over June 1790, plus a rate per league for trans-
portation, plus 5 per cent. for the wholesaler and 10 per cent.
for the retailer. The law affected thirty-nine commodities of
general consumption, but excluded firewood, fish, tobacco,
salt, milk, and poultry. In the case of wages it provided for an
increase of 50 per cent. over rates prevailing in June 1790.[1] An
inquiry conducted in June 1793 had revealed that, taking the
country as a whole, the prices of essential commodities had
doubled, or even trebled since 1790; and that, over the same
period, allowing for wide divergences between districts and
types of work done, wages may have risen, on a broad average,
by 100–150 per cent.[2] With the June inquiry as a basis the
Districts were now instructed to prepare lists of maximum
prices and wages in accordance with the provisions of the law
of 29 September—which meant, of course, that eventually,
when these operations were completed, the existing level of
both prices and wages should be drastically reduced.

It is evident that such a law, enacted in a country depending
on the output of thousands of petty producers and confided, for
its execution, to a government and to officials who believed
basically in the sanctity of private property, would be impossible of operation. Yet, whatever its faults as a piece of social
legislation and whatever its ultimate economic and political

[1] H. E. Bourne, 'Maximum Prices in France, 1793–1794', *American Historical
Review*, xxiii (1917), 107–13; and (by the same author) 'Food Control and Price-
fixing in Revolutionary France', *The Journal of Political Economy*, xxvii (1919),
73–94, 188–209.
[2] *Enquête de juin 1793*. Arch. Nat., F¹² 1547ᶜ, doss. 2. The report comprises
returns from 48 Departments only, covering the prices of 38 articles of consumption and wages in about 15 trades, including those of daily labourers (except in
the case of Paris).

results, it is undoubted that the enactment of the Maximum Général had important immediate consequences that both served to arrest inflation and to strengthen the government's ties with the *sans-culottes*. Taken by itself the law might not act as any great deterrent to hoarding and speculation; but introduced as it was with a host of other measures to strengthen the organs of government, to protect the currency, and to enforce compliance with the law by means of terror, it helped— for a period at least—to stabilize prices and to ensure the provision of adequate supplies to feed both the army and the civilian population. This fact is most graphically illustrated by the sudden reversal in the movement of the *assignat* during the first three months after the law was passed: from 22 per cent. of its nominal value in August 1793, it rose to 33 per cent. in November and to 48 per cent. in December.[1] During these weeks the confidence of the people in the government appears to be based on the double hope that its policy will ensure the supply of cheap and adequate food to feed the citizens and of military victories over the Republic's enemies; so we read in a police agent's report of 30 September:

> Les ouvriers qui se trouvent en grand nombre à la maison commune sur la place, à l'heure des repas, se réjouissent de la diminution des denrées, de l'ardeur de la jeunesse en réquisition, et particulièrement du prochain triomphe de la République.[2]

And, even in late December—when meat, groceries, and vegetables had long been in short supply and rationing cards had been introduced to meet a temporary lack of bread—we are told of the market women's enthusiasm for Robespierre, the Mountain (*la Sainte Montagne*), and the legislators of the Republic: 'Les femmes de la halle sont d'une gaîté charmante: elles chantent les louanges de la Convention.'[3] This loyalty may have survived the longer because, during this period, for the first time, it was the *sans-culottes* themselves who formed the backbone of the Paris administration: their militants dominated the majority of Sectional assemblies and committees—particularly the all-important Revolutionary Committees—and the general assembly and executive of the Commune. Albert

---

[1] Harris, *The Assignats*, pp. 176–85.
[2] Caron, *Paris pendant la Terreur*, i. 241. For similar expressions see also pp. 168, 197.   [3] Ibid. ii. 14.

Soboul has found that, of 454 members of Revolutionary Committees holding office in Paris in the course of the Year II, 9·9
per cent. were wage-earners, 63·8 per cent were shopkeepers,
small workshop masters, and independent craftsmen, while
only 26·3 per cent. were rentiers, manufacturers, civil servants,
and members of the liberal professions.[1] Similarly, Sainte-
Claire Deville has shown that, of 132 General Councillors of
the Commune, holding office between July 1793 and July
1794, and whose occupations are listed, 82 were small manufacturers, craftsmen, and tradesmen; 2 were manual workers
and 9 'blackcoated' workers; while 8 were merchants and contractors, and 31 belonged to the professions.[2] This was, of
course, not just a fortuitous distribution of public servants,
thrown up by the tide of revolution; we shall see in the next
chapter what Robespierre's successors did after Thermidor to
redress the social balance.

Meanwhile the Government's inability to operate the law of
the Maximum in its existing form was proving evident. Even
in Paris, where the Revolutionary Committeees and commissaires aux accaparements were vigilant and strongly backed by
public opinion, breaches of the law by merchants and shopkeepers were becoming daily more blatant. But the real problem
lay elsewhere. The growers, producers, and middlemen who
kept the capital supplied were in a more favourable position to
avoid detection and, finding the margins provided by the law ·
little to their liking, they tended to withhold supplies while
waiting for better times, to sell on the 'black market', or to
enter into illicit deals with retailers or merchants. Consequently the Paris grocers and butchers, having paid their
suppliers above the Maximum, passed the burden back to the
consumer: thus, from December until April, when meat was
rationed, butchers regularly sold at 25–50 per cent. above the
lawful price;[3] while pork butchers, to evade the law, sold only
cooked pork (the price of raw meat alone was controlled).
Meanwhile, an army of mercandiers and revendeurs invaded the

[1] A. Soboul, 'Une Discussion historique du féodalisme au capitalisme', La
Pensée, no. 65 (1956), pp. 28–9.
[2] Sainte-Claire Deville, La Commune de l'an II, pp. 361–79. On the Executive
Council of 48 (Corps Municipal), there were 25 small manufacturers and tradesmen;
4 'black-coated' workers; 4 merchants and businessmen; and 12 members of liberal
professions.   [3] Caron, op. cit. ii. 178, 229, 251, 299, 330; iii. 30; iv. 11.

back streets and markets, selling sugar, butter, and poor cuts of meat above the controlled price;[1] and, in December and January, agents of the Ministry of the Interior reported that butter was being sold in Paris markets at 36–44 *sous* per lb. (controlled price: 22 *sous*) and eggs at 80–100 *sous* for 25 (compared with 21 *sous* in June 1790, 27½ *sous* in June 1793, and 50 *sous* in September).[2] The *sans-culottes*, while complaining bitterly at this evasion of the law at their expense, were inclined to see the merchants and the shopkeepers rather than the Government as the villains of the piece, and called upon the authorities insistently to remedy the abuses by a more continuous and effective use of the organs of repression. It was, in fact, impossible to leave things as they were: either the Government must seek to enforce the existing law by intensifying the Terror, or it must try to win the more wholehearted co-operation of peasants and producers by relaxing the regulations and increasing the margins of profit. It decided on the second course. 'Il fallait guérir le commerce', said Barère, 'et non le tuer.'[3] But it meant losing friends and allies elsewhere. Hébert and his associates, the champions of domiciliary visits and sterner revolutionary justice, who had dominated the Commune since the spring of 1793, were executed on 22 March; a little later the *armée révolutionnaire* was disbanded together with the local popular societies and committees for tracking down hoarders. The currency speculators had already begun to emerge from their hiding-places in late December,[4] and the *assignat* was allowed to slip back again: by July it had fallen to 36 per cent. of its value.[5] Finally, in late March, an amended Maximum was published, which provided for higher prices and profit margins and which, wrote a police agent, seemed to 'favour the merchants and not the people'.[6]

But, some time before this, the *sans-culottes* had begun to pass to more direct forms of protest and, on occasion, to turn their anger against the Government itself. On 20 February, in the crowded popular market of the Place Maubert, a woman encountered no opposition from her hearers when she an-

---

[1] Bourne, op. cit., pp. 206–7 (based on the reports of police agents, Grivel and Siret).   [2] Caron, op. cit. i. 344; ii. 20, 26–27, 102, 185, 251, 310.
[3] *Moniteur (réimpr.)*, xix. 631.   [4] Caron, op. cit. ii. 61, 194, 281.
[5] Harris, loc. cit.
[6] Arch. Nat., F¹ᶜ III Seine 13 (report of 29 March 1794).

nounced: 'Si je ne me retenais, j'enverrais faire foutre le nouveau régime.' The next day, in the same market, butter was seized from a merchant by angry women, and others, assembled in the Halles, held up five cartloads of eggs and butter and com-pelled the drivers to sell the butter at 22 *sous* a pound and eggs at 24 *sous* for 25.[1] The trial and execution of Hébert and his followers aroused confusion and apathy, rather than anger, among the *sans-culottes*: the Père Duchesne, though not loved like Marat, had been a familiar mouthpiece for popular passions and prejudices and his removal snapped the link that bound them to the Paris Commune. 'Qu'allons-nous devenir', women were heard to ask in La Courtille, 'puisque nous sommes trahis par des gens en qui nous avions la plus grande confiance?' 'Le peuple', wrote a police observer, 'ne veut plus se fier à personne'; and, a week later, after Hébert's execution: 'dans les cafés . . . on remarque que ceux qui parlaient beaucoup ne disent plus rien'.[2]

Meanwhile the agitation in the markets continued. On 17 March women rioted over the allocation of eggs and butter in a grocer's shop in the Observatoire Section. On the 19th an unemployed labourer was arrested near the Hôtel de Ville for threatening a grocer and shouting: 'Nous avons une belle liberté, qu'elle était faite pour les riches, et qu'on ne faisait la guerre qu'aux pauvres.' A few days later a laundress was arrested for creating a disturbance at a butcher's in the rue Saint-Paul: she had not been able, she said, to buy eggs or butter for several days. On the 28th an arms worker from an *atelier d'armes* near the Invalides complained to his comrades that, even with higher wages, they were worse off than before: 'avec son argent on ne peut rien avoir'. Two other arms workers were arrested, a fortnight later, in the Arcis Section: one was supposed to have said, 'qu'il fallait que les ouvriers vivent comme les autres', and was sent to prison.[3] And, even more indicative of changing moods, a month later, laundresses of the Faubourg Saint-Marcel, once stalwart allies of the Jacobins, sent General Hanriot, commander-in-chief of the National

---

[1] Caron, op. cit. iv. 237, 263-4.   [2] Schmidt, op. cit. ii. 157, 173, 193.
[3] Arch. Préf. Pol., Aa 198, fol. 260; 139, fol. 410; 70, fols. 418, 439-41; D. Guérin, op. cit. ii. 160. Further examples are to be found in Arch. Préf. Pol., Aa 94 (Butte des Moulins = Palais Royal), 139 (Fidélité = Hôtel de Ville), 201 (Panthéon), 240 (Temple).

Guard, a threatening letter, in which, among other epithets, he is indelicately apostrophized as a 'jean foutre' and a 'foutu satelite de Robespierre'.[1]

But meanwhile an even more serious situation had developed in the workshops. This was, in fact, one of the few periods in the history of the Revolution when the wage-earners showed even more concern for the amount of their wages than for the prices of foodstuffs, and when strikes and deputations about wages were a more frequent and more significant form of social protest than food riots.[2] Even so it does not mark a new stage in the relations between capital and labour as Daniel Guérin would have us believe;[3] it arose rather from a quite peculiar set of circumstances that would not be repeated. As we have seen, the law of the Maximum Général had provided for a reduction in the prevailing rates of wages as well of prices; and the Districts were to take the initiative in drawing up new lists—except in the case of the recently established government workshops for the manufacture of arms, and of Districts in which the government's *représentants en mission* enjoyed unlimited powers, overriding those of the local authorities. The result was a patchwork of widely different schemes, in which the operation, or non-operation, of the *maximum des salaires* varied with the social composition of the authority, the resistance of the local *sans-culottes* to any reductions in existing rates, and the interference of the government or its agents. In Paris the problem was merely twofold: in the case of the workshops for the manufacture of arms the decision rested with the Committee of Public Safety; in that of private industry with the Paris Commune. The government, not being handicapped by the rival pressures of employers and workers, applied the law to the armsworkers without delay: in October and December skilled men in a number of new workshops were awarded 5 *livres* a day, unskilled men 3 *livres*; this became the usual pattern. Meanwhile a severe disciplinary code was introduced and already, in December, we read of penalties being imposed on 'agitators' in a couple of workshops.[4] The main trouble was to come later, as we shall see.

[1] Arch. Nat., AF[II] 47, plaq. 368, fol. 37.
[2] See pages 21–22 above.   [3] Guérin, op. cit. ii. 155.
[4] See A. Aulard, *Recueil des actes du Comité de Salut public* (26 vols., Paris, 1889–1923), vi. 486; ix. 322, 400, 515, 696, 751; C. Richard, *Le Comité de Salut public et les fabrications de guerre sous la Terreur* (Paris, 1922), pp. 699–709.

The 'Hébertists' were still in control of the Commune and as long as they remained so there appeared to be no intention of drawing up a table of maximum wages in accordance with the law of 29 September.[1] It was a period of labour shortage and rising wages; and the report drawn up in January by two government agents, Grivel and Siret, in which they claimed that wages had trebled or quadrupled since 1790, may not be greatly exaggerated:

Tel ouvrier, tel commissionnaire, qui ne tirait de sa journée que 4 ou 5 livres, en tire aujourd'hui 20 et 24 livres et quelquefois davantage.[2]

We find bakers refusing to accept a wage of 15 *livres* a week (including board), where they had lately been earning 8 *livres*; the Paris Department itself, as late as March, introduced new scales for building workers well above double those paid in 1790; and even in the arms workshops, in spite of government intentions, we hear of workers earning two, three, or four times their wages in 1790.[3]

But Hébert and his friends were eliminated in March; and, once they were out of the way, the authorities merely bided their time before putting into operation that part of the law of September 1793 which placed a limit on wages. Meanwhile they took energetic measures to prevent any further increases. When a delegation of tobacco-workers presented itself at the Hôtel de Ville in April, Payan, the national agent of the reconstituted Robespierrist Commune, invoked the Loi Le Chapelier, forbidding associations of workpeople, and referred the matter to the police, who made five arrests. Other strikes and wage-claims followed involving plasterers, bakers, pork-butchers, and port-workers. Besides making further arrests, the Commune threatened to prosecute

[ceux] qui, au mépris des lois, abandonnaient des travaux qui doivent leur être d'autant plus chers qu'ils sont nécessaires à l'existence publique.[4]

[1] See G. Rudé and A. Soboul, 'Le Maximum des salaires parisiens et le 9 thermidor', *Ann. hist. Rév. franç.*, no. 134, 1954, pp. 1–22.
[2] It goes on: 'Ils [les journaliers] n'ont pas honte d'exiger 100 sols pour un léger travail qui eût été payé très généreusement 10 sols, il y a un an' (quoted by Mathiez, op. cit., pp. 586–7). See also Caron, op. cit. ii. 7.
[3] R. Marion, 'Les Lois de maximum et la taxation des salaires sous la Révolution', *Revue internationale de sociologie*, xxv (1917), 487. Marion exaggerates the unwillingness of the Jacobins to apply the Maximum to wages.
[4] Rudé and Soboul, op. cit., pp. 10–12; Mathiez, op. cit., p. 591.

A month's lull followed—possibly due to the efficacy of these threats or to the temporary diversion caused by an attempt to assassinate Robespierre and Collot d'Herbois. But in June the movement started up again and was not to subside until after Thermidor. This time it began with the arms workers, who had kept fairly quiet since December. Alleged ringleaders were arrested in a number of workshops, including both those agitating for higher wages on the spot and others who had left their shops in search of better pay and less restrictive conditions elsewhere.[1] The movement appears to have spread to other branches of government employment, as we find Barère instructing the public prosecutor of the Revolutionary Tribunal, in the name of the Committee, to take proceedings against what he termed

les contre-révolutionnaires qui ont employé des manœuvres criminelles dans les ateliers de fabrication d'assignats, d'armes, de poudres et salpêtres.[2]

Other trades joined in; and in June and July we read of building workers, potters, and workers engaged on a variety of public contracts pressing their claims for higher wages; and on 7 July even the Committee's own printing workers struck work, leading to the arrest of three of their comrades.

While this excitement was still going on, the Paris Commune decided at long last, on 23 July, to publish the new rates of wages to operate in the capital. This disastrous document followed the provisions of the original law of the Maximum Général to the letter, took no account of recent increases in either wages or food prices, and faced the great majority of the working population with substantial reductions, sometimes amounting to one-half or more of their existing earnings.[3]

Such a provocative measure was hardly calculated to make for social peace or to bind the workers more closely to the administration at a time of deep political crisis. After committing this imprudence, the Commune seems to have realized the need to take preventive action in case of further disturbances: on the 25th Hanriot was warned that several arms workers, 'doubtless led astray by the enemies of the people', had left their

---

[1] Richard, op. cit., pp. 709–27.   [2] *Moniteur* (*réimpr.*), xx. 699.
[3] Thus a carpenter earning 8 *livres* would be reduced to 3 *livres*, 15 *sous*; and the highest-paid blacksmith or fitter in the arms workshops would be reduced from 16 *livres*, 10 *sous* to 5 *livres*, 5 *sous*(Rudé and Soboul, op. cit., pp. 16–17).

workshops; and the mayor, Fleuriot-Lescot, on the morning of 9 Thermidor (27 July), obviously unaware of the drama that was already unfolding inside the government Committees and in the lobbies of the Convention, ordered a military force to keep the workers in check on the following day, which was a public holiday.[1]

Meanwhile the political crisis had come to a head. Since the Republic's victory at Fleurus (26 June), the main body of the Convention, whose members sat silent on the benches of the Plain', had shown less inclination to continue their support for a government whose watchwords still appeared to them to be Terror and tightened belts, and the conflicts of principle and personality within and between the two principal Committees —that of Public Safety and of General Security—had broken into the open.[2] In the early afternoon of 9 Thermidor Robespierre was refused a hearing in the Convention, and his arrest was ordered together with that of his principal associates. As the news spread around the capital, a prolonged and involved tussle ensued for the loyalties of the Paris Sections and *sans-culottes* and, above all, for the control of the Parisian armed forces, which nominally still remained largely under the orders of the Commune and its commander-in-chief, Hanriot.[3]

Despite this considerable initial advantage the Commune was, as is known, defeated. And yet this was to all intents and purposes the same armed force with the same commander at its head which, in June 1793, had compelled the Convention to submit to its will; this time it was to abandon the Commune and the Jacobin leaders and rally to their enemies after a few hours of indecision by a minority of its units. When every allowance is made for the bungling of Hanriot and the refusal or inability of Robespierre and Saint-Just to lead a popular revolt against a hostile majority in the Assembly, and for all the chances and mischances in a tangled series of events, the essential fact remains that they had lost the support of the Parisian *sans-culottes*.

[1] Arch. Nat., AF[II] 47, plaq. 368, fol. 38; AF[II] 48, plaq. 374, fol. 10.
[2] See A. Ording, *Le Bureau de police du Comité de Salut public* (Oslo, 1930); A. Mathiez, *Autour de Robespierre* (Paris, 1926), pp. 149 ff.; and, for the part played in this crisis by the Parisian Sections and *sans-culottes*, A. Soboul, *Les Sans-Culottes parisiens de l'an II*, pp. 917 ff.
[3] For the most detailed factual account of the events of 9–10 Thermidor see Sainte-Claire Deville, op. cit., pp. 189–314.

The militants in the Sections had every chance to make up their minds on the important issue presented to them by the two contending parties which, throughout the afternoon and evening, sent mutually conflicting orders, threats, and declarations, appealing to their loyalties: should they rally to the side of 'les patriotes opprimés' or should they reject and abandon them to their fate as men condemned, and finally outlawed, by the lawfully constituted National Convention? The Commune had some early successes: seventeen of the thirty companies of *canonniers* (forming part of the Paris National Guard) remaining in the capital obeyed the call to parade in the Place de Grève; they included two companies from the Faubourg Saint-Antoine, two from the markets, and two from the Bonnet Rouge and Luxembourg Sections on the Left Bank. In addition another dozen Sections sent battalions of fusiliers and pikemen, including a strong force of 1,200 from the Panthéon Section in the Faubourg Saint-Marcel. At one time there were over 3,000 armed men drawn up outside the Hôtel de Ville. But they lacked both direction and purpose; and, as the debate went on in the Sectional committees and assemblies, the whole of this force, left largely idle and unattended, gradually melted away: at 1.30 in the morning of 10 Thermidor, 200 men of the Finistère Section, the last armed support of Robespierre and his associates, marched silently back to the Faubourg Saint-Marcel.[1]

More significant still was the lack of response from the civil authorities in the Sections. That the traditionally *bourgeois* Sections of the west—Tuileries, Champs Elysées, République (Roule), Louvre, Révolutionnaire (Pont Neuf), and even Piques (Robespierre's own Section)—should have quickly declared for the Convention is hardly surprising; but early supporters of the Assembly also included such radical Sections as the Quinze Vingts, Unité, and Maison Commune, as well. Sainte-Claire Deville, who made a detailed study of the actions and affiliations of every local assembly and committee on that day, found that less than one-fifth of all the civil authorities in the capital showed any inclination, however half-hearted, to rally to the side of the Commune: these included twelve Revolutionary Committees, among which that of the Finistère showed the most eager response. Finally—and most conclusive

[1] Sainte-Claire Deville, op. cit., pp. 201-14.

evidence of all—during the night thirty-nine of the Sections
were in permanent session, debating and receiving reports. Of
these, thirty-five declared unequivocally for the Convention;
two others—Sans-Culottes (Hanriot's Section) and Finistère—
hesitated at first, but rallied later; only two—the Observatoire
and Châlier (Cluny) Sections of the Faubourg Saint-Marcel—
showed clearly their sympathies for the Robespierrists; yet,
under the weight of opposing opinion and seeing that the game
was lost, they too surrendered to the majority before the night
was out.[1]

The reports of these proceedings were, in the great majority
of cases, written after the event—at a time when the victors of
Thermidor were already seated firmly in the saddle. The
opinions of the minority who favoured the Commune were
therefore rarely recorded; but here and there we find among
them the voice of a *sans-culotte*, who was not so easily to be
swayed from his past loyalties. In the general assembly of the
Quatre Nations Section, for example, we read of a citizen who
insisted in the face of hostile interruption that a letter from
Hanriot should be read, instead of being ignored as the emana-
tion of 'la Commune conspiratrice'. When challenged to give
his name, he stoutly replies: 'Je me nomme Lanbriné, demeu-
rant rue du Sépulcre, compagnon [*journeyman*] de Graseau.'[2]
Again, we read of Charles Joly, wallpaper worker and corporal
of the Réunion (Beaubourg) Section, who tore up the papers of a
woman newsvendor which announced the arrest of Hanriot; he
was arrested as an accomplice of the Commune and kept in
prison till the following December.[3] But these are but isolated
cases; once the tide had begun to turn, Robespierre's vocal
defenders on that day were but a small and ineffectual body,
whose opinions were quickly submerged in the growing flood
of anti-Jacobin reaction.

More evident still was the particular hostility of the wage-
earners, who had been incensed by the recent publication of the
maximum des salaires by the Robespierrist Commune. Presumably

[1] Ibid., pp. 273–8.   [2] Arch. Préf. Pol., Aa 266, fol. 242.
[3] Arch. Préf. Pol., Aa 163, fol. 293. There is also the rather confused account of
Pierre Rose, gunpowder worker of the Homme Armé (Marais) Section, who was
locked up for reporting to his neighbours what he had heard in the Place de
Grève that night—that anyone publicly announcing the outlawry of Robespierre
and others would be arrested by the Commune (Arch. Préf. Pol., Ab 356, fol. 2).

ignorant of the political struggle that had just broken into the open, workers gathered for a protest meeting in the Place de Grève on 4 o'clock that afternoon: it must have made an impression, as it is recorded in the minutes of five Civil Committees of neighbouring Sections. It must also have been somewhat confusing to observers to see the demonstrators converging on the square almost at the same time as the first military formations were beginning to appear in response to the Commune's summons; so we find in these reports such varying interpretations of the workers' meeting as that it was (rightly enough) 'a revolt because of the Maximum'; that the workers were about to march on the Convention; and even that Robespierre had been assassinated by the demonstrators.[1] The Commune, despite its other preoccupations, took the workers' protest seriously enough and did not invite further disfavour by attempting to disperse them by force of arms: at 8 o'clock that evening, in a proclamation to the citizens, the mayor, Fleuriot-Lescot, publicly saddled Barère, one of Robespierre's principal opponents, with responsibility for the reduction in wages—

ce Barère qui appartient à toutes les factions tour à tour et qui a fait fixer le prix des journées des ouvriers pour les faire périr de faim.[2]

But it was too late to have any effect on the course of events. The workers remained either hostile, or indifferent to such pleas. Earlier that evening, eyewitnesses reported that General Hanriot, seeking to win allies for the arrested deputies, harangued a score of paviors, urging them to leave their work, as their 'protector' and 'father' was in danger. 'Les ouvriers', concludes the report, 'l'écoutent un moment, crient Vive la République, et reprennent leur ouvrage.'[3] Others showed more marked hostility. When, two days later, after Robespierre and his principal lieutenants had been disposed of, the councillors of the Commune were, in turn, being driven to the place of execution, workers are said to have shouted as they passed, 'foutu maximum!'[4] From other accounts, too, it appears that

[1] Arch. Nat., AF[II] 47, plaq. 365, fols. 8, 28; plaq. 366, fols. 1, 6, 34, 50. Sainte-Claire Deville, surprisingly, does not mention this incident.
[2] Arch. Nat., F[7] 4432, plaq. 1, fol. 40.   [3] Ibid., plaq. 9, fol. 4.
[4] A. Aulard, *Paris pendant la réaction thermidorienne* (5 vols., Paris, 1898–1902), i. 11.

the wage-earners, who, in Paris, formed so substantial a part of the *sans-culottes*, had come to believe that the removal of Robespierre and his associates would mean the end of the hated *maximum des salaires* and clear the way for higher wages.[1] In a sense they were right; but the outcome was neither what they hoped nor expected.

[1] It was later reported by a brush-maker of the Lombards Section that his workpeople had greeted the execution of Robespierre and his associates with the observation, 'et voilà le maximum dans le panier!', and promptly put in for a 33 per cent. increase to their wages! (R. Cobb, 'Une "Coalition" des garçons brossiers de la section des Lombards', *Ann. hist. Rév. franç.*, no. 130 (1953), pp. 67–70).

X

GERMINAL-PRAIRIAL

THE popular insurrections of 12th Germinal and 1st–4th Prairial of the Year III (1 April and 20–23 May 1795) marked the final, and the most considerable, effort of the Parisian *sans-culottes* to impose their will on their rulers as an independent political force. After their defeat in Prairial they ceased to play any effective part until the next round of revolutions in the early nineteenth century. To a lesser extent these movements are important as marking the final attempt of the remnants of the Mountain and the Jacobins to recapture their political ascendancy in the Convention and the Paris Sections; but this time, though they gave some political direction to the popular movement which arose in the first place in protest against worsening economic conditions, their intervention was timorous and half-hearted and doomed the movement to failure. To understand its range and significance we must trace the policy of the Thermidorians and the discontent that it aroused among the *sans-culottes* back to the autumn of 1794.[1]

Robespierre's successors lost little time in dismantling the machinery of government created by the Jacobins, and in reverting to a freer economic system that accorded better with the wishes and interests of the new majority in the Convention. By a decree of 24 August sixteen committees were set up to carry out the work previously done by the Committees of

---

[1] For a general account of these events see A. Mathiez, *La Réaction thermidorienne* (Paris, 1929), pp. 186–209, 236–58; G. Lefebvre, *Les Thermidoriens* (Paris, 1937), pp. 111–39. For more detailed studies see E. Tarlé, *Germinal i prairial* (Moscow, 1951; German edition, Leipzig, 1954); K. D. Tönnesson, *La Défaite des sans-culottes: mouvement populaire et réaction bourgeoise à Paris en l'an III* (Doctoral thesis for University of Oslo, 1958). The present chapter is based, more particularly, on R. Cobb and G. Rudé, 'Le Dernier mouvement populaire de la Révolution à Paris: les journées de germinal et de prairial an III', *Revue historique*, October–December 1955, pp. 250–81. The latter draws extensively on police records, which form a particularly fruitful source during this period—including the 'public opinion' bulletins edited by A. Aulard (*Paris pendant la réaction thermidorienne*, i. 1–756), the papers of the Committee of General Security (Arch. Nat., F7 [série alphabétique] [Police générale]), and the *procès-verbaux* of the *commissaires de police* of the Paris Sections (Arch. Préf. Pol., series Aa).

Public Safety and General Security; the latter, while continuing in being, were reduced both in powers and in independence: above all, the armed forces (including the Parisian National Guard) were removed from their control and placed under that of a specially constituted Military Committee, responsible to the Convention. As drastic was the reorganization of local government. The old *comités de surveillance* and Revolutionary Committees which at the local level had been the main props of the Jacobin dictatorship, were swept away wholesale or brought under central control. In the provinces they only survived at the District level. In Paris the Commune was abolished and the forty-eight Revolutionary Committees were grouped together in twelve *comités d'arrondissement*, from which all Jacobin militants were excluded and in which the predominant social element was no longer the small shopkeeper and craftsman, but the merchant, civil servant, or professional man.[1] Similarly the Civil Committees of the Sections were purged, put under the direct control of the Convention, and their numbers made up by persons selected by the Convention's Committee of Legislation; once more a social transformation was effected in the process, and on the committees that emerged the *sans-culottes* and Jacobins of the Year II gave way before the substantial property-owners and 'moderates' who had dominated the Sections before June 1793.[2] In the Sectional assemblies themselves the influence of the *sans-culottes* was further drastically · reduced by the removal of the forty *sous'* compensation; the assemblies were, besides, to meet only once every *décade*, or ten days.[3]

The new government's economic policy was in keeping. In spite of continuing war and shortage, it owed it to its supporters—the large producers of town and countryside, the merchants, and shipbuilders, 'the hard-faced men who had done well out of the war'—to liberate the economy from the controls imposed by their predecessors. As a first step, in October, the Maximum legislation was so amended as to allow prices to rise to a level two-thirds above that of June 1790; on 23 December the Maximum laws were virtually abolished: the price of rationed bread was still maintained at 12 *sous* for the

[1] M. Bouloiseau, *Les Comités de surveillance des arrondissements parisiens* (Paris, 1930), p. 88.   [2] Brit. Mus., F* 61, nos. 11, 20, 21, 27 (printed lists).
[3] Lefebvre, op. cit., pp. 14–110.

4-lb. loaf—though bread was now allowed in addition to be sold on an open market; the basic meat ration of a half-pound every five days was also retained at its new price of 21 *sous* per pound; otherwise, prices were now free to find their natural level. The inflationary movement thus set in motion is reflected in the steady fall in the value of the *assignat* from 36 per cent. in July to 28 per cent. in October, 24 per cent. in November, 20 per cent. in December, 17 per cent. in February, and to 7½ per cent. in May 1795.[1]

Although Paris was a privileged area compared with the large towns in the provinces, where controls were abandoned altogether and whose citizens were to suffer near-famine conditions,[2] the common people of the capital came to face considerable and prolonged hardship as the result of the new policy. There now developed side by side with the closed market, still subject to restriction, an open market not only in unrationed goods—eggs, butter, sugar, firewood, oil, and vegetables—but in meat and bread as well. With the repeal of the Maximum laws and the constantly increasing shortages of every article entering into the poor man's budget, not only did the Parisian *menu peuple* have to purchase all commodities other than bread and meat at the higher, famine prices now prevailing; but the inability of the government to honour its undertaking to provide sufficient quantities of bread and meat at the controlled price,[3] compelled them to spend an ever higher proportion of their income on bread and meat in the open market. Thus, for the first time since the autumn of 1791, the price of bread reappeared as a social problem. Its importance may be judged from the rise in the price of bread in the open market from 25 *sous* on 28 March 1795 to 65 *sous* on 11 April, to 6 *livres* on 21 April, to 9 *livres* on 11 May, and to 16 *livres* a week later—two days before the outbreak of 1st Prairial.[4] Meanwhile the price of meat on the open market rose from 36 *sous* in December to 7 *livres*, 10 *sous* on 1 April.[5] The index of retail prices, based on June 1790, rose from 500 in January to 900 in April.[6]

[1] Harris, *The Assignats*, p. 186.   [2] Ibid., p. 99.
[3] The meat ration was often not honoured at all (ibid., p. 107); the bread ration, fixed at 1–1½ lb. per head in March 1795 (*Moniteur* (*réimpr.*), xxiii. 700), between March and May fell to 8, 6, 4, or even 2 ounces per head (Aulard, op. cit., vol. 1, *passim*).   [4] Aulard, op. cit., i. 610, 654, 675, 715, 729.
[5] Ibid. 341, 629.   [6] Harris, op. cit., pp. 107–8.

We know less about wages for this period. At first the Thermidorians tried to win over the wage-earners by repudiating the scales issued by the former Paris Commune on the eve of its downfall: a revised *maximum des salaires* was, in fact, published on 9 August, which provided for increases of about one-half above those of the ill-fated *maximum* of 23 July.[1] But these gains were rapidly swallowed up by the government's deliberate policy of fostering inflation and of restoring a freely competitive market. From the limited evidence available it appears that the real wages of Parisian workers in April 1795 were far lower than in 1793–4 and had probably fallen back to the catastrophic level of the early months of 1789.[2]

But long before this, and even before the repeal of the Maximum laws in December, the common people of Paris had begun to voice their hostility to the government's policy, though at first in terms of apathy and sullen resentment. The prevailing mood is described by an agent of the Ministry of the Interior in late November:

Complaints and murmurs are continually heard. The long delays in obtaining rationed bread, the shortage of flour, the high prices, in markets and squares, of bread, firewood, wine, coal, vegetables and potatoes, the price of which is increasing daily in the most alarming manner, are plunging the people into a state of wretchedness and despair that is easy to imagine.[3]

The first open clashes with the authorities involved the arms workers, who, since Robespierre's fall, had remained relatively calm. On 17–18 November delegations from two workshops urged the Convention to consider their claims for higher wages; they were followed, a few days later, by 350 workers from the Panthéon workshop, who had compelled their managers to lead them on a march to the Tuileries. Other workshops followed suit; and the Convention, alarmed at what appeared to be the revival of a general wages movement, ordered its two leading Committees to propose suitable measures. It was decided to close down the government arms workshops altogether

---

[1] Rudé and Soboul, op. cit., pp. 20–23.
[2] For the preceding two paragraphs see G. Rudé, 'Prices, Wages and Popular Movements in Paris during the French Revolution', *Econ. Hist. Rev.*, vol. vi, no. 3, April 1954, pp. 261–4.   [3] Arch. Nat., F7 3688⁴ (my translation).

on 20 January. The workers, faced with the prospect of unemployment in mid-winter, reacted vigorously and, after a
series of demonstrations, in the course of which a score of ringleaders were arrested, persuaded the authorities to grant them
a few weeks' respite. The workshops were closed down on 8
February 1795.[1] But after December we hear no more of wages
movements. Once the full effects of inflation were felt, the wage-
earners joined with the rest of the sans-culottes in common protest against the fantastic rise in prices of all consumers' goods;
once more the food riot rather than the strike became the order
of the day.

In fact the repeal of the Maximum laws in late December
touched off a popular movement which, with short lulls, continued till the early summer. A police report of 27 December
warned of growing social unrest: 'La classe indigente donne de
l'inquiétude aux citoyens paisibles sur les suites de cette cherté
excessive.' By early January prices of many goods had already
doubled since the repeal of the Maximum; and workers,
assembled at the Tuileries, threatened merchants and shopkeepers with violence: 'Qu'à l'égard des marchands, c'étaient
des cochons qu'il faudrait tuer.' Some voiced royalist propaganda: 'Au diable la République! nous manquons de tout, il
n'y a que le riche qui ne manque de rien.' It was rumoured that
the Faubourg Saint-Antoine was once more preparing to march
on the Convention, this time to demand a reduction in food
prices; it was even suggested that the Assembly should be
dispersed by force.[2]

But it was not only the rising cost of living that kept this
movement in being: political issues entered into it as well. On
the one hand, there were the measures taken by the Government—the persecution of the 'patriots' of 1793–4, the closure
of the Jacobin Club, the abolition of the 40 sous, the destruction
of the busts of Marat, the encouragement given to speculators
and war-profiteers and to the middle-class youth (or muscadins),
whose arrogance excited the particular fury and hostility of the
sans-culottes; on the other hand, there was the Jacobin propaganda kept up by Lebois's journal, L'Ami du peuple, and the

---

[1] For the above see mainly Procès-verbaux de la Convention nationale, xlvii. 132;
xlix. 244–63; l. 89–90, 115; li. 155–7; liv. 266.

[2] Aulard, op. cit. i. 343, 357–8, 367, 369–70, 377, 380.

clubs and societies that had managed to survive in the Faubourgs Saint-Antoine and Saint-Marcel and the Section des
Gravilliers—prominent among which were the Society of Republican Virtues in the Observatoire Section and the Club de
la Rue du Vert-Bois, the latter said to be composed largely
'd'ouvriers et d'hommes peu instruits, très faciles à égarer'.
Occasionally this propaganda is reflected in the police reports;
as, for example, in late November, when members of the Bonne
Nouvelle Section, marching to the Convention to congratulate
the legislators on their decision to close down the Jacobin Club,
were greeted with cat-calls and derisive shouts of 'Voilà les
petits muscadins de Bonne-Nouvelle qui vont à la Convention';
or, again, when an arms worker, arrested for creating a disturbance at the Tuileries on 9 February, accompanied his criticism
of the Convention for closing the workshops with attacks on the
deputies for feathering their own nests while the people starved,
and for destroying monuments to Marat; while petitioners from
the Sections that had come to applaud these measures were
apostrophized as 'des intriguans, des marchands, des factieux,
un tas de gueux et des hommes à la houppelande'. This atmosphere of class-hostility—reminiscent of that prevailing in the
capital on the eve of the Champ de Mars 'massacre' of July
1791—was further intensified by the counter-measures taken
by the Convention. The remaining clubs were closed down and
some of the local leaders—Babeuf among them—were arrested.
Even more significant perhaps was the suggestion made to the
Committee of General Security that better use might be made
of the anti-Jacobin youth, the *jeunesse dorée* led by Fréron, to act
as a counter-weight to the activities of 'la faction':

Ce contrepoids est d'autant plus nécessaire qu'il [le Comité] n'a
nuls moyens de répression, nulle force armée sur laquelle il puisse
entièrement compter.[1]

The suggestion did not fall on deaf ears, as subsequent events
were to reveal.

It was against this background that the insurrectionary movement developed that culminated in the explosion of 12th
Germinal (1 April 1795). The new element that brought it to
a head was the growing shortage of rationed bread, which began

[1] See Cobb and Rudé, op. cit., pp. 257-9.

to be felt in January and reached near-famine proportions by the end of March. Police reports for the fortnight leading up to the outbreak present a graphic picture of a growing movement of anger and frustration, which may be summarized as follows:

16 March. Meetings of women in the Gravilliers Section.

17 March. Deputations from Saint-Jacques and Saint-Marcel petition the Convention: 'We lack bread and are beginning to regret all the sacrifices we have made for the Revolution.'

18 March. A waiter arrested in the Montagne (Palais Royal) Section complains that 'it was dreadful to see Frenchmen reduced to a ration of one lb. of bread a day and to eating potatoes, which were only fit for pigs'.

21 March. A deputation from the Faubourg Saint-Antoine received by the Convention; workers and *muscadins* come to blows at the Porte St. Denis.

22 March. Bread-ration breaks down completely in Gravilliers and Homme Armé (Marais) Sections; two gentlemen insulted by arms workers in the Palais Egalité (Palais Royal); a paper-worker arrested on Pont Neuf for shouting that 'the rich were all rogues'.

23 March. Women of the Arsenal workshop threaten to throw 'jeunes gens', who had ventured into the Faubourg Saint-Antoine to fraternize with the *ouvriers*, into the river.

24 March. Four persons arrested in Montreuil Section for trying 'to raise the Faubourg'; no bread distributed in Droits de l'Homme, Indivisibilité, Marchés and Lombards Sections.

25 March. A jeweller of the rue Saint-Martin arrested for threatening the Convention and complaining 'that it was not easy to live on a half-pound of bread'.

26 March. Women of rue Saint-Martin accuse men of being 'cowards' for taking no action; women flour-workers try to organize a march to the Convention.

27 March. Extensive bread-riots in Gravilliers and Temple Sections; women and male workers march to Convention and complain of bread-ration of only a half-pound; several arrests; illegal Sectional assemblies in Amis de la Patrie and Gravilliers.

28 March. Agitation in Gravilliers and Temple continues; march on Convention dispersed by National Guard, who arrest eight persons near Opera.

29 March. A father kills two of his three children for fear of famine.

30 March. Bread-riots in Droits de l'Homme and Faubourg du Nord.

31 March. Illegal assembly in Droits de l'Homme addresses petition to Convention; workers strike for more bread; four Sections petition Convention: Quinze Vingts deputation reminds deputies that, on occasion, insurrection a sacred duty and calls for justice for imprisoned 'patriots', for steps to alleviate hunger and for the implementation of the Constitution of 1793.[1]

These demands were voiced on a far larger scale on the following day (12th Germinal). Meetings and processions formed at an early hour. The bread ration failed completely in some Sections; in others, a ration of 4 or 8 ounces was distributed. In the Droits de l'Homme women came to blows at bakers' shops. In the rue Montmartre building workers met to protest against a decree of 31 March, which debarred those living in furnished rooms from buying bread at the controlled price;[2] workers in neighbouring shops were invited to join a protest demonstration to the Convention. The Faubourgs Saint-Marcel and Saint-Jacques joined forces to march to the Tuileries, and the Gravilliers Section was reported to have concerted with thirteen other Sections for the same purpose. While the Assembly's President, Boissy d'Anglas, was in the middle of a speech, the men and women of the insurgent Sections burst in on the Convention, shouting, 'du pain! du pain!'; some wore on their caps the insurgent slogan, 'du pain et la Constitution de 1793'. But the demonstrators lacked leaders and had no settled plan of action: while the spokesman for the Cité called for the Constitution of 1793, those of two other Sections won the applause of the Assembly's majority for their moderate speeches. When Merlin de Thionville, one of the Thermidorian leaders, appeared, escorted by loyal detachments of the National Guard from the western Sections, and by groups of *jeunes gens* (who had previously assembled at the Louvre to meet this situation), the intruders dispersed without offering any resistance. And, far from the deputies of the Mountain playing any active part in these proceedings, it was two of their number that first proposed that the insurgents should discharge their business quickly and leave the assembly-hall in good order.[3]

Minor disturbances followed, both that day and the next, in various parts of the capital. Some Sections—Popincourt, Cité,

---

[1] Ibid., pp. 259–62.
[2] The police considered this decree the main cause of discontent among the workers on 12th Germinal (Aulard, op. cit. i. 627, 630).
[3] Mathiez, op. cit., p. 206.

and Panthéon—went into permanent session; and the gunners of the Gravilliers Section ('composés en grande partie d'ouvriers') talked of marching to the Champs Elysées to release the 'patriots' from prison. But the Convention took stern measures to re-establish order and to prevent a renewed outbreak. Paris was declared to be in a state of siege and its armed forces were placed under the supreme command of a regular Army officer, General Pichegru; local leaders were arrested in the Contrat Social, Gravilliers, Arcis, and Montmartre Sections; a dozen deputies (including Léonard Bourdon, Amar, and Cambon—all opponents of Robespierre in Thermidor) were also arrested; and three of the leaders of the Thermidorian *coup d'état*, but now denounced as terrorists—Barère, Billaud-Varennes, and Collot d'Herbois—were sentenced to deportation.[1]

The authorities showed less energy in dealing with the food crisis. The Convention decreed, on 2 April, that the bread ration, where insufficient, should be supplemented with rice and biscuits, and that priority should be given in their distribution to 'les ouvriers, artisans et indigents'. But this did nothing, of course, to solve the larger problem of supplies, and the shortage of rationed bread continued unchecked: we still read during April and May of distributions of 2, 4, or 6 ounces per head, supplemented by small portions of rice. There were reports, besides, of increasing numbers of beggars, of people dying of hunger in the streets, and of suicides.[2] There was a further revival of royalist propaganda: 'Prenons patience [some were heard to say], nous aurons un roi avant quinze jours; alors nous ne manquerons pas de pain.' But the prevailing mood was one of resignation and despair, tempered by outbursts of militancy.

Yet, despite the attempts to overawe the *menu peuple* by a display of force, the popular movement started up again after a brief lull. On 4 April the familiar complaints were voiced again in the markets; on the 9th a porcelain-painter was arrested at the Porte Saint-Denis for bitterly attacking the Convention before a large crowd and complaining of the insufficiency and poor quality of bread. The next day some 500 women gathered in the Bonnet de la Liberté (Croix Rouge)

[1] Mathiez, op. cit., pp. 201–8.
[2] Aulard, op. cit. i. 660, 714–15, 719, 721, 724, 728.

Section to shouts of 'A bas les armes! nous ne voulons plus de soldats, puisqu'il n'y a plus de pain!' On 17 April women in Gravilliers and Lombards refused to accept their bread ration; on the 20th a domestic servant was arrested in the Pont Neuf Section, charged with saying, 'Il y a huit mois que nous avions du pain; aujourd'hui nous n'en avons plus, nous sommes dans l'esclavage'; while one of two craftsmen arrested for seditious talk, the next day, in Arsenal excused his conduct by saying, 'qu'il croyait que c'était pour cause de pain'.

Similar incidents are reported almost daily during the next month in the public opinion bulletins issued by the police;[1] and, occasionally, we find signs, besides, of a more organized movement once more beginning to take shape. Thus, on 29 April, the Montreuil Section declared itself to be in permanent session for the purpose of discussing food supplies and called on other Sections to follow its example; a similar attempt in the Jardin des Plantes was nipped in the bud by the arrest of a number of ringleaders. On 12 May building workers threatened to go on strike if the bread ration were not increased; and a police agent sadly noted that it would be impossible to arrest all those who cursed the government, 'as it would mean arresting over half the population of Paris'. The next day demonstrators in a number of central Sections—Muséum, Lombards, and Marchés—went from one baker to another to persuade the women to refuse to accept their bread ration. On the 16th, when the ration fell to two ounces per head, police agents spoke of a pending popular insurrection, allegedly inspired by terrorists; and, on the 18th, it was rumoured that, if the ration were not increased, the Faubourg Saint-Antoine would rise again on 1st Prairial (20 May) and invite the rest of Paris to follow its example. The next day, there was general talk of a march on the Convention: in the Invalides Section (reported the police) the *ouvriers* were ready to join with those of the Faubourg Saint-Antoine. Illegal assemblies were held in Droits de l'Homme and Quinze Vingts, where it was urged 'qu'il fallait marcher en masse et en armes pour demander à la Convention du pain ou la mort'. The same evening and the following morning an anonymous manifesto was widely distributed in the *faubourgs* and city centre, bearing the title: *Insurrection du*

[1] Cobb and Rudé, op. cit., pp. 267–70.

peuple pour obtenir du pain et reconquérir ses droits.[1] It was the call to arms for what was to be one of the most remarkable and stubborn popular revolts of the Revolution.

Early on 1st Prairial the tocsin was sounded in the Faubourg Saint-Antoine and in the Jardin des Plantes. Once more, as in October 1789, it was the women that took the initiative and brought their menfolk into action after them. In the Faubourg du Nord (Faubourg Saint-Denis) they called the men out from the workshops at 7 o'clock in the morning. There were food riots and assemblies of women at bakers' shops in Popincourt, Gravilliers, and Droits de l'Homme. In the Tuileries Section bands of women compelled housewives queueing at bakers' shops to join them in a march to the Convention. In the Left Bank Sections of Mutius Scaevola (Luxembourg), Jardin des Plantes, and Finistère (where only two ounces of bread had been distributed that morning), women broke into meetings of the Civil Committees and demanded that their members lead them to the Tuileries. In the Fidélité (Hôtel de Ville) Section women seized a drum to beat a call to arms, 'afin qu'elles marchassent sur la Convention'. In the Arsenal Section near-by, a scandalized merchant observed, 'que ce n'était pas aux femmes de faire les lois'. In the Faubourg Saint-Antoine women forced shops to close and began to march on the Tuileries at 1.30 in the afternoon, followed by groups of armed men, 'many of them wearing in their caps the inscription, *du pain ou la mort*'. According to an eyewitness, as they marched, they compelled women in shops and private houses, and others riding in carriages, to join them. They reached the Place du Carrousel, in front of the Tuileries, at 2 o'clock; pinned to their hats, bonnets, and blouses were the twin slogans of the rebellion, *Du Pain et la Constitution de 1793*. Thus equipped, they burst into the assembly-hall, but were quickly ejected. They returned with armed groups of the National Guard an hour later.

Meanwhile, a general call to arms had been sounded in the Faubourg Saint-Antoine; men quickly armed and prepared to follow the women to the Tuileries. A similar movement began in the Faubourg Saint-Marcel and in the central Sections. In some cases, a minority of insurgents forced the doors of the

---

[1] For a *résumé* of this pamphlet, in which appear all the slogans and political demands of the insurgents of 1st–4th Prairial, see Mathiez, op. cit., pp. 243–4.

armouries, distributed arms to their comrades, and compelled
their commanders to lead them to the Convention. In others,
the 'party of order' retained the upper hand, but marched to
the Convention, nevertheless, in response to the general call to
arms issued by the Government later that morning. It was,
therefore, a mixed force of insurgents and would-be defenders of
the Convention that converged on the Place du Carrousel in the
wake of the marching women at 3.30 that afternoon.[1]

The second invasion of the Tuileries quickly followed. A
deputy, Féraud, who opposed their entry, was struck down and
his head was severed and paraded on a pike. This time the
women were amply supported by armed citizens of the rebellious Sections, though few battalions broke into the building in
full strength. Yet the demonstrators were in sufficient numbers
and their weapons sufficiently imposing to reduce the majority
to silence and to encourage the small remnant of deputies of the
Mountain to voice their principal demands—the release of the
Jacobin prisoners, steps to implement the Constitution of 1793,
and new controls to ensure more adequate supplies of food.
These were quickly voted and a special committee was set up
to give them effect. But the insurgents, like those of Germinal,
lacked leadership and any clear programme or plan of action.
Having achieved their immediate objective, they spent hours
in noisy chatter and speech-making. This gave the Thermidorian leaders time to call in the support of the loyal Sections—
with the Butte des Moulins (Palais Royal), Muséum (Louvre),
and Lepeletier at their head—and the insurgents were driven
out of the Tuileries.[2]

The armed rebellion continued the next day. From 2 o'clock
in the morning, the call to arms had sounded in the Quinze
Vingts. The tocsin tolled before 10 o'clock in Fidélité (Hôtel de
Ville) and Droits de l'Homme. In these two Sections and in
Arcis, Gravilliers, and Popincourt illegal assemblies were held.
The three Sections of the Faubourg Saint-Antoine sprang to
arms and marched on the Convention, led by a West Indian,
Guillaume Delorme, a wheelwright and captain of the gunners

---

[1] Mathiez's account, so valuable in every other way, does not make this clear
(op. cit., pp. 244–5). At least two of the insurgent battalions—those of the Gravilliers and Mutius Scaevola (Luxembourg) Sections—did not appear at the Tuileries
at all (Arch. Nat., W 546–8).

[2] Mathiez, op. cit., pp. 245–53.

of Popincourt. Supported by some Sections of the centre, they appeared on the Place du Carrousel at 3.30 in the afternoon, loaded their guns and trained them on the Convention. General Dubois, who was commanding the Convention's forces, had 40,000 men under him; the insurgents may have numbered 20,000. It was the largest display of military force drawn up for battle that had been seen in Paris since the Revolution began. But no shots were fired: when the Convention's gunners and *gendarmerie* deserted to the opposing side, the insurgents failed to follow up their advantage. Towards evening negotiations began; petitioners were received at the bar of the Assembly, repeated their demands for bread and the Constitution of 1793 and received the presidential embrace. Lulled by vain hopes of promises to be fulfilled, the insurgents thereupon retired to their various Sections.[1]

But the Convention was determined to make an end of the business. On the morning of 3rd Prairial regular army units were mustered, in addition to the *jeunesse dorée* and battalions of the western Sections, and preparations were made to enclose the Faubourg Saint-Antoine within a ring of hostile forces. The *jeunesse* made a premature sortie into the *faubourg* and was forced to retreat, and Saint-Antoine workers rescued from the police one of the assassins of Féraud on his way to execution. But, during the night, the Government overcame the resistance of most of the other insurgent Sections; and, on the 4th, the *faubourg* was called upon to hand over Féraud's murderers and all arms at its disposal: in the event of refusal it would be declared to be in a state of rebellion and all Sections would be called upon to help to reduce it by force of arms or to starve it into surrender. Meanwhile an army under General Menou prepared to advance against the rebels.

Their situation was hopeless; yet some attempt was made in other Sections to bring them relief. In Poissonnière Étienne Chefson, a cobbler and old soldier of the *armée révolutionnaire*, was later arrested for trying to organize building workers of the rues d'Hauteville and de l'Échiquier to march to the help of the *faubourg*; in Arcis, women were heard to shout in the streets: 'Il faut soutenir nos frères du faubourg Antoine, avoir raison des représentants et ne faire aucune grâce aux marchands et aux

[1] Mathiez, op. cit., pp. 254–5; Lefebvre, op. cit., pp. 123–4.

muscadins'; and, in Finistère, there were shouts, even after the battle was lost, of 'aux armes à l'appui du faubourg Antoine'. Other Sections, too, both in the Faubourg Saint-Marcel and the city centre, pledged their support; so much appears from the following report on the situation issued by the police at 5.30 that evening:

The guns [of the rebels] are trained on the city at the former Porte Saint-Antoine; the Grande Rue du Faubourg is filled with platoons of citizens armed with pikes and a few old-fashioned muskets; there are no armed pickets in the rues Charonne, Nicolas, Montreuil, Traversière, &c.; yet the citizens appear determined not to let themselves be disarmed. Women are assembled in every street and are making a great noise. *Bread is the material cause of their insurrection; but the Constitution of 1793 is its soul;* this they admit. It seems that the *Panthéon, Sans-Culottes (Jardin des Plantes), Finistère, Cité,* and *Gravilliers* Sections and a large part of the *Thermes de Julien* have declared in their favour.[1]

But no material support was forthcoming; and the *faubourg* surrendered, a few hours later, without a shot being fired. The movement was totally crushed. Two days later, a police agent noted:

Les rapports de ce jour présentent la position de Paris, pendant la journée d'hier, dans l'état le plus calme ... les hommes regardent, les femmes se taisent.

This time, the repression was thorough and ruthless. It struck both at the leaders—or presumed leaders—of the insurrection itself and at the potential leaders of similar revolts in the future: to behead the *sans-culottes* once and for all as a political force it was thought necessary to strike at the remnants of Jacobinism in the Convention and in the Sectional assemblies and National Guard. Twelve deputies were arrested, including six that had supported the demonstrators' demands on 1st Prairial. On 23 May (4th Prairial), a Military Commission was set up for the summary trial and execution of all persons captured with arms in their possession or wearing the insignia of rebellion. The Commission sat for ten weeks and tried 132 persons; nineteen of these, including six deputies of the Mountain,[2]

[1] Arch. Nat., F⁷ 4743, doss. 3 (my italics).
[2] They were Romme, Duquesnoy, Goujon, Bourbotte, Duroy, and Soubrany. For the dramatice suicide of the first three see Mathiez, op. cit., pp. 256–7.

were condemned to death. The Sections were invited to hold special meetings on 24 May to denounce and disarm all suspected 'terrorists' and Jacobin sympathizers. The result was a massive toll of proscriptions, in which the settling of old scores played as large a part as the testing of political orthodoxy. By the 28th the *Gazette française* already put their number at 10,000; and the eventual total of arrested and disarmed must have been considerably larger, as, in several Sections, all former members of Revolutionary Committees, all soldiers of the *armée révolutionnaire* were arrested or disarmed irrespective of any part they may have played in the events of Germinal or Prairial. The precedent thus established was to be followed on more than one occasion during the Directory and Consulate.[1]

The authorities had no other solution to offer for the crisis that had arisen; it was natural, therefore, that they should wish to represent the insurrections of Germinal and Prairial as the outcome of a conspiracy hatched by dissident Jacobins and former terrorists and members of the disbanded popular societies and clubs. A police report of 1st Prairial puts the official view clearly and succinctly enough:

We are inclined to believe that the shortage of food was the *pretext*—only too plausible, alas—used by the agitators to mislead the credulous, but that the *cause* of the popular movement that has arisen over a long period has been the agitation carried on by the faction of former leaders, who have put the people up to demand not only bread but the revival of the Commune, the Constitution of 1793, and the release from prison of all deputies of the Mountain and members of the old Revolutionary Committees.[2]

Political motives and Jacobin agitation naturally played their part in the movements just described. We saw that, in the months leading up to 12th Germinal, the few surviving popular societies gave a certain political direction to a movement that would otherwise have expended itself in blind outbursts of anger over rising prices and food shortage; so much is evident

---

[1] For the systematic repression of Jacobin and *sans-culottes* cadres during this period see R. C. Cobb, 'Note sur la répression contre le personnel sans-culotte de 1795 à 1801', *Ann. hist. Rév. franç.*, no. 134, January–March 1954, pp. 23–49.

[2] Aulard, op. cit. i. 733 (my italics). The addition of the demand for the restoration of the Commune of the Year II is, no doubt, a piece of deliberate embroidery by the police: there is no trace of such a demand among the slogans and political programmes voiced by the insurgents of Germinal or Prairial.

from the political slogans voiced by the insurgents in Germinal: *liberté des patriotes* and *la Constitution de 1793*. In Prairial, too, we saw that a number of Sections in the *faubourgs* and the centre resorted to the purely *political* action of forming illegal assemblies and declaring themselves to be in permanent session; and, even more significantly, that the insurgents paraded the twin slogans of 'bread' and 'the Constitution of 1793'. The police had some justice in considering the latter slogan as 'the soul of the movement': without it the movement would have lacked coherence and even the beginnings of a conscious political direction. It would be wrong, however, to ascribe anything but a minor role to the small group of Jacobin deputies in the Convention in either of these events: in Germinal, as we saw, they were only too anxious to persuade the demonstrators to leave the assembly-hall as quickly as possible; and, in Prairial, they followed the lead already given by the insurgent Sections and echoed the demands put to them by the women and armed *sans-culottes*.

When all is said and done, however, it was not the political agitation but economic hardship that was the primary cause of the movement. As we have seen, the constantly recurring theme running through all the stages of the movement from its first beginnings in December 1794 was shortage and rising food prices—particularly the shortage of rationed bread and its precipitous increase on the open market: this resulted, in the main, from the deliberate policy of the government, which was one of rapidly freeing the whole economy from controls in a period of war and shortage; but it was further aggravated by natural factors such as the unprecedented severity of the winter of 1795. A sure indication that the bread-and-butter question lay uppermost in the minds of the insurgents was the outstanding part played by the women in both Germinal and Prairial, which was second only to the part they had played in October 1789.

The bulk of the rioters were, as so often before, the men and women of the great popular *faubourgs* and the Sections adjoining the markets and city centre. Of the few hundred persons arrested for direct participation in the events of 1st and 2nd Prairial[1] the occupations of 168 appear in the records

---

[1] These should not be confused with the far larger number of persons arrested and disarmed in the Sections after 5th Prairial (see p. 156).

consulted; of these some 45 to 50 seem to have been wage-earners, while the rest were small shopkeepers, workshop masters, craftsmen, and clerks. They are drawn from no less than 40 Sections—most prominent among them being Popincourt (13 arrests), Arsenal (12), Quinze Vingts (10), and Arcis (10).[1]

But the records of the comparatively few persons arrested give but a limited picture of Sectional participation in the events of Germinal and Prairial. A fuller picture emerges from the events already related. From these it appears that the Sections mainly engaged in the movement culminating on 12th Germinal were Quinze Vingts and Popincourt (*Faubourg Saint-Antoine*); Observatoire and Panthéon (*Faubourg Saint-Marcel*); Cité, Droits de l'Homme, Amis de la Patrie, and Gravilliers (*centre*); and Temple and Faubourg Montmartre (*north*). In Prairial, more Sections were engaged—some fully, others only in part. Leading the movement again were the three Sections of the Faubourg Saint-Antoine and four of the five Sections of the Faubourg Saint-Marcel (Observatoire only excepted). They were closely supported by the central Sections—Arcis, Droits de l'Homme, Fidélité (Hôtel de Ville), Cité, Lombards, Marchés, Gravilliers, and Halle au Blé; and (less wholeheartedly) by the northern Sections of Poissonnière and Faubourg du-Nord, and by Mutius Scaevola (Luxembourg) and Invalides in the south. There were even supporting contingents of women from Muséum and Tuileries in the west; but the western Sections, generally, formed a solid block of defenders of the Convention and its Committees. As we shall see in the next chapter, in Vendémiaire (October 1795) these roles were to some extent reversed.

Why then, with such solid support, were the Parisian *sans-culottes* defeated in May 1795? Partly, as we have seen, it was for lack of a clear political programme and plan of action; partly through the weakness of the deputies of the Mountain; partly through political inexperience and the failure to follow up an advantage once gained; partly, too, through the correspondingly greater skill and experience of the Convention and its Committees and the support that these were able to muster— even without the active intervention of the regular army—from the *jeunesse dorée* and the merchants, civil servants, and monied

[1] In Gravilliers there were 7 arrests, in Bondy (7), Lombards (6), Halle au Blé (6), and—more surprisingly—in Tuileries (6) and Muséum (6).

classes of the western Sections. But, above all, the *sans-culottes* failed to secure and maintain in Prairial, as they had in the great *journées* of 1789–93, the solid alliance of at least the radical wing of the *bourgeoisie*. When this faltered and failed, their movement, as in 1775, for all its breadth and militancy, was reduced to a futile explosion without hope of political gains.[1]

[1] For suggestions as to the longer-term causes of the final defeat of the *sans-culottes* after Prairial see Cobb and Rudé, op. cit., pp. 280–1.

XI

VENDÉMIAIRE

WHILE the story of popular insurrection during the Revolution in Paris closes with the events just described, they do not mark the last occasion on which revolutionary crowds challenged the authority of the government in armed rebellion or street demonstrations. This final episode was constituted by the *journées* of 12–14th Vendémiaire (4–6 October 1795). This episode cannot therefore be left out of account from our present study, even if the nature and aims of the rioters and the pattern of events leading up to the insurrection mark a sharp departure from those described in preceding chapters.[1] On this occasion, far from seeking to drive the Revolution in a more radical direction or to establish or strengthen the Republic, the ultimate aims of the insurrection were to destroy the Republic and to open the way for the restoration of the monarchy. Its promoters, far from being democrats, Jacobins, or *sans-culottes*, were the hard core of the conservative and monied interests established in the western Sections of the capital, who had most eagerly rallied to the side of the Thermidorians against Robespierre and served as the main defenders of the Convention in the revolts of Germinal and Prairial. Of considerable interest, too, in this affair are the role and attitude of the *sans-culottes* who, though crushed in Prairial, were still a factor to be reckoned with. Though facing economic hardships as severe as those described in the previous chapter, they gave no support to the royalist (or near-royalist) rebels; incapable of engaging in an independent movement of their own, they tended rather to rally (somewhat passively, it is true) in support of the constituted authorities against those who attempted to overthrow the Republic by force of arms.

The events of Vendémiaire have a further importance in that they opened up new perspectives in the relations between the government and the citizens of Paris. They revealed, for

---

[1] Thermidor already marks a certain departure from this pattern, it is true; but the differences are not so clear-cut as in the case of Vendémiaire.

the first time since 1789, that the revolutionary Assembly might maintain itself in office and impose its will on the country as a whole even without the active support of any substantial social group or body of opinion in the capital. In Thermidor the Convention had been able to depend on the support, or at least the benevolent neutrality, of the bulk of the Parisian Sections— including those in which the *sans-culottes* were still firmly entrenched—to overthrow Robespierre. In Prairial, in order to overcome the *sans-culottes* and the active Jacobin remnants, it had been able to call upon the armed citizens of the 'respectable' western Sections. In Vendémiaire, when faced with a rebellion from this very quarter, having destroyed the Jacobin cadres and silenced the *sans-culottes*, arrested their leaders, and driven them out of the Sectional assemblies and committees, the Convention had no other resort but to call in the army. The precedent, once established, was not easily abandoned; and from October 1795 the military *coup d'état* already looms on the horizon as the ultimate arbiter of political disputes.

The immediate issue out of which the insurrection of Vendémiaire arose was the decree of 22 August 1795 (the decree of the *deux tiers*), which invited the primary assemblies convened for the new elections to agree to the uncontested return of two-thirds of the members of the outgoing Assembly. This blatant attempt to perpetuate the political existence of a body which, for a variety of reasons, had forfeited most of the respect or devotion that it had once enjoyed, gave the handful of convinced royalists in the capital the pretext and opportunity to rally the majority of the Parisian Sections in opposition to the Convention and to win substantial support for the armed rebellion that followed. In essence this was the political background to the days of Vendémiaire.[1] Yet the picture is grossly oversimplified when presented in such exclusively political terms. Here it is proposed, therefore, before picking up the narrative

[1] For the most complete account of the insurrection and its political background see H. Zivy, *Le Treize vendémiaire, an IV* (Paris, 1898). Though the author makes full use of the correspondence of the Committees of Public Safety and General Security, the minutes of the Sectional assemblies, the police reports edited by Schmidt (*Tableaux de la Révolution française*), and the records of the Military Courts set up on 15th Vendémiaire to judge the arrested ringleaders, his study appeared too early to make use of the fuller police reports edited by Aulard (*Paris pendant la réaction thermidorienne*, vol. 2).

of political events in mid-September, when the opposition to
the decree of the 'two-thirds' was beginning to take shape, to
consider the government's economic policy and its effects on
the various parties concerned.[1]

In spite of the plight of the small consumers, which had become only too evident during the spring and summer, the
Convention and its Committees did nothing to amend their
economic policy, whose effects continued to be aggravated by
the extension of the war and the persistence of unfavourable
natural factors. The *assignat* slumped further to 5 per cent. of its
nominal value in October before virtually fading out of existence.[2] The ration of bread (nominally 1–1½ lb. a head) at the
controlled price of 3 *sous* per lb. continued to be blatantly
dishonoured: up to the end of July, at least, we read of
distributions of only 2, 4, 6, 7, or 8 ounces per head; and
there were frequent complaints of bakers selling bread above
the controlled price.[3] During August there was an improvement:
a half-pound ration became the rule, rising to three-quarters
later in the month; but during September there were frequent
complaints about the poor quality of flour and, before October,
the ration had again dropped to half a pound or below.[4] Meanwhile, on the 'open' market, bread was still sold at 15–20
livres a pound.[5] Meat tended to be unobtainable at its controlled price of 21 *sous*; and, on the 'open' market, its price rose
from 8 *livres* in June and July to 15 *livres* in late September.[6]
Other essential commodities followed a similar course: butter
rising from 16–18 *livres* a pound in July to 30 *livres* in September;
sugar from 11 *livres* in January to 62 *livres* in September; eggs from
9 *livres* per dozen in July to 12 *livres* in September; potatoes from 34
livres a bushel in May to 56 *livres* in October; tallow-candles from
5 *livres* in January to 30 *livres* in June and 50 *livres* in August;
coal from 75 *livres* a *voie* in June to 175 *livres* in October; and
firewood from 160 *livres* in May to 500 *livres* in late September.[7]

[1] The main source used for this purpose has been Aulard, op. cit. i. 755–75;
ii. 1–319 (29 May–14 October 1795).   [2] Ibid. ii. 326.
[3] Ibid. i. 755, 760, 767; ii. 8, 34, 48, 108, 120, 138, 145.
[4] Ibid. ii. 102, 151, 181, 186–9, 199, 208, 210, 213, 277.
[5] Ibid. i. 756; ii. 36, 139; Zivy, op. cit., p. 124.
[6] Aulard, op. cit. ii. 24, 34, 113; Zivy, loc. cit.
[7] Aulard, i. 368, 376, 750; ii. 3, 8, 36, 61, 113, 191, 271, 291, 327. A *voie* corresponds to 56 cu. ft.

The effects of such a continuous rise in the cost of living on wage-earners and other earners of small or fixed incomes may be readily imagined. Workers, striking in August for more bread and assembled at the porte Saint-Martin, ask the pertinent question: 'Est-ce avec 12 francs que nous gagnons par jour que nous pouvons acheter du pain à 15 livres la livre?'[1] The plight of all small property-owners in such conditions is well summarized in an agent's report of 16 July:

> The worker's wage is far too low to meet his daily needs; the unfortunate *rentier*, in order to keep alive, has to sell his last stick of furniture, which adds to the haul of the greedy speculator; the proprietor, lacking other means of subsistence, eats up his capital as well as his income; the civil servant, who is entirely dependent on his salary, also suffers the torments of privation.[2]

More than one observer, in fact, believed that the distress thus caused among the *rentiers* and small proprietors was relatively greater than that suffered by the craftsmen and wage-earners.[3] The point is significant, as it may help to explain the intense hostility shown to the Convention in such western Sections as Lepeletier, Butte des Moulins (Palais Royal), and Place Vendôme—where these social elements abounded—long before the political crisis arose over the decree of the 'two-thirds'.[4] Yet there could, of course, be no effective action from such quarters to end the economic conditions complained of, as the Sections in question were equally the main haunts of the speculators and stock-jobbers, who thrived on inflation and rising prices and whose activities were favoured by the Government's policies.[5]

For their part the *sans-culottes* reacted in characteristic fashion. Some, as in the months before Prairial, gave way to despair and were concerned only with the immediate problems of food and survival.

[1] Ibid. ii. 142.   [2] Ibid., p.86; see also ibid., p. 50.
[3] Ibid. i. 757; ii. 48–49.
[4] For examples of food shortage and complaints in May–July, and even talk of 'une insurrection prochaine où les représentants et les marchands puissent trouver leur tombeau', in Lepeletier, Place Vendôme, and Butte des Moulins, see Aulard, i. 755, 767; ii. 48, 60, 65, 108.
[5] Cf. a report of 5 October (13th Vendémiaire): 'C'est du sein de ces deux arrondissements (Lepeletier and Butte des Moulins: G.R.) que sortent tous les agioteurs, qui, au Palais Égalité, font le trafic le plus infâme au détriment de la fortune publique et des fortunes privées' (ibid. ii. 300).

Le public [wrote an observer in July] paraît ne s'occuper que de ses besoins et . . . la politique est réléguée dans les cafés.

Peu importe le gouvernement [said one citizen], pourvu que j'aie de quoi subsister.

And, in August, another observer reported: 'Le public . . . ne s'occupe ni de lois, ni de Constitution; que ce n'est que du pain qu'il demande.'[1] Others reacted more vigorously: both in June and July we hear of crowds in the Palais Royal cheering working men who raided the stocks of dealers selling bread on the open market; and it was thought advisable to suspend the practice of offering bread at Holy Communion at Saint-Gervais as long as the shortage lasted.[2] Some began to regret the old régime, bitterly denounced the Republic, and placed their hopes in the restoration of the monarchy. In July citizens of the Faubourg Saint-Antoine were heard to say that they did not care if the enemy came to Paris, 'parce que, ne pouvant plus tenir à la cherté, il leur était bien égal d'être Anglais ou Français'; and an observer wrote that the 'lowest orders', while not openly pronouncing in favour of a king, did not appear to be opposed to the monarchy, provided it gave them bread. In August the general refrain in certain public places was said to be: 'Un roi ou du pain'; and an agent wrote that 'comparisons with the old régime . . . do not redound to the credit of the Republic'.[3] Yet, among the sans-culottes, at least, this mood appears to have been short-lived and to have disappeared before Vendémiaire.

More persistent were the effects resulting from a revival of Jacobin agitation. In August there were demands for a return to controls on the price and supply of essentials: 'Le public semble désirer [wrote an observer] que les grains et autres objets de nécessité soient taxés à un prix raisonnable'.[4] Later in the month it was reported that many regretted the time of Robespierre: 'On était plus heureux sous le règne de Robespierre; on ne sentait pas alors le besoin.' On 8 September a soldier in the Palais Royal said things would continue to go wrong 'as long as Terror was not made the order of the day'; and, a fortnight later, a woman was heard to say at the Porte Saint-Martin 'qu'elle regrettait le temps de la guillotine, et

[1] Aulard, ii. 53, 65, 177.
[2] Ibid., pp. 22, 43–44, 67.
[3] Ibid., pp. 70, 77–78, 161.
[4] Ibid., p. 208 (see also p. 143).

qu'elle désirait qu'elle fût permanente'. By the end of the month, with the release of former terrorists in some Sections and the growth of royalist agitation in others, Jacobin principles were once more being openly proclaimed both in the Tuileries Gardens and in the popular districts adjoining the Portes Saint-Denis and Saint-Martin.[1]

Meanwhile, despite their defeat in Prairial, there had been talk of a new *sans-culottes* uprising.

On débite dans les queues et rassemblements [wrote an observer at the end of June] que l'on croit les ouvriers tranquilles parce qu'on les a désarmés, mais qu'ils sauront bien employer les mêmes moyens que dans les commencements de la Révolution pour se procurer du pain.

A week later Inspector Bouillon compares the popular discussion that is going on with that preceding the outbreak in Prairial. On 20 August it was noted 'que les rassemblements d'ouvriers à la porte Martin deviennent de jour en jour plus nombreux'; and, the next day, the general excitement was such 'qu'on pourrait croire qu'il se prépare une insurrection très prochaine'.[2] But, by this time, the political conflict between the Government and the Sections was beginning to emerge: we shall see what effect this was to have on the agitation among the *sans-culottes*.

The primary assemblies (corresponding, in Paris, to the general assemblies of the Sections) had been convened in June. They were invited to approve or reject the newly drafted Constitution and to appoint electors, who were, in turn, to appoint the deputies to the new revolutionary Assembly, due to meet in the autumn. Royalist agitation was increasing and was winning recruits both in Paris, in the provincial towns, and in the countryside;[3] and it was, no doubt, as much with a view to safeguarding the Republic from being overwhelmed by a royalist reaction as with that of perpetuating its own political existence that the majority of the outgoing Convention, on 22 and 30 August, issued its famous decrees of the 'two-thirds'. These invited the primary assemblies to agree that 500 of the deputies to the new Assembly should be selected from the

[1] Ibid., pp. 182, 233, 254, 276.   [2] Ibid., pp. 47, 65, 182, 184.
[3] Lefebvre, op. cit., p. 173; Aulard, ii. 14, 77–78, 161, 182–3.

existing members of the Convention, while the remaining 250 alone should be freely chosen by the electors. Anticipating an unfavourable response, the Convention began to draft regular troops into the capital on the same day; and, to help redress the balance of opinion, former terrorists were permitted, by a decree of 2 September, to attend the primary assemblies.[1]

The Parisian Sections to whom these proposals were put had changed greatly since Thermidor. By a succession of purges all Jacobins had been driven off the committees and out of the weekly general assemblies of not only the western Sections, but those of the *faubourgs* and city centre as well. When the Sections were convened as primary assemblies to vote on the Constitution, a dozen of them—including such recent rebels as Arcis, Droits de l'Homme, Gravilliers, Jardin des Plantes, Lombards, and Thermes de Julien—specifically excluded all former Jacobins from their deliberations;[2] and, in June, the Jardin des Plantes Section had announced the arrest of no less than thirty-eight alleged 'massacreurs des 2 et 3 septembre'.[3] The purge of undesirable social elements had been equally wholehearted: since Prairial, workers and artisans had either been excused service, or specifically excluded from serving, in the National Guard; and, in September, an observer noted 'qu'il n'y a qu'un petit nombre d'ouvriers qui assistent aux assemblées'.[4] The assemblies were, in fact, coming more and more to resemble, in miniature, that 'République des propriétaires' that had become fashionable in governing circles since Thermidor, and whose social philosophy was well expressed by the *Gazette française* of 24 September:

Dans toutes les associations policées, les propriétaires seuls composent la société. Les autres ne sont que des prolétaires qui, rangés dans la classe des citoyens surnuméraires, attendent le moment qui puisse leur permettre d'acquérir une propriété.[5]

Such citizens were not likely to hesitate long before accepting the draft Constitution of the Year III, whose most signifi-

[1] Aulard, ii. 187, 218.
[2] Others were Place Vendôme, Bon Conseil, Ouest (Bonnet Rouge), Lepeletier, Brutus, and Butte des Moulins (Zivy, op. cit., p. 28; Aulard, ii. 223).
[3] Aulard, ii. 9.
[4] Zivy, op. cit., p. 38; Aulard, ii. 227.
[5] Ibid., pp. 267–8.

cant departures from that of 1793 were that it reintroduced the system of indirect election and restricted the suffrage, even at the primary stage, to tax-payers and, at the electoral stage, to substantial property-owners. All Sections had, in fact, accepted the Constitution with large majorities by 6 September.[1] Quite different was the reception given to the decrees of the 'two-thirds'. When, after heated debates and violent recriminations against the Convention and its Committees, the vote was finally announced in the Assembly, it was found that no less than forty-seven of the Parisian Sections had rejected the decrees —the one exception being the Quinze Vingts, in the Faubourg Saint-Antoine, which accepted them by 433 to 139 votes.[2]

It was not only the decrees of 22 and 30 August themselves which aroused the political opposition of the Sections; further hostility was aroused by the drafting of troops into the capital and the decision to allow former terrorists, so assiduously disarmed and disfranchised by the Sectional authorities only a few months before, to attend the assemblies and vote alongside their political opponents. It was the combination of these factors, bitterly resented by the main body of conservative opinion in the capital, which gave the small group of determined royalists their opportunity to build up a centre of opposition, based on the Parisian primary assemblies and involving many who would have rejected their ultimate aims, had they been openly proclaimed.

The main nucleus of this royalist agitation lay in the Section Lepeletier, 'le quartier de l'argent' and centre of finance and stock-jobbing, the monarchist and moderate leanings of whose leaders and military units have been noted in earlier episodes of the Revolution—the Section whose grenadiers had opposed the Marseillais and defended the monarchy in August 1792, which had most eagerly rallied to the Convention against Robespierre in Thermidor, had been the first to destroy the busts of Marat in February 1795,[3] and had led the armed opposition to the insurgents of Germinal and Prairial. At the outset they found allies in the Butte des Moulins (Palais Royal)

[1] Zivy, op. cit., pp. 24–25.
[2] Ibid.; Aulard, ii. 204–65 (passim).
[3] Ibid. i. 467. For the survival of counter-revolutionary intrigue in the Lepeletier Section during the whole period 1789–94 and its social basis see A. de Lestapis. 'Autour de l'attentat d'Admiral', Ann. hist. Rév. franç., 1957, pp. 6–18, 106–20.

Section,[1] and were soon to find more elsewhere. Lepeletier began to take the lead in the Sectional opposition in early September; but its first attempt to create an agitational centre based on a committee drawn from the forty-eight Sections failed.[2] There followed a week of vigorous agitation among the dissident Sections, in the course of which it was reported in the assembly of Unité that 5,000 terrorists had arrived in the capital and a million *livres* had been distributed in the Faubourg Saint Antoine[3]—all so much grist to the mill of royalist propaganda; and, on 16 September, Lepeletier managed to win the support ('expressément et unanimement') of thirty Sections for an Address of the Citizens of Paris to all the Primary Assemblies of France.[4] Meanwhile, in a separate address to the Convention, the Butte des Moulins revived the claim, not heard since the Gironde–Mountain disputes of 1793, that Paris, because of its political and geographical situation, 'doit avoir l'initiative dans la nomination du Corps législatif et du pouvoir exécutif'.[5]

On 23 September (1st Vendémiaire), the results of the voting in the primary assemblies were announced in the Assembly: the Constitution had been accepted by a large majority all over the country; the decrees of 22 and 30 August as well, but with a substantial number of opponents.[6] The primary assemblies were ordered to wind up their business by 2 October; the electoral assemblies should be convened on the 12th, and the new legislative Assembly be summoned to meet on 6 November. These announcements opened a new phase in the conflict. Several of the Parisian assemblies declared that the returns had

---

[1] It is of interest to note, in retrospect, the political sagacity of a *sans-culotte* of the Bon Conseil Section who, in urging armed support for the Faubourg Saint-Antoine on 4th Prairial, had observed: 'Nous foutrons le bal à ces s. . . aristocrates et muscadins des sections de la Butte des Moulins, Le Peletier et autres sacrés coquins' (Arch. Nat., F⁷ 4662, doss. 2). After the primary assemblies' discussions on the new Constitution minority votes for a monarchy were returned in the following Sections: Unité (6), Butte des Moulins (6), Cité (5) (Aulard, ii, 285; Arch. Préf. Pol., Aa 266, fols. 327-8).

[2] Zivy, op. cit., p. 29.   [3] Aulard, iii. 236.

[4] Bib. Nat., Lb⁴¹ 4598; Zivy, op. cit., pp. 31–32. These were: Amis de la Patrie, Arsenal, Bon Conseil, Bondy, Bonne Nouvelle, Brutus, Champs Elysées, Cité, Droits de l'Homme, Fontaine de Grenelle, Halle au Blé, Homme Armé, Indivisibilité, Jardin des Plantes, Lepeletier, Luxembourg, Marchés, Mont Blanc, Observatoire, Ouest (Bonnet Rouge), Place Vendôme, Poissonnière, Pont Neuf, Réunion, Temple, Théâtre Français, Tuileries, Unité.   [5] Aulard, ii. 246.

[6] The voting was: 914,853 for, and 41,892 against, the Constitution; and 167,758 for, and 95,373 against, the decrees (Zivy, op. cit., p. 35).

been faked and prepared to ignore the instruction to disband.[1] Meanwhile, the *jeunesse dorée*, which had rallied to the royalist cause in a number of Sections,[2] began to molest private citizens and came to blows with the army in the Palais Royal: on one occasion, it was accompanied by shouts of, 'A bas les deux tiers! Vive le roi! A bas la Convention! A bas les baïonnettes!'[3] Jacobins, or Convention-supporters, in their turn, were outspoken in their condemnation of the 'meneurs royalistes' in the Sections. During the night of 25–26 September, three such critics were insulted and manhandled in the Mail and Lepeletier Sections, and brought before the police commissioner of the Butte des Moulins for having suggested that the primary assemblies were composed of 'brigands' and for having expressed their support for the Convention in downright terms:

Que quand on battrait demain la générale et qu'on leur donnerait des billets de garde ils s'en torcheraient le derrière si on leur envoyait ces billets illégalement, et qu'en ce cas leur devoir serait à la Convention.[4]

The Sectional agitation continued. Attempts were made to bring the Quinze Vingts into line with the other assemblies, and several deputations called to persuade them to revoke their support for the decree of the 'two-thirds'; yet, after considerable hesitation, they refused. Popincourt, though opposed to the decree, refused, on 28 September, to accept Lepeletier's invitation to appoint commissioners (shadows of 10 August and 31 May 1793!) 'pour rédiger une déclaration'.[5] The next day, however, Lepeletier presented a declaration to the Assembly which, though failing to win the direct support of 'the majority of the Paris Sections', in whose name it purported to speak, yet bore the signatures of twenty-three, including Butte des Moulins, Fidélité (Hôtel de Ville), Fraternité, and Mail, which had

---

[1] These included Amis de la Patrie, Arsenal, Cité, Droits de l'Homme, Fontaine de Grenelle, Mont Blanc, Pont Neuf, Réunion, Théâtre Français, Fidélité (Hôtel de Ville), and Mail—of which the two latter had not signed the Address of 16 September (ibid., p. 36).

[2] They attended the assemblies of Brutus, Lepeletier, and Luxembourg (ibid., p. 33).

[3] Ibid., pp. 36–37; Arch. Préf. Pol., Aa 98 (Butte des Moulins), 480–1, 483–8, 489–90, 502–5. For attacks on individuals in the Palais Royal and elsewhere see Arch. Préf. Pol., Aa 98, fols. 462, 463–4, 465–6, 467–8, 508.

[4] Ibid., fols. 472–8. For similar expressions see ibid., fols. 499–500 and Aa 189 (Muséum), fols. 208, 211. [5] Arch. Préf. Pol., Aa 266, fols. 327–8, 240–1.

not signed the Address of 16 September;[1] it was a direct challenge to the authority of the Convention which, two days earlier, had forbidden the assemblies to deliberate on matters other than those relating to the elections.[2] The government's measures to prevent the Paris Sections from taking joint action with neighbouring communes[3] provoked a more serious threat: on 2 October Lepeletier and Théâtre Français invited the electors of the other primary assemblies of the capital to assemble on the morrow in the meeting-hall of the Théâtre Français (near the present Odéon), escorted by a military force. Twenty Sections accepted the invitation, though only fifteen attended. That night, Lepeletier, Butte des Moulins, Théâtre Français, and four Sections of the centre declared themselves to be 'in a state of rebellion' against the Convention.[4] The insurrection followed soon after.

Yet to all but a small majority of the 'honnêtes gens', or property-owners, of the Sections such steps did not appear as conscious acts of aggression—far less as deliberate attempts to weaken and overthrow the Republic—but as measures of self-defence against an Assembly whose decrees had infringed the sacred principle of popular sovereignty and which was now trying to impose them by military force and by the wholesale release of the dreaded terrorists or *buveurs de sang*. To them the 'Republic of proprietors' was being undermined and threatened, not by the rebellious Sections, but by the Convention itself. Every measure taken by the government to protect itself and the growing restiveness of the *sans-culottes* served to develop a state of mind in many ways reminiscent of the defensive-offensive attitude of the Parisian *bourgeoisie* in the summer of 1789. Faced with the threat from the Sections, the government not only summoned further army units but enrolled and armed a special force of 1,500 volunteers, including many who had been disarmed after Prairial.[5] Meanwhile, with prices rising further, there were threats once more against *marchands* and *accapareurs* in the markets and *faubourgs*, and there were wide-

---

[1] Zivy, op. cit., p. 43.   [2] Aulard, ii. 279.

[3] Two delegates to Paris from Dreux were arrested; and, at Nonancourt, fighting broke out between local militia and troops of the regular army (Zivy, op. cit., p. 44).

[4] They were Brutus, Poissonnière, Temple, and Contrat Social—the latter not a signatory of the declaration of 16 September.   [5] Zivy, op. cit., p. 52.

spread fears of a general pillage, or attack on food-shops, as in February 1793.[1] But, far from joining forces with the rebels in the Sections in order to settle accounts with the Convention, the *sans-culottes* and *ouvriers* moved closer to the Assembly in common defence of the Republic, and castigated the *sectionnaires* as both royalists and *marchands*. The point is illustrated by the following extracts from police reports of September and early October:

10 September. 'Les ouvriers réunis en groupes, dans différents quartiers, se prononcent pour la Convention, et attribuent aux Royalistes et aux meneurs des Sections tous les arrêtés contre les décrets de 5 et 13 fructidor (22 and 30 August).'

1 October. 'Les motions . . . sont très animées contre les Sections, les marchands, les accapareurs.'

2 October. 'Les groupes des portes Martin et Denis, composés en partie d'artisans, sont tous portés pour la Convention, et *leur opinion serait plus prononcée encore, si la cherté des denrées, du bois, du charbon ne venait les attrister*.'

4 October. 'Dans plusieurs quartiers, des ouvriers rassemblés, *quoique se plaignant de la cherté*, disaient qu'en dépit des royalistes qui mènent les Sections, ils soutiendraient la Convention.'[2]

In the Champs Élysées, the workers manning the local fire pumps went even further: they locked the *sectionnaires* out of their meeting-place and threatened the electors that if they joined the rebels, 'ils les mettraient à la raison'.[3]

The same day (12th Vendémiaire), most Sections armed in defence of property, which appeared, from one quarter or another, to be threatened. In several, citizens attended the primary assemblies under arms and openly defied the Convention; in others, they stood ready without any offensive intent, or were too deeply divided to take any action;[4] in others again, they were compelled to arm by their electors against their will or persuaded to do so by tales of invading brigands or escaped prisoners. In Marchés there was talk of terrorists preparing to disarm Paris and cut the throats of its inhabitants. In Mail armed citizens paraded to shouts of 'à bas les terroristes!'

---

[1] Aulard, ii. 283, 290.   [2] Ibid., pp. 232, 283, 290, 297 (my italics).
[3] Ibid., p. 295.
[4] For example, in Lombards the Civil Committee refused the assembly's request to order the general call to arms; it was sounded, however, against the Committee's wishes, the next morning (Arch. Préf. Pol., Aa 266, fol. 176).

Crowds gathered in the Carrefour de Bussy, at the junction of the Luxembourg and Unité Sections, when the rumour spread that prisoners had escaped from Bicêtre. In Théâtre Français, prisons were guarded by armed *sectionnaires*; and, in Unité, citizens were ordered to parade in arms in the Cour de l'Abbaye, 'parce que les comités de gouvernement ont armé ce jourd'hui tous les buveurs de sang, les terroristes et les malveillants'.[1] In Lepeletier alone royalist aims were openly proclaimed: outside the Section's headquarters in the rue des Filles Saint-Thomas (the present Bourse), passers-by were invited to take up arms 'pour combattre la Convention, et les terroristes, disant qu'il n'y a qu'un roi qui puisse nous rendre heureux'.[2]

That night the government ordered troops under General Menou, commanding the military forces in Paris, to advance on the headquarters of the Lepeletier Section and arrest its leaders. Whether through treachery or through a laudable attempt to avoid bloodshed, General Menou parleyed with the rebels and allowed them to return to their homes. The same night Butte des Moulins, Mail, and Tuileries met to shouts of 'A bas les terroristes! vive la République!' and rallied in support of Lepeletier; they were followed by Brutus, Amis de la Patrie, and Théâtre Français. A general staff now emerged under avowedly monarchist direction, with Richer-Serisy, a royalist journalist, as its chairman and General Danican, of the Théâtre Français Section, as commander-in-chief of its forces.[3] An important link between the two main centres of rebellion on the two Banks was established when Arcis, which controlled the vital Pont au Change, declared for the insurgents at 9 o'clock the next morning.[4] By now some 25,000 *sectionnaires* were under arms; but the majority remained on the defensive, waiting for the non-existent *buveurs de sang* to strike; and only 7,000–8,000 of them—mostly from the Sections adjoining Lepeletier and Butte des Moulins—took part in the armed attack on the Tuileries that followed soon after.[5]

Meanwhile the government had organized its defences. In the place of Menou, who had been arrested, Barras was given

[1] Aulard, ii. 293–9. For similar scares regarding 'brigands', 'terroristes', and 'malveillants' in Arcis, Gravilliers, Ouest, and Temple on 12th and 13th Vendémiaire, see Arch. Nat., W 556–8. [2] Aulard, ii. 297.
[3] Zivy, op. cit., pp. 66–9. [4] Arch. Nat., W 557–8, doss. 2.
[5] Zivy, op. cit., pp. 84–5.

command of the Parisian forces, numbering 5,000 troops of the line and a few hundred volunteers, including 250 from the Quinze Vingts.[1] General Bonaparte, who was as yet unknown to the public, was put in charge of the artillery; he sent Murat with 300 men to Les Sablons to fetch forty cannon, converted the Tuileries into a fortress, and manned all its approaches.[2] When the rebels advanced from the north, where they were solidly entrenched in their home territory of Lepeletier and Butte des Moulins, they were met by withering gun-fire—Bonaparte's famous 'whiff of grape-shot'. A stiff battle took place, with heavy casualties on both sides, in the rue de la Convention (the present rue du Dauphin), which connected the rue Saint-Honoré with the Tuileries.[3] At 6 o'clock the rebels were driven back. They still held the church of Saint-Roch, the Théâtre de la République (Comédie Française), and the Palais Royal; but the two latter fell shortly after nightfall. In the Droits de l'Homme Section there were prison riots at the Hôtel de la Force, whose inmates feared—not without justice—a repetition of the September 'massacres'.[4]

The last and best-known incident in this affair, the battle for Saint-Roch,[5] was fought out on the morning of 6 October (14th Vendémiaire). During the night a general call to arms had once more been sounded in Lepeletier, Théâtre Français, and Butte des Moulins; barricades were built; but the response was halfhearted. Saint-Roch quickly fell to General Vachot; and Barras, soon after, occupied the headquarters of the Lepeletier Section. The next day the Committees ordered the disarmament of all grenadiers and *chasseurs* of the Parisian

---

[1] The other hitherto 'loyal' Sections—Montreuil, Popincourt, Gravilliers, Gardes Françaises, and Panthéon—refused to respond. Gravilliers actually voted to join Lepeletier (ibid., p. 69).

[2] Contrary to legend Bonaparte was, at first, only one of half a dozen generals appointed to serve under Barras in this affair. It was only after the fighting was over that, at Barras's request, Bonaparte was officially recognized as his second-in-command (ibid., pp. 73–78).

[3] There were 200–300 killed and wounded on each side (ibid., p. 95). For claims for damage to property in the Tuileries Section as the result of the battle see Arch. Préf. Pol., Aa 252, fols. 378, 417–18. One claimant, of the rue de la Convention, declared somewhat heatedly, 'que la majeure partie des vitres des croisées de sa maison a été cassée, que le dommage qui lui a été fait est un attentat à sa propriété dont la garantie lui est assurée par la loi' (ibid.).

[4] Arch. Préf. Pol., Aa 136, fols. 224–5.

[5] See, e.g., Balzac's *César Birotteau* (1st edition, 1837).

National Guard and of all citizens, without distinction, of the rebellious Lepeletier, now almost universally condemned as 'le foyer du royalisme, de l'agiotage et de l'anarchie'.[1] All primary assemblies were, once more, ordered to close down; and three separate Military Courts were set up to try those of 'the principal authors and instigators of the rebellion' who had not already made good their escape—they were to meet in Théâtre Français, Lepeletier, and Butte des Moulins. On 9 October (17th Vendémiaire), the police reported in familiar and reassuring tones: 'Paris offre le spectacle de la plus parfaite tranquillité'; though they felt obliged to add: 'Les plaintes et les murmures contre la cherté des denrées . . . sont les mêmes.'[2]

Having crushed the revolt the government was anxious not to drive too deep a wedge between itself and the Sections which had nourished it. It was therefore decided to treat the mass of the rebels as ignorant sheep who had been led astray, and to concentrate its repressive measures against a small number of 'instigators'—journalists, known royalists, and presidents and secretaries of Sectional assemblies. Even most of these were allowed to get away, as the barrières were left open: in the Théâtre Section alone, of fifteen persons whom the police wished to arrest or interrogate during the following fortnight, no less than twelve made their escape.[3] Of maybe 200 persons whom the Committees arrested or wished to arrest[4] only thirty were tried (in person or in their absence) before the three Military Courts set up in the main centres of revolt. Of these, two were executed (five others were capitally convicted in their absence), eight were acquitted, and the rest were sentenced to fines or imprisonment. A year later the sentences on those tried in their absence were quashed as part of a general amnesty.[5] In short the rebels of Vendémiaire were treated with far greater leniency than those of Prairial—a fact which did not escape public notice and comment.[6]

[1] Aulard, ii. 306.   [2] Ibid., p. 313.
[3] Arch. Préf. Pol., Aa 243, fols. 23–60.
[4] I have found 66 such cases in 16 Sections, but the police records are very incomplete: there are, for example, no records for Lepeletier for this period (Arch. Préf. Pol., Aa 71, 74, 75, 77, 134, 158, 168, 175, 177, 202, 211, 214, 219, 242, 243, 252).   [5] Arch. Nat., W 556–8; Zivy, op. cit., pp. 99–101.
[6] 'Quelques-uns observent que les révoltés de prairial étaient moins coupables que ceux du 13 vendémiaire, puisque les premiers ne demandaient que du pain et

But, quite apart from the differences in their aims, the participants in these two events were, of course, of a very different kind. Among those killed and wounded in Vendémiaire, the authorities purported to find a predominance of *émigrés* and hardened royalists. 'Parmi les blessés [wrote Barras in his *Memoirs*] on relève surtout des émigrés, des collets verts ou noirs, peu de boutiquiers . . .';[1] and a press report of 12 October speaks of corpses dressed in rough outer garments, but swathed in fine underclothes bedecked with *fleurs de lis*![2] Yet the government and its agents had too obvious an interest in presenting the insurgents as a small minority of royalists for such reports to be given much credence. Such elements may well have existed among the *jeunesse dorée* taking part in the rebellion; but they are no more typical of the insurgents as a whole than those 'ouvriers pris de vin' whom a police observer's report describes as enrolling among the armed citizens of Lepeletier on 12th Vendémiaire.[3] More typical of the active elements, at least, were the few hundred persons whom the Committees arrested, or sought to arrest, after the rebellion had been crushed. Those whose homes and papers were searched by the police in the Sections were (as far as their identity can be traced) mainly journalists, printers, civil servants, deputies, and stock-jobbers; there was also a wine-merchant among them. Those tried by the Military Courts, apart from their official positions in the primary Sections, were professional soldiers, civil servants, and members of the professions; in addition, they included a former officer of the Royal Household, a wholesale grocer, and a shop assistant (the only *sans-culotte* among them).[4] Doubtless, there were other social elements among the rank-and-file of the armed citizens of the Lepeletier, Butte des Moulins, Brutus, Théâtre Français, Arcis, Luxembourg, and other actively rebellious Sections of 13th Vendémiaire; but, apart from those specially recruited for the purpose,[5] they must have been made up, in the main, of the tax-payers, shopkeepers, and property-owners of

que ceux-ci voulaient attaquer et anéantir la représentation nationale; et cependant . . . ceux de prairial ont éprouvé une bien plus grande sévérité et promptitude dans leur jugement que ceux du 13 vendémiaire' (police observer's report of 13 October 1795 [Aulard, ii. 319]).   [1] Zivy, op. cit., p. 85.
   [2] Aulard, ii. 318.   [3] Ibid., p. 297.   [4] See nn. 4, 5, p. 174.
   [5] A few such cases are reported in the records of the Military Courts; but it is impossible to estimate their importance (Arch. Nat., W 556–8).

the capital, who alone had escaped the social purges carried out since Thermidor. Such citizens had applauded the siege of the Bastille and supported, or condoned, the overthrow of the monarchy; but it was the first—and last—time that they themselves formed the predominant element in a revolutionary crowd or bore the main brunt of street-fighting during the years of the Revolution in Paris.

Yet, though playing little part in these events, the *sans-culottes* were, as always since Thermidor, the principal victims. The Convention, it is true, played to the gallery by decreeing on 6 October that all who could afford to do so should forego their bread ration and buy on the open market;[1] but the measure was of little practical value. High prices and scarcity continued and, as winter approached, became more severe. In November the price of bread on the open market rose to 24 *livres* a pound and a *voie* of coal to 300 *livres*.[2] On the 20th, in the Bon Conseil Section, a dealer was forced by a crowd to sell his bread at 10 *livres* a pound.[3] But the prevailing mood was one of hopelessness and despair in the face of mounting hardships to which there no longer appeared to be any hopes of a solution.

Poverty [wrote an observer at this time] is at its lowest depths; the streets of Paris present the grievous spectacle of women and children on the point of collapse from lack of nourishment; the hospitals and almshouses will soon be insufficient to house the army of sick and wretched. Poverty and hunger have almost completely silenced their voices; but when, on occasion, their voices are raised, it is in muttered imprecations against the Government.[4]

The picture is reminiscent of that painted by the police just a year before. As then, it was followed by worse hardships in the months to come: in December, the price of a pound of bread had risen to 45 and 50 *livres*, and to 80 *livres* in May 1796; and the price of meat to 75 *livres* in January and to 97 *livres* in March.[5] But, this time, the Jacobin remnants were silent, the *sans-culottes* militants were dispirited, scattered, imprisoned, or disarmed, and there was no revival of the combative spirit of

[1] Aulard, ii. 308.　　　　　　　　　　　　　[2] Ibid., pp. 375, 434.
[3] Arch. Préf. Pol., Aa 74, fol. 608.
[4] Aulard, ii. 434 (report of 26 November) [my translation].
[5] E. Levasseur, *Histoire des classes ouvrières en France de 1789 à 1870* (2 vols., Paris, 1902), i. 236–44.

the spring of 1795. Parisians were also suitably cowed and restrained by the new element that had entered the political scene since Vendémiaire: the army, brought in to the capital by the Convention, stayed in occupation[1] under the Directory and paved the way for the military dictatorship of Bonaparte. The days of 'revolutionary crowds', whether composed of *sans-culottes* or of dissident *bourgeois*, were over for many a year.

[1] For early examples of the menace to Parisian civilians constituted by the occupying army (pilfering of goods, damage to property, danger to life and limb) see Arch. Préf. Pol., Aa 252 (Tuileries), fols. 356–68, 373–5, 378, 417–19.

PART THREE

The Anatomy of the Revolutionary Crowd

XII

THE COMPOSITION OF REVOLUTIONARY CROWDS

FOR all their diversity of scope, organization, and design, does a common thread run through the various revolutionary commotions and *journées* described in the preceding pages? In the first place, it is evident that there is a certain uniformity of pattern in the social composition of the participants in these movements: with the single exception of the armed rebels of Vendémiaire, they were drawn in their overwhelming majority from the Parisian *sans-culottes*—from the workshop masters, craftsmen, wage-earners, shopkeepers, and petty traders of the capital. Thus, in respect of social origins, a sharp division is revealed between the mass of demonstrators and insurgents and the political leaders directing, or making political capital out of, these operations—the Paris Electors of May–July 1789, the revolutionary journalists, the leaders of the Paris Commune, or the members of the National Assembly, of the Cordeliers and Jacobin Clubs. These, with remarkably few exceptions, were drawn from the commercial *bourgeoisie*, the professions, or the liberal aristocracy.[1] We shall see later how

---

[1] Mirabeau and Lafayette were, of course, nobles—as were such lesser lights as Musquinet de Saint-Félix and the Marquis de Saint-Huruge. Robespierre and Danton were former *avocats*; Desmoulins, Brissot, and Hébert were journalists and Marat a doctor turned journalist. Sieyès and Jacques Roux were priests, Santerre and Legendre prosperous tradesmen, Maillard an usher, and Fournier l'Américain the son of a well-to-do *bourgeois*. Even Hanriot, the so-called *sans-culotte* commander of the Parisian National Guard in the Year II, was a former customs official. Perhaps the only genuine *sans-culotte* (in the purely social sense of that abused term) among the lesser, yet known, leaders of the Revolution was General Rossignol, a former journeyman goldsmith.

far this discrepancy in origins between leaders and participants is reflected in a discrepancy in their social and political aims. Yet, though overwhelmingly composed of *sans-culottes*, the revolutionary crowds taking part in these events were by no means drawn from identical social groups. It would, in fact, be a gross over-simplification to present them as a sort of homogeneous, nameless 'mob' of the lower orders of Parisian society ever ready to spring into action at the behest of political leaders or in spontaneous response to the promptings of hunger or of momentary grievance. Yet such has only too often been the picture of them that has emerged from the pen of the memorialist or historian.

To correct this picture we shall have to consider the motives underlying the revolutionary *journées*; but, before doing so, we must also look once more at the elements taking part in them. The riots of the autumn of 1787 and 1788 broke out, as we saw, in response to the agitation of the Paris *Parlement* in the course of its struggle with the king and his ministers in the period of the *révolte nobiliaire*. The original impulse to them was given by the lawyers' clerks and ushers of the Palais de Justice; yet, as the riots continued, the clerks were joined by the apprentices and journeymen of the Cité and, in 1788, by the *menu peuple* of the markets and the Faubourgs Saint-Marcel and Saint-Germain as well. In fact those arrested were composed, in the main, of small shopkeepers, craftsmen, and journeymen, of whom one-half were wage-earners in a variety of trades.[1] Workshop journeymen and labourers played an even more conspicuous part in the Réveillon riots of April 1789, when the houses of two manufacturers were pulled down by angry crowds in the Faubourg Saint-Antoine. We saw that, on this occasion, special efforts were made by the itinerant bands, who formed the most active elements among the rioters, to enrol wage-earners both at their places of work—at docks, in workshops and manufactories—and in their lodgings; and wage-earners of every sort accounted for over fifty of some seventy persons killed, wounded, or arrested as a result of the disturbances. While this is an unusually high proportion, it is perhaps not surprising in view of the particular hostility aroused among the journeymen and labourers of the *faubourg* and its approaches

[1] See Appendix III.

by the threats that Réveillon had, either by implication or design, uttered against the workers' living standards at a time of acute shortage and high price of bread.[1]

In a very real sense it may be claimed that the Paris revolution of July 1789 was the work of a great part of the population as a whole: those under arms, may, as we have seen, have numbered as many as a quarter of a million. Yet the most active elements in the main episodes of that great upsurge were far fewer and are reasonably well known to us. The immediate assailants of the Bastille, most of whom were members of the newly formed National Guard, were only a few hundred in number. While a handful of these were prosperous merchants or other *bourgeois*, the great majority were craftsmen, shopkeepers, and journeymen, drawn from a wide variety of trades and occupations, though predominantly from the building, furnishing, and luxury crafts of the Faubourg Saint-Antoine and its adjoining districts.[2] At the Bastille, the unemployed country-workers, whose influx into the capital had been one of the more striking manifestations of the economic crisis which heralded the Revolution, played little or no part; and wage-earners in general, even workshop journeymen, appear to have been in a distinct minority. Quite different was the composition of the crowds that burned down the customs posts between 11 and 14 July and raided and sacked the monastery of the Saint-Lazare brotherhood on the 13th. At the *barrières*, as at the Bastille, there was a small number of *bourgeois*—even of nobles—among the most prominent of the insurgents. The aristocratic adventurer, Musquinet de Saint-Félix, was seen at two of the *barrières* on the approaches to the Faubourg Saint-Marcel. Among the incendiaries of two of the northern *barrières* 'il y en avait deux assez bien vêtus'. The leader of the rioters at Longchamp 'avait l'air d'un seigneur'; at Passy, 'il était vêtu d'une redingote blanche'. Among eighty persons for whose arrest writs were subsequently issued by the Procureur-Général, one is described as wearing 'un habit bleu et canne à pomme d'or' and another as being 'monté sur un cheval blanc'. Yet these were exceptional and the description most often given of the rioters by eyewitnesses was of roughly dressed men and women of the people—local tradesmen, craftsmen and wage-earners,

[1] See pp. 35 ff. above.   [2] See Appendixes III–IV and pp. 58–59 above.

among whom wine-merchants and allegedly professional smugglers were much in evidence, but also working housewives, water-carriers, building and barrel workers, and unemployed from the neighbouring *ateliers de charité*.[1] At the Saint-Lazare monastery, too, the work of looting and destruction seems, in the main, to have been carried out by small tradesmen, employed and unemployed labourers, and local poor rather than by craftsmen and journeymen. This was, of course, unlike the two other episodes, a purely local affair and the persons taking part in it were almost all resident in an area adjoining the junction of the rue du Faubourg Saint-Denis and the rue du Faubourg Saint-Lazare on the northern outskirts of the city.[2]

In the case of the march to Versailles on 5 October, which brought Louis XVI back to his capital, there are no lists of participants to enlighten us, and the police reports on those arrested and killed are far too few in number to make it possible to draw any general conclusions from them. Yet we know from Hardy's *Journal* and from the testimony of various other reporters and witnesses that the women of the markets both initiated the whole movement for bread in September and October and played the predominant part in the first great contingent that set out for Versailles; but we have also noted that the women marchers included, in addition to the petty, privileged stall-holders, fish-wives and working women of the markets, well-dressed *bourgeoises* ('des femmes à chapeau', as Hardy called them), and other women of various social classes.[3] And Hardy, in reporting the strange sight presented by the women crowding into the benches of the Assembly at Versailles, observed:

[Que] cet étrange spectacle l'était encore plus par le costume de plusieurs d'elles qui avec des vêtements de femmes assez élégans, faisaient pendre sur leurs juppons des couteaux de chasse ou des demi sabres.[4]

We know a great deal less about the 20,000 *gardes nationaux* that paraded in the Place de Grève that morning and compelled the apparently reluctant Lafayette to lead them to Versailles later in the evening in the wake of the marching women—but it

[1] Arch. Nat., Z¹ᵃ 886.   [2] Arch. Nat., Z² 4691.
[3] See pp. 73–75 above.   [4] Hardy, *Journal*, viii. 506.

appears from the evidence given by witnesses before the Paris
Châtelet and from the handful of arrests made at Versailles that
they were once more composed of the workshop masters, craftsmen, and journeymen of the Faubourg Saint-Antoine and its
adjoining districts.[1] Yet pride of place, on this occasion, undoubtedly goes to the stall-holders and fish-wives of the central
markets. In this event, more than in any other similar event in
the Revolution, women played the leading part and held the
centre of the stage throughout.

After the prolonged lull of 1790 we saw that the popular
movement, fed by the agitation of the democrats and the
Cordeliers Club, started up again in the spring of 1791. This
time it became more widespread, involving probably every
one of the Paris Sections, and took on a distinctly political form.
Its culmination was the meeting round the *autel de la patrie* in
the Champ de Mars on 17 July 1791, when 50,000 people
gathered to sign a petition drawn up by the Cordeliers Club,
calling for the abdication of Louis XVI. Of the 6,000 persons
who had signed the petition before martial law was declared
and the Garde Nationale opened fire, a great number could
neither read nor write and the petition sheets were studded
with circled crosses in the place of signatures.[2] From the indirect
evidence of the police reports we learn that of some 250 persons
arrested on political charges during the summer and autumn
months, or wounded or killed in the demonstration itself, a
little over half were wage-earners, the rest being mainly self-
employed craftsmen, shopkeepers, and petty traders, with a
sprinkling of *rentiers*, *bourgeois*, professional men, and clerks;
about one in twenty were women.[3]

The assault on the Tuileries in August 1792 was, like that on
the Bastille two years earlier, a largely military affair and was
carried out by organized battalions of the Parisian National
Guard, supported by visiting contingents from a number of
provincial cities. As wage-earners had been virtually excluded
from the Paris militia until a few days previously and as women
would only in exceptional cases be enrolled, we should not

[1] See p. 77 above.   [2] Buchez et Roux, op. cit. xi. 113.
[3] See Appendixes IV–V and pp. 90–92 above. For a fuller treatment of the
social composition of the insurgents and rioters of 1789–91 see my article, 'La
Composition sociale des insurrections parisiennes de 1789 à 1791', *Ann. hist. Rév.
franç.*, no. 127, 1952, pp. 256–88.

expect the insurgents of 10 August to be as broadly representative of the Parisian *sans-culottes* as a whole as those involved in the political movement of 1791. Yet, from the lists of those applying for pensions for themselves or their dependents, we have seen that once more it was the *sans-culottes* of the *faubourgs* and markets that played the principal role: of 123 persons whose occupations appear on these lists, the great majority were craftsmen, shopkeepers, journeymen, and 'general' workers, wage-earners accounting for about two-fifths of the total.[1]

As far as we can tell from incomplete records, the crowds taking part in the food riots of the early months of 1792 and 1793 were of a somewhat different complexion. These were, it may be remembered, more or less spontaneous outbursts directed against provision merchants, particularly grocers, at times of steeply rising prices. Not surprisingly, women were much in evidence in these disturbances: grocers' depositions spoke of cohorts of women invading their shops, and laundresses and market-women of the Faubourg Saint-Marcel were picked out for special mention. One woman, Agnès Bernard by name, was sentenced to two years' prison for her part in the riots of 1793;[2] yet the number of women actually arrested—about one in eight of the prisoners—does not fully reflect the part played by them in these episodes. Another feature was the comparatively large number of cooks and domestic servants that were involved; and of the wage-earners arrested (some three-fifths of those appearing in the records), the majority were, in fact, servants, porters, and other unskilled or general workers rather than journeymen of the traditional crafts.[3]

Both women and craftsmen reappear in large numbers in the great popular revolt against Robespierre's Thermidorian successors in Prairial of the Year III (May 1795). In this respect there is a remarkable resemblance between this outbreak and that of October 1789, when Parisians marched to Versailles with the double object of protesting against the shortage of bread and of bringing the king back to the capital. In both

---

[1] See Appendix IV and pp. 105–6 above.
[2] Arch. dép. Seine-et-Oise, series B, Tribunal Criminel de Versailles, May 1793.
[3] See Appendix IV and G. Rudé, 'Les Émeutes des 25, 26 février 1793', *Ann. hist. Rév. franç.*, no. 130, 1953, pp. 46–51.

cases the women of the markets and *faubourgs* played a significant part and an insurrection of tradesmen and craftsmen enrolled in battalions of the National Guard followed closely on
the heels of a women's revolt for bread. In the case of Prairial
this feature is reflected in the lists of civilians arrested for taking
part in the disturbances: alongside a substantial minority of
women we find a prevalence of workshop masters, independent
craftsmen, and journeymen of a wide variety of trades.[1]

From this brief review we may note both the common feature
and certain significant differences in the composition of the
rioters and insurgents of this period. The common feature is,
of course, the predominance of *sans-culottes* in all but one of these
journées. Yet other social elements played some part: overwhelmingly so in Vendémiaire of the Year IV; but there were
also small groups of *bourgeois*, *rentiers*, merchants, civil servants,
and professional men engaged in the destruction of the *barrières*
(possibly as direct agents of the Orleanist faction at the Palais
Royal), in the capture of the Bastille, the Champ de Mars
affair, the assault on the Tuileries, and in the outbreak of
Prairial.[2] Women, as we have seen, were particularly in evidence
in the march to Versailles, the food riots of 1792–3, and in
Prairial. This is, of course, not altogether surprising, as in these
episodes food prices and other bread and butter questions were
well to the fore; we find women playing a less conspicuous part
in such an essentially political movement as that culminating
in the 'massacre' of the Champ de Mars—less still, of course, in
largely military operations like the assaults on the Bastille and
the Tuileries and in the expulsion of the Girondin deputies
from the Convention. Again, while wage-earners played a
substantial part on all these occasions, the only important outbreak in which they appear to have clearly predominated was
the Réveillon riots in the Faubourg Saint-Antoine. The reason
for this is not hard to find: though it cannot be termed a strike
or a wages movement (Réveillon's own workers do not appear
to have been engaged), it was the only one of these actions in
which there is the slightest trace of a direct conflict between
workers and employers. It is also no doubt significant that
craftsmen—whether masters, independent craftsmen, or
journeymen—were more conspicuously in evidence in some of

[1] See Appendixes IV–V.   [2] See Appendix IV.

the *journées* than in others. This seems particularly to have been the case when a district of small crafts became substantially involved—like the Cité in the riots of 1787 and 1788 or the Faubourg Saint-Antoine on various other occasions; but it also appears to have been a feature of the more organized, political movements—such as the Champ de Mars affair and the armed attacks on the Bastille and the Tuileries—when the driving element was no doubt the small shopkeepers and workshop masters who, in many cases, brought their *garçons*, journeymen, and apprentices along with them. In this connexion it is perhaps of interest to note the sustained militancy of members of certain trades such as furnishing, building, metal-work, and dress. Most conspicuous of all were the locksmiths, joiners and cabinet-makers, shoemakers, and tailors; others frequently in evidence were stone-masons, hairdressers, and engravers; and, of those engaged in less skilful occupations, wine-merchants, water-carriers, porters, cooks, and domestic servants. Workers employed in manufactories (textiles, glass, tobacco, tapestries, porcelain) played, with the exception of the gauze-workers, a relatively inconspicuous role in these movements.[1]

A study of these records confirms the traditional view that the parts of Paris most frequently and wholeheartedly engaged in the riots and insurrections of the Revolution were the Faubourgs Saint-Antoine and Saint-Marcel. This is strikingly borne out in the case of Saint-Antoine, whose craftsmen and journeymen initiated and dominated the Réveillon riots, the capture of the Bastille, and the overthrow of the monarchy, and played an outstanding part in the revolution of May–June 1793 and the popular revolt of Prairial; the police reports suggest, in fact, that it was only in the events of 1787–8 and in the Champ de Mars affair that Saint-Antoine played little or no part. The Faubourg Saint-Marcel, on the other hand, while it contributed substantially to the commotions of September–October 1788 and was represented by a score of volunteers at the siege of the Bastille, only began to play a really conspicuous role in the spring and summer of 1791. After this the part it played was

[1] See Appendix IV. We have noted, of course, the particular militancy of the workers engaged in the *ateliers d'armes* in 1794 and the early months of 1795 (see pp. 134, 136, 145–6 above); but these were generally former locksmiths, joiners, and metal-workers from small workshops of whom mention has already been made.

second only to that of Saint-Antoine in the revolutions of August 1792 and May–June 1793, and in the days of Prairial.[1] In Vendémiaire, of course, the pattern was quite different. Although property-owners and 'moderates' had by now taken charge of even the popular Sections, it was not they but the traditional *bourgeois* Sections of Lepeletier (Bibliothèque) and Butte des Moulins (Palais Royal) that took the lead and held the initiative, while—characteristically—it was the Quinze Vingts in the Faubourg Saint-Antoine which alone dispatched a contingent of armed volunteers to oppose the counter-revolutionary rebels.

But even if it can be demonstrated that the overwhelming majority of the participants in all but the last of the revolutionary *journées* were Parisian *sans-culottes*, how far can they be considered typical of the social groups from which they were drawn? Taine and his followers, while not denying the presence in revolutionary crowds of tradesmen, wage-earners, and city poor, insisted, nevertheless, that the dominant element among them were *vagabonds, criminels,* and *gens sans aveu.*[2] In view of the panic-fear engendered among large and small property-owners by vagrants, petty thieves, and unemployed at different stages of the Revolution, it is perhaps not surprising that such a charge should be made: it was certainly voiced on more than one occasion by hostile journalists, memorialists, and police authorities of the day. Yet, in its application to the capital at

---

[1] See Appendix III. According to the records examined other fairly consistently 'revolutionary' Sections were those adjoining the Hôtel de Ville, such as Arcis and Arsenal, and certain central Sections such as Louvre, Oratoire, Mauconseil, Marchés des Innocents, Gravilliers, and Lombards—with occasional striking outbursts of militancy from Temple, Bondy, and Faubourg Montmartre in the north and from Invalides in the south-west. We are, of course, only dealing with the active participation of Sections, or large groups of individuals within Sections, in street demonstrations and insurrections. No account has, therefore, been taken here of such purely preparatory revolutionary initiative as shown, for example, in April 1793 by the Halle au Blé and Bon Conseil Sections. There is, in fact, no close concordance (except for brief periods and, possibly, in the case of the Faubourg Saint-Antoine) between the militancy displayed in the Sectional committee room or general assembly—often taking the form of petitions and resolutions addressed to other bodies—and that of demonstrators and insurgents resident in the same Section. This may well be because the social composition of the two, except for a brief period in 1793–4, was strikingly different.

[2] Taine, op. cit. i. 18, 41, 53–54, 81, 130, 135; P. Gaxotte, *La Révolution française,* pp. 122, 133–4, 146.

least, it has little foundation in fact. Among the sixty-eight persons arrested, wounded, and killed in the Réveillon riots for whom details are available, there were only three without fixed abode—a cobbler, a carter, and a navvy.[1] Of nearly eighty scheduled for arrest after the burning of the *barrières* and four arrested for breaking the windows of the Barrière Saint-Denis, all were of fixed abode and occupation.[2] Of some sixty persons arrested at the time of the looting of the Saint-Lazare monastery in July 1789, nine were unemployed workers without fixed abode, who were caught up in the general drag-net directed against vagrants, *gens sans aveu*, and dwellers in lodging-houses at the time of the July revolution, and probably had no direct connexion with this affair at all.[3] Every one of the 662 *vainqueurs de la Bastille* and of those claiming compensation for themselves and their dependents in August 1792 was of fixed abode and settled occupation.[4] In the weeks preceding the Champ de Mars demonstration one beggar was arrested for abusing the king and queen, another for applauding their flight from Paris, and two more for causing a disturbance and insulting the National Guard; three other persons are described as being *sans état*; the rest of the 250 arrested during this period appear to have been of settled abode.[5] Nor is there any mention in the records of vagrants or beggars among those arrested in Germinal and Prairial of the Year III; nor, even more surprisingly perhaps, among those implicated in the grocery riots of 1792 and 1793. Doubtless these elements mingled with the rioters and insurgents on such occasions, and we know that they caused concern to the Paris Electors during the revolution of July 1789;[6] but they appear to have played an altogether minor role in these movements.

This does not mean, of course, that unemployed workers or workers and craftsmen living in furnished rooms or lodging-houses (the often despised *non-domiciliés*) did not form a substantial element in revolutionary crowds. This was particularly the case in the early years of the Revolution, when, quite apart from the influx of workless countrymen, there was considerable unemployment in a large number of Parisian crafts; this,

---

[1] Arch. Nat., Y 18795, fols. 444–62.
[2] Arch. Nat., Z^{1a} 886; Y 10649, fol. 18.
[3] Ibid., fols. 20–21.   [4] Arch. Nat., T 514^1; F^{15} 3269–74; F^7 4426.
[5] Arch. Préf. Pol., Aa 167, fol. 51; 157, fol. 134; Ab 324, pp. 28–29, 32, 36, 37.
[6] *Procès-verbal des scéances . . . de l'assemblée générale des Electeurs de Paris*, ii. 156 ff.

however, became a declining factor after the autumn of 1791. We find that eight of some fifty workers arrested or wounded in the Réveillon riots were unemployed and that the proportion was somewhat higher among those arrested in connexion with the Champ de Mars affair.[1] In July 1789, too, there is circumstantial evidence to suggest that unemployed craftsmen, journeymen, and labourers (only a handful of whom were from *ateliers de charité*) were among those that took part in the assault on the Bastille: we know, for example, that substantial sums were raised after the fall of the fortress to relieve the distress of the *faubourg* and that, of 900 stone-cutters who later petitioned the Assembly for unemployment relief, several claimed to have been present at its capture.[2] We have seen, too, that unemployed workers from neighbouring *ateliers de charité* played a certain part in the destruction of the *barrières* and the raid on the Saint-Lazare monastery.[3] The *non-domiciliés* formed a substantial proportion of the wage-earners, small craftsmen, and petty traders of the capital, by no means limited to the unemployed or casual labourers, though it was a fiction of the time that the *hôtel* or *maison garnie* provided only for provincials, foreigners, cut-throats, thieves, and *gens sans aveu*: indeed, the *logeurs* or tenants of such premises were compelled by law to keep a daily check and to give a daily report to the police on all their lodgers.[4] In view of their numbers[5] it is hardly surprising to find them fairly well represented among those taking part in these disturbances—perhaps one in four of those arrested in the Réveillon affair, one in ten among the *vainqueurs de la Bastille*, one in five of those most actively concerned with the Champ de Mars movement, and one in six of those arrested and jailed in the grocery riots.[6] But this is, of course, a quite

[1] See Appendix V.
[2] Arch. Nat., C 134, doss. 6, fols. 14–15; S. Lacroix, op. cit., 2nd series, v. 260.
[3] See pp. 180–1 above.
[4] Monin, *Paris en 1789*, pp. 21, n. 5; 419, n. 4.
[5] In the census of 1795—the only census of the period in which the *non-domiciliés* are accounted for—they number 9,792 for 25 Sections (P. Meuriot, *Un recensement de l'an II*, p. 32); but this was a period of mass exodus, which was draining the hotels and lodging-houses of a large part of their residents (J. de la Monneraye, *La Crise du logement à Paris pendant la Révolution* (Paris, 1928), pp. 12–13).
[6] See Appendix V. To take a random sample from Maillard's list of the *vainqueurs de la Bastille*: J. A. Lamoureux, a tinsmith, lodged with one Boichamp, lodging-house keeper of the rue de Lappe; Marc-Antoine Saint-Paul, a master fisherman, lived in a lodging-house in the Faubourg Saint-Marcel; Jean Gabriel,

separate question from that of Taine's *gens sans aveu* and gives no further indication of the number of vagrants involved. The further contention that criminals and bandits played a significant part in the revolutionary *journées* collapses no less readily when looked at more closely. The police in cross-examining their prisoners habitually inquired whether they had served previous terms of imprisonment and it was easy enough to verify whether, as in the case of more serious offences, they had been branded with the notorious V of the thief or G of the galley-convict. The eight commissioners examining the Réveillon prisoners were able to find only three who had incurred previous convictions of any kind—in two cases these had involved short terms of detention in the Hôtel de la Force on minor charges, whereas the port-worker Téteigne was found to be branded with a V.[1] Yet such a case is exceptional. Of those arrested for looting the Saint-Lazare monastery only one had served a prison sentence—the butcher's boy Quatrevaux, who had spent seventeen days in the Force on a previous conviction.[2] Not one of the twenty-one arrested for the murder of Châtel, lieutenant to the mayor, during a food riot at Saint-Denis in August 1789, appears to have had a criminal record; and only three of fifteen arrested in a similar disturbance at Versailles in September had served previous sentences—one for stealing four pieces of wood in 1788 and two for minor breaches of army discipline.[3] Of some 150 persons arrested in the Paris Sections for political offences during the months preceding and follow-ing the Champ de Mars affair, only four appear to have served previous sentences, and these, again, were of a trivial nature.[4] Not one of the thirty-nine tried in the Year IV for alleged com-plicity in the September massacres had appeared in court before.[5] Such information is, unfortunately, not available for the other great *journées* of the Revolution; yet this evidence, as far as it goes, is overwhelming and should prove conclusive. By and

a printer, lodged with a wine-merchant of the rue de Plâtre, off the Place Maubert; and Gambi and Semain, riverside workers, lodged at the Hôtel de Châlons in the rue du Figuier in the parish of Saint-Paul (Arch. Nat., T 514¹).

[1] Arch. Nat., Y 15101, 13454.　　　　　　[2] Arch. Nat., Z² 4691.
[3] Arch. Nat., Y 10497; Arch. dép. Seine-et-Oise, series B, Prévôté de l'Hôtel du Roi. Procédures, 1789, fols. 7–21.
[4] Arch. Préf. Pol., Aa 137, fols. 177–8; 173, fols. 24, 25–26; 215, fols. 451–2. See also Appendix V.
[5] P. Caron, *Les Massacres de septembre*, p. 111.

large it does not appear, in fact, that those taking part in revolutionary crowds were any more given to crime, or even to violence or disorder, than the ordinary run of Parisian citizens from whom they were recruited.

It may, of course, be argued that such persons were not fully typical of the Parisian *menu peuple* in so far as their participation in revolutionary events marks them off as a militant minority. This point should, however, not be pressed too far. It is presumably true enough of the small groups of *meneurs* (or 'hommes de main', as Caron called them), who probably played some part in even the most seemingly spontaneous of all these movements; we shall return to these in a later chapter. Again, the term may no doubt be used of those *sans-culottes*—rarely wage-earners, as we have seen—who played an active part in the Sections in the Year II, or were members of local Revolutionary Committees or even of the Commune: these are they of course to whom the epithet *sans-culotte*, in its socio-political sense, has most generally been applied. Doubtless, too, we should consider as a militant minority the recognized *vainqueurs de la Bastille*, those who stormed the Tuileries in August 1792, or who advanced on the Convention under arms in Prairial, and even those few hundred who denounced the Constituent Assembly and the National Guard in such downright, political terms—we have noted the case of the cook, Constance Évrard—in the spring and summer of 1791. Yet the term can hardly be applied with the same confidence to the labourers and journeymen who destroyed Réveillon's house, to the men and women who invaded grocers' shops and imposed their own, popular, form of price-control in 1792–3, to the many who applauded the September massacres (or even to the *massacreurs* themselves?), or to the women who marched to Versailles in October or who demonstrated for bread and the Constitution of 1793 in Prairial. Where, then, should we draw the line? This, of course, raises wider issues than those we have been considering in the present chapter. It may perhaps be possible to answer the question with greater assurance when we have examined the motives and other forms of compulsion that drew crowds together and released their revolutionary energies.

Note

XIII

THE MOTIVES OF
REVOLUTIONARY CROWDS

AFTER what has been said, it is perhaps not surprising to find Taine and historians of his school insisting that bribery and corruption, and the quest for loot, were among the major factors stimulating revolutionary activity. 'Dans la plupart des mouvements populaires', wrote Mortimer-Ternaux, 'l'argent joue un plus grand rôle que la passion.'[1] The market-women who marched to Versailles in October 1789 had, according to Taine, been hired for the purpose;[2] while de Gallier, a more recent writer, is even more specific in asserting that artisans and journeymen were bribed to take part in the assault on the Bastille: 'On embauche dans les ateliers [he writes] à raison d'un louis par tête.'[3] The battalions that stormed the Tuileries in August 1792 are described by Mortimer-Ternaux as 'les misérables qui empruntèrent le masque du dévouement patriotique pour se livrer impunément au meurtre et au pillage'.[4]

Certainly, there is no lack of contemporary assertion that appears to confirm this view. Both royalist opponents of the Revolution and revolutionary authorities were remarkably free with such charges when it suited them. Montjoie, for instance, the editor of L'Ami du Roi, claimed to have first-hand proof of the distribution of money to the Réveillon rioters:

J'ai interrogé plusieurs de ces misérables [he wrote] ... et il ne m'est resté aucun doute qu'ils n'eussent tous été payés et que la taxe n'eût été de douze livres.[5]

And Besenval, commander-in-chief of the armed forces mustered to quell the riots, claimed on the unanimous testimony of the

[1] M. Mortimer-Ternaux, *Histoire de la Terreur* (8 vols., Paris, 1862–81), viii. 455.
[2] Taine, op. cit. i. 129.
[3] A. de Gallier, 'Les Émeutiers de 1789', *Revue des questions historiques*, xxxiv (1883), 122. [4] Mortimer-Ternaux, op. cit. ii. 105.
[5] Montjoie, *Mémoires*, i. 91–93; quoted by Chassin, *Les Élections et les cahiers de Paris en 1789*, iii. 58.

Châtelet's police spies '[qu']on voyait des gens exciter le tumulte et même distribuer de l'argent'.[1] Both the principal victims of the riots, Henriot and Réveillon, made similar accusations.[2] Again, in July 1789, a witness of the Saint-Lazare affair claimed that he had seen men displaying bags of silver; while, at the *barrières*, a witness reported that he had heard a rioter boast of having been paid by Mirabeau, and a gauze-worker was reputed to have said that he received 9 *livres* a day 'pour commettre ces désordres'.[3] Hardy noted in his *Journal* that the ringleaders among the bread-rioters, who attempted to hang a baker at Versailles in September, were each found with 33 *livres* in their pockets.[4] The Châtelet inquiry set up to investigate the events of 5 and 6 October solicited from numerous witnesses the testimony that soldiers of the Flanders Regiment, Paris market-women, and others of more dubious occupation had been handsomely bribed—presumably by the Orleanist faction which the inquiry set out to discredit. On this source Taine and his followers have drawn freely to give substance to their arguments.[5]

In the period of social tension preceding the Champ de Mars affray critics of the administration were liberally branded as paid agents of the enemies of the new régime. The gossip-sheet, *Le Babillard,* describes the recently disbanded workers of the *ateliers de charité* as 'ces gens soudoyés par les séditieux'.[6] Bailly, mayor of Paris, had earlier ascribed the Faubourg Saint-Antoine riots of May 1790, when three thieves were done to death by excited crowds, to similar motives: 'L'administration est instruite que l'argent a été répandu dans le dessein d'entretenir une dangereuse fermentation.'[7] Nor were such charges of mass corruption voiced merely by those hostile to the Revolution or by constitutional monarchists like Bailly. To the Jacobin deputies and Paris municipal authorities of February 1793 it seemed inconceivable that the grocery rioters should have been moti-

---

[1] Berville and Barrière, *Mémoires du Baron Besenval* (Collection des Mémoires relatifs à la Révolution française. 2 vols., Paris, 1921), ii. 346.
[2] *Exposé justificatif pour le sieur Henriot* (Bib. Nat., Lb³⁹ 1619); *Exposé justificatif pour le sieur Réveillon* (Bib. Nat., Lb³⁹ 1618).
[3] Arch. Nat., Z² 4691; Z¹ᵃ 886. [4] Hardy, *Journal,* viii. 488.
[5] *Procédure criminelle au Châtelet de Paris* (see especially witnesses nos. 20, 29, 45, 71, 87, 89, 91, 144, 161, 164, 373, 387).
[6] *Le Babillard,* no. xxiv, 26 July 1791.
[7] *Moniteur (réimpr.),* iv. 465.

vated purely by their desire for cheaper coffee, sugar, or soap; and, in the reports drawn up by police agents, there are various references to men and women carrying bundles of *assignats* or distributing handfuls of gold and silver.[1] In Prairial, too, it was claimed by the police on the testimony of their agents 'qu'on disait qu'il avait été distribué des assignats dans le faubourg Antoine pour fomenter la rébellion'.[2]

In the case of persons arrested, wounded, or killed in such disturbances, the authorities had, of course, a ready-to-hand method of not only voicing their suspicions but of checking their validity. In their approach to this problem the French police and municipal or government committees of the day were no different from their counterparts in Britain or elsewhere when faced with a challenge to the existing order by 'the inferior set of people': the venality of the masses was taken for granted and the remedy for popular insurrection was sought in the tracking down of presumed conspirators rather than in the removal of social grievances. Thus, after the Réveillon riots, the arrested and wounded are asked in their cross-examination by the police commissioners whether they have any knowledge of the payment of money to instigate disturbances.[3] Jean-Nicolas Pepin, tallow-porter, when questioned in connexion with the looting of Saint-Lazare and the general events of 12 to 14 July at the Palais Royal and elsewhere, is asked 's'il a reçu de l'argent de ces particuliers'.[4] Michel Adrien, Bastille demolition worker, later hanged for provoking a 'sedition' in the Faubourg Saint-Antoine, is asked 'si avant ou depuis le 12 juillet il n'a reçu de l'argent de différentes personnes pour exciter des tumultes à Paris'.[5] François Billon, charged with threatening to hang a baker at the École Militaire in the autumn of 1789, is asked 's'il a été excité à cela par quelques mal intentionnés qui auraient cherché à le séduire en lui remettant de l'argent'.[6] And so we can go on—with those arrested in the

---

[1] Arch. Nat., AF^{IV} 1470 (reports for 26–28 February 1793). See also Mathiez, *La Vie chère et le mouvement social sous la Terreur*, pp. 153 ff.

[2] Aulard, *Paris pendant la réaction thermidorienne*, i. 742.

[3] See the cross-examination at the Hôtel-Dieu of 23 wounded by Commissioner Beauvallet on 1 May 1789 (Arch. Nat., Y 11033).

[4] Arch. Nat., Z² 4691 (29 July 1789).

[5] Arch. Nat., Y 18768 (21 October 1789).

[6] Arch. Nat., Y 18769 (16 November 1789).

summer and autumn of 1791, with those questioned in connexion with the grocery riots, and those summoned to appear
before the Military Commission or the Committee of General
Security in Prairial of the Year III.[1] Usually the answer is a
flat denial; but sometimes it is of greater interest. In 1791, for
example, we find a domestic servant of the Vendôme Section
replying to the familiar question with the unexpected retort
that, far from receiving money for taking part in political
affairs, it has cost him 24 *sous* in the past four months to do so—
apparently a reference to his subscription to the Jacobin Club
of which he was a member.[2] In Prairial a Quinze Vingts gunner,
when asked if he knows of any distribution of money in the
faubourg, answers 'no'; though he adds that '*he has heard several
people say* that money and two pounds of bread were given out'
to stir up rebellion.[3] But in no single instance do we find a
straightforward admission that a prisoner or other witness has
personally been present at such a transaction.

 Moreover the police had the far more effective course of
searching their prisoners and had every motive for making
public the discovery of any suspicious objects or sums of money
found on them. In nearly every case for which we have records
the results of such searches are purely negative. It is true that
a paper-worker, arrested after the Réveillon riots, was found in
possession of 4 *livres* which he admitted having received from
two individuals whom he had met at the Palais Royal—but this
happened a full week after the riots were over.[4] This seems a
pretty shaky foundation on which to base the charges of mass
bribery proffered by Besenval and Montjoie, and repeated by
writers in the *Revue des questions historiques*. Again, one of four
young workers arrested at the Barrière Saint-Denis on 14 July
1789 was found with 157 *livres*, 12 *sous* in silver in his pockets; but
this sum had quite evidently either been stolen at the *barrières* or
(as the prisoner insisted) been picked up in the raid on the Saint-
Lazare monastery.[5] And even Hardy, who was usually a reliable

[1] Arch. Préf. Pol., series Aa; Arch. Nat., W 546, F⁷ (série alphabéthique).
[2] Arch. Préf. Pol., Aa 206, fols. 366–7.
[3] Arch. Nat., F⁷ 4735, doss. 4 (my italics).
[4] Arch. Nat., Y 14119 (5–6 May 1789). See also the examination by Commissioner Odent of 18 corpses, which had been brought to the Montrouge cemetery
for identification (Arch. Nat., Y 15019), and pp. 41–42 above.
[5] Arch. Nat., Y 10634, fol. 149; 15683.

witness, appears to have been completely misled by reports that
the Versailles bread-rioters of September 1789 were found with
considerable sums in their purses: the police reports relating to
the case are completely silent on the matter.[1] As for the far more
substantial charges of bribery made in the course of the Châtelet
inquiry into the events of October, for lack of other evidence
we must largely discount them owing to the vagueness of the
assertions and the dubious nature of the majority of the witnesses.[2]

While, therefore, the evidence of widespread bribery is
negligible, we cannot discount so readily the desire for loot as
a stimulus to participation in revolutionary activities. Yet, even
so, it has been greatly exaggerated and there is little sign at any
stage of indiscriminate pillage. We have seen that a number of
food-shops were pillaged during the Réveillon riots—in itself
significant of the underlying cause of those disturbances.[3] At
the *barrières*, too, there was looting of the personal effects and
savings of customs officials, though it did not reach great proportions.[4] Looting played a far more substantial part in the
raid on the Saint-Lazare monastery; yet even here it was a
by-product of the main operation, which was to cart grain to
the central corn market.[5] It played some part again, though a
minor one, in the grocery riots of 1793.[6] In the other *journées* of
the Revolution it played no significant part at all. Yet we have
noted that one historian ascribed this motive to the assailants of
the Tuileries in August 1792. Considerable looting, it is true,
followed the fall of the *château*; in fact, we have the record of
134 persons detained in the Hôtel de la Force between 10
August and 2 September of that year for pilfering, or being
suspected of pilfering, a wide variety of objects;[7] and several
others were arrested on such charges in the Sections[8]—though
not one of these appears to have been among the armed attackers.
What is more remarkable is that many humble citizens, wage-
earners among them, went out of their way to deposit valuables
found at the Tuileries for safe-keeping with their Sections;[9]

---

[1] Arch. Seine-et-Oise, series B. Prévôté de l'Hôtel du Roi. Procédures 1789,
fols. 7–21.   [2] See pp. 72–73.   [3] See p. 43.   [4] See p. 49.
[5] See p. 50.   [6] See p. 116.   [7] Bib. Nat., Lb³⁹ 6140.
[8] Arch. Préf. Pol., Aa 88, fols. 514–44; 153, fol. 48; 157, fol. 200; 173, fols. 43–
44; 262, fols. 40–42.
[9] Arch. Préf. Pol., Aa 88, fols. 546–71; 219, fol. 32; 262, fols. 42–44. See also
Sagnac, *La Chute de la royauté*, pp. 297–8.

and that even bitterly hostile witnesses felt compelled to admit that the armed battalions, far from condoning or taking part in pillage, summarily executed those weaker brethren among their unarmed supporters who attempted to engage in it.[1] The same fate befell many who tried to pillage during the September massacres.[2]

In response to what motives, then, did the Parisian *sansculottes* participate in such large numbers in these events? And how far did they differ from the aims of those who promoted or initiated them? In the first place, it is evident that revolutionary crowds, far from being mere passive instruments, were impregnated with the slogans and ideas of the political groups contending for power both on the eve and in the course of the Revolution. During the *révolte nobiliaire*, for example, we saw how the rioting crowds of clerks and journeymen on the Pont Neuf burned Lamoignon, the unpopular *garde des sceaux*, in effigy and chanted the slogans of the *parlementaires*, 'A bas Lamoignon!' and 'Vive Henri IV!'[3] Later, during the Réveillon riots, when popularity had already switched to the Third Estate, shortly to meet at Versailles, the demonstrators (though widely believed to have been incited by royalist agents) shouted the revolutionary slogans of the day: 'Vive le Roi! Vive M. Necker! Vive le Tiers État!'[4] The same political rallying cry of 'Tiers État' was voiced by crowds who burned down the *barrières* and sacked the monastery of the Saint-Lazare brotherhood in July[5]—though, on occasion, its meaning appears to have been transformed into a call to action of the poor against the rich.[6] The new ideas of 'liberty' and 'the rights of man' were also gaining ground among the *menu peuple*, and we find a journeyman gunsmith, arrested at Versailles in August for speaking slightingly

[1] Sagnac, op. cit., pp. 136, 195. Sagnac quotes the *Mémoires* of the royalist Madame de Tourzel: 'Il est remarquable que cette armée de bandits s'était interdit le vol aux Tuileries et mettait impitoyablement à mort ceux qu'elle surprenait s'appropriant quelque chose du château.'

[2] Caron, op. cit., p. 111. Roederer told Napoleon: 'Les massacreurs ne pillèrent pas'.

[3] Hardy, op. cit., viii. 49–68. For a large part of what follows in this chapter see G. Rudé, 'The Motives of Popular Insurrection in Paris during the French Revolution', *Bulletin of the Institute of Historical Research*, xxvi (1953), 53–74.

[4] Hardy, op. cit. viii. 299; Arch. Nat., KK 641, fol. 17.

[5] Arch. Nat., Z^{1a} 886; Z^2 4691.

[6] Arthur Young, too, is inclined to identify 'tiers état' with 'the poor' (see, e.g., *Travels in France and Italy* (Everyman edition), pp. 172–3). See also p. 43 above.

of Lafayette, supporting his claim to a fair hearing with an appeal to 'le droit de l'homme'.[1] In the following weeks, as the rift developed in the National Assembly between the constitutional monarchists and the Court Party over the royal veto, the Parisian *menu peuple* openly championed the former against the latter, and we have seen that unemployed workers of the École Militaire and wage-earners and soldiers in the Place de Grève and the Palais Royal expressed their readiness, several days before the actual event, to go and fetch the royal family back to Paris.[2] Another feature of this period was, of course, the adoption by demonstrators and rioters of anti-clerical slogans; and, at Versailles, the marchers treated the deputies of the clergy with scant respect and greeted them with shouts of 'A bas la calotte!'[3]

In the midst of the social calm of the year 1790 Parisians rallied in tens of thousands, at the call of the National Assembly, to the Champ de Mars to celebrate the first anniversary of the Revolution; but, before many months had passed, the social and political ideas of the democrats and Republicans were beginning to find a response among the more active, at least, of the *sans-culottes*. The results of this indoctrination were clearly evident in the Champ de Mars demonstration of July 1791, called by the Cordeliers Club with a purely political object— to sign a petition questioning the king's right to continue in office after his flight to Varennes. Among the 6,000 who had time to sign the petition or scratch their crosses on it before the arrival of the National Guard, there may have been many who did so without a clear understanding of its contents; yet the cook, Constance Évrard, at least, clearly stated under cross-examination that she believed its purposes were 'à faire organiser autrement le pouvoir exécutif'; and of nearly 130 persons sent to the Force prison in connexion with the demonstration, the great majority had been arrested for expressing

[1] Arch. Nat., Y 18766. The examining police commissioner's retort is not without interest: 'Qu'il parle souvent du mot de liberté et des droits de l'homme, ce qui annonce assez qu'il a l'esprit disposé à la sédition.'

[2] See pp. 71–72.

[3] See pp. 65–66. How far the anti-clerical movement of the Revolution and the later 'dechristianization' movement sprang from the deeper feelings and experiences of the *menu peuple* itself, and how far they owed their origins to non-popular sources such as the professional classes or liberal aristocracy, are still matters for debate. The evidence in favour of the latter theory seems fairly strong.

political opposition to the National Assembly, the city administration, or the armed militia.[1]

It is not possible to produce the same documentary evidence in the case of the armed overthrow of the monarchy in August 1792 and the expulsion of the Girondins in May–June 1793; yet this is hardly surprising, as these were insurrections of an entirely different order dependent for their execution, not on unarmed (or largely unarmed) revolutionary crowds, but on the deployment of a centrally organized armed force—the Parisian National Guard, supplemented in the former case by armed units from Marseilles, Brest, and other cities. Yet these actions, too, marked the culmination of many months of political preparation in which the Parisian *sans-culottes* were thoroughly involved. An important new element was the campaign, initiated by the Brissotins, for a revolutionary war against the crowned heads of Europe, which was immensely popular—as was the war itself in its opening stages: we find evidence of this in the long lists of labourers, craftsmen, and journeymen that volunteered to man the frontiers in the autumn of 1791,[2] and in the great numbers of workers in workshops and manufactories who sent their contributions, or *dons patriotiques*, to the Assembly for the feeding and equipment of the armies of 1792.[3] Again, we see a curtain-raiser to the capture of the Tuileries in the mass invasion of the palace on 20 June, when many thousands of citizens of the Faubourgs Saint-Antoine and Saint-Marcel, both armed and unarmed, presented a petition to the king and shouted the current slogans of the 'patriots'; and it was only four days before the revolution of 10 August that a vast assembly of citizens in the Champ de Mars demanded the king's abdication.[4] The same political prepara-

---

[1] See pp. 86–87, 91.

[2] Chassin and Hennet, *Les Volontaires nationaux pendant la Révolution* (3 vols., Paris, 1899–1904), i. 16–136.

[3] A. Tuetey, *Répertoire général*, vol. iv, nos. 258–392, 1403–22, 1747–9. There appeared, it is true, in March 1792, an *Adresse des ouvriers de la Ville de Paris*, signed by about 250 shopkeepers, craftsmen, and journeymen (the latter in a small minority), which was frankly hostile to the Revolution and to the agitation in favour of war (Arch. Nat., C 284, no. 115, fols. 249bis, 250–1 (in MS.): Bib. Nat., Lb^{39} 11162 (printed copy with significant variations)). There seems little doubt that the war became progressively less popular after the autumn of 1792, though it would be difficult to illustrate the point adequately from documentary sources.

[4] See pp. 100, 104.

tion preceded the revolution of May–June 1793. Already in March of that year the reports of police agents revealed that the need for a new insurrection to purge the Convention was being openly canvassed in the clubs and markets; in April, as we saw, the Jacobins decided to give this movement a precise and limited objective and, following their lead, countless deputations and petitions demanding the expulsion of the Girondin deputies preceded the actual outbreak.[1] Finally, in the riots of Germinal and Prairial of the Year III, the crowds that burst into the Convention demanded support for the political programme of the Mountain and the release of Jacobin prisoners; pinned to their caps and blouses they wore, side by side with the word 'bread', the political slogan, 'The Constitution of 1793'.[2]

There is therefore little doubt that these revolutionary crowds enthusiastically supported and assimilated the objects, ideas, and slogans of the political groups in the National Assembly, Cordeliers, and Jacobin Clubs whose leadership they acknowledged and in whose interest they demonstrated, petitioned, or took up arms. These were the objects, ideas, and slogans of the liberal, democratic, and republican *bourgeoisie* (according to the stage reached by the Revolution as it moved leftwards), which the active elements among the Parisian *menu peuple*, from whom the great bulk of these insurgents and demonstrators were drawn, adopted as their own, because they appeared to correspond to their own interests in the fight to destroy the old régime and to safeguard the Republic. Yet they cannot be regarded as the particular demands of wage-earners, small shopkeepers, and workshop masters as such.[3] Therefore, while acknowledging, against the opinion of Taine and his followers, the part played by the political ideas of the leaders in stimulating mass revolutionary activity, we can accept this only as a partial explanation. It does little to explain such non-political movements as the Réveillon riots, the social unrest that

---

[1] See p. 120.   [2] See pp. 149, 152.

[3] It is not suggested that the *sans-culottes*—particularly the shopkeepers, workshop masters, and other small proprietors among them—had, at no stage, any political ideas of their own. In the period June 1793–July 1794 when, as we have seen, such elements were very active in the Paris Sections, there were numerous petitions and resolutions that expressed their particular social and political claims (see Markov and Soboul, *Die Sanskulotten von Paris*, chaps. 2–5, *passim*). These can, however, have played no part in stimulating participation in revolutionary movements, except in that of 4–5 September 1793.

led up to the march to Versailles or the overthrow of the
Girondins, the invasion of the grocers' shops in 1792 and 1793,
or even the essential character of the riots of Germinal and
Prairial—and yet these movements were an intrinsic part of
the Revolution and involved people drawn from (broadly) the
same social groups as those who stormed the Bastille, overthrew
the monarchy, and signed the Champ de Mars petition. Above
all, it does not explain the almost continuous undertone of
social unrest among the *menu peuple*, which characterized the
whole period under review, and without which it would have
been impossible for the contending political groups to mobilize
the popular battalions on the great political *journées* themselves.
To arrive at a more satisfactory explanation we shall have to
find some more constant factor than the changing political
slogans of the leaders, look more closely at the social demands
of the participants themselves, and test the validity of Georges
Lefebvre's contention: 'L'intervention de la foule suppose des
motifs particuliers.'[1]

Perhaps not surprisingly such an inquiry reveals that the
most constant motive of popular insurrection during the
Revolution, as in the eighteenth century as a whole, was the
compelling need of the *menu peuple* for the provision of cheap
and plentiful bread and other essentials, and the necessary
administrative measures to ensure it. We have already observed that, on more than one occasion, this preoccupation,
being at variance with the ideas on free trade and property
held by all *bourgeois* groups, was apt to put a strain on their
alliance with even the most advanced of the political leaders.
It would, of course, have been comforting for the journalists
of the Palais Royal and the deputies and orators of the revolutionary Assemblies and Jacobin Club if the common people of
the markets and *faubourgs* had been content to bedeck themselves with tricolour cockades and *bonnets rouges* and to mouth
patriotic-radical slogans without concerning themselves over-
much with the satisfaction of their own particular needs and
grievances—if the Réveillon rioters, for example, had not
insisted on accompanying their shouting of the unexceptionable
slogan of 'Vive le Tiers État!' with the destruction of the properties of such stalwarts of the official Third Estate as Henriot and

[1] G. Lefebvre, *La Révolution française. La révolution de 1789*, pp. 141–2.

Réveillon; or if the women of the markets had been merely satisfied to march to Versailles to fetch the royal family to Paris —as required by the constitutional monarchists—without agitating so violently and vociferously for more bread and better quality flour. This divergence of interest is perhaps best illustrated in the grocery riots of 1792 and 1793. In the first it was solemnly proposed by the Jacobins that the crisis might be solved if only the small consumers would voluntarily abstain from purchasing such 'luxuries' as coffee and sugar—'ces chétives marchandises', as Robespierre termed them; in the second, the rioters who, when the authorities refused to act, imposed their own particular form of price-control, were castigated by both Marat and Robespierre as the dupes of Pitt and the counter-revolution. 'Les hommes du 14 juillet ne se battent pas pour des bonbons.'[1] It was the old social dilemma that few of the revolutionary leaders—the Jacobins only for a brief period in 1794—were prepared to face. Yet Barnave at least showed some appreciation of the problem and its significance for the Revolution when, in relating the events of October 1789 to his constituents, he clearly distinguished between the purely *political* aims of the *bourgeoisie* and the predominantly *economic* preoccupations of the people—'y mêlant l'intérêt du pain qui commençait à être rare'.[2]

The theme of shortage and high prices (particularly of bread) as a major cause of social disturbance in eighteenth-century France has been given a new emphasis by Professor Labrousse's studies in price fluctuations and budgets in the years preceding the outbreak of the Revolution. He has shown the catastrophic effects on the poorer sections of the urban population in particular of the chronic shortage and high price of wheat during these years, reaching a climax in the period 1787 to 1789.[3] We can appreciate better the Parisian wage-earners' hostility to the old régime and their willingness to join with the *bourgeoisie* in destroying it, when we learn, for example, that the proportion of his income that a Paris builder's labourer would have to spend on bread in order to maintain his normal

---

[1] Mathiez, op. cit., pp. 46–49, 151–7.
[2] Arch. Nat., W. 12, nos. 200–1.
[3] C.-E. Labrousse, *La Crise de l'économie française*, pp. xlii–l.

consumption rose from about 50 per cent. in August 1788 to
over 80 per cent. between February and July 1789.[1]

It is, therefore, not surprising that the price and supply of
bread should emerge so clearly from contemporary documents
as a constant source of popular disquiet during the insurrectionary movements of 1788 and the early years of the Revolution. We saw, for instance, that the movement launched by the
Palais clerks in the Place Dauphine and on the Pont Neuf to
celebrate the recall of the *Parlement* in August 1788 coincided
with a sudden, sharp rise in the price of bread—and that, a few
days later, the *menu peuple* of the *faubourgs* and markets joined
the riots and changed their character. Again, the fact that the
riots, after a fortnight's respite, started up again with renewed
vigour may have been due as much to the further increases in
the price of bread in early September as to the enthusiasm
aroused by the dismissal of Lamoignon.[2] Further rises followed
in November and December and, by the time of the Réveillon
riots in April, the price of the 4-lb. loaf had already, for three
whole months, stood at the unusually high level of 14½ *sous*; in
fact, as we have seen, it was this high cost and scarcity of bread
that served as the prime cause of the disturbances, though it
was not their immediate pretext.[3] Apart from other supporting
evidence, the point is underlined by a report sent to the king
by the lieutenant of police, Thiroux de Crosne, in the middle of
the riots: 'Quoique la sédition paraisse toujours dirigée contre
le sr Réveillon, on demande vivement la diminution du prix
du pain.'[4] After this temporary eruption the bread motive
appears almost continuously as the main stimulus in the protracted popular movement which sprang up at the end of May,
rose to a climax in the days of 12–14 July, again on 5–6 October,
and did not visibly subside until the early days of November,
when the first stage of the political revolution, which placed
power firmly in the hands of the constitutional monarchists, was
already long completed.

In the weeks preceding the July revolution, which culminated
in the seizure of the Bastille, Hardy vividly illustrates in his
Journal the popular mood and the authorities' constant fear of
an outbreak on a larger and more violent scale than that which

---

[1] See Appendix VII, Table 1.   [2] See pp. 31–32; Hardy, op. cit. viii. 72.
[2] See pp. 42–43.   [4] Arch. Nat., C 221, no. 160/146, fol. 48.

had occurred in the Faubourg Saint-Antoine at the end of April. On nine occasions during May, June, and the early days of July he records the posting of special guards in the markets to quell bread riots. On 13 June he noted that the police had forbidden a rise in the 4-lb. loaf from 14½ to 15 *sous*, as requested by the bakers, for fear of social disturbance. A few days before the political revolution itself, a crowd publicly burned the pamphlet, *Espérance du peuple*, which suggested two prices for bread—3 *sous* and 5 *sous* per lb. 'Le but avait été mal saisi par la classe inférieure du peuple', wrote Hardy.[1] During the July revolution the same theme constantly recurs. A major purpose of the organized attack on the Saint-Lazare monastery in the early hours of 13 July was to remove grain stored in its barns to the central markets, and among the local raiders, who looted its rooms, the cry of 'allons chercher du pain' was heard; while to the wage-earners, shopkeepers, and petty traders who burned down the customs posts under orders from the political leaders at the Palais Royal the issue was quite a simple one—to ensure cheaper food and drink: as a locksmith seen smashing the furniture in the office of the Chaillot *barrière* put it, 'nous allons boire le vin à trois sols'.[2]

It has, of course, already been amply demonstrated that the popular insurrection of 5-6 October, which achieved its political purpose of bringing the royal family to Paris, was even more clearly connected with the provision of bread for the hungry Parisian masses. We have seen that the lull following the murder of Foullon and his son-in-law, Berthier, on 22 July was short-lived. After a good harvest the price of bread was reduced to 12 *sous* in early August; but, partly owing to drought, the expected abundance in the bakers' shops did not materialize and the resultant shortage which lasted until November kept the popular movement in a state of continuous animation. There followed the remarkable series of demonstrations of market-women and others at the Hôtel de Ville and at bakers' shops, culminating in the great march to Versailles. Noteworthy features of this *journée* were of course the slogans shouted by the marchers—'Cherchons le boulanger, la boulangère et le petit mitron'—and the persistence with which the

[1] Hardy, op. cit. viii. 310, 312, 320, 332, 341, 344, 348, 351, 378, 384.
[2] Arch. Nat., Z² 4691; Z¹ᵃ 886.

women and their spokesman, Maillard, urged the National Assembly to feed the people of Paris.[1]

The Champ de Mars demonstration, on the other hand, although widely supported by the *menu peuple* in a majority of the Paris Sections, was, in many respects, the most purely political of the great Parisian *journées*. By early November 1789 the protracted social movement of the first months of the Revolution had been brought to an end as the result of the energetic measures taken by the National Assembly and Commune to supply Paris with cheap and plentiful bread and to curb public disorder. The particular problems arising from the collapse of the *assignat* and war-time inflation were yet to come; so it came about that the Champ de Mars demonstration of July 1791 was the only one of the great Parisian *journées* which was not associated in any way with a popular demand for the control of bread or of any other commodity of prime necessity. The demonstration was, it is true, preceded by a considerable wages movement, involving many thousands of journeymen in a variety of trades, and by months of agitation among the unemployed, threatened with starvation by the closure of the *ateliers de charité*. Yet these movements, though taken under the protective wing of the Cordeliers Club and its affiliates, cannot be directly connected with the Champ de Mars demonstration itself, and the demands of these workers are not reflected in the cross-examination of the numerous wage-earners, shopkeepers, and workshop masters arrested during this period in the various Paris Sections.[2] In this respect the Champ de Mars affair appears to fall outside the general pattern of social disturbance that is here emerging. The particular demands of the common people are, in this case, rarely expressed in economic terms.[3]

[1] See Part II, Chap. V.

[2] See Part II, Chap. VI. Despite the political importance of these independent movements of wage-earners—particularly those of 1791 and 1794—they do not appear to have played any significant part in stimulating participation in the *journées* of this period (unless, of course, we include the workers' demonstration at the Hôtel de Ville on 9 Thermidor). The economic motive most frequently impelling the wage-earners was of course the one that they shared with the *menu peuple* as a whole—the need for cheap and plentiful bread. [For a more detailed examination see my article in the *Bulletin of the I.H.R.* (cited in note 3, p. 196 above), pp. 71–74.]

[3] There was, however, the lady who, when accused of insulting Lafayette and the National Guard, retorted that her accuser would not be so willing to assume their defence 'si le comparant avait autant de mal que les autres à gagner le pain qu'il mange' (Arch. Préf. Pol., Aa 153, fol. 7); and the kitchen-maid who, when

Their demands or protests assume, rather, a political form—
as witness the numerous insults hurled at the National Guard
and the complaints against the Assembly and city government by
those arrested in the course of the movement. In a sense, therefore, the Champ de Mars affair and the popular movement of
the spring and summer of 1791 mark an important stage in the
development of the Parisian *sans-culottes* as a force in the Revolution. With the split in the revolutionary *bourgeoisie* and the
determined attempts of the democrats and Republicans to win
a firm basis of support among the people, they are beginning
to play a more independent part: not only are they voicing
the particular programme of the more radical section of the
bourgeoisie, but they are beginning, however hesitatingly, to
express their own social grievances in a political form.

With the spring of 1792 the Revolution entered on a new
stage which was to give a new intensity and a new direction to
the popular movement. The fall in the value of the *assignat* had
already begun to react on prices in the autumn of 1791, but it
was the outbreak of war that ushered in a long period of
catastrophic inflation, during which the attention of the *sans-
culottes* was almost continuously riveted to the problem of prices,
food shortage, and the compelling need to force measures of
control in the price and supply of the necessities of life on unwilling authorities. From the point of view of the social historian
the whole period is dominated by this preoccupation. It was
only by degrees, however, that the Parisian *sans-culottes*, with
the assistance of the Hébertists and, even more, of the Enragés,
found a programme of social demands that corresponded to
their particular needs and which they were eventually to force
for a brief period on the Jacobin Convention in the shape of the
Maximum Général. In the first place their anger was directed
against grocers, as it had previously been directed against
bakers and millers, and found expression in attempts by revolutionary crowds to compel provision merchants (particularly the
more substantial among them) to sell their wares at pre-Revolu-
tion-prices. The first of these movements—that of January–
February 1792—was limited to a few north-central districts and

asked to explain her hostility to the National Guard, said she found difficulty in
buying bread owing to the bakers' lack of small change (Arch. Préf. Pol., Aa 85,
fol. 117).

to the Faubourgs Saint-Antoine and Saint-Marcel and had no immediate consequences: at any rate its connexion with the political *journées* of 20 June and 10 August, which followed shortly afterwards, was only of the slightest.[1] The riots of February 1793 were on a far greater scale and of far greater political importance.[2] On this occasion the movement did not come to a stop after the mobilization of the National Guard, the arrest of a few dozen rioters, and the adoption of a number of minor administrative palliatives. In a general sense it continued unabated after the enactment of the Maximum Général in September 1793, through Robespierre's Revolutionary Government and its fall in Thermidor, to the last outbreak of the *sans-culottes* in Prairial of the Year III, and beyond. More immediately it merged with the wider movement, guided by the Jacobin Club, which led to the revolution of May–June 1793 and the overthrow of the Girondins, by this time identified, in the eyes of the more active *sans-culottes* at least, with the hated *accapareurs* or hoarders of food. It is not proposed to analyse here the daily reports of the police and the National Guard in April and May of that year, but they establish clearly enough that, at the back of the agitation of those months for violent remedies and purges of the Convention, lay deep popular concern at the continuous rise in food prices.[3]

The expulsion of the Girondins, though transferring power to the Mountain, did nothing immediately to allay this unrest. The reports sent in by police agents in June are almost identical with those of April or May. The shortage of bread in bakers' shops had again begun to arouse concern in March, and by the end of August bread queues and bread riots had again become a familiar feature of Parisian life. This was the immediate background to the *journées* of 4 and 5 September 1793, directed by the Commune under Hébert and Chaumette. It was under their stimulus, as we saw, that the Convention decided at last to decree the law of the Maximum Général and to set on foot the long-delayed *armée révolutionnaire* which, as an instrument of the Terror, was intended to ensure the provision of adequate supplies of grain and meat to Paris from the surrounding countryside.[4] Under such consistent popular pressure

[1] See pp. 95–96, 101.   [2] See pp. 114–18.
[3] Arch. Nat., F⁷ 3688²; AF^IV 1470; F^Ic III Seine 27.   [4] See pp. 126–7.

the Convention and the Committee of Public Safety managed, by a policy of controls, to halt inflation and to arrest for several months the fall in the value of the *assignat*. Yet the demands of a revolutionary war and the hostility of the farmers, who tended to hoard their produce in anticipation of better times or failed to produce at all for fear of requisition, kept food in short supply. The resultant hardships and the Committee's attempts to appease the large producers and merchants naturally placed a heavy strain on the alliance between the government and the Parisian *sans-culottes*. We have already shown that the dissatisfaction thus occasioned, together with the particular grievance of the wage-earners at the authorities' decision to enforce the Maximum on wages, served to deprive Robespierre and his associates of the popular support on which they might have counted on the fatal night of 9–10 Thermidor.[1]

Many Parisians of course lived to regret the fall of Robespierre. Yet they took some time to react: the arrest of Jacobin leaders, the purges of local committees, the closure of political clubs, and, even, the destruction of their own creation, the Maximum Général, left them more or less unmoved; but when, largely in consequence of government policy, inflation ran riot and the prices of essential goods soared, a popular movement of formidable proportions took shape, gathered momentum in the early months of 1795, and broke out in the violent eruptions of Germinal and Prairial. As we saw, this movement merged with and drew strength from the political movement directed by the surviving popular societies and Jacobin remnants; but its most consistent and continuous element was the hunger for bread.[2]

Yet we must avoid the temptation, to which some historians have succumbed, of presenting the popular insurrections of the Revolution as being almost exclusively dominated by short-term economic considerations—as though each of these movements were, in essence, an 'émeute de la faim'. This was, of course, far from being the case. Not only have we seen that the *sans-culottes* identified themselves fully with a wide and varying range of political ideas and calls to action as the Revolution advanced; but we noted in particular the essentially political nature of the Champ de Mars demonstration and the whole

[1] See Part II, Chap. IX.　　　　　[2] See Part II, Chap. X.

preparatory movement leading up to it, not to mention the active support of the *sans-culottes* for such exclusively military-political actions as the assault on the Bastille and the Tuileries and the expulsion of the Girondins from the Convention. In the case of the Champ de Mars affair at least, the threat of famine or of rising prices played no part whatsoever. On the other hand, we have noted the abstention of the *sans-culottes* from any direct political intervention in the events of Vendémiaire of the Year IV.—in striking contrast with their active participation, a few months earlier, in the days of Germinal and Prairial, though popular concern with bread-shortage and inflation was as acute in the one case as in the other.[1] The essential difference lay of course in the changed political conditions and in the very differing aims of the rebels of Vendémiaire from those of Prairial:[2] in spite of continuing inflation and near-famine conditions, the active *sans-culottes* were not prepared to carry their hostility to the Thermidorian Convention to the point of giving comfort to the declared enemies of the Republic. The point is of interest: for one thing, it serves to disprove the contention that the *menu peuple*, for lack of political maturity, were prepared to follow the lead of any demagogue irrespective of their own interests or inclinations; for another, it shows that a satisfactory explanation of popular participation in, or abstention from, these movements cannot be given without proper account being taken of both political and economic factors and that concentration on the one to the exclusion of the other will only produce a distorted picture.

Yet, when all is said and done, the inescapable conclusion remains that the primary and most constant motive impelling revolutionary crowds during this period was the concern for the provision of cheap and plentiful food. This, more than any other factor, was the raw material out of which the popular Revolution was forged. It alone accounts for the continuity of the social ferment that was such a marked feature of the capital in these years and out of which the great political *journées* themselves developed. Even more it accounts for the

---

[1] See Part II, Chap. XI.

[2] It is true that there were other factors involved, of which the most important was the purely technical difficulty of staging a concerted action after the crushing defeat of Prairial; but this does not invalidate the argument in any way.

occasional outbreaks of independent activity by the *menu peuple*, going beyond or running counter to the interests of their *bourgeois* allies and castigated by them as 'counter-revolutionary' —such outbreaks as the blind fury of the Réveillon rioters or the more constructive efforts of Parisians to impose a form of popular price-control in the grocery riots of 1792 and 1793. Yet without the impact of political ideas, mainly derived from the *bourgeois* leaders, such movements would have remained strangely purposeless and barren of result; and had the *sans-culottes* not been able to absorb these ideas, as claimed by some writers, their influence on the course and outcome of the Revolution would have been far less substantial than in fact it was.

P

XIV

THE GENERATION OF
REVOLUTIONARY ACTIVITY

YET other questions still remain, to some of which we may attempt an answer. How were the revolutionary ideas and slogans transmitted? How did the particular atmosphere of tension, violence, audacity, or heroism, that marked revolutionary crowds, develop? How were the various *journées* of the Revolution in Paris prepared and organized? What were the links between the leaders and the crowds that often formed in response to their calls to action? To what extent were their actions spontaneous?

It is evident, of course, that popular opinion—the opinion of those who, as individuals, formed the main body of revolutionary crowds—was, in large part, moulded by the direct experience of the *sans-culottes* themselves. Some historians have denied this, but we have already said enough of their reaction to economic crisis and to rising food prices not to have to press the point further. Yet here we are mainly concerned with those ideas and slogans that the *menu peuple* derived and assimilated from other social groups and which, as we saw, both gave them a new political vocabulary and drew them into action as allies of the revolutionary journalists and politicians on the great *journées* of the Revolution. How were these ideas conconveyed to them? In the villages at least, where illiteracy was almost general, such communication must have been largely oral;[1] and even in provincial capitals and market towns, where Arthur Young found such a dearth of newspapers,[2] the reports of the deputies of the Third Estate of 1789 were read aloud to their constituents in the main square or outside the Town Hall.[3] We may assume, too, that Hébert's *Père Duchesne*, which was

---

[1] For peasant illiteracy at this time see E. Champion, *La France d'après les cahiers de 1789* (Paris, 1921), pp. 209–10; and D. Mornet, *Les Origines intellectuelles de la Révolution française* (Paris, 1933), pp. 420–5.

[2] A. Young, *Travels in France and Italy*, pp. 174, 178–9, 182, 185–6.

[3] G. Lefebvre, *La Grande Peur de 1789*, pp. 83–84.

distributed free of charge to army units by the Ministry of War in 1793,[1] served a similar purpose in the barrack-room; and we are told that the Constitution of 1791 was read aloud and discussed at meetings of *ouvriers* and others before its adoption by the Assembly.[2]

Yet it would be wrong to assume that the Parisian *sans-culottes* at least had no direct access to the writings of the political thinkers and journalists. In the capital the degree of literacy appears to have been considerably higher than in the provinces: this is attested by both contemporary observers and police records. Restif de la Bretonne no doubt exaggerated when he wrote in 1789:

Depuis quelque temps, les ouvriers de la capitale sont devenus intraitables parce qu'ils ont lu, dans nos livres, une vérité trop forte pour eux: que l'ouvrier est un homme précieux.[3]

But the police reports of the Châtelet and the Sections on those arrested in riots in this period suggest that the great majority of the small workshop masters and tradesmen, and a large proportion of the adult male wage-earners—the journeymen, in particular—could at least sign their names.[4] While we may perhaps take it for granted that no considerable body of *sans-culottes* read Rousseau or any other *philosophe* first-hand,[5] there is ample evidence that some pamphleteers and political writers addressed themselves directly to them, their women-folk included. This is suggested by the large number of pamphlets not only purporting to reflect the views of the *faubourgs* and markets, but written in popular language. Hébert's *Père Duchesne* is an obvious case in point; and it is interesting to note the remark attributed to a market-woman in a tract of 1789, *Premier dialogue*

---

[1] The number of copies ordered by the Ministry was increased from 8,000 to 12,000 daily as from 18 September 1793 (Tuetey, *Répertoire*, vol. x, no. 2221).

[2] *Mercure national et étranger*, no. viii, 23 April 1791.

[3] Restif de la Bretonne, *Mes inscriptions. Journal intime*, p. 130; quoted by D. Mornet, op. cit., p. 426.

[4] See Appendix V. The incidence of literacy of course varied widely between one type of wage-earner and another—even more between one type of *sans-culotte* and another. It was considerably higher, as we should expect, among workshop masters than among journeymen; higher among journeymen than among 'general' workers or workers in manufacture; considerably higher among men than among women; and, of male workers, lowest among the many unemployed workers and peasants who filled the *ateliers de charité* in the early months of the Revolution.

[5] For a discussion of this question see Mornet, op. cit., pp. 281, 449.

entre une poissarde et un fort de la halle: 'Dame! j'savons lire, j'espère!'[1] The democrats in 1791 made special efforts to reach the wage-earning population: Marat's *Ami du peuple* published letters from journeymen cobblers and building workers;[2] and Louise Robert, in describing the enrolment of 'la classe la moins éclairée de la nation' in Fraternal Societies in May 1791, wrote: 'Les journaux ne lui suffisaient plus: ils lui avaient inspiré le désir de s'instruire.'[3] There is evidence, too, among the police reports drawn up in connexion with the Champ de Mars affair of the same year, which suggests that a fair proportion, at least, of the active journeymen and other workers read the revolutionary press. Thus the cook, Constance Évrard, told the police commissioner of the Fontaine de Grenelle Section 'qu'elle lisait Prudhomme, Marat, Audouin, Camille Desmoulins et très souvent l'Orateur du Peuple';[4] a tobacco-worker, when arrested, was found in possession of *L'Ami du peuple*; a commercial traveller claimed to derive his views from Marat and Prudhomme; and a journeyman cobbler asserted that his opinions were formed through reading the democratic press.[5] It is perhaps significant that, of the 250 persons arrested in the Paris Sections on political charges during this period, twelve were news-vendors, accused of distributing pamphlets and newspapers among such customers.[6] If this is the case with the active wage-earners, we can only assume that the democratic press circulated far more widely among the small workshop masters and tradesmen, who were more literate than their journeymen and often moulded their views.

It seems likely, therefore, that the journals and pamphlets played an important part in shaping popular opinion on the main political questions of the day and, on occasion at least, in preparing such opinion directly for the great revolutionary events in the capital. We have seen the part played by the democratic press and the Cordeliers Club in the agitation of 1791; and Marat's ferocious incitement against merchants and grocers in *Le Publiciste* of 25 February 1793 no doubt contributed

---

[1] Bib. Nat., Lb³⁹ 7577, p. 16.
[2] *L'Ami du peuple*, no. 468, 24 May 1791, p. 7; no. 487, 12 June 1791, pp. 1–5.
[3] *Mercure national et étranger*, no. xxiv, 10 May 1791, p. 376.
[4] See p. 87.
[5] Arch. Préf. Pol., Ab 324, p. 44; Aa 76, fol. 40; Arch. Nat., DXXIXᵇ 36, no. 376, fol. 37.   [6] See Appendix IV.

to the atmosphere of the grocery riots that immediately followed. Again, according to police informers, more than 500 copies of the pamphlet, *L'Insurrection du peuple*, were distributed in appropriately selected districts of the capital on the eve of the revolt of 1st Prairial of the Year III.[1] Yet, by and large, it seems probable that the great body of participants in these events were drawn in by other means.

A more systematic indoctrination of the *sans-culottes* with the ideas of the advanced political groups took place by their enrolment in the National Guard and, above all, in the clubs and societies and Sectional committees. It is interesting to observe how the *sans-culottes*, at first excluded from positions of authority in such bodies, gradually came to 'capture' them and even, for a brief period, to convert them into vehicles for the expression of their own views rather than those of the political leaders who established them. When the National Guard was formed in July 1789, Barnave rejoiced that, in large part at least, it was 'bonne bourgeoise';[2] soon after, 'passive' citizens were implicitly debarred from its ranks;[3] yet such distinctions were abolished in the summer of 1792; and, with Hanriot's appointment as commander-in-chief in May 1793, it became largely composed of *sans-culottes* and, for many months, it remained the obedient instrument of the Jacobin Commune. There seems little doubt that it was under these conditions that the future military cadres of the armed uprising of Prairial developed.

An even more significant part in the political education of the Parisian *menu peuple* in Jacobin principles must have been played by the clubs and popular societies. We have already considered the role of certain of these, the so-called Fraternal Societies, in moulding the opinion of cooks, water-carriers, and other *simples ouvriers* in the months preceding the Champ de Mars demonstration and petition of 1791—at a time when the 'parent' body, the Cordeliers Club, opened its doors to 'passive' citizens by reducing its subscription to 2 *sous* a month.[4] During this period, societies like the Club Fraternel des Jacobins, the Club

[1] A. Aulard, *Paris pendant la réaction thermidorienne*, i. 735.
[2] Arch. Nat., W 12, nos. 197-8.
[3] M. Tourneux, *Bibliographie de l'histoire de Paris pendant la Révolution française* (5 vols. Paris, 1892-1913), ii, no. 6702.   [4] See pp. 85-86.

des Halles, and the Société des Ennemis du Despotisme, largely composed of such elements, were able to attract meetings of 300 to 800 persons.[1] By early 1792 the societies were springing up everywhere and, in May of that year, the complaint is made that the workers of the Gobelins tapestry manufacture 'sont toujours de garde ou de club'.[2] A year later a bookbinder of the Panthéon quarter protests at the scandalous behaviour of the workers employed on the construction of the church of Sainte-Geneviève, 'qui se sont formés en club et se réunissent en dehors et après l'assemblée de la section'.[3]

The Revolutionary Committees were, from the start, largely composed of sans-culottes: at the inaugural meeting of their representatives they petitioned the Commune and the Convention to indemnify their members, 'presque tous des ouvriers qui vivent de leur travail'.[4] Even the Champs Élysées Section, on the western boundary of the fashionable residential quarters, had, in June 1793, a Committee 'composé d'ouvriers, mêlés avec quelques bourgeois'.[5] From figures quoted earlier we saw that in the Year II the overwhelming majority of commissaires were shopkeepers, small workshop masters, and independent craftsmen, while only a little over a quarter were made up of rentiers, manufacturers, civil servants, contractors, and members of the professions.[6] While we know a great deal less of the composition of the Popular Societies in Paris, it appears to have been somewhat similar;[7] the same is true of the Commune of this period;[8] and the regular attendance of a fair body of sans-culottes at the general meetings of the Sections was assured by the payment of 40 sous as compensation for time lost from work.[9]

---

[1] I. Bourdin, Les Sociétés populaires à Paris pendant la Révolution (Paris, 1937), pp. 131-9. Mlle Bourdin's account covers only the period 1790-2.

[2] Arch. Nat., O¹ 2053.

[3] Dutard's report to Garat on 29 May 1793 (A. Schmidt, op. cit. i. 330).

[4] Arch. Nat., F7 250.   [5] Schmidt, op. cit. ii. 52.   [6] See pp. 130-1.

[7] There is only a handful of such lists now surviving for Paris. Of these the most complete that I have seen is that of the Société Populaire et Républicaine de l'Unité in the Théâtre Français Section, whose 280 members in January 1794 comprised some 200 craftsmen and shopkeepers in 60-odd trades (15 joiners, 24 tailors, and 39 shoemakers), 28 clerks, 16 miscellaneous wage-earners, and a score of merchants, contractors, and stock-jobbers (Brit. Mus., F. 827 (5)). What little I know of the membership of provincial societies I owe to Mr. Richard Cobb, who has worked extensively on French provincial records.   [8] See p. 131.

[9] E. Mellié, Les Sections de Paris pendant la Révolution française (Paris, 1898), p. 145.

This being the case, it is not surprising that these bodies often became centres for the propagation of the views of the *sans-culottes* themselves—derived in part, it is true, from the revolutionary leaders—rather than of those of the majority in the National Convention. This, of course, helps to explain why the larger part of the societies was compelled to close down and the independence of the Sections restricted in the spring of 1794[1]—a process that was completed by the more 'moderate' Convention after Thermidor, with the wholesale 'purging' and reconstruction of the Commune, the *comités civils* and *comités révolutionnaires*, and the withdrawal of the 'forty *sous*'.[2] As we have seen, by September 1795, there were no societies, clubs, committees, or assemblies that still directly voiced the opinions of the *sans-culottes* and, when the primary assemblies were convened to discuss the draft Constitution of the Year III, only a handful of *ouvriers* attended their meetings.[3] Henceforward, their agitation and the utterance of their grievances were once more confined to the streets, workshops, and markets.

With all this, a considerable—perhaps the preponderating—part in spreading ideas and moulding opinions must still have been played by the spoken word in public meeting-places, workshops, wine-shops, markets, and food-shops. There is ample evidence for this view in the police reports and other contemporary comment on the disturbances of the period. During the *révolte nobiliaire*, it was the Pont Neuf and Place Dauphine that served as the main focal points of political gossip and revolutionary agitation: this was of course due to their immediate proximity to the Palais de Justice, where the *parlementaires* and their most vocal supporters, the lawyers' clerks and ushers, both had their scene of operations. In June 1789 the centre of agitation, which had lain for a while in the eastern *faubourgs*, shifted to the Palais Royal, where the Duke of Orleans and his retinue of orators, pamphleteers, and journalists had established their headquarters. It was from here that the crowds set out on the night of 30 June to release the eleven Gardes Français from the Abbaye prison, where they had been locked up for refusing to fire on Parisians who had

---

[1] Thirty-nine of these were closed down in Paris during May–June 1794 alone (A. Soboul, 'Robespierre and the Popular Movement of 1793–4', *Past and Present*, May 1954, p. 69).   [2] See p. 143.   [3] See p. 166.

demonstrated at Versailles against the attempt to dismiss Necker a week before.[1] It was at the Palais Royal, too, that Camille Desmoulins and others gave the call to arms on 12 July, which touched off the Paris revolution; and it was from here that parties set out to destroy the *barrières*, to search religious houses and gunsmiths' shops for arms, and to fetch grain to the central markets from the monastery of the Saint-Lazare brotherhood.[2] The Palais Royal played its part again in preparing opinion for the march to Versailles in October: it was in its gardens and cafés that the Marquis de Saint-Huruge and his associates tried to force the pace by inciting Parisians to march at the end of August; and, with greater success, its orators repeated the incitement on 4 October.[3] In the years to come the arcades and gardens of the Palais Royal (soon to be renamed the Maison de l'Égalité) became notorious as a haunt of prostitutes, money-jobbers, speculators, and gamblers rather than of political journalists or orators; but it reappeared as a centre of agitation after Thermidor: it was the scene of verbal exchanges between *muscadins* and *sans-culottes* in the spring of 1795 and of more violent outbreaks between royalist youth and republican troops in the days before Vendémiaire.[4] On other occasions the Palais Royal might be eclipsed by the Place de Grève, lying within easy reach of the popular districts and on the threshold of the city government (we have seen its importance on 13 July, on 5 October 1789, and on 9 Thermidor);[5] or again by the Champ de Mars, the main venue for the great organized demonstrations of celebration, or the Terrasse des Feuillants, at the entrance to the National Convention. Other local rallying centres were the Grande rue du Faubourg Saint-Antoine and the rue Mouffetard.

It is less frequently that we find documentary evidence of the part played in preparing popular opinion by the small workshop, where master and journeyman worked, and often supped

---

[1] Hardy, op. cit. viii. 373; *Relation de ce qui s'est passé à l'Abbaye St. Germain*, Bib. Nat., Lb³⁹ 1882; M. Rouff, 'Le peuple ouvrier de Paris aux journées du 30 juin et 30 août 1789', *La Révolution française*, lxiii (July–December 1912), 430–54.

[2] See pp. 48–51.   [3] See pp. 70–71, 72.   [4] See pp. 148, 169.

[5] See pp. 51–55, 74–75, 137–9. Police soundings on the state of *sans-culotte* opinion tended, in the year 1793–4, to be taken in the Place de Grève; later in 1795, however, the favourite centre for such operations appears to have moved north to the Portes Saint-Martin and Saint-Denis (see Caron's and Aulard's collections of police *rapports* for the period, *passim*).

and slept, under the same roof, and where the former's influence affecting the questions of the day must often have been decisive. Yet we catch occasional glimpses of this relationship in the police reports. We saw, for instance, how the porcelain manufacturer Olivier, deliberately or otherwise, incited his workpeople against Réveillon by relating in lurid detail the speech that the latter was reputed to have made in the local assembly of the Sainte-Marguerite District concerning his workmen's wages.[1] More typical are the cases where masters and journeymen shoulder arms together to participate in the armed uprisings of the Revolution: we saw how the brewer Santerre was followed to the Bastille by one of his journeymen (and there must have been many other such cases that day in the Faubourg Saint-Antoine); again, we saw Pierre Homette, a journeyman cabinet-maker, accompanying his employer to the Tuileries on 10 August 1792; and farmer Guerre of the Invalides Section arranging for the attendance under arms of his two farmhands during the revolution of May–June 1793.[2] On other occasions we hear of workshop masters being accused by hostile witnesses of inciting their workpeople to take part in such movements as the Champ de Mars demonstration and the rebellion of Prairial.[3]

The wine-shop may have been equally potent as a channel of communication for revolutionary ideas. Not only do wine-merchants appear to have been a most consistent revolutionary group—note their numbers at the Bastille and, even more, at the burning of the barrières[4]—but their shops were the common resorts of the menu peuple of the faubourgs and markets who, on Sundays and Mondays in particular, flocked beyond the barrières to the popular taverns of La Courtille, Les Porcherons, and La Nouvelle France. These became ready centres for gossip and exchanges of news and rumour; for this and other reasons it is perhaps no coincidence that so many of the great journées in Paris should have started or gathered momentum at the weekend.[5] Gustave Bord overstates his case, but there may be more

[1] See pp. 40, 43.
[2] See pp. 58, 107, 124.
[3] Arch. Préf. Pol., Aa 153, fol. 6; Arch. Nat., F⁷ 4707, doss. 2; F⁷ 4735, doss. 2.
[4] See Appendix IV and pp. 181, 185.
[5] The Réveillon riots and grocery riots of 1793 were on Mondays; the Paris revolution of 1789 began on a Sunday; the Champ de Mars demonstration of

than a grain of truth in his assertion that many of the assailants of the Bastille were recruited in the wine-shops of the Saint-Antoine quarter.[1] Certainly the marble-dealer, Joseph Chagnot, who was injured by a falling tile during the Réveillon riots, admitted being picked up by an itinerant band of rioters as he sat drinking in a wine-shop; other persons arrested on that occasion told a similar tale.[2] And Jean-Nicolas Pepin, a chandler's tallow-bearer, related, in the course of a detailed account of his experiences during the July revolution, how he joined the insurgents on the night of the 12th near the Barrière Saint-Martin, after spending the evening drinking and dining 'chez le Sr Chevet Md de vin au Soleil d'Or à la Nouvelle France'.[3]

Food-shops and markets were even more obvious centres of agitation. In days of shortage and high prices tempers became easily frayed in the queues that formed at grocers', butchers', and bakers' shops. We have seen, on the evidence of Hardy, the precautions taken by the Government to keep disturbances in check during the weeks preceding the outbreak of the Revolution in Paris by drafting troops into the markets and posting guards at the door of bakers' shops; and how, during the following summer and autumn, when such measures were no longer possible, bakers became, on more than one occasion, the victims of popular violence.[4] Although there was no further resort to 'la lanterne' after 1789, bakers' and grocers' shops continued, as has been amply illustrated, to be common centres of disturbance and starting-points for popular demonstrations that often assumed insurrectionary proportions.

How, then, from such comparatively small beginnings in markets, bakers', and wine-shops did gatherings of craftsmen, wage-earners, and housewives develop into great revolutionary crowds with all the attendant manifestations of fear, heroism, or destructive violence? Historians have shown a certain reluctance to deal with such questions, believing that they belong more particularly to the province of the sociologist or specialist in crowd psychology.[5] Yet the specialist, for lack of historical

July 1791 was held on a Sunday; 2 June 1793 (the crucial day in the anti-Girondin revolution) was also a Sunday; 10 August 1792, on the other hand, was a Friday.

[1] G. Bord, 'La Conspiration maçonnique de 1789', Le Correspondant, 10 and 25 May 1906, pp. 521–44, 757–67.   [2] Arch. Nat., Y 11033, 15101.

[3] Arch. Nat., Z² 4691.   [4] See pp. 67–69, 78.

[5] See Caron, Les Massacres de septembre, p. vi.

perspective or exact documentation, may just as easily go astray, as was the case with Gustave Lebon, the author of a number of books on this subject. According to Lebon revolutionary crowds tended to be formed of criminal elements, degenerates, and persons with destructive instincts, who responded more or less passively to the call of 'leaders'[1]—which suggests both that the author had fed on a surfeit of Taine and that his generalized conception of revolutionary crowds would be equally appropriate to all times and to all places. Georges Lefebvre, on the other hand, has argued that the revolutionary crowd is not an abstraction but a social phenomenon which, though responding to certain general laws of development, arises in particular historical circumstances and as the result of particular social pressures and ideas; so it was in the case of the French Revolution.[2]

In this respect it is of course necessary to distinguish from the rest those occasions when crowds collected in direct response to the call of leaders—for such demonstrations, for instance, as that in the Champ de Mars on 17 July 1791, or such organized military operations as the armed assault on the Tuileries in August 1792 and the expulsion of the Girondin deputies on 2 June 1793. In such cases as these the participants have already been won over, both in general and in particular, to the objects of the demonstration, the collective mentality of the crowd corresponds closely to that of the groups of individuals forming it, and there is no sharp mutation from one state of mind to another[3]—unless, of course, some new and unexpected factor intervenes to upset the balance.[4] A demonstration like that of 20 June 1792 belongs to a somewhat different category: on this occasion, the break-through into the Tuileries

[1] G. Lebon, La Révolution française et la psychologie des révolutions (Paris, 1912), pp. 55–61, 89–93. By the same author: Psychologie des foules (Paris, 1895).

[2] G. Lefebvre, 'Foules révolutionnaires', Ann. hist. Rév. franç. xi (1934), 1–26; reprinted in Études sur la Révolution française (Paris, 1954), pp. 271–87. Although Lefebvre's study is concerned mainly with the year 1789, his conclusions are generally applicable to the whole period 1787–95. I am largely indebted to him for the ideas discussed in the present chapter.

[3] Ibid., p. 272.

[4] As, for example, in the early stages of the Champ de Mars demonstration, when two unknown individuals were found hiding under the 'autel de la patrie' (see p. 89), and the 'treachery' of the Swiss guards who, on 10 August 1792, unexpectedly opened fire on the Marseillais (see p. 104). Both incidents led to panics and provoked massacres.

(which may have been purely spontaneous) transformed a peaceful procession of citizens, headed by their acknowledged leaders, into a riotous and spontaneous challenge to the authority of the king in person.[1]

It is, in fact, this element of mutation or transformation that marks the revolutionary crowd in its most typical form—such as it appeared most frequently in the opening stages of the Revolution,[2] before the creation of the National Guard and the Sections had provided a framework within which the challenge to authority might be more systematically organized. We saw, for example, that the more or less harmless jubilations of the Palais clerks and Cité journeymen in August 1788 were transformed into riots of insurrectionary proportions by the entry of the small masters and journeymen of the *faubourgs* and markets; and this transformation was not brought about by the insidious agitation of leaders (as Taine or Lebon would have us believe), but by the effect on the small consumer of the sudden rise in the price of bread.[3] No such abrupt transformation took place in the course of the Réveillon riots, whose contributory causes were already in being after Réveillon and Hanriot had made their offending speeches on 23 April. But nevertheless they developed from murmuring groups in wine-shops and workshops and marching bands parading through adjoining districts into orgies of destruction—and heroic resistance to bullets—in the Faubourg Saint-Antoine on the night of the 28th: here the tempo and character of the insurrection developed not so much through the intervention of external factors as by the swelling of the numbers of demonstrators by recruitment and the prevailing atmosphere of nervous excitement engendered by the approach of the meeting of the States General.[4]

The classic examples of this kind of transformation are afforded by the two great Parisian insurrections of the summer and autumn of 1789. In the first a more or less peacefully disposed Sunday crowd of strollers in the Palais Royal was galvanized into revolutionary vigour by the news of Necker's dismissal and the call to arms issued by orators of the entourage of the Duke of Orleans. From this followed a sequence of events that could not possibly have been planned or foreseen in detail

[1] See p. 100.
[3] See pp. 31–32.
[2] Lefebvre, op. cit., p. 279.
[4] See pp. 34–36.

by even the most astute and determined of the court's opponents: the parades on the boulevards with the busts of Necker and the Duke of Orleans; the assaults on the *barrières* and the Saint-Lazare monastery; the search for arms in gunsmiths' shops, religious houses, and arsenals; the massive demonstrations outside the Hôtel de Ville, where the new city government was in the process of formation; the storming of the Invalides in search of weapons to arm the newly created *milice bourgeoise*; and finally (partly planned, but mainly the outcome of a whole series of fortuitous events) the frontal assault on the Bastille and the murders of de Launay and de Flesselles.[1] In October we have a similar pattern of growth and development, though the final stages of the insurrection bear the mark of a more conscious political direction. Certainly, to the majority of the housewives and market-women demonstrating for cheaper and more plentiful bread in the early morning of 5 October, as to the casual observer, the opening shots of the uprising must have seemed no more than a continuation of a whole series of similar demonstrations during September. Even the mass invasion of the Hôtel de Ville was but a repetition on a larger and more violent scale of similar forms of protest in preceding weeks. Yet the diversion of the women to Versailles (partly the outcome of weeks of agitation by the 'patriots' and partly of the intervention of Maillard and his *volontaires de la Bastille*) gave an entirely new political content to their demonstration. From this point, although still professing mainly economic aims, it merged with the political insurrection launched by the 'patriots' and supported by the marching contingents of the Parisian National Guard.[2]

We have seen that the transformation in the nature and activities of revolutionary crowds may result from the intervention of widely varying factors. Leaders are undoubtedly an important element, though they do not play the outstanding part assigned to them by Taine and Gustave Lebon; we shall return to them later. But one factor should be noted here, though it is by no means peculiar to the events of the French Revolution and may be, in fact, one of the most constant elements contributing to certain states of collective mentality at all times and in all places. This is the element of panic-fear,

[1] See pp. 48–56.   [2] See pp. 73 ff.

propagated by rumour—particularly liable to develop where communications are scarce and news is slow and hard to come by. Whatever its immediate origins in other circumstances, here it arose from the threat, real or imaginary, to three matters of vital moment—to property, life, and the means of subsistence. In various forms we find such panics arising intermittently during the revolutionary years—both in towns and country-side—and becoming more frequent with the outbreak of war in April 1792. The latter years of the old régime were haunted by the *pacte de famine*, according to which the king and his ministers were credited with the deliberate intention of seeking to starve the people by creating an artificial scarcity of bread. A similar notion gained credence—though this time associated with Turgot and not with the king—at the time of the grain riots of 1775, and probably contributed to their scope and persistence.[1] During the Revolution, the new authorities, and sometimes millers and bakers, were charged with similar designs: we see it in the fermentation in the Faubourg Saint-Antoine in the weeks following the Réveillon riots, in the persistent outcries against *accapareurs*, in the violent assaults on millers and bakers and on Châtel, mayor's lieutenant of Saint-Denis; and the notion is almost continuously present, though diverted temporarily by the 'patriots', in the insurrection of 5–6 October. It reappears in the invasions of grocers' shops in 1792 and 1793; again in Prairial and on the eve of Vendémiaire; and the Revolutionary Government of the Year II was able to turn it to good advantage in its indictment of Hébert and his associates who, in the spring of 1794, were charged, along with other crimes, with the design of creating disorders in order to starve the capital of supplies.[2]

The panic-fear of an attack on property, another recurrent theme, particularly affected the *bourgeoisie*, substantial farmers, and peasant proprietors, but it also vitally concerned the small property-owners among the *sans-culottes*. We see it graphically illustrated in the constant repetition of the scare of 'la loi agraire', used with telling effect to weaken the resolve of Jacobin and other *bourgeois* democrats, who might threaten to effect even a partial distribution of property. Its most famous

[1] See pp. 23–24.
[2] Arch. Nat., W 76, 78; Tuetey, *Répertoire*, vol. xi, nos. 1–171.

expression, however, was the panic that seized large parts of the countryside and affected Paris itself in the summer of 1789—the episode known to historians as 'la Grande Peur'. It had its origins in the combination of rural unemployment and vagrancy, arising from the economic crisis of 1787-9, with the widespread belief that the privileged orders were about to shatter the hopes and illusions aroused by the summoning of the States General. Thus the vagrants of the countryside—the *errants* or *brigands*—were seen as the agents of a *complot aristocratique*, whose assault on small rural properties was hourly expected and aroused widespread panic. In the villages, where the peasants armed to meet a danger that proved illusory, their defensive units soon transformed themselves into aggressive bands that fired *châteaux* and destroyed manorial rolls.[1] In Paris, which felt its backwash, the presence of several thousands of rural unemployed, many of them herded into the *ateliers de charité* on the hill of Montmartre, while others roamed the streets, inspired similar terrors. This was, of course, in part the background to the creation of the Parisian *milice bourgeoise*, set up to meet the double danger of an attack on property by the dreaded *gens sans aveu* and a military *coup* against the capital by the Court Party at Versailles: Hardy echoes these terrors in his relation of events on the morrow of the fall of the Bastille.[2] The theme recurs in the spring of 1791 and, particularly, in the weeks following the king's flight to Varennes: to the Parisian municipal authorities and the majority in the Constituent Assembly, the unemployed, soon to be finally disbanded from the *ateliers de charité*, seemed the actual or potential agents of the *émigrés* at Coblenz—'ces gens soudoyés par les séditieux', as *Le Babillard* called them.[3] Some democrats inclined to this view: the radical journalist Loustalot equated the 'prolétaires' with 'tous les citoyens susceptibles d'être facilement corrompus'; and even Marat, for all his deep compassion for the poor, feared that the inmates of the public workshops might become the ready tools of counter-

[1] G. Lefebvre, *La Grande Peur de 1789*.
[2] 'Le complot infernal qui avait existé de faire entrer, dans la nuit du 14 au 15, 30.000 hommes dans la capitale, secondés par des brigands' (Hardy, op. cit. viii. 395). See also the Chevalier de Beaurepaire's pamphlet of August 1789, in which it is alleged that the Montmartre unemployed were building fortifications for training artillery against Paris-(*Rapport à MM. du district des Petits Mathurins*: Bib. Nat., Lb⁴⁰ 285). [3] *Le Babillard*, no. xxiv, 6 July 1791, p. 3.

revolution.[1] On the eve of the demonstration of July 1791 there was a report of a plot to abduct the royal family and to set fire to the capital with the aid of 40,000 men mainly recruited from the unemployed,[2] and it was widely believed that the poor would stage a spectacular revenge on the propertied classes for the 'massacre' of the Champ de Mars.[3] Such fears might arouse a militant response both among revolutionary democrats and among the conservative elements of the western districts. We find examples of the former tendency in the frequent panics stirred up by rumours of imminent prison outbreaks—the various *complots des prisons*—and the lesser-known episode of the *complot militaire* of the spring of 1794.[4] We have seen a classic example of the second in the panic that swept the Paris Sections on the eve of Vendémiaire, when shopkeepers, civil servants, and proprietors sprang to arms in order to defend their properties and lives against the dreaded terrorists or *buveurs de sang*, who were presumed to be letting loose on them the familiar *brigands* and scum of the prison population. In this case, of course, it was the royalists who turned the panic to their advantage by converting it into an armed rebellion against the Convention.[5]

The third type of panic—arising from a threat to life—is, of course, closely related to the last, and sometimes, as we have seen, they appear together. We saw it in the siege of the Bastille, when de Launay's folly in opening fire on the assembled crowds led to the cry of treachery and the massacre of the Governor and a number of his garrison.[6] An almost identical situation arose during the assault on the Tuileries in August 1792.[7]

---

[1] Jaurès, *Histoire socialiste*, iii. 388; *L'Ami du peuple*, no. 422, 7 April 1791, p. 6. There is certainly ample evidence that attempts were made by counter-revolutionaries in these early years to stir up discontent—with the Revolution and the new authorities—among the wage-earners of the *faubourgs* and, particularly, among the unemployed in the public workshops; but, although taken seriously by the authorities and the democrats, they met with surprisingly little success. (See E. Tarlé, 'La Classe ouvrière et le parti contre-révolutionnaire sous la Constituante', *La Révolution française*, lvii (1909), 304–26, 385–404; and my *Parisian Wage-Earners*, i. 260–9.)   [2] Arch. Nat., DXXIX[b] 33, no. 348, fol. 26.
[3] Ibid., no. 347, fols. 9–10.
[4] R. C. Cobb, 'Le Complot militaire de ventôse an II', *Paris et Île-de-France*, vii (1956), 221–50.
[5] See pp. 170–2 above. The panic of the property-owners engendered, in turn, a panic among the prison population, who feared a repetition of September 1792 (see p. 173).   [6] See pp. 55–56.   [7] See p. 219, n. 4, above.

But these panics were momentary and, though affecting the behaviour of the besiegers and their supporters, did little to alter the course of events. On a far greater scale and more drastic in its consequences was the panic that developed in the days following the expulsion of Louis XVI from the Tuileries, when the departure of the volunteers for the frontiers was accompanied by the rumour that the inmates of the prisons were waiting to break loose and to slaughter the women, children, and aged: thus was created the atmosphere of mass hysteria that led to the September massacres.[1]

Such defensive reactions were typical of the response of *sans-culottes*, small proprietors, and even *bourgeois*, to many of the situations that developed on the eve and in the course of the French Revolution. It is the failure to recognize this fact that has led so many historians and writers from Burke onwards to represent the Revolution as a sort of unbroken chain of innovations or as the systematic unfolding of the long-conceived plans of the *philosophes* by the devotees of 'political messianism'.[2] Quite apart from its other fallacies such a conception once more reduces the role of the *sans-culottes* to that of passive instruments —unless it can be shown, of course, that they, too, were imbued with a desire for 'total renovation'. The opposite is, indeed, the case. At every important stage of the Revolution the *sans-culottes* intervened, not to renovate society or to remodel it after a new pattern, but to reclaim traditional rights and to uphold standards which they believed to be imperilled by the innovations of ministers, capitalists, speculators, agricultural 'improvers', or city authorities. This defensive reaction to events is a characteristic feature of each one of the great *journées* that led up to or marked the progress of the Revolution. The clerks and journeymen who rioted in August–October 1788 hailed Henri IV and acclaimed the *Parlement* as the custodian of 'ancient liberties' against the innovations of the king's ministers. The Réveillon riots arose as a defensive action by Saint-Antoine

---

[1] See pp. 108–10.
[2] See, e.g., J. L. Talmon, *The Origins of Totalitarian Democracy* (London, 1952), in which the Revolution is represented as the logical outcome of the thought of Rousseau, Mably, Morelly, &c., and the thought and deeds of their disciples (Robespierre, Saint-Just, and others)—men 'impelled by a revolutionary impetus of total renovation, and by the idea of a society reconstructed deliberately with a view to a logical and final pattern' (p. 63).

Q

wage-earners against the threats to wages and living standards that were said to have been uttered by two employers of the Faubourg Saint-Antoine. The Paris revolution of July 1789 began as a protest against the dismissal of a popular minister and developed into a massive defensive action against the 'aristocratic plot' visibly being hatched at Versailles. In the following weeks the assaults of peasant bands on the *châteaux* of the nobility and the destruction of fiscal records were a forceful riposte to the innovations of the *seigneurs*, whose systematization of feudal contract and extension of seigneurial obligations constituted an attack on the traditional property rights of the peasantry. The October insurrection took the form of a demand for the restoration of cheaper and more plentiful bread and of a defensive action against the military measures being prepared by the court; and the forcible return of the king to the capital revived an ancient tradition in the relations between the monarch and the people of Paris. Even the overthrow of the monarchy was as much the final act in a movement of self-defence against counter-revolutionary intrigue as the logical outcome of plans hatched by consistent Republicans.[1] We have seen how the majority of the Sections that armed before Vendémiaire, far from considering themselves as rebels against lawfully constituted authority, believed that they were defending themselves against the attacks of a tyrannous Assembly.[2] And what were the repeated outbreaks of popular price-control or *taxation populaire*, but the assertion of the traditional right of the small consumers to protection against the capitalist innovation of the 'free market' and the new-fangled principles of supply and demand? And yet, in the prevailing conditions of revolutionary crisis, each one of these movements, with the exception of that of Vendémiaire, tended to carry the Revolution forwards, to drive another nail into the coffin of feudalism, and to advance the aims of more consciously radical groups.

It is not surprising perhaps that the actions of such insurgents and demonstrators should also tend to be clothed in traditional forms and that in so many *journées* of the Revolution we should catch echoes of past events. There is no innovation about the destruction of the *châteaux* or the violent assaults on individuals who had incurred popular disfavour, such as de Launay, de

[1] See pp. 101–3. [2] See p. 170.

Flesselles, Foullon, and Berthier: they hark back to the *jacqueries* of the fifteenth and seventeenth centuries and other more recent outbreaks of popular fury. The *taxation populaire* of 1789 and 1793 has its antecedents in that of 1752[1] and 1775. Caron tells us that the prison massacres of September 1792 marked the assertion by the people of the ancient right of 'la justice retenue' —the sovereign's prerogative right to dispense justice without recourse to the normal juridical processes—traditionally vested in the king, but since 10 August devolving upon the sovereign people.[2] The march to Versailles to solicit the intercession of the king as protector of his people had precedents in the riots of 1775[3] and, more recently, in the Parisian carriers' strike of 1786.[4] Even the chant of the marchers, 'Allons chercher le boulanger, la boulangère et le petit mitron', expressed sentiments similar to those expressed in the Bordeaux peasants' slogan of 1674: 'Vive le Roi et sans gabelle!';[5] and in the cry of a Parisian master locksmith of May 1775: 'Vive le Roi et que le pain ramende!'[6] The same conception of the king as protector is evident in the assumption by leaders of the rebellious peasantry of July 1789 of the royal authority ('de par le Roi') for their acts of arson and destruction against the property of the nobility; as such it echoes the conviction of the grain rioters of 1775 that the king had personally intervened to reduce the price of corn, flour, and bread to a just level.[7] Apart from the armed insurrections of 10 August and 2 June 1793, it is perhaps only in the petitions of July 1791 and June 1792 and the agitation of the arms workers of 1794 that we find the emergence of new forms of action that look forward to the urban–industrial society of the future.

We should not under-estimate either the degree to which the revolutionary leaders themselves, though steeped in the ideas of the new philosophy, relied upon precedent and, far from following a consistent programme of total renovation, stumbled

---

[1] *Journal et mémoires du marquis d'Argenson*, vii. 229.
[2] Caron, op. cit., pp. 435–45.
[3] G. Rudé, 'La Taxation populaire de mai 1775 à Paris et dans la région parisienne', *Ann. hist. Rév. franç.*, no. 143, 1956, p. 148.   [4] See p. 21.
[5] Traditional.
[6] G. Rudé, op. cit., p. 177.
[7] G. Lefebvre, *La Grande Peur de 1789*, pp. 111–17, 141; G. Rudé, op. cit., pp. 147–60.

from one political expedient to another—in which process the exigencies of war, the needs of social conciliation, and the absence of any traditions of political experience all played their part. Yet their interests, or circumstance, led them to attempt new solutions; and these, as we have seen, on more than one occasion led them into conflict with the *sans-culottes* or involved them in devious attempts to conciliate them or to divert their energies into 'safe' political channels. Such attempts were successful, as we saw, in the preparation of the great political *journées* from the fall of the Bastille to the expulsion of the Girondins. They failed when the *sans-culottes* followed their own head, as in the Réveillon riots and food riots of February 1793; yet these were not irretrievable disasters. Far more serious was the failure of the Jacobins to regain the allegiance of the *sans-culottes* in the summer of 1794, when the gap between them and the Revolutionary Government proved unbridgeable and hastened the fall of Robespierre and his associates in Thermidor.[1] This only goes to show once more that the elements composing revolutionary crowds, though permeated by the political ideas of the Jacobins and advanced democrats, had social claims of their own which they persisted in advancing even against the advice and, on occasion, the interests of the revolutionary leaders themselves.

It remains to consider by what human agency the *sans-culottes* were directly involved in or recruited for the great political demonstrations and insurrections of the Revolution and for those occasions when they acted on their own account. It has become evident of course that each of the great political *journées*, though its exact result might rarely be foreseen, was the outcome of considerable preparations, often carried out in full view of the authorities of the day, involving Sectional resolutions and deputations, speeches, and newspaper articles, or even—as on 10 August, in May–June 1793, and again in Vendémiaire—the creation of a *correspondance*, or *liaison*, committee of the Sections to concert and to conduct operations on the day appointed. This, of course, already goes a long way to explain how the *sans-culottes* became drawn in and their sympathies enlisted—particularly during the years when their most active elements crowded, or dominated, the local societies,

---

[1] See pp. 128 ff.

assemblies, or committees. Again, there is little mystery about the channel of communication between leaders and participants on those occasions when the operation in hand was carried through by military units acting under their own commanders. Yet, in the early months of the Revolution, there is still an element that escapes us and on which the records are too often silent: how and at what stage were the mass of the participants engaged and the slogans and plans of action communicated? Occasionally we catch a glimpse of this process of communication in action—at the burning of the *barrières*, for example, where we learn from the testimony of numerous witnesses that local leaders were acting under the direct orders of the Palais Royal.[1] Again, on 5 October, we find Stanislas Maillard directing operations in consultation with spokesmen for the women; and Fournier l'Américain hurrying back to stir up support for the marchers in his own District of Saint-Eustache, and inciting the *poissardes* at Versailles to call for the king's return to Paris.[2] But such glimpses are rare and the exact mechanism of revolt generally eludes us; yet we may assume from examples such as these that it was through secondary leaders like Maillard and Fournier—and others like Saint-Huruge, Saint-Félix, Théroigne de Méricourt, and Claire Lacombe—that *liaison* was maintained, on these and similar occasions, between the topmost leaders and the rank-and-file participants.

These intermediaries, however, were not of the *sans-culottes* themselves, being drawn from other social groups.[3] Thus the further question arises—did the *sans-culottes* have leaders of their own to co-operate with, or receive the orders of, the agents or emissaries of the *bourgeois* groups and factions, or to inspire and guide them when they acted on their own account? Or was the element of spontaneity considerable in this respect? There is, of course, little doubt that, on these occasions, some showed more spirit, enterprise, and daring, or engaged in more spec-

---

[1] For example, Du Hamel, a former locksmith and leader of the incendiaries at several customs posts, told a witness 'qu'ils avaient des ordres pour en agir ainsi et qu'ils avaient d'autres expéditions à faire'; at the Barrière Saint-Martin, one rioter reproved another with the words: 'Brûlons, s'il le faut, puisque cela nous est ordonné, mais ne volons (pas), puisque cela est deffendu'; and, at the Barrière Blanche, a man called for quiet 'de l'ordre du Palais Royal' (Arch. Nat., Z¹ˢ 886).

[2] *Procédure criminelle au Châtelet* . . ., witness no. 81; *Mémoires secrets de Fournier, Américain.* [3] See p. 178, note 1, above.

tacular acts of violence, than their fellows and, as such, drew the attention of the police, National Guard, or bystanders. In the Réveillon riots, for instance, a leading part was ascribed to one Marie-Jeanne Trumeau, *femme* Bertin, a market-woman, who was sentenced to death (though later reprieved) for having incited the rioters to loot and burn with cries of 'Allons, vive le Tiers État!' and 'A la Réveillon!'[1] Prominent among the *sans-culottes* that burned down the *barrières* were, said witnesses, Bataille, a wine-merchant's assistant, and Dumont (alias Cadet), a docker.[2] In the women's march to Versailles, their chief spokesman, according to Maillard, was the *femme* Lavarenne, an illiterate sick-nurse and wife of a porter, though she herself claimed to have been brought along under compulsion.[3] Among those taking part in the Champ de Mars demonstration we have noted the remarkable cook, Constance Évrard—more remarkable, it is true, for the maturity of her political opinions than for the part she played in the event.[4] During the grocery riots of February 1793, the police recorded that several persons played a prominent part in stirring up dissatisfaction and fixing the price at which sugar, candles, and coffee should be sold. Among these, so ran a detailed report of the commissioner of the Arsenal Section, was

Une femme, assez bien, à nous inconnue . . . de la taille d'environ cinq pieds un pouce, âgée de trente ans . . . vêtue d'un déshabillé de toile fond bleu à dessin courant, un mantelet de taffetas noir et une montre d'or à chaîne d'acier. . . . Cette femme a fait tout ce qui était en elle pour augmenter la sédition . . . ce fut elle qui fixa le prix du savon à douze sols la livre et le sucre à dix-huit.[5]

After the events of Prairial, there were several persons denounced to the Committee of General Security and the specially appointed Military Commission as having played leading parts in the revolt; among these were former members of the *armée révolutionnaire*, of whom some, at least, had been elected to

---

[1] Arch. Nat., Y 13981, 13454.   [2] Arch. Nat., Z¹ᵃ 886.
[3] *Procédure criminelle* . . . , witnesses nos. 81–82.
[4] Arch. Préf. Pol., Aa 148, fol. 30.
[5] Arch. Préf. Pol., Aa 69, fol. 296. In the rue des Lombards, where the riots were supposed to have started, the police picked out for special mention and condemnation Agnès Bernard, a fish-wife of the Section des Halles; she was later sentenced to two years in prison (see p. 183 above).

lead their local units of the insurgent National Guard because of their known record of militancy in the Year II.[1] In such a case, then, we are dealing with experienced cadres of Jacobinism, who have emerged as leaders in the course of the revolutionary years; but this is a later phenomenon and we see little trace of it before the summer of 1791.[2] In the earlier examples cited those reported as playing leading parts may well have had no previous records as militants and probably only distinguished themselves by their vigour or violence on this particular occasion; we may even accept at its face value the frequently voiced assertion that such 'leaders' were present as much by accident as design, or were brought along by the persuasion or compulsion of neighbours or itinerant bands. In fact, may not Marie-Jeanne Trumeau or the *femme* Lavarenne, for all their momentary militancy, have had experiences similar to that of a village woman who appeared to be the leader of the rioters at Brie-Comte-Robert during the grain riots of 1775? When asked by the police to explain her disorderly conduct, she answered simply

Qu'elle a été entraînée . . . et convient que sa tête s'est montée comme celle des autres, et qu'elle ne savait plus ce qu'elle disait ni ce qu'elle faisait.[3]

In such cases there are no leaders in the commonly accepted sense of the term and the distinction between militants, or active elements, and rank-and-file participants disappears. As we have seen, this was not so in the later stages of the Revolution, when the clubs and societies had had time to train and equip militants and leaders from the ranks of the *sans-culottes* themselves. But, in the early years at least, once we have accounted for the efficacy of pamphlets and journals and the spoken propaganda in public meeting-places, food-shops, and markets to generate revolutionary activity, there still remains an element of spontaneity that defies a more exact analysis.

[1] R. Cobb and G. Rudé, 'Les Journées de germinal et de prairial an III', *Revue historique*, 1955, p. 279, n. 2.
[2] We find the earliest signs in the Champ de Mars movement of July 1791: among those arrested in the Sections for protesting at the brutality of the National Guard were three *vainqueurs de la Bastille* (Arch. Préf. Pol., Aa 85, fols. 85–86; 167, fol. 460; 206, fols. 370–2).
[3] Arch. Nat., Y 11441 (interrogatoire de la femme Tanton, journalière d'Yerres).

XV

THE 'REVOLUTIONARY CROWD'
IN HISTORY

WE return to our central question—the nature of the crowds that took part in the great events of the Revolution in Paris. From our analysis these crowds have emerged as active agents in the revolutionary process, composed of social elements with their own distinctive identities, interests, and aspirations. Yet these were not at variance with, or isolated from, those of other social groups. In fact we have seen that the Revolution was only able to advance—and, indeed, to break out—because the *sans-culottes*, from whom these elements were largely drawn, were able to assimilate and to identify themselves with the new political ideas promoted by the liberal aristocracy and *bourgeoisie*. But, even when revolutionary crowds were impregnated with and stimulated by such ideas, they cannot for that reason be dismissed as mere passive instruments of middle-class leaders and interests; still less can they be presented as inchoate 'mobs' without any social identity or, at best, as drawn from criminal elements or the dregs of the city population. While these played a part, it was an altogether minor one and on no occasion corresponded to the unsympathetic picture of the all-prevailing *canaille* painted by Taine and other writers.

Michelet's use of *le peuple* corresponds, of course, far more closely to the facts: we have seen Barnave, for one, applying the term to those participants in revolutionary events who were neither of the aristocracy nor of the *bourgeoisie*. Yet it is too indefinite; for while the *menu peuple*, or *sans-culottes*, taken collectively, formed the main body of rioters and insurgents, the part played by their constituent elements—women, wage-earners, craftsmen, journeymen, petty traders, or workshop masters— varied widely from one occasion to another. This, of course, merely emphasizes the point that revolutionary crowds, far from being social abstractions, were composed of ordinary men and women with varying social needs, who responded to a variety of impulses, in which economic crisis, political upheaval, and the urge to satisfy immediate and particular grievances all played their part.

Are such conclusions only valid within the comparatively restricted context of the French Revolution, or have they a certain validity, as well, in the case of other 'revolutionary crowds', whom historians have been inclined, either for convenience or from lack of sympathy, to depict as 'mobs' or as social riff-raff?[1] It would, of course, be both presumptuous and misleading to generalize too freely and too confidently from the cases examined in the course of the present study; yet, even if we admit that there are no exact historical parallels, there are certain features that are common both to these and to other popular movements arising in Britain and France during the eighteenth and early nineteenth centuries. To that extent, at least, we may perhaps apply our conclusions to a wider field.

We have already noted the similarities between certain 'economic' movements of the Revolution and those of the latter years of the old régime in France—particularly that of 1775. Here we have the same spontaneous reaction to the rising cost of flour and bread; rioting in markets and bakers' shops; the imposition of popular price-control, the terms of which were carried by word of mouth from market to market; the same almost unquestioning faith in the efficacy and benevolence of the royal authority; the role of rumour in stimulating activity; the active participation of different groups of the *menu peuple* of towns and villages, among whom criminal elements and down-and-outs played an altogether insignificant part.[2] Several of these features, though by no means all, reappear in French

---

[1] Sometimes, of course, crowds are given Michelet's more sympathetic, if not more discriminating, label of 'the people' or 'the patriots'. This has generally been the case in British historians' descriptions of the European and South American national movements of the nineteenth century in which crowds were promoting causes with which the writers were manifestly in sympathy. Even, on occasion, from a change of fashion or of official policy, a 'switch' is made, in estimating a given movement, from one attitude to the other. Thus the 'bandits' of yesterday become the 'patriots' or 'freedom fighters' of today. (For an amusing illustration, see Mr. R. H. S. Crossman's account of the 'switch' from Mihailovitch to Tito in the Second World War in the *New Statesman and Nation* of 15 December 1956.)

[2] See the conclusions to my article on the grain riots of 1775 (cited, *int. alia*, on p. 227, note 3, above).

rural riots as late as 1848.[1] In the urban revolutions of the early nineteenth century, too, a large measure of continuity with that of 1789 still persists, though new features emerge with industrial advance and gradual social change. The external appearance of Paris and the geographical distribution of its population remained much the same in 1848 as sixty years before;[2] the small workshop still predominated and, far from disappearing, was increasing its hold;[3] while the main centres of the *menu peuple* were still the Faubourgs Saint-Antoine and Saint-Marcel and the districts north of the markets.[4] As far as can be told from limited records, the composition of the participants in the 'trois glorieuses' of July 1830 was not very different from that of the captors of the Bastille.[5] Like their forbears of 10 August 1792 the *ouvriers* of 1830 left their workshops to take up arms and, far from encouraging looting, shot those who engaged in it out of hand.[6] In 1848, again, masters and journeymen marched together, and jointly manned the barricades and occupied the Chamber of Deputies in the February days.[7] De Tocqueville's descriptions of the popular invasion of the parliamentary sessions of 24 February and 15 May of that year read like accounts of the great demonstrations in the National Convention in Germinal and Prairial of the Year III;[8] and even in the June revolution that followed, when *bourgeois* and *ouvriers* found themselves ranged in armed conflict on opposing sides, we find the insurgents largely belonging to the familiar trades of those who stormed the Bastille and reduced the Tuileries: of 11,693 persons

[1] See R. Gossez's 'carte des troubles' in E. Labrousse (ed.), *Aspects de la crise et de la dépression de l'économie française au milieu du xix siècle (1846–1851)* (Paris, 1956); G. Lefebvre, *La Grande Peur de 1789*, pp. 61–65.

[2] See C. Seignobos, *La Révolution de 1848* (Paris, 1921), pp. 344–5.

[3] L. Chevalier, *La Formation de la population parisienne au XIXe siècle* (Paris, 1950), p. 77.

[4] G. Vauthier, 'La Misère des ouvriers en 1831', *La Révolution de 1848*, xxii (1925), 607–17.

[5] See the very incomplete lists of those killed and decorated as a result of their participation in the events of 27–29 July 1830 in Paris (Arch. Préf. Pol., Aa 369–70, 420).

[6] 'Une Lettre inédite sur les journées de juillet 1830', *La Révolution de 1848*, vii (1910), 272–5. In 1848, too, de Tocqueville noted (without surprise, he added) the absence of looting (*The Recollections of Alexis de Tocqueville*, ed. J. P. Mayer (London, 1948), p. 80).

[7] A. Crémieux, 'La Fusillade du boulevard des Capucines du 23 février 1848', *La Révolution de 1848*, viii (1911), 99–124; F. Dutacq, 'Un Récit des journées de février 1848', ibid. ix (1912), 266–70.   [8] *Recollections*, pp. 51–59, 135–45.

arrested and charged in this affair, there were 554 stonemasons, 510 joiners, 416 shoemakers, 321 cabinet-makers, 285 locksmiths, 286 tailors, 283 painters, and 191 wine-merchants.[1] But the differences are equally, if not more, striking. Even in February the proportion of wage-earners among the insurgents was far greater than it was in 1789: de Tocqueville actually believed that the victors of the Revolution—up to May, at least—were the working classes and that its sole victims were the *bourgeoisie*.[2] This is an exaggeration; yet the fact remains that the wage-earners and independent craftsmen, who played the principal part in the insurrections and *journées* of the period, were now organized in their own political clubs, marched under their own banners and leaders, and, far from responding to the ideas and slogans of the *bourgeoisie*, were deeply imbued with the new ideas of Socialism.[3] The Industrial Revolution of Louis-Philippe's reign had brought in railways and the beginnings of mechanized industry: among the arrested insurgents of June, we note, alongside the joiners, cabinet-makers, and locksmiths of the traditional crafts and small workshops, the names of some eighty railwaymen and 257 *mécaniciens*.[4] As June 1848 marks the first great armed collision between *ouvriers* and *bourgeoisie*, so it marks the final eclipse of the *sans-culottes* and the emergence of the wage-earners as the new shock-troops of insurrection and the predominant element in revolutionary crowds.

We find a similar process taking place in Britain, though it begins at an earlier date. Even more than in France the typical rural riot of the eighteenth century had its origins in the high price of corn, flour, or bread and expressed itself in various forms of direct action, ranging from personal assaults on mill-owners, farmers, or magistrates, the destruction of fences, turn-pikes, houses, or mills, the seizure of stocks of grain and stoppage of food convoys, to great demonstrations of farm-workers,

---

[1] *Liste générale en ordre alphabétique des inculpés de juin 1848.* Arch. Nat., F7* 2585–6.
[2] *Recollections*, pp. 78 ff.
[3] Seignobos, op. cit., pp. 24–25, 57–58, 67–70, 89–106, 138–9; Suzanne Wasser-mann, 'Le Club de Raspail en 1848', *La Révolution de 1848*, v (1908–9), 589–605, 655–74, 748–62; R. Gossez, 'L'organisation ouvrière à Paris sous la Seconde République', *1848. Revue des révolutions contemporaines*, xli (1949), 31–45.
[4] F7* 2585–6. See also G. Duveau, *La Vie ouvrière en France sous le Second Empire* (Paris, 1946), pp. 42–43.

miners, and rural craftsmen in the local market towns. Such activities are, of course, reminiscent of those engaged in by French peasants and village tradesmen during the same period; but none is more strikingly similar than the widespread resort to the *taxation populaire*, or popular price-control, examples of which seem to have been even more abundant in the English countryside than in the French: for the year 1766 alone Dr. Wearmouth has recorded no less than twenty-two such instances from market towns and villages all over the country;[1] and local records would no doubt reveal many more. It was only in the rural districts of England and Wales that this type of riot—with its emphasis on popular, or 'natural', justice—persisted well into the nineteenth century, at a time when such manifestations had long been superseded in urban communities. Perhaps the latest, and certainly the most spectacular, example of it was seen in the Rebecca Riots which broke out in West Wales in 1839 and again in 1842—ostensibly directed against toll-gates, but actually expressing the accumulated grievances of the Welsh peasantry over tithe, 'alien' landowners, tyrannical magistrates, church rates, high rents, and the New Poor Law, besides.[2] Here again, even at this late date, there are striking resemblances with certain of the French riots and insurrections, both urban and rural, of the late eighteenth century—the appeal to tradition in both the propaganda and the costume of the rioters;[3] the sporadic emergence of local leaders or 'Rebeccas';[4] the visible expression of 'natural justice' in the destruction of toll-gates and workhouses; the joint action of farmers and farm-labourers; and the spontaneous spreading of rioting, as though by contagion, from one area to another.[5] But new social forces were at work; and it is certainly significant that 'Rebecca's'

---

[1] R. W. Wearmouth, *Methodism and the Common People of the Eighteenth Century* (London, 1945), pp. 19–50, 51–76, 77–91.

[2] David Williams, *The Rebecca Riots* (Univ. of Wales Press, 1955).

[3] 'Rebecca's' letters reminded the Welsh of their enslavement by the English 'sons of Hengist' (ibid., p. 192) [cf. the English radical tradition that Englishmen had been enslaved by the 'Norman yoke']; and rioters commonly disguised themselves by blackening their faces or by dressing up as women (the last was a charge insistently made against the Parisians who marched to Versailles on 5 October 1789).

[4] These were most often tenant farmers, though occasional reports speak of 'gentlemen', publicans, and even labourers (ibid., pp. 190, 195, 198, 221, 250).

[5] Ibid., p. 212. Some of these features appear in the English agricultural labourers' revolt of 1830–1, the last movement of its kind in rural England.

nocturnal antics were called off and gave way to mass meetings and petitions to Parliament—not so much owing to successful government repression as to the farmers' change of heart when faced with their labourers' insistence on pressing their own particular claims.[1]

It was similar changes in the relations of social classes that transformed the nature of English urban riots. During the eighteenth century, despite the wide variety of issues involved, there is a certain continuity of pattern which, again, is reminiscent of the French. In market towns and all but the largest cities the prevailing form continued to be the food riot. In London it rarely took this form, though the high price of food might be a contributory cause of disturbance.[2] The constant repetition by historians of such catch-phrases as Tory or Wilkite 'mobs' has of course tended to obscure the true nature of such disturbances and the fact that crowds taking part in them were both socially identifiable and were impelled by specific grievances and by motives other than those of loot or monetary gain. The East London riots of July 1736 were largely the work of journeymen and labourers, who had been roused to violence against the local Irish by the employment of Irish workers at lower rates of wages;[3] yet other factors, such as the Gin Act of that year and memories of Walpole's threatened Excise, entered into the picture. In the 'Wilkes and Liberty' riots of 1768–9 and the Gordon Riots of a dozen years later, those taking part were mainly journeymen, apprentices, servants, labourers, small craftsmen, and petty traders. Though the immediate causes of disturbance were very different in the two cases, both movements were movements of social protest, in which the underlying conflict of poor against rich (though not yet of labour against capital) is clearly visible beneath the surface. All these move-

[1] Ibid., pp. 243, 262.
[2] This was probably so in the anti-Irish and Gin Riots of 1736 and in the 'Wilkes and Liberty' riots of March–May 1768, though probably not so in the Wilkes movements of 1763 or 1769, or in the Gordon Riots of 1780. (For these and other points relating to these movements see G. Rudé, '"Mother Gin" and the London Riots of 1736', to appear shortly in *The Guildhall Miscellany*; 'Wilkes and Liberty, 1768–69', ibid., no. 8, 1957, pp. 3–24; 'The Gordon Riots: a Study of the Rioters and their Victims', *Transactions of the Royal Historical Society*, 5th series, vol. vi, 1956, pp. 93–114.)
[3] Despite their origins, these riots, like the Paris Réveillon riots of fifty years later, had little in common with the nineteenth-century type of wages movement.

ments are typical of French and English urban popular movements of the period, in which the *menu peuple* of wage-earners, craftsmen, and small tradesmen, led by local captains, dispense a rough and ready kind of natural justice by breaking windows, burning their enemies of the moment in effigy, or 'pulling down' their dwelling-houses, pubs, or mills.[1] In the Gordon Riots this activity reached alarming proportions, settled claims for damage to private buildings and personal property alone amounting to over £70,000. This particular feature was due not so much to the deeper social antagonisms as to the immediate panic-fear of the consequences of the believed increase in the numbers and influence of the Roman Catholics: it was even rumoured that Lord Mansfield, the Lord Chief Justice, 'had made the king one' overnight! An interesting by-product of all this was that the merchants and householders of the City of London, facing a double threat—to their liberties from the Government's military measures and to their properties from the destructive zeal of 'the inferior set of people'—anticipated the request made nine years later by their counterparts in Paris for the institution of a *milice bourgeoise* to defend their interests.[2]

Such forms of popular demonstration did not long survive the arrival of the new industrial age. With the growth of urban population and the dawn of the factory system at the end of the century, trade unions became more frequent and more stable, and direct conflicts between wage-earners and employers a more common feature of industrial and urban communities. From the 1780's onwards strikes were beginning to eclipse food riots and other movements of natural justice as the typical form of social protest. At the same time, as we have seen, the wage-earners were beginning to replace such social groupings as 'the urban poor', 'the inferior set of people', or the *menu peuple*—terms appropriate to an earlier age—as the main participants in urban social movements. In Britain this process was not attended by as much violence or as rapid a maturing of political ideas as was witnessed in France in 1848; but the general

[1] These features also appear in the 'Church and King' riots of 1790–2 in Birmingham and Manchester; but in these cases other elements enter which require to be separately studied.

[2] G. Rudé, 'I "tumulti di Gordon" (1780)', *Movimento Operaio* (Milan), 1955, p. 852. Not surprisingly the request was coldly received and had to be dropped.

process started sooner and, by the advent of Chartism in the 1830's, it was already completed.

From these few examples it would appear, then, that a new type of 'revolutionary crowd'—to use the term in its broadest possible sense—with new social objectives and new modes of expression was evolving in western Europe in the first part of the nineteenth century; with the advance of capitalist industry it was to spread rapidly elsewhere. This newer type of crowd is probably easier to identify than the older type that prevailed at the time of the French Revolution, and historians of the Trade Union and Labour movement, in particular, have not been backward in using available sources of inquiry to bring it to light. But bad old habits die hard, and the general historian is inclined in such matters to cover up his tracks by resorting to a convenient and ready-to-hand vocabulary which, though hallowed by time, is none the less misleading and inadequate. The term 'mobs', in the sense of hired bands operating on behalf of external interests, doubtless has its place in the writing of social history; but it should be invoked with discretion and only when justified by the particular occasion. In so far as any conclusion of general validity emerges from the present study it is, perhaps, that such occasions are rare and that Taine's 'mob' should be seen as a term of convenience, or as a frank symbol of prejudice, rather than as a verifiable historical phenomenon.

APPENDIX I

Paris Sections of 1790–5

(The first name given is that of 1790–1; later names are in brackets.)

1. TUILERIES
2. CHAMPS ÉLYSÉES
3. ROULE (République)
4. PALAIS ROYAL (Butte des Moulins. Montagne)
5. PLACE VENDÔME (Piques)
6. BIBLIOTHÈQUE (1792. Lepeletier)
7. GRANGE BATELIÈRE (Mirabeau. Mont Blanc)
8. LOUVRE (Muséum).
9. ORATOIRE (Gardes Françaises)
10. HALLE AU BLÉ
11. POSTES (Contrat Social)
12. PLACE LOUIS XIV (Mail. Guillaume Tell)
13. FONTAINE MONTMORENCY (Molière et la Fontaine. Brutus.)
14. BONNE NOUVELLE
15. PONCEAU (Amis de la Patrie)
16. MAUCONSEIL (Bon Conseil)
17. MARCHÉS DES INNOCENTS (Halles. Marchés)
18. LOMBARDS
19. ARCIS
20. FAUBOURG MONTMARTRE (Fbg. Mont-Marat)
21. POISSONNIÈRE
22. BONDY
23. TEMPLE
24. POPINCOURT
25. MONTREUIL
26. QUINZE VINGTS
27. GRAVILLIERS
28. FAUBOURG SAINT - DENIS (Fbg.-du-Nord)
29. BEAUBOURG (Réunion)
30. ENFANTS ROUGES (Marais. Homme Armé)
31. ROI DE SICILE (Droits de l'Homme)
32. HÔTEL DE VILLE (Maison Commune. Fidélité)
33. PLACE ROYALE (Fédérés. Indivisibilité)
34. ARSENAL
35. ÎLE SAINT-LOUIS (Fraternité)
36. NOTRE DAME (Cité. Raison)
37. HENRI IV (Pont Neuf. Révolutionnaire)
38. INVALIDES
39. FONTAINE DE GRENELLE
40. QUATRE NATIONS (Unité)
41. THÉÂTRE FRANÇAIS (Marseille. Marat)
42. CROIX ROUGE (Bonnet Rouge. Bonnet de la Liberté. Ouest)
43. LUXEMBOURG (Mutius Scaevola)
44. THERMES DE JULIEN (Beaurepaire. Chalier. Régénérée. Thermes)
45. SAINTE-GENEVIÈVE (Panthéon Français)
46. OBSERVATOIRE
47. JARDIN DES PLANTES (Sans-Culottes)
48. GOBELINS (Lazowski. Finistère)

APPENDIX II

The Population of the Paris Sections in 1791–5

Section[1]	Wage-earners in 1791[2]		'Active' citizens in 1791[3]	Population: in		Population density in 1800: inhabs. per 4,000 sq. metres[6]
	Employed workers	No. of employers		1792[4]	1795[5]	
1. Tuileries	646	40	1,654	12,600	15,148	74
2. Champs Élysées	..	..	873	8,000	8,000	11
3. Roule	1,497	106	1,289	12,850	11,377	23
4. Palais Royal	1,334	92	2,395	20,400	16,719	251
5. Place Vendôme	..	..	1,030	14,000	13,428	75
6. Bibliothèque	782	46	1,517	12,987	9,930	147
7. Grange Batelière	1,197	55	856	11,570	10,920	39
8. Louvre	1,094	61	2,023	11,800	22,691	259
9. Oratoire	1,677	77	1,902	6,612	12,567	444
10. Halle au Blé	621	37	1,870	7,011	11,640	294
11. Postes	..	..	1,809	9,869	12,567	330
12. Louis XIV	969	71	1,394	13,000	9,500	266
13. Fontaine Montmorency	298	29	1,087	12,472	9,424	224
14. Bonne Nouvelle	2,389	128	1,607	9,950	14,860	360
15. Ponceau	5,288	242	1,607	13,645	16,648	360
16. Mauconseil	1,866	115	1,708	11,000	13,818	388
17. Marchés des Innocents	1,705	61	1,072	14,722	13,146	555
18. Lombards	1,421	110	2,504	12,550	14,811	438
19. Arcis	..	..	1,753	12,000	11,600	580
20. Faub. Montmartre	1,242	78	687	13,800	10,104	51
21. Poissonnière	1,517	97	834	12,000	8,435	43
22. Bondy	..	..	1,439	13,315	12,404	32
23. Temple	1,273	99	1,662	25,000	11,988	48
24. Popincourt	1,358	84	1,268	13,747	10,933	17
25. Montreuil	1,330	84	1,478	15,000	13,479	45
26. Quinze Vingts	1,831	141	1,958	12,550	18,283	27
27. Gravilliers	4,699	339	3,305	11,000	24,774	364
28. Faub. Saint-Denis	3,217	101	1,330	13,840	11,630	62
29. Beaubourg	2,932	165	2,285	11,015	16,320	315
30. Enfants Rouges	1,015	102	1,784	8,974	10,481	132
31. Roi de Sicile	1,028	67	1,811	10,500	12,321	239
32. Hôtel de Ville	..	..	1,729	11,230	12,231	304
33. Place Royale	1,172	75	1,883	14,500	11,836	123
34. Arsenal	890	58	1,407	21,000	10,264	82
35. Île Saint-Louis	305	28	1,032	5,257	4,862	204
36. Notre Dame	..	..	1,657	11,780	11,402	310
37. Henri IV	459	54	883	3,581	5,126	297
38. Invalides	767	30	1,100	11,000	10,401	17

Section[1]	Wage-earners in 1791[2]		'Active' citizens in 1791[3]	Population: in		Population density in 1800: inhabs. per 4,000 sq. metres[6]
	Employed workers	No. of employers		1792[4]	1795[5]	
39. Font. de Grenelle	985	71	2,100	10,878	12,554	86
40. Quatre Nations	2,310	164	3,900	21,516	21,601	204
41. Théâtre Français	2,207	105	2,600	16,600	14,400	275
42. Croix Rouge	1,669	118	1,551	17,600	16,744	67
43. Luxembourg	1,061	84	2,100	17,000	17,633	52
44. Thermes de Julien	1,139	72	2,000	14,490	12,394	325
45. Sainte-Geneviève	2,136	129	2,762	22,645	24,977	320
46. Observatoire	1,133	55	1,700	19,907	13,193	32
47. Jardin des Plantes	1,695	66	2,178	16,000	15,185	60
48. Gobelins	613	38	1,200	12,741	11,775	35
Totals	62,743	3,776	82,270	635,504	636,772	..
	(41 Sections)					

[1] Names of Sections as in 1790–1. (For later changes see Appendix I.)

[2] From F. Braesch, 'Un Essai de statistique de la population ouvrière de Paris vers 1791', La Rév. franç. lxiii (July–Dec. 1912), 289–321. For a discussion of the gaps in M. Braesch's figures see my Parisian Wage-Earners, i. 46–51.

[3] From E. Charavay, Assemblée electorale de Paris (3 vols., Paris, 1890–5), vol. ii, pp. v–vii.

[4] From N. Kareiev, La Densité de la population des différentes sections de Paris pendant la Revolution, pp. 14–15.

[5] Arch. Nat., F[7] 3688[4], doss. 1 (January 1795).

[6] Kareiev, loc. cit.

APPENDIX III

Paris Sections and Insurgents of 1787–95

(Numbers arrested, killed, wounded, or participants in *journées*)

*Sections	(1) 1787–8	(2) Réveillon Riots (April)	(3) Bastille (July)	(4) Champ de Mars (July 1791)	(5) 10 August 1792	(6) Grocery Riots 1792–3	(7) May–June 1793	(8) Prairial Year III	(9) Vendémiaire Year IV
1. Tuileries	..	..	2	3	6	2	68	6	1
2. Champs Élysées	..	..	..	1	5	..	..	..	..
3. Roule	..	1	2	3	..	1	660	5	..
4. Palais Royal	1	..	1	6	6	3	229	2	1
5. Vendôme	1	1	1	4	4	1	331	1	2
6. Bibliothèque	..	..	2	1	2	..	59	1	4
7. Grange Batelière	..	..	2	3	1	1	527	4	..
8. Louvre	1	1	1	8	1	2	270	6	..
9. Oratoire	7	1	2	7	3	4	46	4	..
10. Halle au Blé	..	..	6	5	3	1	315	6	..
11. Postes	1	..	4	4	7	1	191	1	..
12. Louis XIV	..	..	..	7	1	1	..	1	..
13. Fontaine Montmorency	..	..	..	4	1	..	..	3	..
14. Bonne Nouvelle	..	..	..	6	7	..	..	4	..
15. Ponceau	..	..	3	9	11	1	..	..	..
16. Mauconseil	4	1	4	8	5	3	1,400	3	..
17. Marché des Innocents	6	..	6	3	1	2	..	4	..
18. Lombards	4	..	5	4	12	..	..	6	..
19. Arcis	1	1	3	17	9	..	..	10	2
20. Faubourg Montmartre	..	..	..	7	16	..	1,438	..	..
21. Poissonnière	..	1	1	1	4	..	194	5	2
22. Bondy	..	1	4	3	5	2	813	7	..
23. Temple	..	..	9	4	2	..	662	5	3
24. Popincourt	..	6	87	4	6	..	970	13	..
25. Montreuil	..	13	139	3	18	1	2,946	6	..
26. Quinze Vingts	..	13	193	3	58	..	2,039	10	..
27. Gravilliers	4	..	3	9	15	6	1,457	7	1
28. Faubourg St. Denis	..	..	1	2	6	..	..	2	..
29. Beaubourg	2	..	5	9	3	..	678	1	1
30. Enfants Rouges	..	1	2	5	3	..	..	..	..
31. Roi de Sicile	1	..	3	3	6	1	..	2	..
32. Hôtel de Ville	..	6	18	5	2	..	700?	1	..
33. Place Royale	..	..	17	2	..	..	..	5	6
34. Arsenal	..	3	23	2	2	1	618	12	2
35. Île Saint-Louis	..	1	..	..	..	..	..	1	1
36. Notre Dame	2	1	1	7	3	..	..	..	..
37. Henri IV	3	..	2	4	..	..	13	2	..
38. Invalides	1	..	5	3	5	..	1,358	..	..
39. Fontaine de Grenelle	1	..	2	5	3	1	190?	1	..

* Names of Sections are as in 1790–1. For later changes see Appendix I.

*Sections	(1) 1787–8	(2) 1789 Réveillon Riots (April)	(3) Bastille (July)	(4) Champ de Mars (July 1791)	(5) 10 August 1792	(6) Grocery Riots 1792–3	(7) May–June 1793	(8) Prairial Year III	(9) Vendémiaire Year IV
40. Quatre Nations	2	..	6	12	4	2	225?	..	..
41. Théâtre Français	1	..	6	3	12	..	..	..	1
42. Croix Rouge	..	..	2	4	5	..	1,458	1	1
43. Luxembourg	2	..	7	3	7	..	432	3	..
44. Thermes de Julien	4	3	3	11	6	1	..	4	1
45. Sainte-Geneviève	6	1	10	15	7	..	400?	1	..
46. Observatoire	2	..	3	4	18	..	907	3	..
47. Jardin des Plantes	..	1	3	1	1	..	..	3	..
48. Gobelins	..	3	3	3	19	5	660	5	..
Outside Paris	1	3	..	..	..	1	..	..	..
Totals	58	63	602	240	316	45	22,860	168	29

* Names of Sections are as in 1790–1. For later changes see Appendix I.

Sources:

(1) Arch. Nat., Y 13014, 9491, 9989, 11206, 11517, 15309A, 18751, 18795; X^{1b} 8989.

(2) ,, ,, Y 10491, 10530, 11033, 13582, 15019, 15101, 18795.

(3) ,, ,, T 514$^{(1)}$: *Noms des vainqueurs de la Bastille.*

(4) Arch Préf. Pol., Aa (25 cartons), Ab 324; Arch. Nat., W 294, T 214. [For details see p. 91, n. 5.]

(5) Arch Nat., F^{15} 3269–74; F^{7} 4426.

(6) Arch. Préf. Pol., Aa 9, 11 (arrestations); Ab 325, 327; *Ann. hist. rév. franç.* no. 130, p. 33.

(7) Arch. Nat., BB^{3} 80, doss. 7, 11. Figures for Sections nos. 32, 39, 40, 45 are estimates based on incomplete returns.

(8) Arch Nat., W 554–5, F^{7} (various); Arch. Préf. Pol., Aa (various).

(9) ,, ,, W 556–8.

APPENDIX IV

Paris Trades and Insurgents of 1787–95

(Figures in brackets denote probable wage-earners)

Trades	(1) 1787-8	(2) Réveillon Riots	(3)* Burning of barriers	(4)* Saint-Lazare affair	(5) Bastille	(6) Champ de Mars	(7) August 1792	(8) Grocery Riots 1792-3	(9) Prairial Year III	(10) Vendémiaire Year IV
1. Food, Drink										
Bakers	..	3 (2)	..	1 (1)	5	1 (1)	1	..	2 (1)	..
Brewers	..	..	..	..	2 (1)	..	..	..	..	..
Butchers	..	..	..	1 (1)	5 (3)	..	2 (1)	2	..	..
Cafés, Restaurants	1	1 (1)	..	..	4	3 (1)	1	1 (1)	..	..
Chocolate	..	..	..	..	..	1	..	..	..	..
Cooks	1	..	..	..	2 (2)	7 (7)	..	3 (3)	..	..
Fruiterers	1	..	..	..	..	4	2	..	2	..
Grocers	..	..	1 (1)	..	..	2 (2)	1	..	..	1
Inkeepers	..	..	..	..	2	1	..	..	..	..
Pastrycooks	1 (1)	..	..	..	4	1 (1)	..	1 (1)	..	..
Tobacco	..	..	..	..	..	1 (1)	..	..	..	..
Wine-merchants	1	1	17 (3)	..	11	2 (1)	1 (1)	..	4	..
2. Building, Roads										
Carpenters	..	..	..	..	3	4 (3)	3 (1)	..	..	..
Glaziers	..	..	..	..	..	2 (1)	..	..	..	..
Locksmiths	3 (3)	3 (3)	3	..	41 (8)	2 (2)	3	1 (1)	12 (6)	..
Monumental masons	1 (1)	1 (1)	..	..	9 (1)	1 (1)	..	..	1	..
Navvies	..	2 (2)	1 (1)	3 (3)	2 (2)	6 (6)	..	..	1	..
Painters	2 (1)	1 (1)	..	..	4	1	3	..	3 (2)	..
Paviors	..	1 (1)	..	..	..	..	..	..	..	..
Plasterers	..	..	1 (1)	..	..	..	..	..	..	..
Quarrymen	1 (1)	1 (1)	..	2 (2)	..	..	..	..	..	..
Sawyers	..	..	..	..	4 (1)	..	..	..	..	..
Sculptors	..	2 (1)	..	..	20 (1)	1 (1)	..	..	1	..
Stone-cutters	..	..	..	..	4 (4)	4 (2)	1	..	2 (2)	..
Stonemasons	1 (1)	2 (2)	2	1 (1)	7 (5)	6 (6)	2 (1)	1 (1)	4 (1)	..
Surveyors	..	..	..	..	..	1	..	..	1	..
Tilers	..	..	..	..	..	..	1 (1)	..	..	..
3. Dress										
Belt-makers	..	..	..	..	..	..	1	..	..	..
Boot and Shoe	3 (2)	3 (3)	2	3 (2)	28 (5)	17 (13)	12 (2)	2 (2)	10	..
Dressmakers	..	..	1 (1)	..	..	..	..	..	..	..
Dyers, cleaners	1 (1)	..	..	..	3	2 (1)	..	..	..	..
Florists, gardeners	1	..	2 (1)	..	6 (3)	2 (3)	1	1 (1)	1 (1)	..
Furriers	1	..	..	..	2 (1)	..	..	..	..	..
Hairdressers	2 (1)	2 (1)	..	1 (1)	10	6 (3)	4 (3)	..	5	..
Hatters	1 (1)	..	..	..	9 (4)	3 (1)	4 (2)	..	..	..
Ribbon-weavers	..	..	..	1 (1)	3 (3)	..	..	..	..	..
Stocking- ,,	..	..	..	..	4 (4)	2 (1)	1 (1)	..	..	..
Tailors	2 (1)	..	..	..	7 (1)	11 (7)	1	3 (1)	5	..
4. Furnishing										
Basket-makers	..	..	..	..	2	..	..	..	..	..
Box- ,,	..	..	..	..	1	..	..	..	..	..
Cabinet-makers	..	2 (2)	..	..	48 (9)	..	2	..	3 (1)	..
Chandlers	..	..	..	..	..	2 (2)	1 (1)	..	..	..
Fancy Ware	2 (1)	..	..	..	9 (1)	3 (3)	1	1 (1)	3 (1)	..
Joiners	..	5 (5)	1 (1)	3 (3)	49 (8)	12 (7)	8 (4)	2 (2)	8 (2)	..
Upholsterers	..	1	..	..	4 (1)	3	2 (2)	1	..	..
5. Transport										
Bargemen	..	..	..	..	3 (3)	..	..	..	..	..
Blacksmiths	..	..	..	..	..	..	1	..	..	..
Carters	..	2 (2)	2 (1)	2 (2)	5 (5)	1 (1)	1 (1)	..	1 (1)	..
Coachmen	..	1 (1)	..	3 (3)	2 (1)	6 (5)	1 (1)	3 (2)	..	..

Trades	(1) 1787–8	(2) Réveillon Riots	(3)* Burning of barriers	(4)* Saint-Lazare affair	(5) Bastille	(6) Champ de Mars	(7) August 1792	(8) Grocery Riots 1792–3	(9) Prairial Year III	(10) Vendémiaire Year IV
Farriers .	..	1	1	..	4 (1)	2 (2)	..	..	..	..
Harness, saddlers	1 (1)	1 (1)	1	..	5	1	1 (1)	1	..	..
Porters .	2 (2)	2 (2)	3 (3)	5 (5)	16 (16)	6 (6)	2 (2)	3 (3)	4 (4)	..
Riverside workers	..	4 (4)	2 (2)	..	5 (5)	..	..	1 (1)	2 (2)	..
Shipyard workers	..	..	..	..	5 (5)	..	..	..	..	..
Wheelwrights .	..	..	2 (1)	1 (1)	..	3 (2)	1 (1)	..	3 (1)	..
6. Metal										
Braziers .	..	2 (2)	..	..	7 (1)	..	..	..	1 (1)	..
Button-makers	..	..	..	1 (1)	3	1	..	..	1	..
Cutlers .	..	..	..	..	..	1	2	..	4 (1)	..
Edge-tool makers	..	..	..	..	2	..	..	1 (1)	..	..
Engravers, gilders .	2 (1)	..	..	..	13	6 (1)	2	1 (1)	2	..
Founders .	..	1 (1)	..	..	9 (2)	2	2	..	1 (1)	..
Goldsmiths .	3 (2)	..	..	..	6 (1)	5 (3)	2 (1)	..	..	..
Instrument-makers	..	..	..	..	..	..	..	2 (1)	..	..
Jewellers .	..	..	..	..	5	3	1	..	1 (1)	..
Mechanics .	..	..	..	..	..	..	..	..	..	..
Nailsmiths .	..	..	..	..	9 (1)	..	..	..	..	..
Pewterers .	..	..	..	..	2	1 (1)	..	..	..	..
Stove-makers .	..	..	..	..	5 (3)	..	..	..	..	..
Tinsmiths .	..	..	..	..	5 (2)	..	1	..	1	..
Watchmakers .	..	..	..	..	3	1	1	..	1	..
7. Wood										
Coopers .	..	1	1	..	3 (1)	1 (1)	..	..	..	..
Turners .	1	1 (1)	..	..	10	1	..	1 (1)	..	..
8. Textiles										
Cotton .	..	1 (1)	..	..	..	..	..	1 (1)	1 (1)	..
Gauze .	..	1 (1)	..	..	22 (22)	..	6 (6)	..	..	..
Silk .	..	..	..	..	1 (1)	..	..	..	..	..
Weavers .	..	..	..	..	1	1 (1)	1 (1)	..	..	..
9. Leather										
Curriers .	..	..	..	..	..	..	..	..	3 (1)	..
Leather, skin dressers	1 (1)	..	..	..	2	..	..	..	..	..
10. Print and Paper										
Bookbinders .	..	..	..	..	..	..	1	..	..	..
Booksellers .	1	..	..	..	..	..	..	..	..	..
Paper-makers .	1 (1)	5 (1)	..	..	1	..	..	..	..	..
Printers .	1 (1)	..	..	..	8 (4)	3 (1)	2 (1)	1	1 (1)	..
11. Glass, Pottery										
Earthenware .	..	..	..	..	1	2 (2)	..	..	3 (2)	..
Potters .	..	..	..	..	7	1	..	..	..	..
Royal Glass Factory	..	2 (2)	..	..	1 (1)	..	2 (2)	..	..	..
12. Miscellaneous										
Actors, artists, musicians, &c.	..	..	..	..	..	6	2	1	..	..
Beggars .	..	..	..	..	..	3 (3)	..	..	..	..
Bourgeois .	..	1	6	..	..	7	2	2	1	..
Business men .	..	..	..	..	4	2	..	..	..	1
Charcoal-burners	..	..	..	..	3	..	..	..	..	..
Civil Servants .	..	..	..	..	..	4	..	..	4	7
Clerks .	1 (1)	..	..	..	5	7 (2)	2	..	..	..
Domestic servants, cleaners	1 (1)	..	..	..	..	11 (11)	9 (9)	9 (9)	2 (2)	..
Deputies .	..	..	..	..	..	..	..	..	11	..
Fishermen .	..	..	..	..	2 (1)	..	..	..	..	..
Housewives .	..	..	..	3 (3)	..	..	..	..	..	..
Journalists, publishers .	..	..	..	..	..	6	..	..	..	..
Labourers (miscell.) .	2 (2)	1 (1)	6 (6)	2 (2)	2 (2)	4 (4)	2 (2)	..	4 (4)	..
Launderers .	..	..	1	..	3 (1)	..	2	1	4 (4)	..
Newsagents, vendors .	..	..	..	..	..	13 (12)	..	..	..	..

Trades	(1) 1787–8	(2) Réveillon Riots	(3)* Burning of barriers	(4)* Saint-Lazare affair	(5) Bastille	(6) Champ de Mars	(7) August 1792	(8) Grocery Riots 1792–3	(9) Prairial Year III	(10) Vendémiaire Year IV
Peasants .	..	1	4 (2)	1 (1)	..	..	..	..	1	..
Priests .	..	1	..	..	..	1	..	..	1	1
Professional (architects, law, medicine)	..	..	..	..	..	5	3	..	1	3
Shopkeepers, assistants .	10	2	1 (1)	..	22 (1)	..	..	..	5	1 (1)
'Smugglers' .	..	..	15	..	..	..	..	..	..	..
Teachers .	..	..	..	..	..	4	..	..	2	..
Trades (miscell.)	2	5 (2)	1 (1)	3	56 (1)	8	8 (2)	6 (1)	7 (2)	..
Army, police, National G'd: (a) Officers, N.C.O.s	..	..	..	..	..	6	..	..	4	8
(b) Others .	1	1	..	..	77	..	..	5	41	..
Totals . . .	55 (28)	68 (52)	77 (26)	37 (33)	662 (149)	248 (128)	123 (51)	58 (35)	186 (46)	22 (1)

Sources:
(3)* Arch. Nat., Z¹ª 886; Y 10649.
(4)* Arch. Nat., Z² 4691; Y 14240, 10649; Arch. Saône et Loire, B 705. Sources for nos. (1)–(2), (5)–(10) are as in Appendix III.

APPENDIX V

Parisian Insurgents and Rioters of 1775–95

Age, sex, literacy, origin, previous convictions, &c.

Riots, &c.	(1) Nos. arrested, &c.	(2) Wage-earners	(2) Unem-ployed	(3) Women	(4) Av. age	(5) Per cent. literate	(6) Previous convictions (%)	(7) Born in provinces (%)	(8) Living in lodgings (%)
1. Corn Riots of 1775	139	102	18	14	30	33	15	80	37*
2. Riots of 1787–8 .	55	28	?	1	23	60	?	31	10
3. Réveillon Riots .	68	52	8	1	29	62	13	66	25
4. Barrières . .	77	26	?	9	?	?	?	?	?
5. Saint-Lazare affair . .	37	33	..	13	..	..	..	..	..
6. Bastille . .	662	149	..	1	34	..	..	63	10
7. Champ de Mars	248	128	44	13	31	80	2–3	72	20
8. 10 August 1792 .	123	51	..	3	38	..	..	..	..
9. Grocery Riots of 1792–3 . .	58	35	..	7	30	..	..	..	17
10. Prairial Year III	186	46	..	20	36	85	..	72	..
11. Vendémiaire Year IV .	30	1	..	0	44	100	..	..	..

Sources:

For Corn Riots of 1775 see G. Rudé, 'La Taxation populaire de mai 1775 à Paris et dans la région parisienne', *Ann. hist. rév. franç.*, 1956, p. 239.
[Other sources as for Appendixes III–IV.]

* In the case of those resident in Paris it was 46 per cent.

APPENDIX VI

The Revolutionary Calendar[1]

Vendémiaire Sept.–Oct.	Brumaire Oct.–Nov.	Frimaire Nov.–Dec.	Nivôse Dec.–Jan.	Pluviôse Jan.–Feb.	Ventôse Feb.–March	Germinal March–April	Floréal April–May	Prairial May–June	Messidor June–July	Thermidor July–Aug.	Fructidor Aug.–Sept.	Jours sans-culottides September
1 22	1 22	1 21	1 21	1 20	1 19	1 21	1 20	1 20	1 19	1 19	1 18	1 17
2 23	2 23	2 22	2 22	2 21	2 20	2 22	2 21	2 21	2 20	2 20	2 19	2 18
3 24	3 24	3 23	3 23	3 22	3 21	3 23	3 22	3 22	3 21	3 21	3 20	3 19
4 25	4 25	4 24	4 24	4 23	4 22	4 24	4 23	4 23	4 22	4 22	4 21	4 20
5 26	5 26	5 25	5 25	5 24	5 23	5 25	5 24	5 24	5 23	5 23	5 22	5 21
6 27	6 27	6 26	6 26	6 25	6 24	6 26	6 25	6 25	6 24	6 24	6 23	
7 28	7 28	7 27	7 27	7 26	7 25	7 27	7 26	7 26	7 25	7 25	7 24	
8 29	8 29	8 28	8 28	8 27	8 26	8 28	8 27	8 27	8 26	8 26	8 25	
9 30	9 30	9 29	9 29	9 28	9 27	9 29	9 28	9 28	9 27	9 27	9 26	
10 1	10 31	10 30	10 30	10 29	10 28	10 30	10 29	10 29	10 28	10 28	10 27	
11 2	11 1	11 1	11 31	11 30	11 1	11 31	11 30	11 30	11 29	11 29	11 28	
12 3	12 2	12 2	12 1	12 31	12 2	12 1	12 1	12 31	12 30	12 30	12 29	
13 4	13 3	13 3	13 2	13 1	13 3	13 2	13 2	13 1	13 1	13 31	13 30	
14 5	14 4	14 4	14 3	14 2	14 4	14 3	14 3	14 2	14 2	14 1	14 31	
15 6	15 5	15 5	15 4	15 3	15 5	15 4	15 4	15 3	15 3	15 2	15 1	
16 7	16 6	16 6	16 5	16 4	16 6	16 5	16 5	16 4	16 4	16 3	16 2	
17 8	17 7	17 7	17 6	17 5	17 7	17 6	17 6	17 5	17 5	17 4	17 3	
18 9	18 8	18 8	18 7	18 6	18 8	18 7	18 7	18 6	18 6	18 5	18 4	
19 10	19 9	19 9	19 8	19 7	19 9	19 8	19 8	19 7	19 7	19 6	19 5	
20 11	20 10	20 10	20 9	20 8	20 10	20 9	20 9	20 8	20 8	20 7	20 6	
21 12	21 11	21 11	21 10	21 9	21 11	21 10	21 10	21 9	21 9	21 8	21 7	
22 13	22 12	22 12	22 11	22 10	22 12	22 11	22 11	22 10	22 10	22 9	22 8	
23 14	23 13	23 13	23 12	23 11	23 13	23 12	23 12	23 11	23 11	23 10	23 9	
24 15	24 14	24 14	24 13	24 12	24 14	24 13	24 13	24 12	24 12	24 11	24 10	
25 16	25 15	25 15	25 14	25 13	25 15	25 14	25 14	25 13	25 13	25 12	25 11	
26 17	26 16	26 16	26 15	26 14	26 16	26 15	26 15	26 14	26 14	26 13	26 12	
27 18	27 17	27 17	27 16	27 15	27 17	27 16	27 16	27 15	27 15	27 14	27 13	
28 19	28 18	28 18	28 17	28 16	28 18	28 17	28 17	28 16	28 16	28 15	28 14	
29 20	29 19	29 19	29 18	29 17	29 19	29 18	29 18	29 17	29 17	29 16	29 15	
30 21	30 20	30 20	30 19	30 18	30 20	30 19	30 19	30 18	30 18	30 17	30 16	

[1] The Revolutionary (or Republican) Calendar was in official use between 22 September 1793 (1st Vendémiaire of the Year II) to the end of 1805 (11th Nivôse of the Year XIV). In leap-years (1796, 1800, 1804), 11th Ventôse corresponded to 29 February and the extra day of the Republican Year was 'found' by adding a sixth 'jour sans-culottide' (or 'jour complémentaire') to the five shown above.

APPENDIX VII

Prices and Wages in Paris, 1789–93

[Reproduced from *The Economic History Review*, vol. vi, 1954, no. 3, pp. 248–55]

TABLE 1. *Percentage of income spent on bread by Parisian workers in 1789*

Occupation	Daily wage[1]	'Effective' daily earnings[2]	Expenditure on bread as percentage of income			
			At 9 s.	At 14½ s.	At 13½ s.	At 12 s.
Labourer in Réveillon's factory .	25 s.[3]	15 s.	60	97	90	80
Builder's labourer . . .	30 s.	18 s.	50	80	75	67
Journeyman mason . . .	40 s.	24 s.	37	60	56	50
Journeyman locksmith, carpenter, &c.	50 s.	30 s.	30	48	45	40
Sculptor, goldsmith . . .	100 s.	60 s.	15	24	22½	20

[1] Wages given here, unless otherwise stated, are from L. Biollay, *Les prix en 1790* (Paris, 1886), pp. 14–79. Nearly all these, for lack of other evidence, are for 1790. What material there is for 1789 suggests, however, that the differences between the two years are very slight. A notable exception is the case of the journeymen tailors who, in August 1789, obtained an increase of 10 *sous* per day by concerted action (Hardy, *Journal*, viii. 438–9).

[2] In computing 'effective' earnings, allowance has been made for the numerous unpaid Feast Days of the *ancien régime*. Here these are assumed to number 111 per year (G. M. Jaffé, *Le Mouvement ouvrier à Paris pendant la Révolution française*, pp. 26–27). Further allowance should also be made for sickness.

[3] *Exposé justificatif pour le sieur Réveillon.* Bib. Nat. Lb[39] 1618.

TABLE 2. *Hypothetical budgets of Parisian workers in June 1789 and June 1791*

	Budget of a builder's labourer (wage 30 s.; 'effective' income 18 s.)		Budget of a journeyman carpenter, locksmith, &c. (wage 50 s.; 'effective' income 30 s.)	
	June 1789	*June 1791*	*June 1789*	*June 1791*
4 lb. bread	14½ s.	4 lb. bread 8 s.	4 lb. bread 14½ s.	4 lb. bread 8 s.
Rent	3 s.	Rent 3 s.	Rent 3 s.	Rent 3 s.
		½ litre wine 4 s.	½ litre wine 5 s.	1 litre wine 8 s.
		1¼ lb. meat 2½ s.	½ lb. meat 5 s.	½ lb. meat 5 s.
Balance for oil, vegetables, clothing, &c.	½ s.	Balance ½ s.	Balance 2½ s.	Balance 6 s.
TOTAL	18 s.	18 s.	30 s.	30 s.

TABLE 3. *Hypothetical budgets of Parisian workers in June 1790 and June 1793*

Budget of a journeyman carpenter				Budget of a journeyman locksmith			
In June 1790 (wage 50 s.; 'effective' income 30 s.[1])		In June 1793 (wage 80 s.; 'effective' income 57 s.)		In June 1790 (wage 50 s.; 'effective' income 30 s.)		In June 1793 (wage 110 s.; 'effective' income 78 s.)	
4 lb. bread	11 s.	4 lb. bread	12 s.	4 lb. bread	11 s.	4 lb. bread	12 s.
Rent[2]	3 s.	Rent	6 s.	Rent	3 s.	Rent	6 s.
1 litre wine	10 s.	1½ litres wine	24 s.	1 litre wine	10 s.	1½ litres wine	24 s.
¼ lb. meat	5 s.	¼ lb. meat	9 s.	¼ lb. meat	5 s.	1 lb. meat	18 s.
Balance for vegetables, oil, clothing, &c.	1 s.	Balance	6 s.	Balance	1 s.	Balance	18 s.
TOTAL	30 s.		57 s.		30 s.		78 s.

[1] 'Effective' earnings are here based on the assumption of a 5-day working week. Many of the old Feast Days had, by this time, been abandoned, but the Revolutionary Calendar, which considerably increased the number of working days per year, had not yet been introduced.

[2] For lack of exact information on rent, I have assumed an increase of 100 per cent. on charges made in 1790, which is roughly in proportion to the rise of other prices.

For budgets and tables of wages and prices for 1793–5, see *Econ. Hist. Rev.*, vol. vi, 1954, no. 3, pp. 257–64. In view of their greater lack of detail and the need for more textual explanation they are not included here.

GLOSSARY[1]

Accapareur. A hoarder (most frequently used of a real, or believed, hoarder of food).

Armée révolutionnaire. A citizen army, reputedly composed of trustworthy *sans-culottes*, raised in various centres in the autumn of 1793, primarily for the purpose of compelling agrarian producers to release their stocks for Paris and other cities. Discredited and disbanded after the fall of the 'Hébertists' in the spring of 1794.

Assignat. Revolutionary paper-money, in general use after the summer of 1791.

Autel de la Patrie. A civic altar, dedicated to the Nation and erected in the centre of the Champ de Mars (see below).

Barrières. The customs posts surrounding the City of Paris, erected by the Farmers General shortly before the Revolution.

Bourgeoisie. Here used as a generic term more or less synonymous with urban middle classes—bankers, stockbrokers, merchants, large manufacturers, and professional men of every kind.

Buveur de sang. A term of abuse applied to Jacobins in general and to Robespierrists in particular after Thermidor of the Year II. Variations on this theme are: 'septembriseur' and 'terroriste'.

Cahiers de doléances. The lists of grievances drawn up by specially convened meetings of citizens and villagers, and of representatives of the three Estates, in preparation for the meeting of the States General in 1789.

Champ de Mars. Originally the chief military parade-ground of the city, lying on the Left Bank (where the Eiffel Tower stands today). Used during the Revolution as the main centre of civic festivals and pageantry (e.g. Festivals of the Federation on 14 July and Festival of the Supreme Being), also as a popular centre for the drafting of petitions (e.g. those of 16–17 July 1791 and 6 August 1792).

Comité civil. The political or administrative committee of the Section (see below).

Comité révolutionnaire (originally *comité de surveillance* and, after Thermidor, *comité d'arrondissement*). The local committee attached to the Section and charged with duties relating to police and internal security.

Commissaires aux accaparement. Officers appointed by the Sections to ensure the local operation of the laws of the Maximum (see below) and to investigate charges of hoarding food and drink.

Committee of General Security. One of the two main Committees of government in which the power of the Jacobin dictatorship was vested in the Year II. Specifically charged with responsibility for police and internal security.

[1] This Glossary claims no more than to give very rough-and-ready definitions or explanations of certain terms used in the text that might cause confusion or misunderstanding. For fuller and more exact definitions the reader is referred to Marion's *Dictionnaire des institutions de la France aux XVII* et XVIII* siècles* and to Bourssin and Challamel's *Dictionnaire de la Révolution française*.

Committee of Public Safety. The more important of the two leading Government Committees of the Year II. Generally responsible for the conduct of both internal and external affairs, its powers overlapped with those of the Committee of General Security in police and judicial matters.

Commune. This title, fraught with tradition and revolutionary implications, was given to the Paris local government that emerged after the fall of the Bastille. It disappeared shortly after Thermidor and reappeared (briefly) in 1848 and 1871.

Complot aristocratique. The name popularly ascribed to attempts made by the Court Party (see below) to overawe Paris by a show of arms and to disperse the newly formed National Assembly in the summer of 1789. Used subsequently in relation to other genuine, or believed, plots of counter-revolutionaries.

Constitutional Monarchists. A term here somewhat loosely applied to the new majority that emerged in the National (and Constituent) Assembly after the 'parti anglais' (who favoured the Absolute Veto and a Second Chamber) had been defeated and broken up in the October 'days'. Their leaders in the Assembly were Barnave, Duport, and the Lameths and, in the Paris administration, Bailly and Lafayette. (See also *Feuillants.*)

Cordeliers Club. The more 'plebeian' of the two great Parisian Clubs of the Revolution. It lay in the Théâtre Français Section on the Left Bank, charged a lower subscription than the Jacobin Club, and generally adopted more advanced policies (e.g. in July 1791 and the spring of 1794). Its best-known leaders were Danton, Marat, Hébert, and Ronsin.

Counter-revolutionary. Here used in a relative, rather than in an absolute, sense to denote an opponent of the Revolution at any one of its stages.

Court Party. A term here applied, in particular, to the group led by the Comte d'Artois in the summer of 1789; more generally, applied to those enjoying the confidence of the king and queen, and their supporters in the press and the Assembly, at all stages up to August 1792.

Décade. The 10-day periods into which the Republican 30-day month was divided.

Districts. In April 1789, Paris was divided into 60 Districts for electoral purposes. With the July revolution, however, they virtually assumed the powers of local government organs. They survived as such until May–June 1790, when they were replaced by the Sections (see below).

Enragés. The extreme revolutionary group, led by Jacques Roux, Théophile Leclerc, and Jean Varlet, who, while condemned by Cordeliers and Jacobins alike, yet had considerable influence on the *sans-culottes* in the spring, summer, and autumn of 1793.

Faubourgs. Originally lying outside the walls of the old City, the *faubourgs* (literally, 'suburbs') had, by 1785, all become enclosed within the City boundaries. Here the term is applied both to these former 'suburbs' in general and to the most famous among them—the Faubourg Saint-Antoine and the Faubourg Saint-Marcel—in particular. The term is sometimes used (incorrectly) by historians to denote 'working-class districts'.

Fédérés. The armed units from the provinces that came to Paris to attend the Festival of the Federation on 14 July 1792. Here applied, in particular, to the men of Marseilles, Brest, &c., that took part in the assault on the Tuileries.

Feuillants. Name given to the group of royalist deputies and journalists who broke with the Jacobins to form their own Club in protest against the campaign to depose the king or suspend him from office after the Flight to Varennes in June 1791.

Garde Nationale (or *milice bourgeoise*). Citizens' army, or militia, originally raised by the Paris Districts in July 1789.

Gardes Françaises. The main body of royal troops stationed in the capital on the eve of the Revolution. While loyal to the Government in the Réveillon riots of April 1789, they began to be won over by the revolutionaries in June and generally sided with the people in the July insurrection.

Gens sans aveu. Vagrants or persons without a fixed abode.

Girondins. Name originally given to a group of Left-wing deputies in the Legislative Assembly, who supported Brissot's policy of a 'revolutionary war' in the autumn and winter of 1791 and many of whom (like Brissot) came from the Gironde region. Later applied to a wider group sharing a more or less common political and social programme in opposition to that of the main body of Jacobins.

Jeunesse dorée. Bands of anti-Jacobin youths organized by the journalist Fréron after the overthrow of Robespierre. In Vendémiaire of the Year IV they supported the royalist uprising against the Convention. (See also *muscadins.*)

Journée (or *journée révolutionnaire*). A day of revolutionary struggle in which crowds (generally composed of *sans-culottes*) participate.

Marais (or *Plaine*). Name given to the Centre group in the Convention of the Year II which, by withdrawing its support from Robespierre on 9th Thermidor, made it possible for his enemies to isolate and arrest him.

Maximum. There were two laws of the Maximum: that of May 1793 imposing a limit on the price of grain only; and that of September 1793 extending price-control to nearly all articles of prim enecessity, including labour (*maximum des salaires*).

Meneur. A leader (often used in a derogatory sense).

Menu peuple. The common people: wage-earners and small property-owners. (See also *sans-culottes.*)

Mountain. Name given to the Jacobin deputies led by Robespierre and Danton, who sat in the upper seats of the National Convention when it assembled in September 1792. It was from their ranks that the Revolutionary Government of the Year II was formed after the expulsion of the Girondins.

Muscadins. Term applied by the *sans-culottes* to *bourgeois* citizens and middle-class youth in the period after Thermidor. It suggests foppishness and fine clothes.

Noblesse de robe. Wealthy magistrates of the old régime who, by purchase or inheritance of office, had acquired the status of nobility.

Non-domiciliés. Persons living in hotels, lodgings, or furnished rooms (*chambres garnies*) and, as such, generally omitted from the population censuses of the period and excluded from the franchise until June 1793.

Ouvriers. Term applied in the eighteenth century to all town-dwellers who worked with their hands, whether as small manufacturers, independent craftsmen, or wage-earners.

Pacte de famine. The policy, popularly imputed to various governments under Louis XV and Louis XVI, of deliberately withholding stocks of grain from the market in order to force up prices and create famine.

Poissarde. Literally, fish-wife. By extension applied to market-women in general.

Prévôt des marchands. The senior magistrate of the royal government of the City of Paris prior to the Revolution. The last holder of the office, Jacques de Flesselles, was lynched by an angry crowd after the surrender of the Bastille on 14 July 1789.

Procès-verbal. The formal record of the cross-examination of a prisoner by the *commissaire de police.* Not to be confused with a *rapport de police,* which might be a 'situation' report or a record of the state of public opinion.

Révolte nobiliaire. The revolt of the nobility and *Parlements* of 1787–8, which served as a 'curtain-raiser' to the Revolution of 1789.

Sans-culottes. Here used in its purely social sense as an omnibus term to include the small property-owners and wage-earners of town and countryside: in its Parisian context, the small shopkeepers, petty traders, craftsmen, journeymen, labourers, vagrants, and city poor. Contemporaries tended to limit its application to the more politically active among these classes or to extend it to the 'popular' leaders, from whatever social class they might be drawn. Historians have frequently used the term in this political sense.

Sections. The 48 units into which Paris became divided for electoral (and general political) purposes, in succession to the 60 Districts, by the by the municipal law of May–June 1790.

Sociétés fraternelles. Name given to the early radical clubs and societies that were formed in 1790 and 1791 as associates or affiliates of the Cordeliers Club.

Sociétés populaires. General term applied to the local clubs and societies after the summer of 1791. Many were affiliated to the Jacobin Club but, owing to their tendency (in Paris, at least) to promote advanced views and independent policies, were frowned on by the Revolutionary Government of the Year II. Many (particularly the purely *Sectional* societies set up after 9 September 1793) were closed down after the fall of Hébert; more were closed after Thermidor; a few survived until the early months of 1795.

Taxation populaire. The compulsion of bakers and grocers, &c., to sell their wares at lower prices by the intervention of riotous crowds (examples here given: May 1775, January–February 1792, February 1793).

Terror. The term is used here not so much to describe a method as to define a period—the period September 1793 to July 1794, when the Jacobin government imposed its authority by varying means of compulsion—military, judicial, and economic.

Thermidor. The month in the Revolutionary Calendar covering parts of July and August (see Appendix VI). Here used more frequently to refer to the two days in Thermidor (9th and 10th) of the Year II which saw the overthrow of Robespierre and his closest associates.

Third Estate (*Tiers État*). Literally, the representatives of the non-'privileged' of the three Estates (or Orders) summoned to attend the meeting of the States General. More generally it is here used to denote all social classes other than the aristocracy, upper clergy, or privileged magistrates—i.e. *menu peuple* as well as *bourgeoisie*.

Vainqueurs de la Bastille. The title given to those 800–900 persons who were able to establish their claim to have participated actively in the capture of the Bastille.

BIBLIOGRAPHICAL NOTE

A FULL record of source-materials used in the preparation of this volume appears in the footnotes, either directly or by reference to other published work. Here it is not proposed to recapitulate the titles of the numerous secondary works that have been consulted, and whose repetition would be needlessly wearisome for author and reader alike.

What follows is a summary of primary sources only—both manuscript and printed; but, of the latter, only those documents are cited which are not easily accessible in the form of memoirs, correspondence, or published collections—such as those edited by Aulard, C. Bloch, Caron, Charavay, Chassin, Lacroix, Monin, Tourneux, and Tuetey.

Manuscript Sources

ARCHIVES NATIONALES

Series AA   (Section législative et judiciaire), nos. 46–47.
     „   AF   (Section administrative. Secrétairerie d'État), nos. II. 47–48, 50, 57; II*. 294, 298; IV. 1470.
     „   BB   (Justice): BB^3 73, 76, 80, 222; BB^{16} 702; BB^{30} 17, 79, 87.
     „   C   (Procès-verbaux des Assemblées nationales), nos. 27, 31, 35, 71, 75, 134, 167, 184, 203, 221, 238, 246–7, 251.
     „   D   (Comités des Assemblées), nos. III, IV, VI, XXIX^b, XLIII.
     „ F^{1c} III (Esprit public. Élections), Seine 13, 27.
     „ F^7 (Police générale), nos. 2476, 2491, 2513, 2523, 3299, 3688, 3281, 4387, 4411–4776 (65 bundles used), 6504.
     „ F^{7*} (Registres), nos. 2497, 2505, 2507, 2517, 2520, 2585–6.
     „ F^{12} (Commerce et Industrie), nos. 1430, 1544, 1546–7.
     „ F^{13} (Bâtiments Civils), nos. 1137–8.
     „ F^{15} (Hospices et Secours), nos. 3267–74, 3564.
     „   H   (Généralités, Bureau de la Ville), nos. 1453, 2121.
     „   KK   (Monuments historiques. Registres), nos. 641, 647.
     „ O^1 (Maison du Roi), nos. 500, 1036, 2053, 2057.
     „   T   (Section domaniale. Séquestre), nos. 214, 514.
     „   W   (Section judiciaire. Tribunal Révolutionnaire), nos. 12–13, 24, 76, 78, 81, 170, 174, 294, 319, 343, 357, 444, 546–8, 556–8.
     „   Y   (Archives du Châtelet de Paris), *Chambre criminelle*: nos. 9828–10598 (some 25 bundles used); *Registres*: 10626, 10634, 10648–50; *Archives des commissaires au Châtelet*: nos. 10790–16022 (some 150 bundles used for 1775, 1787–90); *Prévôté de l'Île-de-France*: nos. 18748–70, 18794–6.
     „   Z   (Juridictions spéciales et ordinaires), nos. I^a/640, 886; 2/4691.

ARCHIVES DE LA PRÉFECTURE DE POLICE

Series Aa   (Sections de Paris. Procès-verbaux des commissaires de

police, 1790–An IX), nos. 9–266 (some 80 bundles used for 1790–Year IV).
Series Ab (Registres d'écrou des prisons), nos. 132 (Conciergerie), 319 (Sainte-Pélagie), 324–7 (Force), 356 (misc.).

ARCHIVES DE LA SEINE

Series V.D.* (Sections 1790–An IV), nos. 645, 650, 826, 1012, 1635, 1656, 1661–2, 1681.

ARCHIVES DE SEINE-ET-MARNE

Series B (Justice), nos. 2247, 2387, 2695, 3698.

ARCHIVES DE SEINE-ET-OISE

Series B. *Versailles*: Prévôté de l'Hôtel du Roi. Procès, 1775; Greffe, 1789; Procédures, 1789; Tribunal criminel de mai 1793. *St. Germain-en-Laye*: Prévôté Royale. Pièces du Greffe, 1775.

BIBLIOTHÈQUE NATIONALE

Fonds français, nos. 6680–7: Hardy, *Mes loisirs, ou journal d'événements tels qu'ils parviennent à ma connoissance* (8 vols., 1764–89); 11697 (Bailly–Lafayette correspondence, 1789–91).
Nouvelles acquisitions françaises, nos. 2654, 2666, 2669, 2670, 2673, 2678, 2716, 2811, 3241.

Contemporary Printed Sources

Pamphlets, petitions, lists of citizens, Sectional reports, &c., have been consulted in series Lb 39–41 in the *Bibliothèque Nationale* and in series F, F.R., and R (Croker Collection) in the *British Museum*.

Some use has been made of the Revolutionary Press, particularly of: *L'Ami du peuple*, *Le Babillard*, *Le Journal de la Révolution*, *Mercure national et étranger*, *Les Révolutions de France et de Brabant*, and *Les Révolutions de Paris*.

The following contemporary (or near-contemporary) accounts of events have also been freely consulted (but have yielded comparatively little). Buchez et Roux, *Histoire parlementaire de la Révolution française* (40 vols., Paris, 1833–8); Mavidal et Laurent (ed.), *Archives parlementaires* (1st series, 1789–99, 80 vols., Paris, 1868–1914); *Réimpression de l'ancien Moniteur* (31 vols., Paris, 1858–63); and the *Procès-verbaux* of the Constituent and Legislative Assemblies, and of the National Convention.

INDEX

Alexandre, Charles-Alexis, 99 and n. 3, 101, 103.
Amar, André, 150.
Argenson, Marquis d', 22–23.
Aristocracy, 12–14, 27, 34, 45, 61, 73, 178 and n. 1, 180.
Aristocratic revolt, see *révolte nobiliaire*.
Armée révolutionnaire, 127, 132, 154, 156, 206, 230.
Artois, Comte d', 13, 47, 59.
Assignats, 17 n. 4, 96 and n. 1, 125, 130, 132, 144, 162, 193, 204, 207.
Ateliers de charité, 19, 64, 82–3, 181, 188, 192, 204, 223.
Audouin, Pierre-Jean (journalist), 87, 212.
Augeart, Farmer General, 62.
Auger and Monnery (dyers), 97, 101.
Aulard, Alphonse, 3, 4, 5, 8.

Babeuf, Gracchus, 147.
Bailly, Jean-Sylvain, 59, 61, 69, 72, 74, 78, 82, 89, 94, 192.
Barère de Vieuzac, Bertrand, 118, 128 n. 1, 132, 136, 140, 150.
Barnave, Pierre-Joseph, 52 and n. 2, 62, 63, 70, 72, 210, 213, 232.
Barras, Paul-Jean, 172–3, 173 n. 2, 175.
Barrières (customs posts), 10–11, 14, 16, 25, 48, 49 n. 1, 64, 82, 203, 217; see also Revolutionary 'days': *Barrières*.
Bastille, 1, 2, 3, 10, 11, 12 n. 7, 14, 15, 19 n. 8, 26 and n. 2, 27, 35, 53 ff., 64, 73, 81, 82, 83, 104, 108, 122, 176; see also Revolutionary 'days': *Bastille*.
Beaurepaire, Chevalier de, 64, 223 n. 2.
Bernard, abbé, 70, 71.
Berthier de Sauvigny, 56, 203, 227.
Besenval, Marquis de, 191–2, 194.
Billaud-Varenne, Jean-Nicolas, 128, 150.
Biron, Maréchal de, 32.
Blanc, Louis, 3, 4.
Boissy d'Anglas, François-Antoine, 149.
Bonaparte, Napoléon, 173 and n. 2, 177, 196 n. 2.

Bord, Gustave, 57 n. 5, 217–18.
Bourbotte, Pierre, 155 n. 1.
Bourdon, Léonard, 150.
Bourgeois, bourgeoisie, 9, 12, 14, 24, 27, 28, 30, 33, 34, 57, 61, 62, 63, 80, 83, 86, 90, 117, 138, 143, 158–9, 160, 163, 166, 170, 175–6, 177, 178, 180–1, 184, 186, 200, 205, 222, 229, 232, 235.
Braesch, F., 17.
Brienne, Loménie de, 28–29, 30, 31.
Brissot de Warville, Jacques-Pierre, 95, 119, 178 n. 1, 198.
Brunswick, Duke of, 103, 109, 112.
Buchez and Roux, 90.
Buirette-Verrières, 81, 91.
Burke, Edmund, 1, 2, 4, 225.
Buzot, François-Nicolas, 120.

Cahen, L., 12.
Cahiers de doléances, 22 n. 1, 46, 54, 70.
Calonne, C.-A. de, 11, 28, 30.
Calvet, Henri, 124.
Carlyle, Thomas, 2, 4.
Carnot, Lazare, 128 n. 1.
Caron, Pierre, 8, 111, 190, 227.
Chambres garnies, see *non-domiciliés*.
Châtel (mayor's lieutenant, Saint-Denis), 67, 189, 202.
Châtelet, Duc du, 36.
Chaumette, Anaxagoras, 126, 206.
Cobb, Richard C., 214 n. 7.
Colbert, J.-B., 16.
Collot d'Herbois, Jean-Marie, 128, 136, 150.
Collot, J., 38.
Commard (merchant-grocer), 96, 97.
Committee of General Security, 7, 137, 142 n. 1, 143, 145, 147, 161 n. 1, 194, 230.
Committee of Public Safety, 5, 128, 134, 136, 137, 143, 145, 161 n. 2.
Commune, Paris Commune, 8, 17, 70, 78, 84, 89, 94 n. 4, 98, 99, 103, 105, 114; and the grocery riots of 1793, 117–18; and the Enragés, 119–20, 124, 126; and the *sans-culottes*, 130–1, 131 n. 2; and Hébert, 132–3; and the *maximum des salaires*, 134–6; and 9–

Commune, Paris Commune, *Cont.*
10 Thermidor, 137–41; abolished,
143; 156 and n. 2, 190, 204, 206, 214.
Complot aristocratique, 46, 59, 223 and
n. 2, 226.
Constitutional monarchists, 61 ff., 78,
80, 197, 201.
Conti, Prince de, 47.
Cordeliers Club, Cordeliers, 72, 80; and
the agitation of spring–summer 1791,
83–88; and the Champ de Mars
petition, 88–89, 91, 93, 120, 126, 128,
182, 197, 199, 204, 212, 213.
Couthon, Georges, 128.

Danican, General, 172.
Danton, Georges-Jacques, 69, 72, 113,
119, 178 n. 1.
Decrees of the 'Two-Thirds', 161–2,
163, 165–6, 167, 168–9, 170, 171.
De Launay, Marquis, 54 ff., 221, 224,
226.
Democrats, 80–88, 91, 93, 100, 212,
222, 228.
Desmoulins, Camille, 48, 69, 70, 72,
83, 87, 106, 178 n. 1, 212, 216.
Dubois, Chevalier, 32.
Dubois, General, 154.
Dumouriez, Charles-François, 98, 119.
Duport, Adrien, 69, 70.
Duquesnoy, Ernest-Dominique, 155
n. 1.
Duroy, Jean-Michel, 155 n. 1.
Dussaulx, Academician, 55 n. 1, 62, 70.

Enragés, 119–21, 205.

Fabre d'Églantine, 111.
Farmers General, 11.
Faubourgs, 12, 14–17, 24–25, 30–31,
47, 67, 91, 101, 151, 157, 166, 170,
200, 202, 215, 217, 220, 224 n. 1.
—Saint-Antoine, 10, 15–18, 23, 31, 33–
39, 54, 56, 58–59, 67, 73, 76, 77 n. 1,
78, 81, 83, 88; and the Champ de
Mars affair, 92–93; and the grocery
riots of 1792, 96–97; and 20 June
1792, 98–99, 101; and the overthrow
of the monarchy, 103–6; 109, 114,
123, 138; and Germinal-Prairial,
146–55, 158, 164, 167, 168; and
insurrections of 1787–95, 185–6, 192,
203, 206, 218, 222, 226, 234.

— Saint-Denis, 10, 16, 96.
— Saint-Germain, 10, 32 n. 2, 33.
— Saint-Honoré, 13, 58.
— Saint-Jacques, 10, 16, 17, 148, 149.
— Saint-Laurent, 16.
— Saint-Marcel, 10, 16–18, 35–36, 38,
58, 81 n. 3; and the Champ de Mars
affair, 93–94; and the grocery riots
of 1792, 96–98; and 20 June 1792,
98–99, 101, 102; and the overthrow
of the monarchy, 106, 109, 115, 123,
133; and 9–10 Thermidor, 138–9;
and Germinal-Prairial, 147–9, 152,
155, 158; and insurrections of 1787–
95, 185–6, 198, 206, 234.
— Saint-Martin, 10, 16, 81 n. 3.
— Saint-Victor, 10, 16.
Féraud, Jean, 153, 154.
Flesselles, Jacques de, 53, 56, 221,
227.
Fleuriot-Lescot, J.-B., 137, 140.
Fleury, Cardinal, 23.
Foullon de Doué, 56, 203, 227.
Fournier (L'Américain), Claude, 57
n. 3, 58 n. 8, 73, 76, 77, 92, 93, 102,
104 n. 1, 178 n. 1, 229.
François (baker), 78.
Fréron, Louis-Marie, 147.

Gardes Françaises, 25, 29, 32, 36, 49,
51, 55.
Gens sans aveu, see Vagrants.
Gironde, Girondins, 95, 98, 99, 102,
111, 113, 119, 120–2, 199, 206.
Goujon, Jean-Marie, 155 n. 1.
Grande Peur, 223.
Guadet, Marguerite-Élie, 120.
Guérin, Daniel, 126, 134.
Gunsmiths, 50–51.

Hanriot, François, 122, 133, 136, 137,
139, 140, 178 n. 1, 213.
Hardy, Sébastien (diarist), 8, 21, 24 ff.,
29 ff., 43 ff., 52 ff., 60, 65 ff., 75,
181, 192, 194–5, 202–3, 218, 223.
Hébert, Jacques-René (Le Père
Duchesne), 120, 126, 132, 133, 135,
178 n. 1, 205, 206, 210, 211, 222.
Henriot (powder-manufacturer), 35 ff.,
192, 201, 220.
Henri IV, 13, 31, 32, 196, 225.
Hôtel des Invalides, 53, 55, 56 n. 1,
133, 221.

Hôtel de Ville, 15, 47-48, 51, 53, 54, 55, 56, 60, 65, 67, 69, 71, 73, 74, 78, 93, 105, 118, 133, 135, 138, 204 n. 2, 221.
Hulin, Pierre-Augustin, 55.

Insurgents, insurrections, see Revolutionary Crowds, Riots, &c.

Jacobin Club, Jacobins, 5, 80, 81, 83, 85, 88, 98, 102, 111, 113, 114; and the grocery riots of 1793, 117-18; and the Enragés, 119-20; and the revolution of May-June 1793, 121-2; and the insurrection of September 1793, 126-7, 128, 137; and the Thermidorians, 137, 142-3, 146-7; and Germinal-Prairial, 149, 153, 156, 158, 160; and Vendémiaire, 164-6, 169, 176, 192, 194, 199-201, 207, 222, 228, 231.
Jaurès, Jean, 5, 14, 38, 57, 58, 80 n. 1.
Jeunesse dorée, jeunes gens, 147, 149, 154, 158, 161, 169, 175; see also Muscadins.
Journées, see Revolutionary 'days', Riots, &c.

Labrousse, C.-E., 5, 20 n. 3, 21, 201.
Lacombe, Claire (Rose), 122 n. 3, 229.
Lafayette, Marquis de, 50, 61, 62 and n. 3, 64, 68, 71, 72, 74, 76, 77, 81, 89, 91, 92, 102, 181, 197, 204 n. 3.
Lambesc, Prince de, 48.
Lamoignon, G.-F. de, 30, 31, 196, 202.
La Tour du Pin, 72.
Lebon, Gustave, 219, 220, 221.
Lefebvre, Georges, 4 n. 2, 46, 200, 219 and n. 2.
Lefevre, abbé, 53.
Legendre, Louis, 178 n. 1.
Lettres de cachet, 30, 81.
Lindet, Robert, 128 n. 1.
Lodgers, lodging houses, see non-domiciliés.
Loi Le Chapelier, 85, 135.
Louis XIV, 13, 16.
Louis XV, 12, 23, 45.
Louis XVI, 35, 70, 77, 87, 88, 95, 98, 100; his overthrow, 101-5, 108, 113, 181, 182, 198, 225.
Loustalot, É. (journalist, 58, 69, 87, 223.

Madelin, Louis, 3 n. 2.

Maillard, Stanislas, 57 and n. 3, 64 n. 2, 73, 74, 75, 178 n. 1, 204, 221, 229, 230.
Mallet du Pan, 34, 45.
Malouet, Pierre-Victor, 71.
Marat, Jean-Paul, 69, 71, 78, 85, 87, 110, 113, 118, 119, 133, 146, 147, 167, 178 n. 1, 201, 212, 223-4.
Marie-Antoinette, 47, 77.
Mathiez, Albert, 5, 7, 62, 69, 118.
Maximum laws (prices), 119, 127, 129, 131-2, 145-6, 205, 206, 207; (wages) 127, 129, 134, 135 and n. 3, 136 and n. 3, 139, 140-1, 141 n. 1, 145, 207.
Menou, Jacques, General, 154, 172.
Menu peuple, 11, 15, 22, 31, 33, 44, 50, 61, 63, 66, 67, 71, 78, 80 n. 1, 85, 88, 91, 93-95, 114, 119, 121, 129, 144, 150, 190, 196, 197 and n. 3, 232-3; see also Sans-culottes.
Mercier, Sébastien, 13, 16, 26.
Méricourt, Théroigne de, 229.
Merlin (de Thionville), Antoine-Christophe, 149.
Michelet, Jules, 1, 3, 4, 59, 232, 233 n. 1.
Milice bourgeoise, see National Guard.
Mirabeau, Vicomte de, 47, 62, 76, 192.
Monin, H., 13.
Montjoie (journalist), 41, 191, 194.
Mortimer-Ternaux, M., 5, 191.
Murat, Joachim, 172.
Muscadins, 146, 147, 155, 216; see also Jeunesse dorée, jeunes gens.

National Guard, 48, 52, 57, 59, 61, 65, 71, 73; and the march to Versailles, 76-77 and n. 1, 81, 82; and the Champ de Mars affair, 82, 84, 86, 89-92, 97; and 20 June 1792, 98-101; and the overthrow of the monarchy, 102-7, 111, 113; and the grocery riots of 1793, 115-16; and 9-10 Thermidor, 137-8, 143, 149; and Prairial, 152-5, 166, 173-4, 182-3, 197, 204 n. 3, 205-6, 213, 230-1.
Necker, Jacques, 11 and n. 5, 12, 28, 31, 34, 37, 46, 47-48, 196, 216, 220-1.
Noblesse, nobility, see Aristocracy.
Non-domiciliés, 11, 12 and n. 1, 18 n. 7, 36, 149, 188 and ns. 5 and 6.

Olivier (porcelain-manufacturer), 40, 41 n. 3, 43, 217.

Orleans, Philip Duke of, 14, 30, 47, 48, 49, 62, 64, 69, 101 and n. 1, 215, 220–1.

Ouvriers, definition of, 18 and n. 5; 31, 35, 39, 56, 81, 86, 91, 124, 130, 148, 150, 151, 165, 166, 171, 211, 213, 234.

Pacte de famine, 23, 46, 68, 222.

Palais Royal, 2, 13, 14, 15, 47, 48, 50, 51, 63, 65, 69–72, 90, 148, 164, 169 and n. 3, 173, 194, 197, 200, 215, 229 and n. 1.

Parlement, 20, 23, 27, 29 ff., 32, 33, 196, 202, 225.

Parochet, abbé, 90–91.

Paroy, Marquis de, 76.

Payan, Claude-François, 135.

Pétion de Villeneuve, Jérôme, 98, 99, 100, 102, 103, 104, 109.

Pichegru, General, 150.

Police, 6–7, 8, 21, 25–26, 35–38, 41, 61–62, 86–87, 90, 92, 94, 96–97, 103, 118, 142 n. 1, 155.

Polignac, Comtesse de, 30.

Popular (Fraternal) Societies, 83, 85, 87, 91, 121, 147, 213, 214 and n. 7, 215–16.

Population of Paris, 11 and n. 5, 12, 18.

Prices, of bread, flour, wheat, 21–22, 23 and ns. 1 and 6, 24, 25 n. 2, 31, 33, 37, 42, 43, 45, 46, 63, 67–68, 74, 78, 80–81, 94, 118 and n. 4, 125 n. 3, 143–4, 157, 162, 163, 176, 180, 202, 203; of meat, 125, 131, 143–4, 162, 176; of groceries, 96, 118, 114, 125; in general, 20 n. 3, 125, 129 and n. 2, 131, 146, 157, 168, 170, 176.

Prieur (de la Côte d'Or), 128 n. 1.

Prieur (de la Marne), 128 n. 1.

Prisons, Abbaye, 109–10, 111, 215; Bicêtre, 23, 51 n. 3, 110; Châtelet, 14, 110; Conciergerie, 81, 98, 110; Hôtel de la Force, 30, 42, 51 n. 3, 90, 91, 93, 94, 110, 173, 189, 195, 197; Salpêtrière, 110; Sainte-Pélagie, 110; Temple, 14.

Restif de la Bretonne, 211.

Réveillon (wallpaper-manufacturer),

34 ff., 68, 192, 201, 202, 220.

Révolte nobiliaire, 9, 27 ff., 196, 215.

Revolutionary Committees, 124, 130–1, 143, 156, 190.

Revolutionary Crowds, behaviour of, 29–30, 31–32, 35–37, 40, 49, 50, 67, 73–77, 89, 100, 104–5, 109–10, 115–17, 122, 126, 149, 152–5, 173, 219–27, 229–31; composition of, 29–30, 32–33, 39, 49, 50, 56–59, 67, 69 n. 1, 73, 90–92, 98, 100–1, 105–8, 111, 117, 122–5, 126, 157–8, 175–6, 178–90; motives of, 40–44, 49, 54, 78, 108–9, 114, 156–7, 191–209.

Revolutionary 'Days'—Barrières, 11, 48–49, 51, 64, 69, 180, 192, 203, 221; Bastille, 1, 2, 3, 26, 27, 53–59, 180, 191, 201, 202–3, 218; Champ de Mars, 80–81, 84, 86, 87, 88–94, 147, 182, 192, 197, 204, 208, 224; Germinal, 147, 149–50, 157, 199; Grocery riots (1792), 96–98, 183, 205–6; Grocery riots (1793), 114–18, 171, 183, 191–2, 206, 230; May–June 1793, 113 n. 1, 122–5, 137, 200, 208; June 1792, 98–101, 219–20; October 1789, 1, 2, 3, 61–63, 65–66, 73–77, 151, 181–2, 191–2, 195, 201, 221, 226, 227; Prairial, 7, 152–9, 161, 165, 170, 174 and n. 6, 183–4, 193, 194, 199; Réveillon riots, 35–44, 179–80, 191–2, 193, 199; Saint-Lazare, 49–50, 51, 181, 192, 193, 203; September Massacres, 109–12, 166, 173, 196, 225, 227; September 1793, 8, 126–7, 206; Thermidor, 1, 111, 128, 137–41, 160 n. 1, 161, 204 n. 2, 207, 215, 228; Tuileries (August 1792), 1, 3, 7, 64, 101, 104–8, 176, 182–3, 191, 195, 198, 206, 208, 217, 219 and n. 4, 224; Vendémiaire, 7, 9, 158, 160–1, 208, 224 and n. 5, 226; see also Riots.

Revolutionary Press, L'Ami du peuple, 69, 78, 85, 146, 212; Le Babillard, 83–84, 90, 91, 192, 223; Le Journal de la Révolution, 94; Les Révolutions de Paris, 69, 87, 89 n. 5; Mercure national et étranger, 85; L'Orateur du peuple, 87, 212; Le Père Duchesne, 120, 210, 211; Le Publiciste, 212.

Riots, over bread, 22, 23, 24, 43, 73–74, 78, 118–19, 126 n. 4, 148–9, 152, 192,

206; corn riots of 1775, 23–25, 28, 41, 96, 117 n. 3, 159; of 1787, 29–30, 179; of 1788, 31–33, 179, 196, 202; miscellaneous, 48, 66, 67, 68, 69, 81, 125–6, 236–7; *see also* Revolutionary 'Days'.
Robert, François, 85, 88.
Robert, Louise, 85, 212.
Robespierre, Augustin (the Younger), 120.
Robespierre, Maximilien, 1, 76, 83, 85, 88, 95, 102, 111, 113, 128, 130, 134, 136; and 9–10 Thermidor, 137–41, 141 n. 1; 142, 145, 150, 160, 161, 164, 167, 178 n. 1, 183, 201, 206, 207, 225 n. 2, 228.
Roederer, Pierre-Louis, 104, 196 n. 2.
Roland de la Platière, 119.
Roland, Madame, 88.
Romme, Gilbert, 155 n. 1.
Ronsin, General, 254.
Rossignol, Jean, General, 178 n. 1.
Rouff, Marcel, 6, 21.
Rousseau, Jean-Jacques, 211, 225 n. 2.
Roux, Jacques, 118, 119, 126, 178 n. 1.
Roy, abbé, 41.

Saint-André, Jeanbon, 128 n. 1.
Saint-Félix, Musquinet de, 178 n. 1, 180, 229.
Saint-Génie, 70.
Saint-Huruge, Marquis de, 70, 178 n. 1, 216, 229.
Saint-Just, Louis-Antoine, 128, 137, 225 n. 2.
Sainte-Claire Deville, Paul, 8, 121 n. 1, 131, 138.
Sans-culottes, 8, 9; definition of, 12 and n. 5, 22, 33, 80 and n. 1, 100, 106, 113, 114, 120; and the revolution of May–June 1793, 122–3, 127–8; and the Paris administration of 1793–4, 130–1; and protests against the food policy of the Revolutionary Government, 131–3; and 9–10 Thermidor, 137–41; and Germinal-Prairial, 142–3, 146, 156 n. 1, 157–8, 159 and n. 1; and Vendémiaire, 160–1, 163–5, 168 n. 1, 170, 176–7, 178 n. 1; and their role in revolutionary crowds, 178 ff., 196–9, 205–9; degree of literacy, 211–12; &c.
— Adrien, Michel (labourer), 78, 193;

Advenel, Jean (metal-worker), 78; Audu, Louis-Reine, 105; A. Auger (Téteigne), 42; Bataille (wine-merchant's journeyman), 230; Benoit, E. (port-worker), 108; Bernard, Agnès (fish-wife), 183, 230 n. 5; Billon, Nicolas (mill-worker), 78, 193; Blin, François (market-porter), 78; Buté, Henri (jeweller), 107; Chagnot, Joseph (marble-dealer), 218; Charpentier, Marie-Anne (laundress), 58; Chauvet, Louis (water-carrier), 107; Chauvin, Louis (master locksmith), 108; Chefson, Étienne (cobbler), 154; Delorme, Guillaume (wheelwright), 153; Dénot (cook), 56 n. 1, 57 n. 3; Dumont, Pierre (gauze-worker), 107; Dumont (docker), 230; Dusson, Charles (edge-tool-maker), 58; Évrard, Constance (cook), 86–87, 190, 197, 212, 230; Farcy, Edmé (journeyman goldsmith), 77 n. 1; Gervais, Eugène (cook), 65 and n. 5; Gilbert, J. (blanket-maker), 37; Gomy, Jean-Marie (brewer's j'man), 58; Guerre (farmer), 124–5, 217; Homette, Pierre (journeyman cabinet-maker), 107, 217; Joly, Charles (wallpaper-worker), 139; Lanbriné (journeyman), 139; Lavarenne, *femme* (sick-nurse) 230–1; Le Blanc, J. (journeyman harness-maker), 40; Le Roy, Louis (j'man goldsmith), 107; Lhéritier, Jérôme (journeyman cabinetmaker), 76 and n. 1, 77 n. 1; Lobjois, Antoine (master glazier), 107; Mary, Jean-Baptiste (scrivener), 37; Pepin, Jean-Nicolas (tallow-porter), 51, 193, 218; Pergaud, Joseph (military pensioner), 71; Pinché (button-maker), 94; Pourat, A. (porter), 37; Primery, A.-E. (fancy-ware worker), 88 n. 6, 92; Rose, Pierre (gunpowder-worker), 139, n. 2; Salabert, Bernard (mill-worker), 75; Sirier, C. (paper-worker), 41, 42; Trumeau, Marie-Jeanne (market-woman), 37, 39, 230.
Santerre, Antoine-Joseph, 57, 58, 81, 93, 99, 103, 104 n. 1, 109, 115, 178 n. 1, 217.
Schmidt, A., 8.

Sections, Paris Sections (for alternative names, see Appendix I)—*Arcis*, 93, 107, 116, 133, 150, 153, 154, 158, 166, 172 and n. 1, 175, 186 and n. 1; *Arsenal*, 115, 151, 152, 158, 168 n. 4, 169 n. 3, 186 n. 1, 230; *Beaubourg*, 18 n. 2, 96, 139, 168 n. 4, 169 n. 3; *Bibliothèque*, 105, 163, 166 n. 2, 167 n. 3; and Vendémiaire, 167, 168 and n. 4, 169 and n. 2, 170, 172, 173, 174 and n. 4, 175; *Bondy*, 115, 168 n. 4, 186 n. 1; *Bonne Nouvelle*, 18 n. 2, 123 n. 3, 147, 168 n. 4; *Champs élysées*, 138, 168 n. 4, 171, 214; *Croix Rouge*, 123, 138, 150–1, 166 n. 2, 168 n. 4, 172 n. 1; *Enfants Rouges*, 115, 139 n. 3, 148, 168 n. 4; *Faubourg Montmartre*, 123, 150, 158, 186 n. 1; *Faubourg Saint-Denis*, 18 n. 2, 148, 152, 158; *Fontaine de Grenelle*, 86, 107, 115, 168 n. 4, 169 n. 3, 212; *Fontaine Montmorency*, 166 n. 2, 168 n. 4, 169 n. 2, 170 n. 4, 175; *Gobelins*, 97, 98, 99, 106, 110, 123, 138, 139, 152, 155; *Grange Batelière*, 115, 168 n. 4, 169 n. 3; *Gravilliers*, 18 n. 2, 93, 96, 109, 115, 117, 118, 123, 147, 148, 149, 150, 151, 152, 153 and n. 1, 155, 158, 172 n. 1, 173 n. 1, 186 n. 1; *Hôtel de Ville*, 115, 138, 152, 153, 158, 169 and n. 1; *Halle au Blé*, 120, 124 n. 6, 158, 168 n. 4, 186 n. 1; *Henri IV*, 89, 106, 124, 125 n. 1, 138, 151, 168 n. 4, 169 n. 1; *Île Saint-Louis*, 93, 106, 169; *Invalides*, 107, 123, 124, 125, 151, 158; 186 n. 1, 217; *Jardin des Plantes*, 151, 152, 155, 166, 168 n. 4; *Lombards*, 18 n. 3, 115, 117, 141, 148, 151, 158, 166, 171 n. 4, 186 n. 1; *Louvre*, 18 n. 3, 93, 115, 123 n. 4, 125 n. 1, 138, 151, 153, 158, 186 n. 1; *Luxembourg*, 138, 152, 153 n. 1, 158, 168 n. 4, 169 n. 2, 172, 175; *Marchés des Innocents*, 18 n. 3, 115, 148, 151, 158, 168 n. 4, 171, 186 n. 1; *Mauconseil*, 18 n. 2, 20, 123 and n. 3, 166 n. 2, 168 n. 4, 176, 186 n. 1; *Montreuil*, 97, 103, 106, 107, 123 and n. 3, 124 n. 6, 148, 151, 173 n. 1; *Notre Dame*, 149–50, 155, 158, 168 n. 4, 169 n. 1; *Observatoire*, 106, 123, 133, 139, 147, 158, 168 n. 4; *Oratoire*, 18 n. 3, 93, 115, 116, 173 n. 1,

186 n. 1; *Palais Royal*, 115, 148, 153, 163, 166 n. 2, 167, 168, 169, 172, 173, 174, 175; *Place Louis XIV*, 93, 169 and n. 1, 171, 172; *Place Royale*, 106, 115, 116, 148, 168 n. 4; *Place Vendôme*, 138, 163, 166 n. 2, 168 n. 4, 194; *Poissonnière*, 18 n. 2, 109, 154, 158, 168 n. 4, 170 n. 4; *Ponceau*, 18 n. 2, 93, 109, 115, 148, 158, 168 n. 4, 169 n. 1, 172; *Popincourt*, 107, 114, 123, 149, 152, 153, 154, 158, 169, 173 n. 1; *Postes*, 150, 170 n. 4; *Quinze Vingts*, 93, 106, 107, 108, 115, 117, 123; 138, 149, 151, 153, 158; and Vendémiaire, 167, 169, 173; 194; *Quatre Nations*, 93, 124, 138, 139, 168 and n. 4, 172; *Roi de Sicile*, 115, 124 n. 6, 148, 149, 151, 152, 153, 158, 168 n. 4, 169 n. 1, 173; *Roule*, 106, 115, 138, *Temple*, 148, 158, 168 n. 4, 170 n. 4, 172 n. 1, 186 n. 1; *Sainte-Geneviève*, 93, 123 n. 4, 125 n. 1, 138, 150, 155, 158, 173 n. 1; *Théâtre Français*, 168 n. 4, 169 n. 1, 170, 172, 173, 174, 175, 214 n. 7; *Thermes de Julien*, 93, 139, 155, 166; *Tuileries*, 100 n. 3, 115, 138, 152, 168 n. 4, 172, 173 n. 3.

Sieyès, Emmanuel-Joseph, abbé, 34, 43, 178 n. 1.

Sillery, Marquis de, 37.

Soboul, Albert, 8, 130–1.

Sombreuil, Marquis de, 53.

Soubrany, Pierre Amable de, 155 n. 1.

States General, 27, 28, 29, 30, 31, 33, 44–47, 59.

Strikes, 20–21, 24, 84, 104 n. 2, 143, 135–6, 163; *see also* Wages Movements.

Taine, Hippolyte, 1, 2, 4, 42, 72, 105, 106, 186, 189, 191–2, 199, 219, 220, 221, 232, 239.

Talmon, J. L., 225 n. 2.

Taxation populaire, 24, 96, 115–17, 117 n. 3, 118, 125–6, 133, 176, 226, 236.

Terray, abbé, 23 and n. 1.

Third Estate (Tiers État), 11, 28, 34, 35, 39, 43, 45, 46, 47, 70, 80, 196, 200–1, 210.

Thiroux de Crosne, 35, 36, 37, 38, 39, 202.

Thompson, J. M., 106.

Thuriot de la Rozière, Jacques-Alexis, 54.

Tinto, Baron, 70.

Tocqueville, Alexis de, 234 and n. 6, 235.

Tuetey, Alexandre, 6.

Tuileries, 3, 75, 100, 103–4, 108, 122 and n. 3, 145–7, 149, 152–4, 165, 172–3, 225.

Turgot, Anne-Robert, 23, 24, 28, 30, 222.

Unemployed, unemployment, 17, 19, 33, 34, 50, 51, 52, 64, 72, 82–84, 82 n. 2; and their part in revolutionary crowds, 187–8, 223, 224 and n. 1.

Vachot, General, 173.

Vagrancy, vagrants, 19 and n. 8, 50, 51, 52, 59; and their part in revolutionary crowds, 186–7.

Vainqueurs de la Bastille, 7, 56 ff., 64, 181, 188, 190.

Varennes, 87–88, 95, 197, 223.

Varlet, Jean, 119, 123 n. 1.

Vergniaud, Pierre-Victurnien, 120.

Vincent, François-Nicolas, 126.

Volontaires de la Bastille, 64, 73, 74, 221.

Wage-Earners, 15, 17, 18, 19–20, 22 n. 1, 32, 39 and n. 2, 40, 44, 52, 57–58, 82, 84, 85, 91, 104 n. 2, 106, 107, 117, 124, 126, 131, 133, 134–7; and 9–10 Thermidor, 139–41, 146, 151, 158, 163, 171; as part of revolutionary crowds, 179–80, 184–5, 185 n. 1, 201–2, 216–17, 235.

Wages, 20–21, 34, 35, 40, 42, 64, 68, 84, 125, 129 and n. 2, 134, 136 n. 3, 141 n. 1, 145, 163, 201–2; see also Maximum laws (wages).

Wages Movements, 39, 64–65, 84–85, 134–6, 145–6; see also Strikes.

Walpole, Sir Robert, 25, 237.

Watt, James, 15.

Wearmouth, R. W., 236.

Wilkes, John, 25, 237 and n. 2.

Young, Arthur, 45, 46, 196 n. 6, 210.

PRINTED IN GREAT BRITAIN
AT THE UNIVERSITY PRESS, OXFORD
BY VIVIAN RIDLER
PRINTER TO THE UNIVERSITY

— no class interest in demands for cheaper bread,

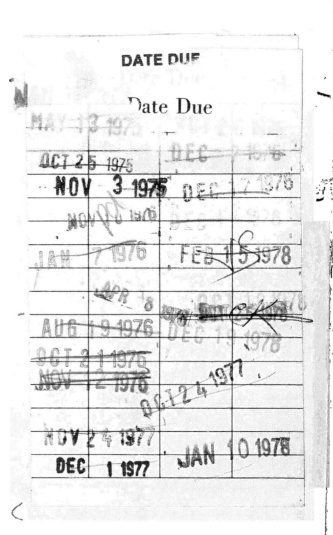

CPSIA information can be obtained
at www.ICGtesting.com
Printed in the USA
BVHW050153090223
658191BV00027B/779

9 781014 601290